The Economics
of Collective Choice

The Economics of Collective Choice

Joe B. Stevens

Oregon State University

A Member of the Perseus Books Group

Copyright © 1993 by Westview Press, Inc. A Member of the Perseus Books Group

Published in 1993 in the United States of America by Westview Press, Inc., 5500 Central Avenue, Boulder, Colorado 80301-2877, and in the United Kingdom by Westview Press, 36 Lonsdale Road, Summertown, Oxford OX2 7EW

Library of Congress Cataloging-in-Publication Data
Stevens, Joe B.
  The economics of collective choice / Joe B. Stevens.
    p.   cm.
  Includes bibliographical references and index.
  ISBN 0-8133-1566-2 — ISBN 0-8133-1567-0 (pbk.)
  1. Social choice.   2. Economic policy.   I. Title.
HB846.8.S74   1993
361.6'1—dc20   92-35195
                                                                      CIP

Printed and bound in the United States of America

       The paper used in this publication meets the requirements
       of the American National Standard for Permanence of Paper
       for Printed Library Materials Z39.48-1984.

15   14   13   12

PERSEUS
POD
ON DEMAND

For Ashlyn and Chris

Contents

Tables and Figures

Tables

Figures

Acknowledgments

A provocative book will often give rise to several journal articles, but less often will an article stimulate the writing of a textbook. That is what happened in this case. My grateful thanks to my friend and mentor William C. Mitchell for his "Textbook Public Choice: A Review Essay" (*Public Choice*, 1982) and for many subsequent discussions that helped a novice understand the literature and write a text that may help students appreciate the collective choice way of thinking.

I also offer my thanks to Tom Husted, Laura Langbein, and Michael Munger for using draft versions of the manuscript in their classes and for providing timely and valuable criticism; Randall Holcombe, Larry Kenny, and Jeffrey Berry for kind words of encouragement; Paul Barkley for teaching me how to write; Jerry Spencer for answering late-night calls and helping me understand the publishing world; and Gene Nelson and Dave Ervin for administrative encouragement.

No one should ever write a book without Bobbie and Ray Glass alongside to do the final typing, formatting, and artwork. I thank them for their patience and their computer skills. Mary Brock, Marianne LeDoux, Claire Renard, Linda Hazlewood, Tjodie Templeton, and Donna Atto also helped prepare the copy, and I appreciate their efforts.

I heartily commend the folks at Westview Press to prospective authors. Spencer Carr, who understood what I was trying to do, passed on his enthusiasm to Marykay Scott, Julie Seko, Shena Redmond, and Ellen Kresky, who helped us put it together. My thanks to all of you.

Teachers who write textbooks know that their students—past, present, and future—are really the ones who deserve the main thanks: for their questions, scowls, and occasional blank looks, and then, their grateful nods when they "see it." May this book expedite that process.

Joe B. Stevens

1

Introduction

1.0 Economics and Collective Choice

Neighbors get together to discuss what they can do about preventing burglaries in their part of town. At the state capitol, the legislature debates a proposal to reduce air pollution. At a nearby convention, manufacturers of electronic equipment discuss a legislative proposal to raise tariffs on imports from Japan. In the countryside, angry farmers debate how to deal with a neighbor who sells his milk as usual instead of dumping it to support their boycott. A voter wonders whether reading the voter's pamphlet is worth the time it takes, and indeed, whether voting itself is worth it.

These situations all involve collective choice, and they all involve economics. The purpose of this book is to present a set of economic concepts that allow a better understanding of collective choice situations and to show how much they have in common. Many of the economic concepts have been developed in the past thirty years, but many of the issues are as old as civilization. It might not be difficult to imagine the cave people, all armed with large clubs, and all with strong opinions about who should go out and fight a marauder and who gets to stay in the cave. Our present means of resolving issues may be more sophisticated, but we still worry about marauders and we still debate who should do battle and who gets to stay in the cave.

Economics and collective choice are terms that need to be defined and explained. Economics can be defined, as usual, as the allocation of scarce resources among alternative uses, but collective choice requires more attention because it is probably less familiar to students of economics.

1

1.1 Elements of Collective Choice

Participants, methods of choice, and criteria for choosing are the key elements of collective choice. Let's deal briefly with each of these.

1.11 Participants

A simplistic view of collective choice is that everyone in a group comes together to decide a matter of common interest. This invites images of community, belonging, and responsibility, but it characterizes only a small part of collective choice. For one thing, participation—or the lack of it—is an outcome of an incentive system. Participation in collective choice is usually voluntary, but unless social pressure, civic pride, or the prospects for gain cause one to participate, voluntary may mean nonparticipatory. You might participate by voting, but your vote is only one of many, and its absence probably won't be noticed. Thus, you may decide not to vote. You can work to elect a candidate to serve in the U.S. Senate, but the election bid may not be successful. You can apply to work for a government agency where you can participate in collective choice by helping to carry out—and maybe bend—legislative enactments.

Voters, senatorial candidates, and government workers aren't the only ones who participate in collective choice. Business firms, trade associations, labor unions, nonprofit organizations, and many other interest groups may also participate. There may be many—or few—participants in collective choice. They may be elected, they may be appointed, they may be hired, or they may volunteer to participate. And they may have very different points of view about how to resolve an issue.

1.12 Methods of Choice

The second element of collective choice is the method of making decisions. There are several methods of choice, and more than one is usually used in a particular situation. A dictator might make all major decisions in a very centralized fashion with religion, tradition, or military power as the basis for authority. This extreme method of making decisions doesn't sound very attractive, but even its critics admit that it can save on the use of resources. Serfs and vassals in feudal times had very few rights and civil liberties, but they didn't have to spend much time on matters of collective choice.

At the other end of the spectrum is agreeing collectively to use the market as a decentralized way to make decisions: Individuals choose what they will buy and sell. To a great degree, people make their own decisions about where to live, where to work, what clothes to buy, and where to do the grocery shopping. We collectively decide to allow individual choice to work when we resist centralized control over these types of decisions. Others could, after all, make these decisions for us.

Another method for making collective choices leans heavily on competence or expertise, drawing on the advice of someone with special skills that are usually technological or scientific. In *After the Revolution* (1970), Robert Dahl noted that the passengers aboard an aircraft that has developed engine trouble aren't likely to insist on voting on what to do; they expect the pilot and crew to be trained to deal with such emergencies. People aren't always willing to follow the voice of competence; many still use tobacco, for example, in spite of scientific evidence that smoking may cause cancer. Should people always (or usually) defer to competence? Hank Jenkins-Smith (1990) has recently examined the tensions that exist between authority and democracy in an increasingly technical society; not surprisingly, the issues are complex.

Consensus is another way to make collective decisions. With this method a group doesn't decide until everyone agrees on the fundamental issues, even though they may still disagree on the details. The League of Women Voters has operated with this method for many years. Despite its factions, Congress occasionally passes major legislation by a nearly unanimous vote, which indicates that the members have reached consensus on that issue. But the process of reaching consensus can be slow, and sometimes matters won't wait. Whether a consensus is right can also be debated. The dissent by Senators Wayne Morse (Ore.) and Ernest Gruening (Alaska) on the Gulf of Tonkin Resolution early in the Vietnam War, for example, was later hailed as an act of courage and wisdom.

Because we often can't wait for a consensus to emerge, we often use voting to decide an issue. Before we vote, we have to decide what we're voting on, decide on a voting rule, and decide who can vote. Issues need to be defined; they don't just appear, full-blown, out of thin air. Should we use majority rule, unanimity, plurality, or some other method of voting? We usually vote by majority rule. Our founders, however, weren't overly impressed with the wisdom that the working class of the late eighteenth century might display in voting. An example of this attitude toward majority rule, one held by Gouverneur Morris, an aspiring young politician from New York and soon-to-be statesman and diplomat, was cited by historian Richard Hofstadter. As Morris saw the working-class voters, "The mob begin to think and reason. Poor reptiles!

. . . They bask in the sun, and ere noon they will bite, depend upon it. The gentry begin to fear this" (1974, p. 6). The franchise, the matter of who can vote, can also be thorny. Mental competence may be required by voting laws, and minimum ages usually apply.

Another way to make collective choices is through representation—by electing people to represent us on school boards, city councils, and in state legislatures and Congress. This is a practical alternative. Usually the question is not whether we should have representation but what type of rules and incentives will cause representatives to be responsive to our needs and wishes. As we'll see later on, this isn't a trivial matter.

We could choose to have governance by the elite, by those who have somehow risen above the masses. If force was the basis for this elite authority, we would probably regard the elite as dictatorial, but if their authority is based on competence, as is the case with the captain of an airliner, this type of governance might be more acceptable. In his classic study of Middletown (1961), Robert Dahl found that most of the major community decisions were made by a few local leaders, many of whom were business and professional people rather than elected officials. Dye and Ziegler (1990) believe that the elite have historically dominated collective choice in this country but that they have often done so with considerable sympathy for democratic values.

Another method, although somewhat startling at first thought, is for volunteers to make collective choices. This might seem like an invitation to dictatorship, but our representative process actually involves a great deal of voluntarism by those who run for Congress, work for government agencies, or serve interest groups and other nongovernmental organizations. Because they are volunteers, they are likely to have strong views on certain issues, and this often invites participation by other volunteers with opposing views.

1.13 Criteria

The third key aspect of collective choice involves *criteria* (or reasons) for choosing one collective action over another.[1] We have come to accept simple criteria for some decisions. A common criterion for enrolling a child in public kindergarten, for example, is that the child must be five years old by October 1. The usual age criterion for obtaining a driver's license is that the driver must be sixteen years old. As issues become more complex, however, simple criteria are not adequate for collective choice. Instead, we often need to consider several reasons for taking a particular course of action.

Most likely, however, the criteria for collective choice are not stated, are vaguely stated, or are misstated by individuals and groups who are interested in particular outcomes. One reason for the lack of clear, accurate statements of criteria is that it may be hard or even impossible for people to identify their reasons for supporting an action. People might like small neighborhood parks and public libraries, but they might be hard-pressed to say exactly why they feel this way. Fortunately, it isn't usually necessary to agree on criteria if a course of action can be agreed upon. I might like parks because they provide open space; you might like them because trees and grass release oxygen. Together, we can agree that we should have parks, but maybe for different reasons. Charles Lindblom (1959) characterized this as *muddling through*, a collective-choice process that features agreement on actions rather than agreement on objectives, one that stresses means rather than ends. According to Lindblom, this method is sound and practical despite its name.

The misstatement of criteria, however, is often a result of incentive structures. That is, it may be advantageous to be vague or misleading about one's reasons for opposing or supporting certain courses of collective action. Suppose that a real estate developer buys a pleasant pasture across from your house and proposes to turn it into a subdivision of tract houses. As an adjacent homeowner, you may not like this. How should you argue your case before the local planning council? You could try to protect your self-interest by saying that the development would ruin your view. Others, however, might say, "That's tough; it ruined someone else's view when you built your house." People in these situations tend to appeal to the "public interest" with a collective rationale for fighting the subdivision: It would ruin *our* view (not just my view), it would clog *our* streets, it would increase the crime rate in *our* community.

Whether these claims are valid depends on the situation, but the incentives for exact and honest statements of criteria for choice are often weak. Morris Fiorina, a political scientist, puts it concisely: "History provides too many examples of special-interest wolves wearing public-interest fleeces" (1989, p. xvi). Because of the weak incentive structure for stating one's reason for doing something, another political scientist, William Riker (1986), greatly downplays the role of criteria; he focuses instead on political manipulation through the formation of coalitions, and through strategic voting and the manipulation of voting dimensions. We'll consider these in Chapter 6; each strategy is designed to secure an outcome that is desired by those who promote the strategy.

In light of the very real difficulties in stating criteria for collective action and because of the incentives for people to misstate their real reasons for action, economists like to think in terms of two criteria for collective choice. The first is *economic efficiency*, or, so to speak, the size of the economic pie. The second criterion is *equity*, or how the economic pie is divided among members of society. Equity, ethics, fairness, justice, distribution: All fall within the second criterion as desirable goals that a society might seek. Economists tend to lump them together in a rather cavalier manner because they have no special expertise or authority on these matters. Economic efficiency, however, is unique to economics. It is based on the notion that, other things equal, a larger set of goods and services is better than a smaller set, something that we'll discuss more in Chapter 2.

If economists are going to advise policymakers, they need to state the criteria that lie behind their recommendations. As an individual, I may buy a blue shirt if I like blue shirts. And maybe it's all right if I vote for Senator Smith because he looks like my grandfather. As an economist and policy adviser, however, I (or we) need to be able to justify my (our) advice on the basis of explicit criteria that others can accept or reject. This is all the more important when the two criteria of efficiency and equity fail to work in the same direction on an issue. What is efficient may not be fair, and what is fair may not be efficient. Thus, trade-offs between efficiency and fairness often have to be made in collective choice. Both of these actions—making criteria explicit and dealing with trade-offs—can help economists in assisting with collective choice.

Economists might agree that it would be handy to consider only efficiency and equity as criteria, but it is usually difficult to compress policy outcomes into just these two criteria. Practitioners in the academic field of public policy analysis often think in terms of *multiple attributes of outcomes* (Stokey and Zeckhauser, 1978) or *multiple-criteria decision-making* (Zeleny, 1982).[2] To cite Stokey and Zeckhauser,

> If the assortment of possible outcomes of a policy choice is measured in terms of a single attribute, such as dollars, it isn't difficult to decide that more is better than less (or worse, if you're talking about costs). . . . The trouble is that most policy proposals . . . serve a variety of objectives, and their outcomes are described in terms of more than one characteristic, some of which may be unfavorable. These characteristics we call *attributes*. Except by extraordinary good luck no one outcome will be best with respect to all attributes. Which of the combinations of attributes is preferable is rarely self-evident. . . . Nor is there any mechanism ready at hand for reducing all attributes to a common denominator. It is this ubiquitous problem, termed *the multiattribute problem*, that makes it tough to determine our preferences among outcomes. (1978, p. 117)

Stokey and Zeckhauser's advice is that analysts should first define a comprehensive and measurable set of attributes. A likely next step would be to predict outcomes—to determine the effects of policy alternatives on each of the attributes. Finally, the outcomes would need to be subjected to some method or methods of comparison; Stokey and Zeckhauser offer five possibilities. Comparisons of alternative policies are easiest, they argue, if the objectives of the policymakers are known in advance, and if it is known how each attribute relates to the objectives.

Zeleny takes a slightly different slant; criteria are "those attributes, objectives, or goals which have been judged relevant in a given decision situation by a particular decision maker" (1982, p. 17), and attributes are "descriptors of objective reality" (p. 15) from which decisionmakers can form objectives. For example, city officials might adopt an air quality objective of reducing auto emissions (an attribute), provided that the cost of doing so (another attribute) does not exceed a certain level.

Whether decisionmakers use only efficiency and equity as criteria for collective action, whether they use other descriptors of outcomes, or whether they use some other system, a third key aspect of collective choice is thus having some means by which outcomes can be evaluated and judged.

1.2 Examples of Collective Choice

One way to better understand collective choice is to read a newspaper or news periodical, or to listen to a newscast. In this section, five news items are boiled down to their essentials. In the next section, major linkages among these news items are identified. Many other news items could serve the same purpose, but these five include a rich variety of insights into collective choice.

1.21 Interstate Highways

The first news item relates to the condition of our highways, particularly the U.S. interstate highway system. According to a 1989 article in the *Wall Street Journal*,

> The Federal Highway Administration, which now spends about $13 billion a year on repairs and construction, figures that bringing the roads up to "minimum engineering standards" would cost a stunning $565 billion to $655 billion over the next 20 years. For comparison, the huge bailout of the nation's failed savings and loans, perhaps the biggest financial debacle in history, is expected to cost about $166 billion. (August 30, 1989, p. A1)

It is also pointed out that the present system was designed for a much lighter traffic level than now exists, and that businesses now move 75 percent of their freight by highways. Not surprisingly, this concentration of highway use generates political demands for road improvements, but with many of the costs to be paid by others:

> Trucking companies, which pay special federal taxes to help fix the roads, have long been the most vocal lobby for more federal spending on highways. Experts say, however, that their extra tax assessment doesn't come close to compensating for what the big rigs do to roads. The Transportation Department estimates that a single 80,000-pound truck does as much damage to an interstate as 9,600 cars. (p. A8)

1.22 Federal Deposit Insurance

A second example of collective choice relates to the use of federal money to pay back investors whose deposits were lost through poor investments made by savings and loan institutions and banks, starting in the mid-1980s. "Bailouts," it has been argued, are needed to maintain investor confidence in a financial system that has helped make home ownership a reality for millions of Americans. Because each deposit has been insured up to at least $100,000 (many are fully insured) by the Federal Savings and Loan Insurance Corporation (FSLIC) or the Federal Deposit Insurance Corporation (FDIC), the average citizen has been free from worry about putting savings in the hands of these institutions. The flip side of the coin, however, has been that the legal liability of the thrifts and banks has been limited to the losses of their own capital; thus, the true risks of their investments are not taken into account. The *Wall Street Journal* notes:

> Born in the Depression with the modest aim of protecting Mom and Pop depositors, deposit insurance has grown into a monster that defends major depositors at banks deemed "too big to fail." Out of fairness, regulators routinely back all deposits at most other banks as well.
>
> Regulatory precedent and policy have rendered meaningless the limit emblazoned in every bank lobby in the country: "Each depositor insured to $100,000." In practice, the only depositors held by regulators to the $100,000 cutoff are those with their money in certain small institutions that can't be sold. Thus, deposit insurance now protects the nation's biggest and most sophisticated investors. And as hundreds of failed thrifts have lately proved, deposit insurance gives bankers the license to bet big, with taxpayers covering the risk. (August 30, 1989, p. A16)

One participant described it this way in a newscast: "You play the game with your own money 'til it's all gone, then you play with the government's money."

Although depositor losses are being met through higher insurance premiums paid by financial institutions and from U.S. treasury receipts, the system is being revised through reorganization of regulatory agencies, the takeover of several hundred insolvent thrifts, and the encouragement of "depositor discipline." The latter would expose depositors to the threat of some degree of loss (10 to 15 percent) on individual deposits over $100,000. This, it is argued, would encourage depositors to investigate the soundness of their bank or thrift.

These proposed revisions have not gone unnoticed by vested financial interests. While the thrift industry was posting losses of $17 billion (1987-1988), it was also contributing $1.85 million to the campaigns of selected House and Senate candidates (*Wall Street Journal*, February 7, 1989, p. A20). Among the 163 PACs (political action committees) sponsored by the FSLIC-insured thrifts and their trade associations, contributions to House and Senate candidates rose by 42 percent between 1983-1984 and 1987-1988. Banking, construction, and related industries were also observing the scene with keen interest.

1.23 *Veterans' Housing Loans*

The third example of collective choice comes from state government. In Oregon, as in several other states, qualified veterans are able to buy homes at low interest rates through a veterans' loan program because the state has chosen to use its borrowing power to issue tax-free bonds to finance the program. The program has not been controversial because a deserving clientele is thought to be served by a program that appears costless to taxpayers. Veterans are expected to pay off the bonds, as well as pay the operating costs of the program. A major Oregon newspaper editorialized: "As the Legislature looks into the long-term financial problems of the Oregon veterans loan program, it should keep one thought firmly in mind: Responsibility for making the fund solvent should rest with those who borrowed from it, not Oregon's taxpayers as a whole" (*Oregonian*, January 28, 1987, p. B8). Even if the veterans pay all the out-of-pocket costs, there is still another cost that is borne by all the citizens of the state. The bonds are tax free; investors who buy them pay no taxes on their interest earnings. There is, however, a sacrifice of potential tax revenues because the bonds could have been issued on a taxable basis. Economists call this a *tax expenditure*, or a revenue loss to government because of tax laws. The federal tax exemption on interest paid for home mortgages is one example. Programs like this are often popular for several reasons. They seem to serve a deserving clientele, their true cost is not well understood by voters, and few politicians want to jeopardize their electoral position by educating the voters on the issue.

1.24 Timber Management

A fourth situation deals with conflicts between timber and amenity uses of federal forests in the Pacific Northwest and with the intense political struggle between producer groups and environmental groups. By 1989, several environmental groups had gained court injunctions that blocked numerous timber sales; these injunctions were based on a 1989 U.S. District Court decision that ruled the Forest Service had not done adequate planning for protection of the spotted owl, which was then under consideration for inclusion on and later was placed on the list of endangered species. These sales, many of which were on old-growth forest habitats of the spotted owl, involved 2 billion board feet of standing timber. This was a sizable fraction of the total sales volume of 5 to 6 billion board feet that had been sold by the federal government in Oregon and Washington in 1988.

These court injunctions brought intense political pressures by timber interests for measures that would restore the flow of timber for harvest. On June 24, 1989, a unique timber summit was held in Salem, Oregon. A small and carefully selected group of Northwest congress members, governors, industry leaders, and environmental leaders met and bargained in a fishbowl atmosphere. To the surprise of many observers, substantive proposals were offered even though a settlement was not reached. A local news commentator described the outcome in these critical terms: "Environmentalists missed the bus on last week's federal timber supply compromise offered by Oregon's governor and congressional delegation. The timber industry caught it. The difference wasn't necessarily that one side wanted this kind of deal and the other didn't; rather, one side was able to reach a consensus and speak with one voice. The other wasn't" (*Oregonian*, July 2, 1989, p. D2).

The sticking point for the environmental groups was that most of them didn't want to compromise their key bargaining chip, which was the ability to seek court injunctions to block timber sales, but their informal alliance lacked a formal structure for quick decision-making. Three months after the timber summit, the environmental coalition agreed to release about half of the timber sales, provided that court review of new sales be accelerated and that the Forest Service expand and protect spotted owl habitat (*Oregonian*, October 8, 1989).

1.25 *Public School Finance*

The fifth situation, this one at a local level, involves the consequences of majority rule voting on levels of property tax support for public schools in Oregon. In 1914, a property tax "base" was set for each Oregon school district. Each base specified the total amount of property taxes that a district could collect without a popular vote. The law permitted these bases to increase by 6 percent annually without a popular vote. Inflation and enrollment growth soon caused the 6 percent growth rate to be inadequate, and many districts became dependent on annual voter approval of nearly their entire operating budget. By the mid-1980s, more and more school budgets were being defeated. Several schools had been temporarily closed for lack of funds, and the state's largest business lobby had declared school funding to be the number one business problem in Oregon.

An innovative proposal was made and approved in 1987. If a district's operating budget had not received voter approval by September 30, a month after the start of school, a "safety net" could be declared by the school board. Under this plan, a district could simply collect, without further voting, the same amount of property taxes it had collected in the previous year. Instead of being jubilant, however, most school officials fought the idea tooth and nail. One savvy political commentator described it this way:

> "I think you and I have been here before," former Senate President Jason Boe said with a grin. We were standing in the lobby outside the Senate chamber watching a parade of school superintendents on the Capitol's closed-circuit television system. The educators were opposing the Senate-passed safety net to prevent future school closures. Boe, now a lobbyist, was the author of a similar safety net in 1977 when he presided over the Senate. Not much has changed in a decade. "I think certain elements of education have a dog-in-the-manger attitude. They know voters have to give in eventually under the present system. They really don't want it changed unless they get it changed their way," Boe said in a recent interview. (*Oregonian*, February 16, 1987, p. B6)

By saying that voters "have to give in eventually," the commentor meant that prior to the safety net, voters begrudgingly approved larger-than-desired budgets rather than see their schools close. (This is discussed further in Section 9.63.) The safety net meant that schools wouldn't close, but it also meant that school boards could no longer threaten voters with the consequences of an inadequate tax base. This, according to the commentator, is what was worrying school officials, "They argue that by taking away the threat of closure, the Legislature is taking away any incentive voters have to approve higher spending levels" (*Oregonian*, February 16, 1987, p. B6).

1.3 Linkages Among the Examples

These news stories involve different issues and different levels of government, but they have a number of things in common. All three elements of collective choice are reflected in each example. Some of the participants are elected, some are appointed, some are self-selected, and some are more powerful than others. There are one or more methods of collective choice in each story, and there are criteria or reasons for making these choices, although these are often implicit rather than explicit.

1.31 *Governments Do Many Things*

One of the more obvious linkages among the issues is that governments do many things. Governments build roads, operate schools, regulate financial institutions, and insure against risk, among other things. Historically, a primary role of government has been to produce goods and services that were not being produced in appropriate amounts by profit-seeking firms or other suppliers. Defense against invaders, for example, was a valuable economic service that bound the feudal classes to the nobility. Later, governments furnished roads and utilities because markets weren't providing enough of these goods and services.

But governments now do much more than produce goods and services. They also make major transfers of income, wealth, and utility from one group to another. The term *transfer society* has been coined to indicate that the dominant role of government today is transferring income, wealth, and utility, rather than producing goods and services (Anderson and Hill, 1980). We see in each issue that some people or groups are made better off because of taxes, expenditures, subsidies, and regulatory decisions.

1.32 *Some People Gain, Some People Lose*

A second linkage among these issues is that some gain and others lose because of collective action. When freight transport on interstate highways is subsidized by charging less than the full costs of big rig operation, someone else—usually the taxpayer—ultimately has to pay for maintenance and repair of the system. When veterans are subsidized by enabling them to buy homes at lower-than-market interest rates, taxpayers either have to pay more taxes or make do with fewer public services. In both cases, there are far more taxpayers (losers) than there are truckers and veterans (gainers), and the per capita gains to truckers and veterans are probably much larger than the per capita costs to taxpayers. As a consequence, truckers and veterans have more incentive to propose and support political action than individual taxpayers have to oppose it.

1.33 Some Interests Are Better Represented Than Others

All five issues clearly show that some interests are better represented than others in the political process. Producers in the two national issues are well represented by powerful interest groups in the trucking, manufacturing, banking, and savings and loan industries. The story is often the same at the state and local levels. In Oregon, for example, the construction and wood products industries support the veterans' housing loan program because these industries gain from an aggressive loan program.

In general, the private participants in all these issues tend to be self-selected based on their expected gains and losses. Those who anticipate a net gain, even after the costs of participation are taken into account, tend to be active participants in collective choice. Those who anticipate net losses if they don't participate may also be active, especially if the expected losses are large. Those who see small gains or losses, however, will tend not to participate, especially if the costs of participation are high.

Mancur Olson pointed out in his influential book *The Logic of Collective Action* (1965) the pervasiveness of *latent groups*, that is, the lack of action by individuals in situations where the overall gain to a group will be large if action is taken but the expected gain for any one individual is inadequate to trigger action. There are latent groups in each of the previously outlined issues: motorists, depositors, recreationists, homeowners, and taxpayers. In each case, they are unlikely to take action as individuals even though the group might benefit if they did.

Two other participants in collective choice are presumed to consider all the various interests in a democratic society, including those of latent groups. These are the elected representatives and the administrators of government agencies. These parties may view themselves as spokespersons for latent groups, they may try to balance the interests of self-selected groups and latent groups, they may serve the interest of self-selected groups, or they may serve their own self-interest. Chapters 7 through 11 are devoted to this topic.

1.34 Decisions Are Delegated

None of the five issues was decided by a dictator, and none was left strictly to the market. Instead, the real action was somewhere in between. Although we rely fairly heavily on markets to allocate resources, governments often modify these markets in a variety of ways. Most of the issues were about how and whether markets should be modified: whether to change shipping costs by raising user charges for eighteen-wheelers, whether to regulate the investment portfolios of savings and loan associations and thrifts, whether to modify the mortgage markets for veterans' home loans.

One way to decide these issues is through competence or expertise. In the highway case, heavy reliance might be placed on physical safety. No one wants a poorly designed bridge to collapse, and detailed safety standards have been developed by engineers to avoid this. Competence and expertise are also important in financial issues. How can we regulate investors to enhance financial safety? How can we borrow low-cost money for veterans and still maintain a solvent loan program? The timber management issue reflects a strong need for biological expertise so that forest resources can be managed to have more lumber, more water, more wildlife, and more recreation, or to at least minimize conflicts among these uses.

But the political nature of each issue suggests that although we want to be advised by competence and expertise, we don't want to be ruled by technocrats; we would probably say that biologists alone should not rule the forest. With one exception, however, none of the five issues were resolved by a direct vote of the people. In fact, the Oregon school finance example is interesting largely because of its uniqueness as a participatory rather than a delegated decision.

In most of the issues, collective choice involves decisions to modify or replace markets. These decisions are made through representation, reinforced by voluntarism and elitism, and implemented by competence. In each issue, an elected body, whether Congress, a state legislature, or a school board, exercises control over a facet of our economic lives: highway safety, the safety of our financial institutions, conflicts among natural resource uses, the education of children. The representatives are often not "plain folks." Each member of the U.S. House of Representatives represents a half-million people or more; they must be able to raise large amounts in campaign contributions to be reelected. They are assisted (or resisted) in their efforts by key volunteers, many of whom are also drawn from the elite in terms of education, income, and social status. Some represent vested economic interests—trade groups representing savings and loan associations, for example. Others represent citizen-based interest groups that focus on particular concerns such as the environment, health, or product safety. The National Wildlife Federation and the Sierra Club, for example, have played major roles in timber management. Other volunteers represent interest groups that are particularly concerned about democratic processes. Common Cause and the League of Women Voters are examples. The administration of policies on highways, forests, housing, and schools is delegated to nonelected administrators in government agencies because of the competence each agency possesses. Thus, what we may call representation as a method of collective choice is, in a modern and complex society, really a blend of elected representatives, voluntary interest groups, and nonelected administrators.

1.35 Criteria Are Fuzzy

A final and crucial linkage among the five issues has to do with the criteria for choice. In general, the criteria are fuzzy rather than sharp, implicit rather than explicit, multiple rather than singular. We want the highways to be safe and adequate, but we want them to be reasonable in cost. Those concerned with deposit insurance seem to want financial safety as well as asset growth. Those concerned with veterans' loans want a system that favors veterans, but they also want a financially solvent and self-supporting system. One side of the timber management issue wants to maintain the ecological integrity of the forest, the other side wants higher harvest levels. Oregon legislators and school supporters want to stabilize funding of the public schools, but at different levels.

As noted earlier, muddling through as a method of collective choice involves agreement on means rather than ends. Economists, however, have never felt comfortable with this method. Instead, they favor a more explicit decision method that Lindblom (1959) called *rational-comprehensive decision-making*. In this method, an objective is agreed upon, the alternatives for reaching this objective are evaluated, and a decision is made. Ends or objectives are first decided, then appropriate means are selected. Although the criterion of equity or fairness may temper economists' advice, many are reasonably comfortable with the idea that economic efficiency should be a major social objective and that we should endeavor to follow the rational-comprehensive method for obtaining efficiency. Collective choice, however, usually muddles through with vague criteria.

1.4 Objectives of the Book

1.41 *Understanding Economic Efficiency*

One major objective of this book is to help students understand the strengths and the weaknesses of the economic efficiency criterion in guiding public action, because it—rather than the equity criterion—is unique to economics. The fact that the political process doesn't always seem rational and comprehensive, at least to the economist, suggests that a second objective of the book is also important. The second objective is to use economic models to understand how the political process works.

First we have to distinguish between economic efficiency, on one hand, and markets, on the other. The two are related, but they aren't the same thing. Even after students have taken a course or two in economics, their understanding of economic efficiency is likely to be jumbled together with their understanding of how markets work. True, markets can be efficient. Students may learn that the market for designer jeans is an efficient method for providing jeans to those who want them the most and have the greatest purchasing power. But economic efficiency is an end, an objective, or a goal; markets are simply a means or a method by which this goal might be achieved. Methods other than markets also exist. On paper at least, a central planner could allocate resources efficiently.

Markets can be an efficient or an inefficient way to allocate resources, as we'll see in Chapters 2 and 3. In many cases, we have chosen to replace or modify markets with government action if we think that markets will produce inefficient results. The provision of national defense and the public ownership of wildlife resources are two examples of government action. We have also tried to patch up inefficient markets through government intervention to force polluters to bear the costs of pollution. In other words, even if economic efficiency is a goal of collective choice, markets may not be an efficient way to reach that goal.

Comparing Alternatives. Let's go back to one of the news items to illustrate the idea of economic efficiency. We have decided that government should have a major role in providing interstate highways. There are many ways, however, to build and maintain roads and highways; that is, there are many attributes or descriptors of construction outcomes. The roads can be ten lanes wide, they can be two lanes wide with passing lanes, or they can be just two lanes wide. Roads can be straight lines between two points or they can follow the terrain. Roads can go through urban areas or they can bypass these areas. They can be well maintained, moderately maintained, or receive almost no maintenance. One might say, "Leave it to the highway engineers; this is what they're paid to do." But even though we want to draw on engineering competence, there is no assurance that engineers will produce the most efficient highway system, at least as economists use the term.

Imagine that two engineering alternatives have been defined for a new stretch of highway between two cities. Only one alternative can be built. The first would be a two-lane highway with several passing lanes on hills. This highway would largely follow the contour of the land. The second alternative is a straight four-lane highway involving much more modification of the landscape. Other consequences of the two alternatives are these:

- The narrower, more winding road would cost less to build and maintain, even though it would be slightly longer than the straight road. It would be more scenic and there would be less environmental damage due to road construction.
- The straighter, wider road would require less travel time, and shipping costs for freight would be lower. It would be relatively safer; fewer accidents and traffic fatalities would be expected.

It is easy to see that different outcomes would be involved for each alternative; these outcomes can be viewed as gains and losses to a variety of people. Further, these gains and losses appear to be largely noncommensurable or noncomparable. Some of them would be reflected in markets. More construction workers, for example, would have to be hired to build the more expensive alternative. Shorter travel times, however, would reduce shipping costs; these gains might be passed on to consumers. Most environmental gains and losses would go unpriced. Siltation from construction might reduce water quality and impair fish habitat, but the more scenic nature of the winding road would be a gain to consumers.

The Need for a Common Denominator.   Some of the consequences of the two highway alternatives might be estimated in physical or monetary terms. The straight road, for example, might cost $7.3 million more to build than the winding road. According to engineering estimates, it would save four more lives per year, it would save 74,000 more hours of motorists' time, and it would reduce shipping costs by $300,000 per year. But it would also cause 7.2 more tons of sediment to be deposited in nearby streams during construction. All of these factors appear calculable, but unless we can reduce the estimates to a meaningful common denominator, we're simply trying to add apples and oranges.

How can we compare the gains and the losses? As we've seen, many of them aren't priced in markets, so a market measure of value isn't available. Nor can we compare gains and losses in *utility*; economists concluded long ago that utility, or the satisfaction provided to people by goods and services, is entirely subjective, and that it isn't comparable among individuals. Gainers and losers could probably vote on which road to build, but as we'll see in Chapter 6, voting doesn't usually allow people to show how strongly they favor or oppose something.

Because of these types of difficulties, economists have developed the idea of *net economic value* as a common denominator for comparing gains and losses. We'll deal with this idea in detail in Chapter 2. Net economic value is the dollar sum of the value of a good or service to consumers and producers. Each of the two highway alternatives will lead to changes in the availability of certain goods and services. Either choice of highway design will make some of these goods and services more available and other goods and services less available. The straight road will make traffic safety and shipping services more available to motorists, but it will also make certain environmental services (scenic views, water quality, and fish) less available. Someone will have to pay taxes to finance either alternative; this will reduce consumption of other goods and services. The most efficient road plan overall, then, is the one with the largest increase in net economic value, taking into account all affected goods and services.

1.42 Understanding the Political Process

The second objective of the book is to allow students to gain a better understanding of the political process. Over the past thirty years, economic models have been developed that allow powerful insights into why governments tax, spend, subsidize, regulate, and deregulate. The fact that economic models can be applied to political issues doesn't mean that students shouldn't study political science. Even though they are different, the focus and methods of the two disciplines can reinforce each other. The focus of political science is often on the concrete and the specific. How are legislative committees structured, for example, and what voting rules do they adopt? Economists are more inclined to take an abstract and deductive model-building approach to understanding political issues. This is often called a *rational choice* approach, one in which participants are assumed to maximize self-interest. The term *rational* is unfortunate, because it seems to imply that any other way of looking at the political process is irrational. In the rational choice approach, the means are assumed to be consistent with the ends, whatever those ends might be. From a rational choice perspective, if a firm attempts to maximize profits, we would expect it to use productive inputs. And a voter who wishes to maximize utility may choose not to vote in an election, particularly if many voters are involved, because the chance of one vote being decisive is very small in this situation.

Rational Choice Models. Five books published between 1957 and 1971 have probably been the most influential works in the rational choice literature. These are *An Economic Theory of Democracy* by Anthony Downs (1957), *The Calculus of Consent* by James M. Buchanan and Gordon Tullock (1962), *The Theory of Political Coalitions* by William H. Riker (1962), *The Logic of Collective Action* by Mancur Olson (1965), and *Bureaucracy and Representative Government* by William A. Niskanen, Jr. (1971).[3] The methodology of these books is largely that of economics, but the subject matter is that of political science. The idea has been that insights can be gained into government that cannot be gained through two separate disciplines. Economics has some natural building blocks with its established theories about consumption and production, about labor supply, and about markets in general. Each of these theories is based on assumptions of self-interest. Consumers and labor suppliers are assumed to maximize utility, firms are assumed to maximize profits, and markets allow voluntary exchanges among self-interested participants.

The rational choice approach to the political process draws on this foundation by adding three other types of participants: voters, elected representatives, and appointed administrators (or as Niskanen labeled them, bureaucrats). Each is assumed to maximize some dimension of self-interest, just as firms try to maximize profits and consumers try to maximize utility. Voters are seen as a special type of consumer, those who may choose to participate in collective decisions made by voting. Elected representatives are assumed to maximize the prospects of (re)election; appointed administrators are usually assumed to maximize budget size, or at least to attempt to do so. Each assumption, of course, flies in the face of popular sentiment that voters should vote and that representatives and administrators should serve the public rather than themselves.

Criticisms and Limitations. Today there is both major criticism and adept defense of rational choice, primarily within political science, where the approach is more controversial than in economics. These can be found in presidential addresses (Lowi, 1991), honorary lectures (Wilson, 1990), exchanges in periodicals (Steiner, 1990, 1991; Johnson, 1990; Stephens, 1991), and scholarly works (Monroe, 1991). One criticism is that rational choice, especially the public choice variety, is too politically conservative. According to Lowi, "If public choice had not already existed as a sub-discipline, the Republican administrations of the 1970s and 1980s would have had to invent it. As laissez-faire ideology calling for limited government . . . , a supporting political theory was needed to demonstrate . . . the irrationality of politics. Public choice is the purest expression of this economic ideology within political science" (1991, p. B-2). Although there is some substance to this charge, things are changing. Some rational choice analysts clearly believe that less government is better government. Others, however, are less swayed by ideology; they are more interested in such things as election rules for aggregating voter preferences, experimental evidence on free-riding, and voting records of and campaign contributions to elected representatives. Many who regard themselves as rational choice analysts see this approach as simply an extension of economic reasoning from the realm of market processes into the realm of political processes.

A second criticism is that the rational choice approach, based on self-interest motivations, is too narrow and too egoistic an interpretation of human nature. One major critic, Steven Kelman, puts it this way:

> They all start with the assumption that there is no difference between economic man and romantic man or political man. People act everywhere as they do in the marketplace. They are out only for themselves, and typically in relatively gross, money-seeking ways like . . . "pigs at the trough."
> My own view is that this . . . is a terrible caricature of reality. It ignores the ability of ideas to defeat interests, and the role that public spirit plays in motivating the behavior of participants in the political process. (1987b, pp. 80-81)

We can agree that ideas and public spirit should prevail in politics, but whether they actually do prevail is another matter. There may be a great deal of difference between *normative models* of government, the way we might like to see government work, and *positive models*, the way it actually works. Many would argue that perverse incentive systems often stack the deck against ideas and public spirit.

A major part of this second criticism is definitional. Exactly what does "self-interest" mean? Does it mean selfishness and materialism, as Kelman implies, or does it mean enlightened self-interest, where individuals take a less self-centered and less materialistic point of view? Kristen Monroe's (1991) recent book of readings on self-interest explores these issues in great depth. The assumption throughout the remaining chapters of this book is that either meaning may be appropriate. Some older voters will vote for higher taxes to help educate young people, for example, but other older voters will not. Both may be rational; they simply think differently and have different preferences.

A third criticism of rational choice is that the pursuit of self-interest is inevitably bad for society. The "public interest," as we will see in Chapter 2, is a very tricky thing to define. It is possible that legislators, for example, might actually serve the public interest even though they have a self-interest motivation. If this seems paradoxical, so did Adam Smith's observation in *The Wealth of Nations* ([1776] 1937) that the baker works not to serve the needs of his customers but to turn a profit for himself. Competition in the political process may cause self-interested legislators to listen to the people, just as competition in economic markets may replace bakers who don't bake good bread.

A fourth criticism is that rational choice models fail to predict because they "understate the role of deliberation, the influence of norms, and the power of passion in human affairs" (Wilson, 1990, p. 560). According to Wilson, rational choice maintains that people will be apathetic about voting. But many do vote. For reasons we will explore later, rational choice also suggests that political parties will probably be much alike—but they are not. A third expectation is that large interest groups will probably not exist because of free-riding—but they do. These are serious charges and they have to be faced.

A final criticism is that the rational choice approach will lead young minds astray. A classic statement of this charge appeared in a recent periodical. "What disturbs me about rational choice is something else . . . I object when rational choice theorists give implicitly or explicitly the impression to their students that human beings *by their very nature* are calculating selfish utility maximizers. As I argued in my earlier piece, this may easily become a self-fulfilling prophecy, in the sense that students take explanation for justification" (Steiner, 1991, p. 431). Students, teachers, and authors should approach rational choice, like any topic, with open eyes and questioning minds. No one wants to be led astray. One should be careful, however, not to mistake method for conclusions. For example, many people today fear that powerful interest groups are thwarting the democratic process with their large contributions to political candidates. This is an understandable concern. To criticize rational choice analysts for developing models of "legislative markets" that facilitate these contributions, however, is like shooting the messenger who brings bad news to the king. This book is dedicated to the proposition that it may be worthwhile to listen to the messenger even if the news is bad.

1.5 Summary

The key elements of collective choice are the participants, the methods of choice, and criteria or reasons for choosing. Participants are often self-selected because of opportunities for gain or fear of losses. As to method, a dictator could make all choices. Or we could allow decisions to be made through voluntary and decentralized markets. We could draw on the competence or expertise of certain people, we could wait for consensus to emerge, we could vote on the issues, we could let representatives decide, we could let the elite make decisions, or we could leave the decisions to volunteers, including interest groups. Often, we do some of each.

The proposed criteria or reasons for collective choice are usually vaguely stated and even misstated by participants as they jockey for political position. To aid in collective choice, economists have developed two criteria for evaluation of proposed actions—economic efficiency, or the size of the economic pie, and equity, or the distribution of the pie among members of society. Even simple actions may lead to outcomes that have many different attributes or characteristics. Comparing proposed actions is seldom easy. Economists have developed the idea of net economic value—the sum in dollar terms of the value of goods and services to consumers and producers—as a common denominator for making efficiency comparisons. The most efficient proposed action is the one that would result in the largest increase in net economic value, considering all affected goods and services. One objective of the book is to help students understand the strengths and weaknesses of the economic efficiency criterion in guiding public action.

A second and equally important objective is to use economic reasoning to help students gain a better understanding of political outcomes when firms, workers, consumers, voters, interest groups, elected representatives, and appointed administrators are motivated by self-interest. This may not sound like a happy situation. It is not an unlikely situation, however, and it deserves our attention.

Terms and Concepts for Review

criteria
muddling through
economic efficiency
equity
multiple attributes of outcomes
multiple-criteria decision-making
tax expenditure
transfer society
latent groups
rational-comprehensive decision-making

utility
net economic value
rational choice
normative models
positive models

2

Efficiency and Equity as Reasons for Collective Action

2.0 The Efficiency Criterion

*2.01 Introduction

One view of the "right" role for government is that it should ensure the efficient use of resources in both the private and the public sectors of the economy. In this view, efficient quantities of all goods and services would be produced, whether through markets, nonprofit organizations, or by government itself. An alternative view of the right role for government is that it should make sure that economic outcomes are fair and equitable. In this chapter, economic efficiency and equity are explored as two major criteria for collective action, and an explanation is offered for economists' tendency to be efficiency advocates in collective choice.

Efficiency and equity are both normative criteria; they suggest how things should be, not necessarily how things are or how they got that way. Neither is sufficient for deciding what government should do. Trade-offs between the two usually have to be made. What is efficient may not be fair; what is fair may not be efficient. Efficiency is important, but equity also matters; surely feelings about ethics, fairness, and justice are indispensable to a humane society.

Although economists aren't particularly competent in saying what is equitable, they do have something special to say about the efficiency of resource use. Moreover, the incentive system within the political process suggests that few people other than economists will be very concerned about efficiency, at least in the particular sense that economists define it.

---

* Starred sections offer a brief survey of efficiency concepts.

For these reasons, we need to understand what efficiency is, what it offers as a norm, and what can be done about its limitations.

* 2.02 What Is Efficiency and Why Is It Important?

One way to think about the meaning of economic efficiency is with a supply and demand diagram for a market good. An instructor in a principles of economics class would expect students to know that a price above the intersection of supply and demand curves wouldn't be an equilibrium price if the market for the good were competitive. At price P_h, for example, too much would be offered for sale but too little would be demanded (Figure 2.1). Hence, price would tend to fall toward the intersection of the two curves (P^*). At price P_w, too much would be demanded, too little would be offered, and the price would rise.

If we are to look at Figure 2.1 from an efficiency perspective, not just a price-equilibrium perspective, we need to focus on whether an efficient quantity of a good or service will be produced. As economists define it, the most efficient quantity is that which maximizes the *net economic value*, or the value of a good to consumers and producers. The demand function (DD) reflects the *marginal benefit* (MB) to consumers; the benefit or utility of an additional unit of the good can be expected to decline as more is consumed per unit of time. The supply function (SS) reflects the *marginal cost* (MC) of producing the good; the cost of producing an additional unit often rises as more is produced per unit of time.

If the good in Figure 2.1 is exchanged in competitive markets, an equilibrium price (P^*) and quantity (Q^*) equates supply and demand. This equilibrium also equates the marginal benefit to consumers with the marginal cost to producers. Because consumers are willing to pay more than P^* for all units of the good except the last unit, they enjoy a *consumers' surplus*. In dollar value, this surplus is the area abP*. Producers also enjoy a *producers' surplus* (area P*bc) because they are able to sell all units of the good at price P^* even though their marginal costs of production are less than P^* for all except the last unit.

Together, the consumers' surplus and the producers' surplus make up net economic value; the value of the good or service to society is equal in dollar value to area abc. Although this value usually accrues to both consumers and producers, there is no particular reason that it will be divided equally. Try drawing supply and demand functions with various slopes and you will quickly see that the two surpluses can be very different in size.

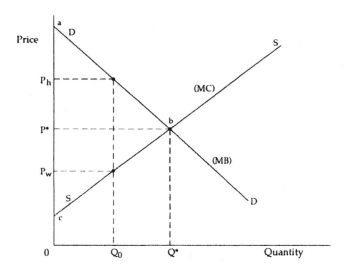

FIGURE 2.1 Supply and Demand for a Good or Service

Let's bring the ideas together with summary statements:

- The most efficient level of output is that which maximizes net economic value, or the sum of consumers' surplus and producers' surplus.
- Net economic value is maximized at Q^*, where the marginal benefit to consumers equals the marginal cost to producers.
- The most efficient output is Q^*.

Another concept can also be introduced. An output level is *Pareto efficient*[1] only if it is not possible to make someone better off without making someone else worse off. Output Q^* has this characteristic. But consider output Q_0, where Q_0 is a smaller output level than Q^*. Q_0 is not Pareto efficient. Why? At Q_0, the marginal benefit to consumers exceeds the marginal cost to producers. This implies that consumers could pay what it costs to produce the good and still have something left over. Consumers would be willing to pay P_h, but producers would need only P_w to cover their costs. For the Q_0 unit of output, this difference, P_hP_w, would accrue to society as a surplus. In a very real sense, someone (the consumers) could become better off without making anyone else (the producers) worse off.

We need to recognize, however, that there are many goods and services that aren't bought and sold in markets. Traffic safety and scenic views are two nonmarket goods that were instrumental in the highway example in Section 1.41. In principle, we can ask whether an efficient amount of any good or service is produced. Deciding whether output Q* has been reached will be more difficult with nonmarket goods, of course, than with market goods; this is largely because the supply function doesn't play its usual role and because price isn't used as a rationing device. As we'll see in Chapter 3, something may be a nonmarket good because it is a *public good*, one from which it is difficult or impossible to exclude those who don't pay and one that can be used at the same time by several people. Clean air, for example, is difficult to withhold from users, and it can be used simultaneously by several voters.

In contrast to determining output levels for market goods, there is no built-in incentive to consider *opportunity cost* in determining the level of output for public goods. However, the concept of Pareto efficiency is still relevant; the resources that are used to produce either nonmarket goods or market goods almost always have opportunity costs or values in alternative uses. These costs are what labor and capital could earn by doing other things. If an entrepreneur uses resources to produce a market good, these resources can't be used to produce another good. As a nonmarket good, clean air also has an opportunity cost. Whether we like it or not, clean air could be used for waste dilution. Having clean air is costly because valuable labor and capital resources must be used to treat wastes instead of using the air to dilute these wastes. The challenge in evaluating the efficiency of a nonmarket good is to determine the nature and size of the opportunity costs, but the concept of Pareto efficiency remains the same.

The size of the consumers' surplus and the producers' surplus are also different for a nonmarket good because price isn't used as a rationing device. Access to forest wilderness areas, for example, is usually made available to users without charge; thus, users receive a larger consumers' surplus than if they had to pay an access fee. If a zero price is placed on wilderness access, the consumers' surplus would be the entire area under the demand curve up to the available output. If output were Q*, total consumers' surplus would be the area abQ*0. Because the resources that produce the good have an opportunity cost of S = MC per unit of output, however, area abQ*0 overstates the value of using the area as wilderness. Opportunity costs equal to cbQ*0 would exist; logging, for example, might need to be forgone to maintain the area as wilderness. Thus, the net economic value of wilderness at quantity Q* would be

$$(abQ^*0) - (cbQ^*0) = (abc). \qquad (2.1)$$

The opportunity costs of the forest resources are thus relevant even though wilderness access may be priced at zero.

2.03 Consumer Choice

Now that some basic concepts about efficiency have been summarized, let's go over them in a more thorough manner. Let's also consider some concepts that weren't discussed.

One key concept is *consumer choice*. People often complain that economists are too materialistic, but consumption doesn't have to be materialistic. Watching a sunset, enjoying clean air, and eating an ice cream cone are all acts of consumption; nothing is consumed although its form may be changed. Each of these acts, however, produces a sense of *utility* or want satisfaction for the consumer.

A basic concept of consumer choice is that a consumer (*i*) has a *utility function*, U^i, where:

$$U^i = U^i(q_1^i, q_2^i ..., q_n^i), \tag{2.2}$$

where q_1 through q_n are goods and services, or commodities, to use a shorthand phrase. We assume that the consumer attempts to maximize utility from the consumption of these commodities given that limited amounts of money or time are available to be spent.

One key assumption of consumer choice theory is that the consumer is able to compare different bundles or combinations of commodities in terms of their ability to provide utility. Most people would rather have two steaks and two desserts each week, for example, than have two steaks and only one dessert each week. The first combination (*a*) yields greater utility than the second (*b*), and it is located on a higher *indifference curve* represented by U_1 in Figure 2.2. (Graphical analysis limits us to comparing two commodities.) It is not possible (or even necessary) to say how much more utility U_1 yields than U_0, only that all combinations along U_1 are of constant utility, and that the consumer prefers any combination along U_1 to any combination along U_0. Those combinations of commodities toward the upper right in Figure 2.2 are preferred to those in the lower left. In the consumer's own opinion, he or she becomes "better off" as they reach higher indifference curves on their *indifference map*.

Another important characteristic of indifference curves is that they have a negative slope; if less of one good is consumed, more of the other good has to be consumed to keep the consumer at a constant utility level. The geometric slope of an indifference curve reflects the *marginal rate of*

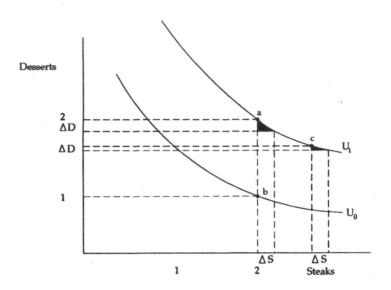

FIGURE 2.2 Indifference Curves for a Consumer

substitution (MRS) between goods, or the rate at which one good might be substituted for another, holding utility constant. Moving from left to right along either indifference curve in Figure 2.2, the MRS diminishes as more of one good is obtained at the expense of having less of the other. At *a*, for example, the consumer would give up ΔD desserts to get ΔS steaks per week. Toward *c* and farther to the right, as steaks become plentiful and desserts become scarce, the MRS of desserts for steaks ($\Delta D/\Delta S$) becomes smaller and approaches zero as the indifference curve flattens out.

2.04 Pareto Efficiency in an Exchange Economy

Economists usually make a value judgment that the preferences of consumers are valid. One might not always agree that consumers should rank commodity bundles the way they do, but there is a strong tradition in economic analysis of accepting the idea of *consumer sovereignty*. That is, we rule out the possibility that someone else can declare that one dessert and two steaks are actually better for the consumer than two desserts and two steaks. This quickly rings a warning bell, because eating too many desserts *or* steaks may not be nutritionally wise! We generally assume, however, that consumers, especially informed consumers, are in the best position to make these decisions; to argue otherwise threatens our traditions with respect to individual rights, liberties, and responsibilities.

Now imagine a simple *exchange economy*, where the amounts of two tradeable goods are fixed at certain levels. Indifference curves can help us understand the meaning of Pareto efficiency. Assume, for example, that there are ten steaks, ten desserts, and two consumers. A random initial allocation gives Jones seven of the ten steaks, but only three of the ten desserts. Smith has three steaks and seven desserts. The initial allocation is shown as *a* in Figure 2.3. Jones's indifference map, consisting of indifference curves J_0 and J_1, looks normal, but Smith's indifference map may look strange at first. This is because it is turned upside down and superimposed on Jones's indifference map. This is not just to aggravate students but to show that there are fixed amounts of the two goods. The left and right sides of the *Edgeworth box diagram*[2] are ten steaks high, so to speak, and the bottom and top of the diagram are ten desserts wide.

At *a*, Jones's utility level is represented by indifference curve J_0. Smith's utility is represented by indifference curve S_0. For simplicity, assume that the two consumers have *independent utility functions*; each derives utility from her own consumption but not from consumption by the other person. Both parties in Figure 2.3 can benefit by exchange. The slopes of the two indifference curves are not equal at *a*; therefore, Smith

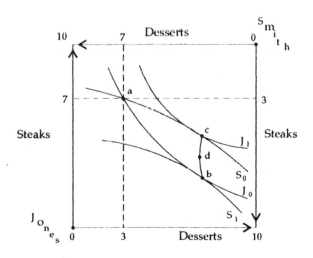

FIGURE 2.3 Trading in an Exchange Economy

and Jones must have different marginal rates of substitution between the two goods.[3] Thus, there is an incentive for exchange because the consumers value the two goods differently. Jones would be willing to trade some steak for Smith's dessert, and Smith would be willing to trade some dessert for Jones's steak.

If exchange were costless, one possibility would be to move to b, where Jones is no better off (but no worse off) than with the initial allocation; she is still on indifference curve J_0. At b, Smith is better off; exchange has allowed her to increase utility from S_0 to S_1. This is a *Pareto improvement* in efficiency because someone (Smith) has been made better off without making anyone else (Jones) worse off. Exchange could also have taken them to c, where Jones is better off and Smith's utility remains constant. The range of mutually beneficial outcomes is between b and c. Both Smith and Jones could gain by moving to d, for example, where two additional indifference curves (not shown) would be tangent. Through exchange, the two parties could move from a to any point along the *contract curve* between b and c; someone could gain without anyone else losing. All points along the contract curve are *Pareto superior* to a, the starting point. Both parties would gain; this is why exchange would occur. Each point along the contract curve is *Pareto efficient*; once the contract curve has been reached, it is no longer possible to make someone better off without making someone else worse off.

The overall set of concepts is often referred to as *Pareto efficiency*, which is an umbrella term for three more precise terms that have just been defined (*Pareto improvement, Pareto superior,* and *Pareto efficient*). The implication is that if someone becomes better off without someone else becoming worse off, a social surplus has been created. In normative economic terms, this has historically been viewed as a good thing.

2.05 *Pareto Efficiency in a Production Economy*

The exchange example suggests that economic efficiency is an attractive reason for deciding how resources should be allocated. After all, it is hard to argue against someone becoming better off when it doesn't hurt anyone else. It has to be admitted, however, that the exchange example is more useful for defining efficiency than it is for describing reality; the real world is far more complex than a simple exchange economy.

The Demand Curve. As we move to a more realistic setting, the idea of Pareto efficiency can be defined somewhat differently to allow it to become more general. Assume now that goods are produced and sold to consumers through markets in a production economy. Think of a competitive industry that produces prerecorded stereo cassettes. The consumer wants to maximize utility from many commodities, including cassettes, subject to that consumer's limited income and the price of cassettes. If we think of money as a proxy for access to all other commodities, the consumer has the option of exchanging a limited income (Y_0 in Figure 2.4) for cassettes at any point along the straight line P_0. This is called a *price line* or *budget constraint*.[4] Its slope reflects the price of cassettes; the higher the price of cassettes, the steeper the price line. With the price at P_0, the consumer could buy Y_0/P_0 cassettes if he or she spent all available income on cassettes, but more cassettes (Y_0/P_1) could be bought at the lower price of P_1.

The highest indifference curve that this consumer can reach with limited income Y_0 and the price of cassettes at P_0 is U_0. This establishes a *consumer equilibrium* at a, where q_0 cassettes are purchased during a given time period. At this equilibrium point, the P_0 price line is tangent to the U_0 indifference curve. This means that the rate at which the consumer is willing to give up money to get cassettes (the slope of the indifference curve or the marginal rate of substitution) is exactly equal to the rate at which money has to be given up to get cassettes (the slope of the price line or the price of cassettes). The consumer is maximizing utility, given the circumstances.

The *market demand curve* for cassettes is shown as DD in Figure 2.5. As one point on this demand curve, Q_0 cassettes would be purchased by

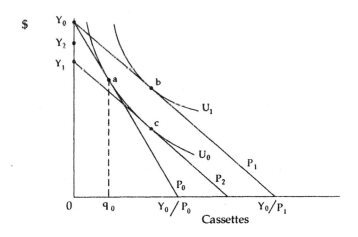

FIGURE 2.4 Consumer Equilibrium and Consumer's Surplus

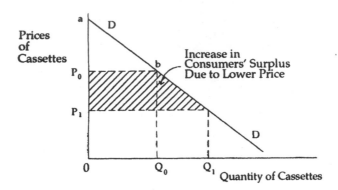

FIGURE 2.5 Market Demand Curve for Cassettes

consumers per unit of time if P_0 was the price of a cassette. Consumers would purchase more (Q_1) if the price was lower, say P_1. A key question is, Why would more cassettes be purchased at a lower price? The answer is that consumers would be better off, individually and collectively, if the price of cassettes was lower. That is, they would enjoy a greater consumers' surplus at lower prices.

The Consumer's Surplus. The extent to which consumers become better off because of a lower price is usually thought to be nonmeasurable because utility is an ordinal (ranked) rather than cardinal (counted) construct. That is, the magnitude of utility increases for consumers due to a lower price can't be measured in any sense that allows comparison. Consumers may feel that they have become "better off," but it is not easy to visualize a unit of measurement for determining how much they are better off, or whose utility has increased the most.

In 1939, a way to finesse this problem and thus provide comparability was presented by J. R. Hicks, an English economist. Hicks felt that economists and policymakers needed a "money measure" of the extent to which a consumer is made better off when the price of a good falls. To accomplish this, he defined the *consumer's surplus* as the maximum amount of money that a consumer would be willing to give up in order to buy a good at a lower price. In Figure 2.4, this lower price is shown as P_1. More cassettes could be bought with the same amount of money (Y_0), and the consumer would reach a new equilibrium, b, on a higher indifference curve, U_1.[5] If one were to draw P_2, a fictitious price line that is parallel to P_1 but tangent to the original indifference curve U_0, another tangency would occur, this time at point c. At c, the consumer is exactly as well off (on U_0) as she was to begin with. The purpose of this procedure is to identify a vertical distance on the money axis, Y_0Y_1, as the extent of the consumer's surplus. This distance shows the maximum amount of money that the consumer would pay for the opportunity to buy cassettes at the new and lower price. The consumer would gladly pay any amount less than Y_0Y_1 (such as Y_0Y_2), because this would leave her better off than at U_0, but she would be worse off if she had to pay any amount larger than Y_0Y_1.

If we consider all those who buy cassettes, the *consumers' surplus* (now in plural form) associated with a lower price is the aggregation of all Y_0Y_1 money amounts, or the money measure of the extent to which consumers are better off because it now costs less to buy the good. Buyers were already enjoying some consumers' surplus (area abP_0) at price P_0; the increase in consumers' surplus is shown as the shaded area between prices P_0 and P_1 in Figure 2.5. Consumers pay a lower price for the same amount of the good that they were previously consuming ($0Q_0$), but an additional amount (Q_1Q_0) has been added to their consumption. The extent of an individual consumer's surplus may be very different among consumers, of course, depending on the strength of their preferences for the commodity. It should also be noted that economists have many definitions for consumer's surplus. This definition is called the compensating variation measure of consumer's surplus. It is most appropriate when, as in this case, a seller has the property rights to a commodity and the buyer has to induce the seller to part with it.

The same general idea of the consumer's surplus is applied in Figure 2.6 to nonmarket goods and services, those that aren't allocated by markets. Note the absence of a price line. If the level of air quality in a community was Q_0, for example, a consumer with Y_0 income would be on the U_0 indifference curve (point a) because air quality (whether good

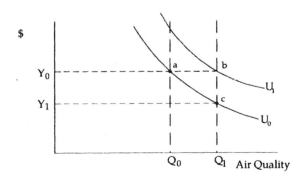

FIGURE 2.6 Consumer's Surplus for a Nonmarket Good

or bad) is available without charge. If air quality improved to Q_1 because of tighter regulations on industrial polluters, the consumer would find himself better off on the U_1 indifference curve (point b) because he would still have Y_0 income. (It is assumed for convenience that the consumer pays none of the cleanup costs.) In the nonmarket case, the consumer's surplus is the maximum amount of money ($Y_0Y_1 = bc$) that the individual consumer would be willing to pay to obtain the good in larger quantities (Q_1 compared to Q_0). The consumer would be willing to pay any amount less than Y_0Y_1 because this would leave him on an indifference curve above U_0. By the same reasoning, payment of an amount larger than Y_0Y_1 would make him worse off than he was to start with.

Actually tapping the consumer's willingness to pay for nonmarket goods may, of course, be fraught with all kinds of problems. Consumers may feel that they shouldn't have to pay for better air quality, and it may be physically impossible to prevent them from enjoying an air quality improvement. These problems will be considered in Chapters 3 and 5. At this point, our purpose in defining the consumer's surplus is simply to establish the idea of a money measure of gain that can be compared with a money measure of loss, thus providing a common denominator for efficiency analysis in collective choice.

The Producer's Surplus. The counterpart to the consumer's surplus is the *producer's surplus,* the idea that an individual producer would enjoy a money measure of gain if a product or service could be sold at a higher price. One complication is that many producers might be involved in producing a stereo cassette, for example, even though the consumer might be just one individual. These producers jointly create value by producing the cassettes, and this value is distributed among them in the form of wages, salaries, interest, dividends, and rent.

Consider just one of the producers, a worker who packs cassettes into shipping containers. Beyond the time required for eating, sleeping, and personal maintenance, this worker's available time (T^*) can be allocated either to work, thus earning money, or to leisure, which is itself a commodity. This choice is shown in Figure 2.7. The upward slope of the indifference curves indicates that to remain at the same utility level (U_0, for example), the worker must receive a higher level of income if she gives up leisure time by working.

Assume that at a wage rate of W_0, the worker chooses to work x_0 hours per week, taking the remainder of her time in leisure. This is point a on indifference curve U_0. Now imagine that the price of stereo cassettes increases because of a surge in demand and that this causes profits to increase in the cassette industry. Assume that the worker's wage rate increases from W_0 to W_1 and that she is able to choose a new allocation of work and leisure that maximizes her utility. At the higher wage rate,

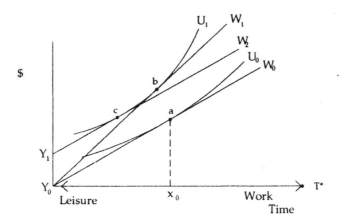

FIGURE 2.7 Producer's Surplus from an Increased Wage Rate

the worker chooses point *b*. She works fewer hours, makes a higher wage, and enjoys more leisure—the best of all worlds.

The producer's surplus in this case can be defined as the minimum amount of money that the worker would accept in order to forgo the wage increase. To determine this amount, draw a fictitious wage line (W_2) parallel to the old wage line (W_0) but tangent to the new and higher indifference curve (U_1). This tangency occurs at *c*, and it indicates the worker's allocation of time if she had to work for the original wage rate but she could still reach the higher utility level. This identifies a vertical distance on the money axis, Y_1Y_0, as the producer's surplus for this worker. The producer would gladly accept any amount larger than Y_1Y_0; this would make her better off than would the wage increase. She would not accept any amount less than Y_1Y_0, however, because this would leave her worse off than would the wage increase.

As with consumer's surplus, the economic literature has many definitions of producer's surplus. The one used here is the equivalent variation measure. It is appropriate because the worker has the right to withhold her labor.

2.06 The Net Economic Value of a Good or Service

Having seen that consumers would gain from price decreases and that producers would gain from price increases, let's put the two ideas together in a market diagram (Figure 2.8). First, however, we need to

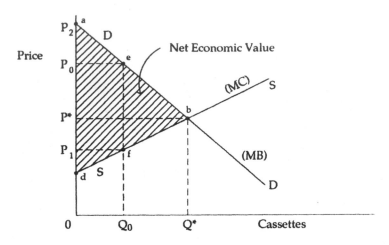

FIGURE 2.8 Consumers' Surplus, Producers' Surplus, and Net Economic Value

distinguish between two related definitions of economic value. The first is *total economic value*, which is the value of all quantities of a commodity up to and including some particular level of output. This value may accrue to either consumers or producers. The gain in consumers' surplus from being able to buy output Q^* at price P^*, for example, as compared to buying output Q_0 at the higher price P_0, is the area P_0ebP^*. This is the maximum amount of money that consumers would pay for the opportunity to buy at the lower price of P^* rather than P_0. Producers would gain producers' surplus on all quantities up to Q^* if they were able to sell Q^* at P^* rather than sell Q_0 at P_1; this gain would be area P^*bfP_1. This is the minimum amount of money that they would accept in order to forgo a price increase from P_1 to P^*. Both the consumers' surplus and the producers' surplus are considered over all quantities of the commodity through Q^*.

The second definition of economic value is the *marginal economic value*, or that associated with a particular output level. Demand curves show the marginal benefit (MB) of a good to consumers. At output Q_0, the marginal value of cassettes to consumers would be e (or P_0). At output Q^*, the value at the margin would fall to b (or P^*) because cassettes would be more abundant. The SS supply curve shows the marginal cost (MC) to producers; the good may be increasingly expensive to produce as certain inputs become more expensive, more constraining, or less productive.

Now let us bring together the two definitions of economic value—total and marginal. If output Q^* could be produced without cost and simply given to consumers, the total consumers' surplus would be area abQ*0; consumers would gain the entire area under the demand curve up to and including output Q*. Because the good is not free, however, but available on the basis of those costs reflected in the SS supply function, the total cost to society would be the area under the supply curve up to Q*, or dbQ*0. Assume for now that only producers and consumers of cassettes are involved and that there are no significant effects on others; externalities will be discussed in Chapter 3.

The difference between the total cost and the total consumers' surplus at zero price is the *net economic value* of the good. This shaded area in Figure 2.8, abd, is the sum of consumers' surplus and producers' surplus, taking into account all quantities of the good. This sum is the greatest when the marginal benefit to consumers just equals the marginal cost to producers. "Maximizing the net economic value of a good" means that the good contributes most to society when produced at output level Q*, where supply and demand curves intersect.

Output level Q* is also Pareto efficient, and not by coincidence. Consider the case when for some reason output is limited to Q_0. At Q_0, the marginal benefit of cassettes to consumers (e) exceeds the marginal cost to producers (f). Demanders would be willing to pay P_0, but suppliers could sell for only P_1 and still cover their full costs of production. Therefore, there could be a Pareto improvement in efficiency if output were expanded beyond Q_0. Expansion of output to Q* would allow someone to be made better off without anyone being made worse off. In fact, both consumers and producers would be made better off by output expansion from Q_0 to Q*. Consumers would gain P_0ebP^* in consumers' surplus, and producers would gain P^*bfP_1 in producers' surplus. Both would have an incentive to expand output. This explains why competitive markets with no externalities would tend to move toward an equilibrium output at Q*; someone gains and no one loses.

2.07 What Role Should Government Play?

In a strictly efficient world, the role of government would be to ensure that all goods and services are produced in Pareto efficient quantities. If they weren't, it might be possible for government to make someone better off without making anyone else worse off. If less-than-efficient quantities of some goods were produced, government could intervene to ensure that greater quantities were produced. If too much was produced, government might cause production to be reduced so that the marginal benefit to consumers would equal the marginal cost to producers.

Several things should be noted. One is that an efficient size of government isn't readily apparent; an efficiency role may not translate directly into numbers of government workers or public buildings. Government could be small in budget size yet have great impact in a variety of ways. It might give those in the private sector monetary incentives to do or not do certain things. It might require that firms use a particular technology in producing a good. It might subsidize production by paying part of the cost. It might give money to those consumers who are likely to buy a certain good, or it might produce the good itself. A second note is that some goods and services wouldn't be produced in an efficient world. Unless a positive "net economic value" triangle could be created, it would be more efficient for society that the good not be produced at all. California condors, snail darters, and Edsels might all fall by the wayside.

Finally, as a somewhat contentious statement of general tendencies, the reasons for expecting less-than-efficient quantities to occur are different than the reasons for expecting greater-than-efficient quantities. To the left of Q^*, the Pareto efficient output in Figure 2.8, lies the range of "market failure," where consumers may conceal their preferences and producers may withhold their supplies. Private firms will be given inadequate incentives to produce, and private markets will fail to produce efficient amounts. Chapters 3 through 5 will explore these issues. To the right of Q^* is the range of "government failure," where self-interest on the part of legislators and bureaucrats may result in excessive output. Exceptions to these generalizations are clearly possible; private firms, for example, may produce too much for some periods of time, but the profit incentive provides a built-in tendency to move back toward Q^*. Governments, too, may produce too little of certain goods and services. Many rational choice analysts, however, tend to feel that there are strong self-interest incentives in the public sector that move us from left to right, from lesser to greater public sector output. Chapters 6 through 11 will explore this theme.

2.1 There Are Many Efficient Outputs: Is There a Best One?

The beauty of the efficiency model is perhaps its simplicity; if someone can be made better off without making someone else worse off, why not do it? There is, however, a crucial limitation to the efficiency model. This limitation is that there is nothing unique about Q^*, the Pareto efficient output in Figure 2.8. Instead, it changes every time there is a shift in the demand curve or the supply curve! Because there can be several Q*'s, an obvious question is, Is there a "best" Q*? This has been a key question in theoretical welfare economics for many years. The question can't be answered, but it is useful to highlight the issues that underlie the debate.[6] The crux of the problem is that economic efficiency and equity are related. If one wants to say which Q* level of output is best, an ethical judgment has to be made that the distribution of income that gives rise to some particular Q* is more appropriate than any other distribution of income among consumers.

Think back to the market for stereo cassettes; suppose that the government launched an ambitious program of grants and loans for college students. This program would enable some students to attend college who wouldn't otherwise attend, but it would also allow others to use these grants and loans rather than their own money for tuition and living expenses. This would release some personal funds that otherwise would have been spent for college expenses. Some of this money might be saved by students, but part of it would probably be spent for goods and services other than education.

Let's say that the scholarship program was large enough that the demand for cassettes would shift from D_0 to D_1 in Figure 2.9. More cassettes would be bought at any given price. For convenience, assume that the S_0 supply function is perfectly flat, meaning that cassettes would be supplied at (say) $8.95 each. Without the scholarship program, Q* would have been the efficient output of cassettes. With the D_1 demand for cassettes, however, the marginal value of cassettes (*a*) would exceed

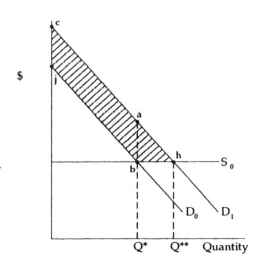

FIGURE 2.9 The Market for Cassettes, With and Without the Scholarship Program

the marginal cost (*b*) at the Q* output level, and Q* would no longer be the most eficient output. Now, Q** would be the most efficient output! The net economic value of cassettes (all of it consumers' surplus, in this case) would increase by the shaded area, chbj, as a result of the scholarship program. This is no surprise; we've already said that the scholarship program would release some resources for spending elsewhere in the economy.

Which output of cassettes, Q* or Q**, is best? There isn't any scientific answer to this question. Instead it depends on which distribution of income is most appropriate. In this case, it depends on whether the scholarship program is an appropriate activity for government to undertake. Many students might think that it is a great program; many taxpayers would disagree. The choice of a best output is clearly a value judgment. A major limitation of economic efficiency as a criterion for public policy, therefore, is that it is usually not clear whether an explicit and collective value judgment has been made with respect to equity and the distribution of income.

2.2 Efficiency and Equity: Making Trade-Offs

2.21 When We Choose to Be Inefficient

An obvious question is this: If Pareto efficiency is as good as it sounds, why not have government make sure that all goods and services are produced at output Q*, as in Figure 2.1? At that point, the benefit from an additional amount of a good is equal to the marginal cost of producing it, and the net economic value, which is the sum of consumers' surplus and producers' surplus, is maximized. We dealt with a technical answer to this question in the previous section; Q* isn't unique. Instead, it depends on who has the purchasing power; change the tax laws and Q* will change. If the rich are very rich, the efficient output of jewelry will be large compared to what it would be if there was a more equal distribution of income.

Aside from this, the simplest answer to why Pareto efficiency isn't necessarily "good" is that society may care, and indeed care greatly, about who benefits—and conversely, who does not benefit—when a good or service is produced and consumed. Because we care, we may be willing collectively to give up something to ensure that particular groups are benefited. And if the "something" we give up is a portion of the net economic value triangles, we are making trade-offs between equity and efficiency.

Historically, we have been willing to make these trade-offs. As a society, we have chosen to use some of our tax revenues to make income transfers to people who are older, younger, poorer, and less healthy than the average taxpayer. We have also used tax revenues to finance public investments that create economic opportunity for target groups rather than just transfer income to them.

The fact that we have made these trade-offs, however, should not be construed to mean that all income transfers and public investments are "rational trade-offs" of economic efficiency for greater equity. For one thing, we may not need to give up efficiency to gain equity; we may be able to have more of both. Investments in early childhood education among the disadvantaged, for example, may have a high economic payoff and may also enhance equity. Second, some trade-offs turn out to be income transfers to the well-to-do. Promoters of water resource development in the arid West, for example, have generally portrayed these developments as productive national investments and as opportunities for small farmers. Some water projects have been economically productive with social benefits in excess of social costs, but many others have not (Reisner, 1986). In general, the program has redistributed income from the urban East to the rural West, and often to large corporate farmers. Whether this is rational depends on your point of view.

We are thus troubled by whether, when, and where to make trade-offs between efficiency and equity, and how to assess whether trade-offs have been rationally made. It is not an easy problem to resolve, and one should be skeptical of those who counsel otherwise.

2.22 Some Heavy-Duty Theory

If any one efficient output isn't necessarily the best output, what *is* the best output? Welfare economists have developed three theoretical concepts for thinking about this question. Each concept is quite abstract; not one lends itself to measurement. The first is the *utility possibility frontier*; this concept shows the most utility that can be generated from a fixed set of resources for two groups of users (F_0F_0 in Figure 2.10). It is based on three assumptions; these are only summarized here because of their technical complexity.[7]

The first assumption is that all goods and services are produced as efficiently as possible. The second is that all goods and services are exchanged efficiently; recall from Figure 2.3 that Smith and Jones improved their well-being through exchange. Once the possibilities for mutual gain were exhausted, one person could become better off only if the other became worse off. The third assumption is that the consumption of goods and services is aligned with production technology by means of costless income transfers among consumers. If the technology for apple production is more advanced than the technology for wheat production, for example, the economy will be more efficient if apple lovers have greater purchasing power than bread lovers. If these three assumptions are met, no utility gains can be squeezed out of a fixed set of land, labor, and capital resources. All points on the (F_0F_0) frontier are Pareto efficient; it isn't possible to make someone better off without making someone else worse off.

Suppose that points *a* and *c* in Figure 2.10 show the most utility that could be derived from two efficient but very different plans for managing public forest resources for the benefit of two groups, the amenity users and the timber users.[8] Let's say that point *c* would result from an intensive timber harvest plan. This would involve a large timber harvest each year, but it would also have negative impacts on amenity uses of the forest environment. The building of logging roads, logging, and log hauling would reduce wildlife and fish habitat, impair recreation use, and reduce the scenic attractiveness of the forest. In spite of this, the intensive timber harvest plan would call for amenity users to be made as well off as possible, given that a large timber harvest would occur. In fact, there are even more destructive alternatives that would have outcomes below and to the left of *c*. At *b*, for example, less timber and even fewer amenities would be produced. Trees might be cut and left lying across

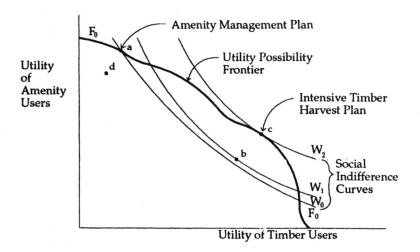

FIGURE 2.10 The Utility Possibility Frontier and Social Indifference Curves

small streams. This would waste timber, allow stream temperatures to rise, and impair fish habitat. An amenity user might not like the intensive timber harvest plan, but things could be worse!

The amenity management plan would result in point *a*. Although it would allow some timber harvest, the primary focus would be to ensure a high level of amenity uses. Less efficient combinations of the two uses, such as *d*, could occur, but the amenity management plan would be the most efficient way to favor amenities over timber production. Along the utility possibility frontier, all possibilities for making both types of users better off have been exhausted, and the only way to make one user better off is to make the other user worse off. Hence, *a* and *c* (and all other points along F_0F_0) are Pareto efficient.

Not surprisingly, the amenity users would prefer *a*, but timber users would prefer *c*. Which plan is best? This leads to a second concept, the *social welfare function*, which has been touted as a way to determine the "best" output. In principle, this would be a way for society to decide which of the two plans should be selected. In more general terms, it can be defined as a means for making collective rankings of the relative deservedness of various people or groups within society.

We are referring to collective decisions, it should be noted, and not individual decisions. This calls for special attention. If collective decisions are to be made, we have to somehow add our likes and dislikes, or in the language of economics, we need to aggregate preferences. One way to do this is through voting. When we vote, however, we usually vote on candidates or issues. Should we reelect Senator Smith? Should we approve the construction of a new school building? These types of issues are usually decided by a particular aggregation procedure, majority voting, which will be discussed in Chapter 6.

A social welfare function involves a different type of preference aggregation. Instead of voting on candidates or issues, a society would somehow make explicit judgments on whose utility we value most highly. With the forest resource management alternatives, social welfare (W) would depend on the utility of the various affected groups:

$$W = W (U_T, U_A, \ldots U_O), \qquad (2.3)$$

where $U_T, U_A, \ldots U_O$ are utility levels for timber users, amenity users, and others in society. If a method actually existed for making social welfare rankings between timber users and amenity users, it might be that social welfare would depend more on the utility of timber users (U_T) than on the utility of amenity users (U_A). This might happen if timber users were mostly low-income renters and first-time home buyers, for example, and amenity users were in the upper-income brackets. It might even be that society could assign different weights to the two groups, such as

$$W = (1.0 + \lambda)(U_T) + (1.0)(U_A),\qquad(2.4)$$

where $\lambda > 0$. If we knew λ and if we could translate management plans into utility levels for the two groups, we could determine which forest management plan would contribute the most to social welfare. In reality, of course, these are very big ifs.

The third concept, *social indifference curves*, is related to the social welfare function. Social indifference curves, if they could be derived empirically, would look like indifference curves for an individual consumer. That is, if the utility of timber users declined, society could be kept at a constant level of total welfare only if amenity users were made better off (W_0, W_1, or W_2 in Figure 2.10). If it were possible to make both groups better off, society would move to new and higher levels of collective welfare (W_1 rather than W_0, W_2 rather than W_1).

We can now bring together these three theoretical concepts. The utility possibility frontier shows all Pareto efficient combinations of utility for amenity and timber users; the social indifference curves, derived from social welfare functions, show society's preferences toward the two groups. As Figure 2.10 is drawn, *a*, the amenity management plan, lies on W_0, the lowest of the three social indifference curves, because this plan favors the group that is least favored in the social welfare function (Equation 2.4). The intensive timber harvest plan, point *c*, lies on a higher indifference curve, W_2. It would involve more utility for the group most favored by society, the timber users.[9]

In short, an explicit value judgment has to be made about equity between amenity users and timber users if we are to say which forest management plan is "best." Society may not always want to be efficient. Instead, we may wish to sacrifice some efficiency to gain additional utility for a certain group. Point *b*, which involves inefficiency in the production of both timber and amenity values, might actually be preferred to *a*, the more efficient amenity management plan because it generates a larger timber harvest and more utility for a socially favored group, the timber users. This equity gain, as society sees it, is large enough to counteract some loss of efficiency due to wasted logs and warm rivers.

How useful are these theoretical concepts in everyday collective choice? For several reasons, the answer is, "not very." For one thing, we have a very knotty aggregation problem that is difficult, if not impossible, to resolve. How can we add your preferences for collective action to mine? As we'll see in Chapter 6, the mathematical logic of aggregation has been researched for many years. In particular, Kenneth Arrow's major result, known as the *Arrow theorem* (1951), was that there is *no* aggregation procedure that meets minimal and reasonable requirements for collective choice. In other words, we can't add preferences in any logical and orderly manner except in very simple and unrealistic situations. This is a sobering conclusion.

But in spite of the Arrow theorem, we do have an aggregation procedure that we use for making collective decisions in the real world. We call it the political process. The issue, of course, is how well it works in adding up individual preferences. Have social indifference curves really been defined when Congress decides on a forest management program? Probably not. More likely, timber interests have prevailed by promising to support key legislators on other issues in exchange for their support on the forest issue. Is this an appropriate way to aggregate preferences? Some would say, "No!" but some would say, "Yes, that's the way the political process works."

In spite of their impotence in an operational sense, the three concepts are still useful in thinking about and debating the trade-offs between efficiency and equity. Efficiency is neither inherently good nor inherently bad, but something to be considered along with equity in deciding how the rewards from resource use should be distributed.

2.23 Kaldor-Hicks Compensation Tests: A Practical Alternative

One shortcut for defining a social welfare function is the *Kaldor-Hicks compensation test*, named after two British economists, Nicholas Kaldor (1939) and J. R. Hicks (1939). According to this test, a policy should be regarded as adding to social welfare if it has the potential for making someone better off without making anyone else worse off. Kaldor and Hicks argued that if the gainers could compensate the losers and still have something left, then the policy should be adopted because it would represent a *potential Pareto improvement*.

In devising this test, Kaldor and Hicks assumed that efficiency and equity could be separated for purposes of economic policy. They felt that if society is unhappy with the distribution of income brought about by a policy, distribution could be changed through a variety of payments and charges. The Kaldor-Hicks test has had great pragmatic appeal among economists because almost any economic policy will create both gainers and losers. Restricting policy advice to circumstances where there are no losers usually relegates the policy adviser to a great deal of silence, and no adviser likes to remain silent.

The Kaldor-Hicks concept can be applied, for example, to the scholarship program that we discussed earlier. One outcome of the program might be that it would move taxpayers and students from utility combination *a* without the program to *b* with the program (Figure 2.11). Making grants and loans available would make some students better off, but it would make many taxpayers each slightly worse off. There are no scales on either axis; we simply assume that higher incomes mean greater utility and lower incomes, less utility. Also, there is no pretense that social indifference curves are available to help us decide on a course of action.

The Kaldor-Hicks test asks whether it would be arithmetically possible to redistribute the gains from the scholarship program to allow *both* groups to reach the shaded area, or at least the edge of the shaded area. This is the area of Pareto improvement, where at least one group would be better off without the other group becoming worse off. If the gains from the program exceeded the costs, a potential Pareto improvement would exist and the Kaldor-Hicks test would be satisfied. The taxpayers' initial utility level of T_0 could be restored, for example, by a system of charges to students and payments to taxpayers, thus moving from *b* back to *c*. This would leave students somewhat better off than they were without the program, but it would leave taxpayers no worse off. Perhaps both groups could be made even better off, by moving from *b* to *d*, for example. If the scholarship program resulted in gains that were less than the costs of the program, however, the shaded area couldn't be reached through charges and payments and the Kaldor-Hicks test wouldn't be met. It would be an inefficient program.

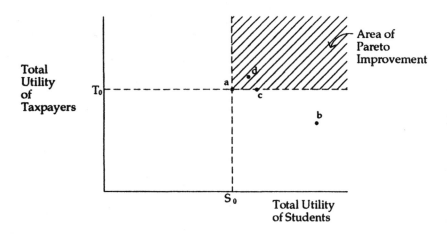

FIGURE 2.11 Kaldor-Hicks Compensation Tests

One question about the Kaldor-Hicks test is how society could redistribute the utility gains from the scholarship program, moving from *b* to *c*, for example. One way would be through more aggressive repayment policies. Students might be required to pay back a certain percentage of their future earnings instead of paying back a certain amount. If future earnings are high, taxpayers as well as students might benefit from the program.

A second question is whether the gains from the scholarship program would exceed the costs. *Benefit-cost analysis* is a set of procedures for identifying and measuring the benefits and costs of public programs such as the scholarship program. Consider higher education, the commodity that the scholarship program would attempt to enhance (Figure 2.12). The demand function for higher education reflects the value of the increased skills, knowledge, and personal satisfaction acquired by students, some of which could be translated into increased lifetime earnings. The supply function reflects the private and public costs of education, including administration of the scholarship program. If education was being produced in less than Pareto efficient quantities, Q_0 for example, and if the scholarship program would cause enrollment to increase from Q_0, to Q^*, the net benefits of the scholarship program would be positive. If higher education was costless, the benefits of the scholarship program would be Q_0abQ^*, the area under the demand curve between the two levels of output. These benefits would be greater than the cost of providing the education, which is the area under the supply curve between the two output levels (Q_0cbQ^*). Thus, there would be an increase in net economic value of area abc. If education was already being produced at greater than Pareto efficient levels, however, the change in net economic value because of the scholarship program would

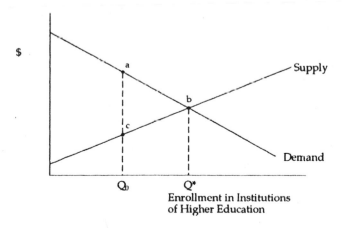

$

a

b

c

Supply

Demand

Q_0 Q^*

Enrollment in Institutions
of Higher Education

FIGURE 2.12 Demand and Supply for Higher Education

be negative. Whether the net value of a particular scholarship program would be positive or negative is obviously an empirical matter.

The advantage of the Kaldor-Hicks compensation test is that it addresses the efficiency criterion; its main limitation is that it addresses *only* the efficiency criterion. It asks only whether gains would exceed costs, whether gainers would be able to compensate losers. It does not ask whether actual redistribution would be appropriate; thus, it is an incomplete criterion for collective choice. It simply ignores the equity issue. And in general, it does matter to society whether gainers compensate losers or whether they are allowed to keep all of the gains.

2.24 Economists as Efficiency Advocates

As policy advisers, economists usually find themselves in an ambiguous position. On one hand, Pareto efficiency sounds good; the possibility of making someone better off without making anyone else worse off has a strong pragmatic appeal. And as a means of implementing this concept, Kaldor-Hicks compensation tests can often be used to compare the size of gains and losses. On the other hand, economists don't have any particular competence in gauging whether these effects are good or bad in an equity sense. Nevertheless, economists often tend to be efficiency advocates in the policy process, partly because most other participants tend to focus on equity aspects and give inadequate attention to efficiency aspects.

One reason for this can be found in how groups make decisions. As we noted in Chapter 1, one major method of group decision-making is the rational-comprehensive method (Lindblom, 1959). First, members collectively agree on their objective; then they explore all the alternatives for attaining that objective. Finally, they select the most expeditious of these alternatives. Objectives are clarified and agreed upon before policies are discussed. All policy alternatives are explored before the best one is selected; the best one is simply the most appropriate way to reach the agreed upon objective.

According to a dictionary definition, the second method, muddling through, is "to think or act in a confused or aimless way." Lindblom, however, argued that this is not only the way groups make decisions, it's the way they *should* make decisions! The problem lies in defining objectives. Advocates of muddling through maintain that there is usually no practical way to define objectives except insofar as they can be attained through particular policies. I might be hard pressed, for example, to say exactly why I favor public libraries, but I do favor them. You might like city parks, but it might be difficult to state their advantages.

Even if we could specify all the appropriate objectives, some policies are too complex and too uncertain to be considered. There are also substantial limitations on our ability to process information; these limitations keep us from being fully rational and comprehensive. A final and crucial characteristic of muddling through is that the test for the "best" policy is whether agreement can be reached among those who have a vested interest in the outcome. If those who are involved in decision-making agree that a policy is good, then it is good irrespective of any objective tests.

To contrast the two methods, suppose that a university is considering razing several older buildings to build a parking lot. Some faculty members and students object, claiming that the older buildings add to campus character. At least two objectives can thus be identified: one, to create parking space and two, to maintain campus character. The approach of the two decision methods might be as follows.

Rational-Comprehensive Decision-Making. The rational comprehensive method would require that agreement be reached on the two objectives before considering policy alternatives. Either the campus community would have to delete one objective or it would have to agree on a set of weights that specify the importance of each objective. If enough meetings could be held, perhaps the campus community could agree that parking should account for 60 percent of total importance and campus character should account for the remaining 40 percent.

Once agreement was reached on a set of weights, all policy alternatives would need to be explored. These might include encouraging people to walk to work, maintaining other scenic sites on campus, and limiting the right to park on campus. Each alternative would be evaluated on its ability to contribute to the two objectives. The policy that would make the greatest contribution to the two objectives, given the set of agreed upon weights, would be selected as the most appropriate policy.

Muddling Through. The muddling-through process would not require agreement on objectives or weights. Instead, the issue would be resolved through give and take among partisans, including administrators, students, and faculty. Some partisans, like those on the campus planning committee, would be formally designated; others would be self-selected. The number of proposed alternatives would likely boil down to two or three. If a compromise could be reached, it would be because the partisans decided that that was the best they could do at the time.

Why not muddle through? It seems clear that most groups do muddle through. But should we feel comfortable with outcomes that are reached by a group of partisans, most of whom are self-selected because they will benefit or be hurt by proposed actions? Those who espouse muddling through often assume that there will be spokespersons to represent those who will benefit or be hurt. This assumption can often be questioned. In particular, it is unlikely that Pareto efficiency will usually have a spokesperson. Those with only slight preferences about outcomes may be affected in large numbers, but the incentive system may not encourage them to participate in group decision-making. Thousands (or millions) of people might each be a little worse off or a little better off because of a policy, but few may have sufficient incentive to actively oppose it or promote it.

Because of this unevenness of incentives in collective choice, many economists feel that they need to be efficiency advocates. This doesn't mean that they are oblivious to justice and equity, but they often stress efficiency because they feel that others will give it inadequate attention. And in particular, they often feel that voters, legislators, and administrators—the self-interested participants in a rational choice approach to politics—will give it much less than adequate attention.

2.3 Summary

Economic efficiency is espoused by economists as a criterion for collective choice because it stresses the net economic value of market and nonmarket goods and services—and because few others espouse it. In an efficient world, each good or service is produced at an output level that equates the marginal benefit to consumers with the marginal cost to producers. These output levels are Pareto efficient; it is not possible to make someone better off without making someone else worse off. Even if someone is made worse off, the Kaldor-Hicks compensation test can be used to ensure that the gainers are able to compensate the losers and still have something left. This constitutes a potential Pareto improvement and hence, economic efficiency is enhanced.

But economic efficiency has its blemishes. One is its incompleteness. People *do* care about who benefits and who loses. Another blemish is ambiguity; the efficient output of costly jewelry, for example, will change as the distribution of income within society changes. To decide *which* efficient output is "best" means that society has to be able to make ethical decisions about the distribution of income. This is something we can do on paper with utility possibility frontiers, social welfare functions, and social indifference curves, but few people believe that the political process does it in an unambiguous manner.

Terms and Concepts for Review

net economic value
marginal benefit
marginal cost
consumers' surplus
producers' surplus
Pareto efficient
public good
opportunity cost
consumer choice
utility function
indifference curve
indifference map
marginal rate of substitution
consumer sovereignty
exchange economy
Edgeworth box diagram
independent utility functions
Pareto improvement
contract curve
Pareto superior
Pareto efficiency
production economy
price line or budget constraint
consumer equilibrium
market demand curve
consumer's surplus
producer's surplus
marginal economic value
total economic value
utility possibility frontier
social welfare function
social indifference curves
Arrow theorem
Kaldor-Hicks compensation test
potential Pareto improvement
benefit-cost analysis
bliss point
welfare maximization

3

Markets:
Will They Be Efficient?

3.0 Introduction

In Chapter 2, the focus was on economic efficiency as a criterion for the "right" role for government. If it doesn't matter who gains from the distribution of goods and services, government could see that all goods and services are produced at the level where the marginal benefit to consumers is just equal to the marginal cost to producers. Obviously, it does matter who gains from the distribution of goods and services, but it is still useful to think about what an efficient world would look like. One reason for this, as we'll see in Chapters 7 through 11, is that legislative and administrative government may cause inefficiencies because of self-interested behavior.

Decisions about how to allocate resources can be made in a variety of ways. On one hand, the government can make all decisions about what goods and services will be produced. On the other hand, individuals can make all these decisions through voluntary market transactions. The latter has been much closer to our experience in the United States, so we'll start by specifying the conditions that would have to be met for markets to bring about efficient resource use. Then, if those conditions aren't met, we will consider the advantages and disadvantages of government intervention. We could do it the other way around, starting with the government making all decisions about resource use, but to start with markets is to start with a more familiar setting.

3.1 Markets and Government

First, we need to explore the meanings of the terms *markets* and *government*. When economists talk about markets, they refer to situations where buyers and sellers make voluntary and independent decisions that result in equilibrium prices and quantities for goods and services. The number of people involved in this process can range from a single buyer and a single seller to large competitive markets where many buyers and sellers each have an imperceptible influence on prices and quantities.

The relative absence of *coercion*, the ability to make free and independent decisions, is central to any distinction between markets and government. The basis of a market is voluntary action. Buyers are free to buy or not buy. Sellers are free to sell or not sell. Government may constrain or limit individual actions, however, to attain group ends. As we saw in Chapter 1, governments levy taxes to build highways, they require that thrift institutions provide deposit insurance, and they issue tax-free bonds in competition with the taxable bonds issued by other borrowers. In each case, markets and would-be voluntary participants are constrained in their economic actions. Some other goods and services such as prostitution have been declared illegal, and heavy taxes are levied on liquor, tobacco, and similar goods to discourage their consumption. On the supply side, workers under a certain age can't be hired because of child-labor laws. Minimum-wage laws exist, and safe working conditions need to be maintained. All of these involve coercion through threats of punishment by government. As political scientist Michael Laver has characterized government, "The government is the agency that controls a monopoly of legitimate force" (1983, p. 8).

It is simplistic, however, to say that governments coerce people but that markets do not. Markets also coerce people in very real ways. The rich and the poor aren't equally free to make economic decisions. If you are poor, you are free to work for low wages or to withhold your labor, depending on your preferences about eating. If you are an unemployed coal miner or steel worker, no one tells you that you have to move to another city or state, but you are coerced nonetheless by market forces. Nevertheless, there is a distinction between markets and government, one that depends on the relative degree to which free and willing buyers and sellers determine prices and quantities. The greater the degree of voluntary action, the more we say the market is allowed to work. The greater the constraints imposed by government on voluntary action, the less the market works.

It would be difficult to imagine any market existing without a legal currency and without some system of property rights for enabling parties to make binding contracts; these functions are usually taken for granted as minimal roles for government. Even a pure market would have property rights and a currency. Without these, force would probably be observed, but not, to use Laver's terms, just the legitimate force of government.

3.2 When Markets Will Be Efficient

The extent to which markets will result in an efficient allocation of resources depends on whether four assumptions are met. The first is that goods or services are what economists call *private goods*, for which the following are true:

- The consumption of private goods is rival. If I consume them, you can't consume them at the same time.
- The consumption of private goods is excludable. Their services can be withheld from a potential consumer.
- Both the production and consumption of private goods are divisible. They can be sold and consumed one unit at a time.

A pair of shoes, for example, is about as close as one can get to a purely private good. If you wear them, I can't wear them at the same time. They are divisible; you can buy them by the pair. Because of these characteristics, the collective demand for a private good like shoes involves horizontal summation of the demands of individuals, that is, adding the quantities that would be purchased by different individuals at any particular price. The marginal benefit or demand curves for two individuals are shown in Figure 3.1 as D_a and D_b; horizontal addition of these demands at each price allows us to derive the collective demand, $D = MB$. If the price was P_0, for example, the two individuals would purchase quantities Q_a^0 and Q_b^0; together, they would purchase quantity Q^0. At price P^*, they would individually purchase Q_a^* and Q_b^*; together, they would purchase Q^*.

The second assumption about efficient markets is that all of the value or utility of the good to potential consumers is reflected in the demand function for that good. There are no bluffs, no threats and no games, just an accurate and honest revelation of preferences by all consumers. The third assumption is that all of the costs of producing the good are reflected in $S = MC$, the supply function. This function is shown as flat in Figure 3.1 to simplify the presentation. The marginal costs of production are assumed to be constant, and each unit of the good is sold for its cost of production; thus, there is no producer's surplus. No unpaid costs are imposed on others. All factors of production earn their opportunity costs, that which they could earn in other endeavors, but no more. Fourth, it is assumed that markets are competitive. No single producer or consumer can affect price, all resources are mobile among uses and locations, and firms have to produce as efficiently as possible to survive.

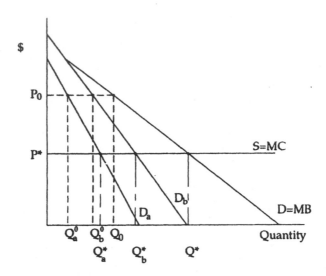

FIGURE 3.1 Private Good

As far back as 1776 and Adam Smith's classic book *The Wealth of Nations*, it has been a premise of economics that if all four of these assumptions are met, an "invisible guiding hand" will cause self-interested suppliers and demanders to arrive at efficient outcomes. The market output in Figure 3.1, for example, would be Q*, because all parties would find it in their best interests to reach this level. The two consumers would maximize their individual consumer's surplus by purchasing quantities Q$_a^*$ and Q$_b^*$, respectively, at price P*. Self-interest would prevent output from expanding past Q* because self-interested buyers would find that their marginal benefits are less than the cost of the good.

3.3 When Markets Won't Be Efficient

There are at least two major problems with an unswerving allegiance to the market. One is that efficiency is not all that matters to society, something that we discussed in Chapter 2 and will discuss further in Chapter 4. Second, the extent to which the four assumptions are actually met in any given situation is usually a subject of debate. When are markets perfectly competitive? To what extent do the gains accrue to those other than the consumers who purchase a good, and to what extent are costs imposed on third parties who are not compensated? Some economists prefer to let even an imperfect market allocate resources because they fear that government would do worse. Others view the violations of these assumptions as more frequent and more serious and tend to call more quickly for government intervention.

The question of *market failure*, whether markets would lead to inefficient outcomes, shouldn't be settled by dogma and ideology. If any of the four assumptions about efficient markets aren't met, it may be that the government should intervene in some manner to promote more efficient use of resources. The real problem, of course, is that the four assumptions relate to a very abstract and hypothetical world, and to conclude that real-world political processes would improve the situation is to use faulty logic. Imagine a music competition with only two contestants, and suppose that the judge hears the first opera singer, but then awards first place to the other without even listening to her sing! If markets have defects, government intervention might improve the situation, but not necessarily. Political processes have problems of their own, as we'll see in later chapters. The substantial literature that economists have developed on market failure is useful, but only if kept in perspective with the potential shortcomings of government in making decisions about what to produce.

3.31 Market Failure Due To Characteristics of Goods and Services[1]

Public Goods. The most common explanation for the need for governments to produce certain goods and services is that these would not be adequately provided by the private sector. National defense, it is argued, wouldn't be produced by profit-seeking firms because it would not be profitable. Once defense services are produced, they can't very easily be withheld from those who don't pay. By the same token, it might be difficult to withhold the use of streets and highways.

These arguments may sound plausible, but they don't explain why governments also provide public housing and public libraries. Access to these two services could be denied and profits could probably be made by suppliers. The defense issue does illustrate, however, that there are *public goods* that markets don't provide very well because of characteristics that prevent suppliers from capturing the full benefits of their actions. These goods (which may actually be services) have the following characteristics:

- The consumption of a public good is "nonrival." I can consume it without reducing your consumption of the same good.
- The consumption of a public good is nonexcludable. A public good can't be withheld from a potential user.
- Both the production and the consumption of a public good are indivisible. A public good can't be divided up and sold.

Iain McLean offers this example:

> We need to understand the key phrase 'public goods.' Consider the view from the lip of the Grand Canyon. The air is remarkably clear, so that you can see for perhaps ninety miles. The view, and the clean air that makes it possible, are public goods. A pure public good is defined as a good requiring indivisibility of production and consumption, non-rivalness, and non-excludability. The production and consumption of clean air are indivisible. Everybody who could pollute the atmosphere must cooperate in refraining from doing so; and you cannot take away a pound of clean air from the stock and sell it on a market stall. It is non-excludable: you cannot practicably prevent anybody from enjoying it, whether they have paid to do so or not. 'Non-rival' means that it is not subject to crowding. The view I get from the lip of the Grand Canyon is of equal value to me whether I am the only person who is getting it or not. (1987, p. 11)

If a pure public good is provided, one that has all three of the previously stated characteristics, it is provided simultaneously to all. The collective demand for such a good is obtained by vertical summation of the individual demands (Figure 3.2), instead of horizontal summation as with private goods. This vertical summation simply indicates that the marginal benefit of a good is its marginal benefit to me *plus* its marginal benefit to you. As a public good, it is equally available to all, but it isn't necessarily valued to the same extent by different consumers. If the good was available in quantity Q_0, for example, one person might value it to the extent of P_a^0, and a second person might attach a value of P_b^0 to it. Together, they would place a value of $P^0 = P_a^0 + P_b^0$ on that unit of the good. If the quantity of the good was larger, say Q^*, all the marginal benefits would be smaller. The individual valuations would be P_a^* and P_b^*, respectively, and the summed marginal benefit, or the collective demand function, would be $P^* = P_a^* + P_b^*$.

Now that we have a definition of public goods, it should quickly be admitted that there is probably no single real-world commodity that satisfies the strict definition of a pure public good. Even national defense and crime protection aren't equally available to all. Remote Alaskan villages aren't defended as well as Washington, D.C., or Omaha,

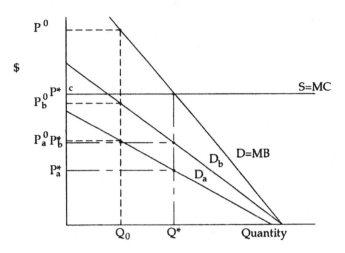

FIGURE 3.2 Public Good

Nebraska, and New Yorkers are likely to have different degrees of police protection, depending on whether they live in Harlem or in a richer district. Steiner has this to say about the definition of public goods:

> This kind of very narrow definition was designed to demonstrate that there may be a type of activity that is socially desirable but that will not be achieved by the unaided private market. It serves well the purpose of showing the existence of public goods. It can prove a hindrance, however, if it leads to the view that such goods are *the only* class of goods which Government can legitimately provide. In fact, examples are hard to find, not ubiquitous, and the great bulk of (nondefense) public expenditures are for goods and services that do not meet the definition. Roads, schools, welfare payments, recreational facilities, housing, public power, irrigation (among others) are important classes of public expenditures that some can be precluded from enjoying, that can be consumed in whole or in part, and that technically can be made subject to user charges. (1977, pp. 30-31)

The nature of the public good/private good dichotomy is *not* that it neatly defines which goods the government should produce and which goods the market should produce, but that it recognizes a continuum between two fictitious extremes. One extreme is the perfectly rival, excludable private good that markets do a good job of providing; the other is the perfectly nonrival, nonexcludable public good that markets will not provide at all. To the extent that public good characteristics exist in a commodity, both the need for consumers to pay for it and the incentive of suppliers to provide it are undercut. Whether consumers would pay for something that would be available in any event and whether sellers could collect from buyers: These are the two key questions about whether markets can efficiently provide commodities that have public good characteristics.

Markets will tend to produce those commodities with public goods characteristics in inefficiently small quantities. Neither individual in Figure 3.2, for example, would purchase a socially efficient (Q*) amount of the good if S was the supply curve. One individual would buy nothing if the price was P*, the other would maximize his or her consumer's surplus by purchasing some amount less than Q*. Neither would value the public good enough to purchase an efficient quantity, no matter how great each individual's demand, if the two parties acted independently. Whether they might jointly and voluntarily purchase an efficient quantity through collective action is something that we will discuss in Chapter 5.

The size and role of an efficient government will thus depend on the meanings of "excludable" and "rival." In general, market output will be inefficiently small if exclusion costs are high, if consumption tends to be nonrival, and if the prospects for payment and profit are low. Exclusion of users may be virtually impossible in some cases, as with the use of ambient air. In other cases, exclusion might be physically possible but costly and perhaps counterproductive; controlling access to a scenic wilderness area by building a high fence is an example. To the extent that exclusion is physically difficult and therefore costly, the profit incentive to a potential supplier is reduced. Collective action may be needed to supply the good in efficient quantities. In other cases, exclusion might be possible at low cost, but we may still choose not to exclude users. Access to public libraries is an example.

Whether goods are rival in consumption depends on space, time, the nature of use, and the degree of use. Two cars can each use a stretch of highway without reducing the amount available for consumption by the other, but only up to some degree of congestion. Beyond this point, the amount of space available to the other will be reduced, and use will become rival. Travel time will increase, drivers will become frustrated, and accidents or gridlock may result.

Externalities. The second and third assumptions for markets to be efficient were that all marginal benefits to users are reflected in the demand curve for a commodity and all marginal costs are reflected in the supply curve. If these assumptions aren't met, *externalities* result; these are situations where some gains or costs to society are not reflected in market prices. The buyer may gain some of the benefits and the seller may bear some of the costs, but gains or costs are also generated for others who aren't part of the market transaction.

Environmental pollution is a classic example of a negative externality. If making paper products kills fish because of the discharge of toxic chemicals, the price of paper is too low. It fails to reflect a cost imposed on someone else—the cost of dead fish. But externalities may also be positive. Our support of public schools and public libraries is based on the perception that schools and libraries generate positive values for others as well as for the primary user.

Let's look at why externalities would lead to inefficient output levels, starting with positive externalities. Assume that all marginal costs of producing a good or service are reflected in the SS supply function of Figure 3.3. Assume also that all market demands are reflected in the DD demand function; these are the demands by consumers from whom the good could be withheld. Output Q_0 might appear to be Pareto efficient, but it is not. If positive externalities exist, the consumption of the good by the primary consumer also creates values or gains for others. These latter values are reflected by D_eD_e, the external demand function. These values should be vertically added to the DD market demand to create a collective demand function of D^*D^*. If only Q_0 was produced, too little of the good would be produced because the sum of the marginal benefits to primary and external users ($a = b + f$) exceeds the marginal cost of production (b). Increasing output from Q_0 to Q^* would increase net economic value by area abc.[2]

The relationship between public good and externality in this case is that the collective demand function in Figure 3.3 involves the vertical

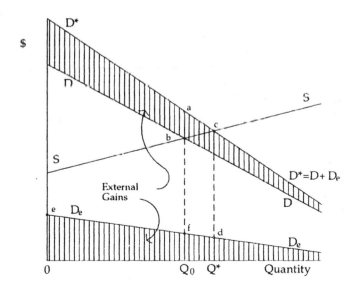

FIGURE 3.3 Positive Externality

summation of two lesser demand curves, that is, adding "my value" to "your value" for the same unit of the commodity. An externality exists because the production of the commodity has a public good aspect. The good lacks the excludability and rivalness that would characterize a pure private good. Uncompensated gains "spill over" to others. Even at efficient output Q^*, external users enjoy marginal benefits of dQ^*, and because they face a zero price, they enjoy a consumers' surplus of edQ^*0.

This positive externality exists because there is no market for tapping the value of the services received by external users. This absence of a market may be due to a variety of reasons. In some cases, it may be physically impossible to collect from the external beneficiaries. In fact, it may not even be possible to identify the beneficiaries except as members of a community or as types of people. In other cases, it may be possible but costly to identify the external users and to collect from them. In yet other cases, we may encourage the positive externality and not wish to exclude others from the benefits. An example of this is our providing free inoculations against contagious diseases.

Negative externalities involve exactly the reverse reasoning (Figure 3.4). Instead of causing gains for others, negative externalities involve the imposition of costs on others. The costs paid by the producer are SS, but unpaid and external costs of S_eS_e (the equal-sized shaded areas) are imposed on others who have no control over the decisions of the producer. The total costs of production are the sum of the two, or S^*S^*. The market output would be Q_0, given the market demand curve of DD. This output level is not Pareto efficient, however, because the marginal benefit to consumers of the Q_0^{th} unit is only b, which is less than the marginal cost of that unit (a). Considering all costs, not just those actually paid by the producer, net economic value would increase by abc if output was reduced from Q_0 to Q^*. Negative externalities would still be produced, but not as many of them.

As in the case of positive externalities, nonexcludability and nonrivalness are responsible for negative externalities. Again, the problem is the absence of a market through which those who bear external costs can express their preferences. This may be due to the physical characteristics of the good, or it may be due to the way society has decided to deal with the issue. The absence of a market for reducing air pollution on downwind communities, for example, might reflect the high costs of identifying and bargaining with external parties. Or the external parties may be very easy to identify, but the law may give the polluter the legal right to generate the externality. (Market solutions to externalities are discussed in Chapter 5.) This type of externality is defined by the legal and institutional nature of society, rather than by the physical nature of the good. In effect, we have decided to allow the externality to happen.

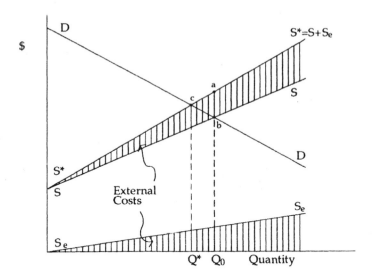

FIGURE 3.4 Negative Externality

3.32 *Market Failure due to Characteristics of Markets*

The situations we have been discussing are those in which it is difficult or impossible to make markets work because of the physical nature of particular goods and services. This next category of market failure is largely one of degree rather than kind. Markets may exist, but they might not be very efficient. That is, "Efficient markets frequently suppose adequate information, sufficient competition, timely adjustment, and modest transaction costs" (Steiner, 1977, p. 36). If these things don't happen, collective action may increase the efficiency of resource use.

Imperfect Competition. One of the oldest questions of economic regulation is antitrust policy, or how government should deal with firms that have enough economic power to influence market price or quantity. The particular market may be well established and the good may be rival and excludable, yet one firm or a few dominant firms may be able to impose costs on society by creating or utilizing barriers to entry, controlling the market, and charging more than the marginal cost of production. In contrast with firms that impose negative externalities outside the market, imperfectly competitive firms impose extra costs within the market.

If we assume that competitive firms and imperfectly competitive firms would face the same demand curve and the same costs of production,

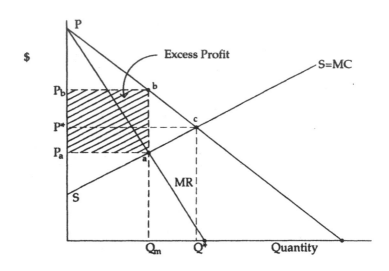

FIGURE 3.5 Imperfect Competition

competitive markets would lead to a Pareto-efficient output of Q* at a price of P* (Figure 3.5). Output levels in imperfect markets, however, are less than Pareto efficient; this outcome is designed to increase profit for imperfectly competitive firms. These firms have enough market power that they can individually affect price; hence, they would need to consider this in setting their profit-maximizing level of output. In contrast to competitive firms that can sell all they want at the existing price, imperfectly competitive firms face the market demand curve and can sell additional output only at a lower price. This leads to a declining *marginal revenue* (MR) curve that shows the addition to total revenue of the seller from each additional unit of output. The firm would maximize profit by setting output at Q_m, where the marginal revenue from that unit of output is equal to the marginal cost of producing that unit. The marginal benefit of this unit to consumers, however, is P_b, which exceeds the marginal cost of production, P_a; this gives rise to *excess profit* for the firm ($P_b baP_a$). The market fails because a Pareto-efficient output is not reached; net economic value is less than it could be (area abc) because of imperfect competition.

    Inadequate Information. Another reason markets might be inefficient is that buyers or sellers may be uninformed about an aspect of the market and make decisions that result in the production of too little or too much of a commodity. Buyers may have faulty information about the price, quality, or availability of goods and services, and sellers may be uncertain about consumer preferences. If consumers think that a product will be high in quality but find that it has major defects, a greater than Pareto-efficient output will have been produced. Hindsight may be better than foresight.

Both buyers and sellers need to acquire, evaluate, and use information, but the information may be incorrect or incomplete. To complicate the situation, information almost always has public good characteristics. When crash tests are conducted on new cars, for example, I can read an evaluation of the tests or listen to a report without reducing the amount of information available for your use. Whether I might be excluded from using this information will depend on incentive frameworks. Certain types of information are treated as private property to encourage innovation and to reward the innovator. Patents and copyrights are examples.

Incentive frameworks won't always encourage the acquisition of information. The costs of product testing, for example, are likely to exceed the benefits to an individual buyer even though the total gains for all consumers might easily exceed the costs of testing. If so, a positive net economic value can be created if markets can develop (as many have) for testing products and providing information to prospective buyers while excluding nonpayers from access to this information.

Time Lags. Markets may react slowly to changing conditions, resulting in output levels that tend to remain greater or less than those that would be Pareto efficient. Production isn't usually instantaneous. Long time periods may be needed to expand or reduce output, especially if biological processes are involved. High citrus prices, for example, may lead to expanded plantings by farmers; these may take several years to come into production. Prices may then plummet. Occupational training may be a time-consuming process, depending on the level of skills that are needed. If the education or training process in some occupations is lengthy, earnings may soar and then sag when newly trained people join the labor force.

This type of market defect is closely related to inadequate information as a source of market failure. The supply of new chemical engineers, as an example, is a time-consuming process, and one fraught with many uncertainties about future earnings. What might appear to be a market failure because of inefficient output levels, however, may really be an issue of equity or income distribution. If society trains too many chemical engineers, their earnings may be much lower than they had anticipated, yet their services may be efficiently used by employers. The price of lemons may seem woefully low to lemon growers, but a Pareto efficient amount of lemons will be produced and consumed if output Q^* exists.

High Transactions Costs. *Transactions costs* are those involved in making and carrying out a market transaction, agreement, or contract between two or more parties (Coase, 1937). These include the costs of

- obtaining and evaluating information
- establishing a bargaining position
- locating a bargaining partner
- negotiating a formal or informal contract
- monitoring the contract

Any of these costs could be zero, but their sum will most likely be greater than zero. Producers may attempt to contract with each other, or producers and consumers may be involved. Transactions may be very different in size and formality, but they almost always involve costs to participants over and above the costs of producing the good or service itself. A clothing store owner and the consumer both benefit when the consumer buys a shirt. The consumer can be reasonably sure that the shirt may be returned if it has major flaws, and the owner can be assured that the customer's check or credit card will be good. Transactions costs can be kept sufficiently low by legal and social means so that the purchase can take place.

In other cases, however, a transaction might not take place because transaction costs are too high. Markets may fail because of high transactions costs and thus prevent voluntary agreements that might have resulted in an increase in net economic value to society. For example, those people who would benefit from reduced air pollution might enjoy gains that would be large enough in total to be able to pay polluters to reduce pollution. The beneficiaries might want to locate others with similar preferences and convince them to become part of the bargaining process so that they do not have to deal individually with the polluters. These search costs could be prohibitively high and thus prevent this type of solution.

3.4 Three Examples of Market Failure

Any particular example of "market failure" is essentially raising the age-old question about the proper role of the state. It may be helpful, however, to consider three situations. We'll start with a seemingly trivial case of mosquito control, then move on to two other cases—public education and subsidies for home ownership. Keep in mind that reasonable people may reach different conclusions. What we're looking for is a productive way to discuss whether markets would result in efficient resource use. This discussion can be enhanced if these three questions are considered in this sequence:

1. Will a market produce a Pareto-efficient amount of a particular good or service?
2. If not, would some form of intervention by government bring about an increase in Pareto efficiency such that there would be gainers but no losers?
3. If there were losers, would the Kaldor-Hicks compensation test be met such that gainers would be able to compensate losers and still become better off?

In other words, we need to identify the good or service, ask whether it would be undersupplied or oversupplied by markets, and then consider whether collective action might improve the outcome.

3.41 Mosquito Control

The simplest market outcome for mosquito control occurs when people take actions that result in household gains that exceed household costs. They may buy flyswatters and screen doors but they probably won't spray outdoor breeding and hatching areas, especially those that aren't located on their property. If I spray, this may or may not affect you, depending on how far away you live. The effects may be substantial if you live next door, but not if you live ten miles away.

If I decide to spray the breeding grounds in the ditch near my house, the service that I provide has strong public good characteristics. It is nonrival; my dead mosquito is your dead mosquito. High transactions costs, however, would likely discourage me from identifying other beneficiaries and creating a market by which I could tap the gains from my actions. My neighbors might not know that I have sprayed, they might not believe me when I tell them so, or we might simply disagree on whether my spraying has helped them. Thus, spraying is basically nonexcludable because of its physical nature and high transactions costs. The market would underproduce mosquito control because of public goods and externality problems; a more efficient level of output would require collective action. Mosquito control thus seems to be a prime candidate for public provision, and indeed it has been a recognized function of local government for many years.

With respect to the second question, however, it isn't clear that public intervention would produce Pareto-efficient gains in the strict sense of the definition. Consider the rich urban family that moves to the beach each summer, trying to avoid the heat and mosquitoes, then complains because the city council uses part of its tax money for mosquito control back in the city. Remember, the definition of Pareto efficiency isn't satisfied if even one person is made worse off. The rich family is a loser in this case, although they probably won't get much sympathy from the rest of the community. The Kaldor-Hicks test for a potential Pareto improvement might easily be satisfied, however. The gains by other city residents might be large enough that they could pay the rich family's share of the cost (if they had to) and still come out ahead.

3.42 Education

It is often assumed that providing education is a role of the public sector, but we also have a tradition of private education in this country. Access to private schools depends on choice and the ability to pay. Today there are many types of these schools, including trade and vocational schools. Some operate on a not-for-profit basis, some are profit-seeking. There are also many private colleges that operate without direct public financing, although students may receive grants and loans from government.

The mosquito example might seem trivial, but the provision of education involves exactly the same issues. That is, the efficiency of the market depends on the rivalness and excludability of the output. If these private good characteristics exist, the market can be relied on for efficient provision of education.

It is clear that there are means of excluding students from access to education. As with public libraries, the door can be closed to those who don't pay. What is crucial for efficient provision, however, is not whether nonpayers can be excluded from the classrooms but whether nonpayers can be excluded from the services produced therein. As with mosquito control, transactions costs might be very high for those students who would like to appropriate all the gains that have been made possible by their education. In some aspects of basic education, there are external gains that students would have great difficulty in appropriating. There is a great deal of nonrivalness and nonexcludability in some of the services that are provided through formal education, and as a society, we think this should be encouraged. We become better citizens by learning to read, write, and engage in dialogue, and we become more productive and better-informed citizens because of public education. Others will benefit from these acquired traits of mine and I will benefit from theirs.

Few would deny that certain positive externalities are generated through education and that society should encourage their provision. Some other types of gains, however, may be more nearly excludable and less nonrival. In particular, increased incomes may accrue to students because of certain skills and abilities acquired through education; these skills and abilities can be withheld from those who don't pay for their use. Milton Friedman (1962) has long maintained that there are substantial private gains from education that are reflected in the higher incomes of those with certain acquired skills. Dentists and veterinarians are valuable resources, but Friedman argues that their contributions to society are largely and perhaps entirely reflected in their professional incomes. In his view, they could and should pay a larger proportion of their tuition in the publicly supported professional schools.

If the gains from education are totally rival and excludable, markets for education would result in efficient resource use. There could still be some inefficiencies, however, because of imperfect competition, inadequate information, time lags, and high transactions costs. One type of market failure could occur because of time lags and uncertainty. Education is a slow process; the uncertainty of future earnings and the certainty of present costs may inhibit an efficient level of investment. In this case, the public sector may need to encourage education through grants and loans in order to attain an efficient output.

Dating back to the work of T. W. Schultz (1961, 1971) and Gary Becker (1964), there has been a great deal of research on the economic returns to investment in human capital. Much of this research has shown that the economic returns to society have been greater than the forgone earnings by students and the costs of instruction. This is another way of saying that education would be produced in inefficiently small quantities by markets and that the Kaldor-Hicks compensation test would be met. The gainers (students and others) could have compensated the losers (taxpayers and the students who gave up some earnings) and still be better off. This doesn't mean that all types of educational investment have passed this test, but it suggests that education has often been an efficient public investment because it has increased private earnings, generated positive externalities, and reduced time lags and uncertainty.

3.43 Veterans' Housing Loans

Several state governments instituted housing-loan programs for military veterans shortly after World War II and after the Korean conflict. These popular programs were generally seen as offering thanks to veterans for their services in time of need. The borrowing power of state government was used to finance the programs through the issuance of general obligation bonds to raise money for housing loans. These bonds have been popular with investors because the interest is usually exempt from federal and state taxation. As a result, they can be sold to investors at a discount that enables veterans to take out housing loans at a reduced interest rate and with reduced monthly payments. Because of the downward sloping demand curves for housing, more veterans buy homes. Not coincidentally, they also receive an increase in consumers' surplus because of reduced housing costs.

The commodity at issue is access to long-term financing of home ownership among veterans; the efficiency question is whether the market would bring about a Pareto-efficient quantity of this type of financing. There is, in fact, an active market for such loans. This market seems to be reasonably competitive. Commercial banks, savings and loan associations, credit unions, and other investors compete to loan money to veterans. Whether this market would reach a Pareto-efficient output, however, would depend on whether there were any associated externalities; this depends, as with mosquito control and education, on whether there are gainers or losers outside the market. The usual argument is that there are gainers, that home ownership by veterans (or anyone else) gives rise to positive externalities and should be fostered, that others gain from neighborhood stability, social integration, and tender loving care to house and yard. The magnitude of these gains can be debated; I'm glad my neighbor is a home owner, but it is probably more important to me that she is literate and law-abiding.

It is unlikely, however, that this type of housing program satisfies the strict definition of Pareto efficiency; someone is bound to gain and someone else is bound to lose when the government intervenes in the market for veterans' loans. Interest earned on conventional housing loans is usually taxable; thus, the use of tax-free loans means that governments receive less tax revenue. Other citizens lose in the sense that less tax revenue means that the level of public services will decline or that another tax has to be used to generate the same amount of tax revenue. This is called a tax expenditure, as we saw in Chapter 1. Taxes are forgone to reach an objective (more and better housing for veterans, in this case); ordinarily, taxes are collected to reach an objective (building a school, for example).

Whether the Kaldor-Hicks compensation test would be met depends upon the relative increase in consumers' surplus for veterans and the reduced consumers' surplus and producers' surplus for others. On balance, it could be that the net gains are close to zero, that surpluses are simply shifted around as we modify the market for veterans' housing loans. Yet it seems that something must be "produced," because the loan programs have continued to win popular acceptance. In reality, the state has helped veterans become better off, individually and collectively. The market for housing loans has failed not because of inefficiencies in the provision of housing but because of society's dissatisfaction with incomes, opportunities, and rewards for veterans.

This third example thus marks a transition from the idea that markets may fail for efficiency reasons, which has been the focus of Chapter 3, to the idea that markets may fail for equity reasons, which is the focus of Chapter 4.

3.5 Summary

Markets will be an efficient way to allocate resources only if certain conditions are met. One is that all goods and services are private goods: excludable, divisible, and rival in consumption. Unless this happens, two or more people can use the goods simultaneously. If public good characteristics exist (nonexcludability, indivisibility, or nonrivalness), this undercuts both the consumers' willingness to pay for the good and the incentive of suppliers to provide it. Markets thus "fail" for efficiency reasons.

The essence of externalities as a source of market failure is that a public good characteristic is produced as a by-product of another decision. Chemical plants may produce toxic wastes as well as valuable chemicals (negative externality); inoculated people may slow the spread of infectious diseases (positive externality). In either case, a market-determined output would likely be inefficient because of unpaid external costs (pollution) or uncompensated external gains (inoculation).

Those who generate positive externalities might like to create a market for these services. In some cases they can if the transaction costs are low enough. In other cases the transaction costs of identifying beneficiaries and charging them for services rendered will be too high and markets won't emerge. In yet other cases—inoculations, for example—we want others to become better off. Those who generate negative externalities, however, often prefer to avoid markets for these services and thereby impose costs on others.

Terms and Concepts for Review

markets
government
coercion
private goods
market failure

public goods
externalities
imperfect competition
marginal revenue
excess profit
transactions costs

4

Markets:
Will They Be Fair?

4.0 Introduction

As we saw in Chapter 3, markets may fail for efficiency reasons if too little or too much of something is produced. In this chapter, we consider why markets might fail for equity reasons. Very simply, society may choose not to allocate resources through markets if some people would be rewarded too poorly, or too well, by the market.

The chapter is organized around three issues. First, what do we mean by market rewards? The amount of income earned in a market is one reward, but not the only one; opportunity itself is important to many people. Although the promise of opportunity has often outpaced reality, it has offered hope and a spur to individual initiative.[1] Second, how evenly are market and other economic rewards distributed in the United States, and how has this changed over time? The third issue is how best to define equity or fairness in the distribution of rewards. Several major philosophic approaches to equity are presented through an example in which one group is taxed in order to transfer income to a less well-off group.

Two nagging questions about market failure need to be considered first. One is, How can we tell when a market has failed? The second is, Has the market failed from an efficiency viewpoint, from an equity viewpoint, or from both? Most economists would probably agree that it is far easier to detect market failure due to inefficient resource use than to detect market failure due to distributional inequity. For one thing, an economist is no more (and no less) able than anyone else to advise society on equity. Economic efficiency is the economist's forte. Moreover, it is often possible to compare the net economic values that are diminished by negative externalities with those values that are created through the production processes that give rise to the externalities (e.g., Freeman,

1979). In the case of air pollution from a manufacturing plant, for example, it may be possible to compare the pollution damages to nearby farm crops with the value of the manufacturer's product. If air pollution helps to create $4,000 worth of product but imposes $5,000 in costs on downwind farmers, the air isn't being used efficiently.

It is much more difficult, however, to show that markets have failed due to an inequitable distribution of income. We may have strong feelings about equity and fairness, but society has to somehow make an explicit and collective judgment on the issue before we can really say that a market has failed in a distributional sense. (This, it might be remembered, is the basic problem with the social welfare function that we discussed in Chapter 2.) Even if the present law forces farmers to suffer air-pollution damages, does this mean that society has made a collective judgment that the polluting firm and its workers are more deserving than the farmers? Possibly. More likely, it may mean that the manufacturer has more political clout or that the laws are out-of-date and need revising. The farmers will no doubt feel that the pollution laws are inequitable. Proving that this is so is difficult.

Thus, it isn't easy to say what should or can be inferred from collective decisions about income distribution. One can argue, for example, that an explicit decision was made in the United States in the 1930s to move away from allowing incomes to be determined strictly by markets. The Great Depression of the 1930s resulted in so much human suffering that Social Security (OASDI), unemployment compensation, and other income-support programs were able to win broad acceptance among voters. By now, however, it is an open question whether the same widespread support still exists for these programs, or whether they are now politically sacrosanct (Social Security in particular) because of a strong coalition of retirees, people nearing retirement, politicians catering to retirees, and interest groups of those who serve the needs of retirees.[2] It has been clear for some time that as a group, those over sixty-five are no longer as economically disadvantaged as they were in the past. According to economist Lester Thurow,

> In 1967 the incidence of poverty among the elderly (29.5 percent) was more than twice that of the entire population (14.2 percent). But a just society does not economically discard its citizens simply because they have reached 65 years of age. As a result, social security was expanded to lower the incidence of poverty among the elderly. The poverty gap hasn't quite been eliminated—in 1980 the poverty numbers were 15.7 percent versus 13 percent—but almost.
>
> The same gains are evident across the entire income spectrum. The average per capita elderly household income has risen to 89 percent of

that of the entire population. Forty percent of that income comes from social security. If in-kind benefits, such as medicare, are included, the elderly may have reached parity with the living standards of the rest of the population. (*Newsweek*, October 26, 1981, p. 71)

Today, proposals to tax COLA's (cost-of-living allowances made to alleviate the effects of inflation), reduce benefits, or extend the retirement age are politically risky. The Social Security program presents a good example of how difficult it can be to discern whether a social welfare function has been defined or whether a particular group, the retirement lobby in this case, simply has a substantial amount of political clout.

4.1 Distributional Sources of Market Failure

When we reject the market for equity or distributional causes, we may do so for a variety of reasons. At one extreme, we may believe that markets would deprive participants of fundamental civil liberties. As an obvious example, slavery was rejected in this country well over a century ago. Some rights and liberties can be lessened in particular cases through voluntary agreement of the affected parties. One could agree, for example, not to sue another person over an auto accident, although the general right to bring suit is a fundamental civil liberty.

Markets might also be rejected if they result in the "wrong" patterns of consumption. Concerned that children may not drink enough milk and read enough books, we subsidize school lunches and libraries. We worry that their parents might be unable to own their homes, so we subsidize home ownership. As a society we are concerned about the general well-being of citizens, but we are more likely to be specifically concerned about what they consume or don't consume. We discourage the consumption of certain items through taxing their use (cigarettes and liquor, for example) and by prohibiting their use (certain drugs, for example). People aren't usually hesitant to give this type of advice to others, but the resulting policies aren't always very effective. The prohibition era, for example, proved that we couldn't simply outlaw markets for alcohol and expect it to stick; instead, people made gin in their bathtubs and beer in their cellars.

A third reason for rejecting markets is that they may provide inadequate opportunities for certain types of people. Mainstream labor market opportunities don't exist for many ghetto youths; thus, the underground economy has developed as a set of illegal markets for willing buyers and willing sellers, many of them poor. We may have to accept the existence of these markets if they are the only means by which opportunity can be generated, but we try to offer alternatives such as retraining programs to make illegal markets less attractive and regular markets more attractive to participants.

A fourth reason for rejecting markets is that the income distribution resulting from markets may not be appropriate. The distribution of income is easy to measure compared to "opportunity," but the two are not the same. Historically, the political process has promised people opportunity, not income. We have offered land for homesteaders, water for arid lands, and books for hungry minds. But as economist Robert Lampmann has said, "While many deplore inequality of *opportunity*, no American president has ever made it his declared intention to reduce inequality of *income* in the United States" (Editor's Comment, *Wilson Quarterly*, Winter 1987, p. 6). We still attempt to improve opportunities for certain groups, but the increasing use of entitlements (the rights to certain benefits) suggests that income share, not just opportunity, is becoming a paramount consideration in our demands on the political system.

4.2 The Distribution
of Money Incomes, 1947-1990

Although it is easier to measure income than opportunity, there are still a variety of ways to measure the distribution of income. In selecting an appropriate measure for a particular purpose, one set of issues relates to how income is defined and a second set involves the definition of "units" to which income is distributed.

4.21 *The Definition of Income*

One way to define income is to include only that obtained through one's own labor, through capital or land, or through entrepreneurial abilities. This is usually called earned income, although a Marxist would insist that capital earnings are really expropriated labor earnings. Let's finesse this by calling it *market income*; its distribution would give us some idea about the rewards for having certain skills, abilities, and other resources.

A second and broader measure of income would add *transfer income*, including Social Security payments, pensions from private employers, welfare payments, farm subsidy payments, and unemployment compensation. These tend to reduce the inequality in market incomes because most of these programs are based, in part at least, on need. This is not true for every type of transfer income; the largest farm subsidy payments, for example, are usually made to those farmers who have the highest market incomes.

Another choice in defining income is whether to consider it on a before-tax or after-tax basis. Measurements after taxes would narrow income inequality if the well-off pay proportionately higher taxes than do the poor. Federal and state income taxes and Social Security (FICA) taxes would be the major difference between the two measures. The data on these taxes are reasonably reliable because of withholding procedures for wage and salary incomes. The amount of sales taxes and property taxes that households pay is known with much less certainty.

Imputed or in-kind benefits may also be considered in the distribution of income. The values of these benefits are often difficult to assess in a monetary sense, but estimates can be made of the value of work done by homemakers in preparing meals, caring for children, and performing other household tasks, for example. These amounts would have to be paid to others if the services were not voluntarily provided to the household. Owner-occupied dwellings also have an imputed value; rent would have to be paid if the dwelling weren't owned by the household. Other examples of inputed benefits include food stamps and school lunches.

4.22 The Definition of Units

The second set of issues about income distribution relates to the recipient units to which income is distributed. One division of historical interest has been that between labor and capital earnings. Other units of more recent interest include the distribution of income among households or families, the distribution by type of person (for example, whether the household head has graduated from high school), the distribution by region or state, and the distributions by industrial sector and occupational class.

The measure of income distribution that seems to be most widely used is the distribution of *money income* among U.S. families (Table 4.1). This measure, released annually since 1947 by the U.S. Census Bureau, includes wages and salaries; net self-employment income; capital earnings, including dividends, interest, trust earnings, net rental incomes, and royalties; and transfer payments, including Social Security, public assistance, veterans' payments, unemployment compensation, workers' compensation, and government and private employee pensions. These are the money incomes regularly received by U.S. households before pay-

TABLE 4.1 Distribution of Money Income Among U.S. Families, 1947-1990 (in percentages)

	Top 5%	High- est Fifth	Next Highest Fifth	Middle Fifth	Next Lowest Fifth	Lowest Fifth
1990	17.4	44.3	23.8	16.6	10.8	4.6
1989	17.9	44.6	23.7	16.5	10.6	4.6
1988	17.2	44.0	24.0	16.7	10.7	4.6
1987	17.2	43.8	24.0	16.8	10.8	4.6
1986	17.0	43.7	24.0	16.8	10.8	4.6
1981	15.3	41.8	24.4	17.4	11.3	5.1
1976	15.6	41.1	24.1	17.6	11.8	5.5
1971	15.6	41.0	23.8	17.6	12.0	5.5
1966	15.6	40.5	23.8	17.8	12.4	5.6
1961	16.6	42.2	23.8	17.5	11.9	4.7
1956	16.1	41.0	23.7	17.9	12.5	5.0
1951	16.8	41.6	23.4	17.6	12.4	5.0
1947	17.5	43.0	23.1	17.0	11.9	5.0

Source: U.S. Bureau of Census, *Current Population Reports,* Series P-60, No. 159, Table 12 (1947-1966), and No. 174, Table B-5 (1971-1990)

ment of any taxes such as income taxes or Social Security (FICA) taxes and before deductions such as union dues or Medicare premiums. Market incomes and transfer payments are included on a before-tax basis, but imputed and in-kind benefits are excluded. For the year-round worker with a monthly paycheck, annual money income would amount to the paycheck times twelve. These data are fairly easy to obtain from the roughly 60,000 households in the Current Population Survey (CPS), conducted in March of each year, and this measure avoids many sticky issues about the value of in-kind benefits.

4.23 The Trends in Money Incomes

Table 4.1 shows that money incomes are distributed quite unequally in the United States and that this has changed very little in the past forty-five years. In 1990, the richest 20 percent of all families received well over 40 percent of total money income; the poorest 20 percent received less than 5 percent. (Remember that money income includes Social Security and public assistance payments.) Moreover, a recent major study shows that the United States has more inequality in the distribution of incomes, even after taxes, than almost all of the other major industrial nations (Haveman, 1988b, pp. 238-239). Over the four decades shown in Table 4.1, money income appears to have become somewhat more unequally distributed, and according to Haveman, it may have become even more unequal compared to other countries.

The extent to which the federal and state governments have narrowed this gap through redistributional efforts has also been estimated by Haveman. He found that in 1950, the bottom quintile of families received only 1.5 percent of total market income; this share had fallen to 1.3 percent by 1985 (1988b, pp. 110-113). When cash and in-kind transfers such as Social Security, welfare, food stamps, and Medicaid were considered, the share of the bottom quintile was raised to 2.5 percent of total income in 1950 (a 67 percent increase over market incomes alone) and to 6.0 percent in 1985 (a 346 percent increase over market incomes alone). The percent of the population in poverty (counting government cash benefits) also fell from 41 percent in 1949 to 15 percent in 1983.

Whether the gas tank is half full or half empty depends on your point of view; one might conclude that substantial redistribution is needed to reduce social unrest and to ensure that the income shares don't become even more unequal over time. Haveman's conclusion is a bit more upbeat:

> Perhaps most important, the redistribution system has greatly reduced the uncertainty faced by all of the nation's citizens—uncertainty regarding what happens when a job is lost, when an accident occurs, when a spouse dies, when a family splits. These events spell pain and adversity, and they potentially affect all of us. With this system in place, the pain and adversity associated with these risks are far smaller than they would otherwise be; we are far less a "nation at risk." (1988b, p. 113)

4.24 The Reagan-Bush Decade

The effects on income inequality of various social and economic forces were a topic of great interest in the 1980s. No small part of this interest was due to the wave of conservatism that resulted in three terms of Reagan and Bush administrations. Again citing Haveman,

Beginning about 1960, . . . government again accepted explicit responsibility for intervening in the social affairs of the nation, reasserting the commitment that was made in the New Deal programs of the 1930s. It responded to issues of poverty, discrimination, and ultimately to riots in the streets. The transformation of government priorities is reflected in the enactment of the War on Poverty, the Great Society, Medicare, Medicaid, Community Action, and expansions in Social Security benefits. By the mid-1970s, however, the enthusiasm for these efforts had waned, and by 1980 the pendulum had swung back. Until then, the government was increasingly concerned with domestic problems of discrimination, insecurity, and gaps among important groups. But the Reagan administration shifted government away from social intervention toward more traditional military-infrastructure activities. (1988b, p. 105)

By promoting tax cuts that favored the rich and budget cuts for social services that penalized the poor, the Reagan administration quickly became a prime target of those favoring greater equality of opportunity and incomes. In 1984 the Urban Institute reported that the disposable (after-tax) income of the bottom quintile of U.S. families had declined by 7.6 percent since 1980, and the income of the top quintile had risen by 8.7 percent (*Wall Street Journal*, August 16, 1984). Much of this tilt was due to a cut in upper-bracket tax rates through the 1981 Tax Act, designed to spur economic growth through "supply-side economics." The Urban Institute report was careful not to attribute all the widening of the gap to Reagan policies, concluding that budget cuts and the recession had contributed about equally to the rise in poverty between 1979 and 1982. By 1992, however, the Congressional Budget Office (CBO) was reporting an increase in income inequality over the entire decade of the 1980s, one even more marked than the 1984 estimate by the Urban Institute. The CBO estimated that the top 20 percent of U.S. families had seen a 77 percent rise in pretax income between 1977 and 1989; the bottom 20 percent had seen their pretax incomes fall by 9 percent (*New York Times*, March 5, 1992, p. A1). Moreover, the top 1 percent of families had received 60 percent of the total after-tax income gain; the top 5 percent had received 74 percent of the gain.

The relative impacts of the conservative Reagan and Bush administrations, on the one hand, and of various social, economic, and demographic trends, on the other hand, were heatedly debated by economists and columnists throughout the 1980s. Was there an acceleration in the trend toward inequality, as economist Lester Thurow argued early in the decade, or were we in a prolonged period of general economic stagnation that kept the improved income figures from surfacing? And if we weren't moving toward more inequality, wasn't it taking a lot of effort just to maintain the status quo? According to Haveman, less than 30 percent of the federal budget in 1965 was devoted to income transfers such as Social Security, welfare assistance, and veterans' benefits, and to helping people buy essential health services such as Medicare and other social services. After 1965, however, more and more of the federal budget went toward these purposes: "In the years from 1965 to 1985, federal spending on income transfers increased more than tenfold; programs designed to help people buy essentials increased about thirtyfold. These programs were America's main growth industry during this period. By 1980, the nation's income redistribution system had grown to over half the federal budget" (Haveman, 1988a, p. 10).

Total federal expenditures increased from $118 billion to $946 billion in current dollars between 1965 and 1985, by a factor of eight. Total redistributional expenditures, however, increased from $36 billion to $465 billion, by a factor of thirteen. By comparison, national defense expenditures, long thought to be large and burdensome, increased from $51 billion to $253 billion, by a factor of only five. This massive redistribution, however, hasn't made much of a dent in income distribution. Haveman concludes that "the incidence of poverty today is only slightly lower than when the War on Poverty was announced in 1964 and inequality is, if anything, greater" (1988a, p. 10).

What are the social, economic, and demographic trends that affected income distribution in the 1980s? One was the increased number of working women, particularly the wives of high-income males. This meant more inequality when measured in family incomes. As Thurow noted, most wives of low- and middle-income males were already working for pay; now, the high-income spouses were coming back into the labor force (*Newsweek*, October 5, 1981). A second trend was the baby boom generation hitting the labor market, where they had to compete with each other and with older workers. Third, there was a marked decline in economic productivity, that is, a reduction in the amount of goods and services produced per unit of labor and capital. There is little doubt that productivity growth slowed in the 1980s; the growth rate amounted to only 1.2 percent per year during that decade, compared to 2.5 percent annually between 1947 and 1973 (R. Samuelson, *Newsweek*, September 19, 1988, p. 49).

A fourth factor that contributed to income inequality was the persistence of entrenched poverty in certain types of families. Only 16 percent of the poorest quintile of families in 1986, for example, had even one full-time, year-round worker (Samuelson, 1988). A fifth and more problematic trend, the growth of "bad jobs," was raised by liberal econo-

mists Bennett Harrison and Barry Bluestone. They released a report to
Congress in 1984 showing that most of the new jobs created in the
Reagan years paid no more than $7,000 per year. Their critics objected to
this conclusion on a variety of grounds, including the choice of time
periods and the exclusion from analysis of certain high-growth and
higher-paying types of jobs. Finally, analysts generally agreed that the
stagnant economy in the 1980s most adversely affected those people who
were least prepared to compete in a market economy. In *Dollars and
Dreams* (1988), Frank Levy estimated that for two thirty-year-olds, one
with a college degree, the other with only a high-school diploma, the gap
in expected lifetime earnings grew from a 15 to 20 percent difference in
the 1970s to nearly a 50 percent difference in the late 1980s.

Nevertheless, some forward strides were made in the 1980s with
those groups that have traditionally been the most vulnerable. The
black-white income gap, for example, narrowed considerably, particularly
for couples. Women's earnings have expanded from more work, but not
necessarily from better pay. And the incidence of poverty among the
elderly fell below the rest of the population during 1985 (Haveman,
1988a, pp. 11-12). Now, Haveman argues, we have a trio of new income
inequalities that have to be faced in the 1990s. The first is that of young
people, particularly minorities; the second is those who live in single-
parent families; the third is the elderly who live alone, especially
minorities.

Haveman urges that we address inequalities of opportunity, not just
inequalities of outcome. This could be done, for example, by scaling back
Social Security benefits for high-income retirees and using the money for
education and training of minority youths and others who have dim job
prospects. Chapters 6 through 11 will develop several dimensions of
collective choice that will be instrumental in deciding whether this is
likely to happen. These dimensions will include interest groups,
coalitions, voting behavior, political support, and political competition.
Unfortunately, they all suggest that high-income retirees will prevail over
low-income youth as a political force in deciding the outcome.

4.3 Philosophic Approaches to the
Question of Equity

As citizens, how can we defend or challenge a certain distribution of
income as unfair or fair, as equitable or inequitable?   One way of
thinking about this age-old question is with a tax example that illustrates
four different philosophic approaches to the question of equity.

4.31 A Tax Example

Let's assume that the workers in one group called High have substantial earning abilities. Born poor and still poor, the workers in Low have no earning ability. Either through their desire for charity or their fear of social unrest, those in High are considering implementing a tax on their own earnings in order to transfer income to Low. At present, the two groups are at point N in Figure 4.1. High's earnings are now untaxed; those in this group can keep all the money they make. Those in Low have no income. Alternative tax rates are proposed, ranging from 15 percent to 100 percent of High's hourly earnings.

How would those in High respond to the different tax rates? As shown in the appendix to this chapter, the labor-supply response of those in High would depend on their preferences for leisure, as well as on their preferences for goods that could be purchased with labor earnings. The tax would reduce the effective price of labor, so those in High would have less income at higher tax rates. Leisure, however, would also be less expensive; less would be given up by choosing an hour's leisure rather than working that hour. In technical terms, the net effect of the tax would depend on the relative size of the substitution and income effects associated with changes in the wage rate.

The straight NL line (N = L) shows how income might be redistributed from High to Low *if* High worked the same amount irrespective of the tax rate. If this happened, all of High's earnings could simply be transferred to Low up to a 100 percent tax rate (point L). This probably wouldn't happen; High's labor supply would most likely change as the tax rate became higher.

A likely consequence of the alternative tax rates is shown as the curved line, NO. If the tax rate were to rise from zero to 15 percent, for example, those in High might choose to work 7 hours per week rather than 6 so that their total earnings would increase and they might defend their initial income position (Table 4.2). In technical terms, the income effect of the wage change would have dominated the substitution effect, causing those in High to work more (point A). Above a 15 percent tax rate, however, those in High might choose to work less. In this case, the substitution effect of the wage change would dominate the income effect (points M and G). It seems almost certain that they wouldn't work at all if the tax rate were 100 percent. Leisure would be free, and nothing would be sacrificed by not working.

Although this particular type of labor-supply response is quite plausible, the general relationship of tax rates to government revenues is

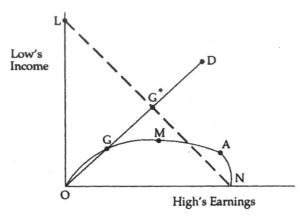

FIGURE 4.1 Taxing High to Pay Low

Source: Adapted from Richard A. Musgrave and Peggy B. Musgrave, *Public Finance in Theory and Practice*, 5th ed. (New York: McGraw-Hill, 1989), pp. 82-85. Reprinted by permission.

TABLE 4.2 Effects of a Tax on High's Labor Earnings

		High				
Point	Tax Rate	Hours Worked Per Week	Pre-Tax Earnings ($10/hr)	After-Tax Earnings	Low's Income	Total Income
N	0%	6.0	$60.00	$60.00	$0.00	$60.00
A	15%	7.0	70.00	59.50	10.50	70.00
M	30%	5.0	50.00	35.00	15.00	50.00
G	50%	2.5	25.00	12.50	12.50	25.00
--	80%	1.0	10.00	2.00	8.00	10.00
O	100%	0.0	0.00	0.00	0.00	0.00

Source: Musgrave and Musgrave (1989, pp. 82-85). Reprinted by permission.

often a matter of controversy. More often than not, at least some of the contentions are based on dogma rather than empirical analysis. The *Laffer curve*, for example, was enthusiastically adopted by the Reagan adminis-tration in the early 1980s. This was the notion that taxation is invariably burdensome, and that a lowering of tax rates would allow government revenues to increase because of enhanced consumption, investment, and productivity.[3]

A more conventional analysis would grant that tax-rate reductions stimulate the economy but would conclude that the associated revenue gain wouldn't be nearly as great as the revenue lost from lower tax rates. Most economists believe that total government revenue would fall if tax rates were reduced. The curved line, NO, reflects an increasing tax rate from right to left, starting with a zero tax at N. Because the vertical axis shows, in effect, government revenues, all of which would be taxed from High and redistributed to Low, the Laffer controversy can be illustrated with Figure 4.1. The Laffer proponents imply that we are somewhere between points O and M, that government revenues will increase if tax rates fall (read the horizontal axis from left to right). The conventional analysis is that we are between M and N, that government revenues will decline if tax rates fall. The empirical research on the issue clearly supports the conventional wisdom. Fullerton (1982), for example, argues that because labor-supply schedules are generally quite inelastic, workers would continue to work nearly as much and government revenue would keep rising as the tax rate increased (read from right to left). Maximum revenue wouldn't be reached until the marginal tax rate rose to perhaps as high as 80 percent. The relevant range is thus clearly between N and M, and not, as the Laffer proponents argue, between O and M.

4.32 *The Endowment Approach*

Without a tax, High would earn N, but Low would earn nothing. If we accept point N as desirable or good, we support an *endowment approach* to the philosophic question of equity. As the terms "conservative" and "liberal" are used today, the endowment approach is much more conservative than it is liberal; it says that it is good and just that people are rewarded to the extent—but only to the extent—that their brain, brawn, and position allow them to be rewarded.

In his insightful book on ethics and efficiency, philosopher Allen Buchanan (1985, Chapter 3) critically examined three arguments that have been used in support of the endowment approach. The first argument comes from late nineteenth-century social Darwinism; those who emerge as fittest from competition in the market are those who have personal characteristics that are most essential to survival of the market system. People who take this view want to minimize government intervention, such as taxes, because they feel that these interfere with the Darwinian process of natural selection. Certain traits like initiative would appear to benefit not only those who possess the trait, but society in general. Buchanan points out, however, that there are other traits—avarice and duplicity, for example—that may benefit the individual but pose a burden to society. Both types of traits may be sharpened and refined by their use in markets. It isn't clear that N is the best position for society as a whole or that markets are the best way to reach that position even if N is the best point.

A second and closely related argument in support of the endowment approach is the so-called argument from desert. It says that those who have certain traits such as frugality or those who exhibit certain behaviors such as hard work are the most deserving and should be rewarded. A major problem with this position, according to Buchanan, is how one should account for luck or chance in determining outcomes. Some of those who have the most wealth may have won it, inherited it, or stolen it.

These questions of rights and entitlements have led to a third and more modern argument for the endowment approach, which is the *libertarian view* (e.g., Nozick, 1974). According to this view, "people are entitled to whatever they get through voluntary exchanges, so long as their initial holdings were justly acquired" (Buchanan, 1985, p. 53). In a libertarian view, the use of force to cause High to pay taxes would be legitimate only if the taxes were used to protect citizens from physical harm, to deter or to punish the perpetrators of harm, or to enforce a voluntary contract. Paying taxes to support Low is not found within these reasons. Would those in High view the tax as a voluntary exchange by which they would gain utility from the knowledge that Low had been made better off by their donations? If so, they could make a private donation to Low and gain the same feeling without the use of coercive taxes. Thus, a libertarian would argue that government action isn't usually needed for redistribution. Buchanan responds by pointing out that charity is a public good; even if we would all benefit from income redistribution, the logic of collective action is that we may wait for others to donate first. We'll see this in Chapter 5.

Private rights to property are paramount in a libertarian view, including the right to the fruits of one's labor, unless others are made worse off and not fully compensated. If this happens, an exchange wouldn't truly be voluntary and those who are made worse off wouldn't be expected to consent. If someone in High is rich because he attended a prestigious law school, one that he was able to afford only because his father was a slumlord, for example, his earnings might not have been justly acquired.

4.33 Three Utilitarian Approaches

If points A, M, or G in Figure 4.1 are chosen as "best" in an ethical sense, one of three *utilitarian approaches* to the question of equity would be implied. In general, a utilitarian philosophy involves the general principle of greatest happiness, not just of an individual but of society. A utilitarian philosophy says that the well-being of society (U*) depends on the well-being of the members of that society, or

$$U^* = U^*(U_{High}, U_{Low}), \tag{4.1}$$

where U_{High} and U_{Low} are the aggregated utilities of the two groups (Oser, 1970, pp. 109-114; Spiegel, 1983, pp. 340-343). Although A (additive utility), M (maximum utility), and G (egalitarian utility) are all utilitarian, they are not the same.[4] They do, however, have four things in common. First, each involves the idea of utility, something that can't be compared among individuals because of its subjective nature. Second, each considers both the High group and the Low group in reckoning the total utility of society. Third, each is a feasible point; they all lie on the curved line NO, which is generated by High's decisions on labor supply. Fourth, each might be called outcome-oriented, in contrast to the libertarian position, which is very process-oriented. The three utilitarian approaches are based on utility outcomes as perceived by High and Low. The libertarian approach stresses whether those in High feel that their rights have been violated.

With this overview, we can examine the three utilitarian approaches in more detail. The *additive utility* position (A) implies that Equation 4.1 should be based on summation,

$$U^* = (a_1)(U_{High}) + (a_2)(U_{Low}), \tag{4.2}$$

and, even more specifically, that the summation should be with equal weights ($a_1 = a_2$). In this case, money income (I), rather than utility (U), has to be summed because of measurement problems,

$$U^* = 1.0 \, (I_{High}) + 1.0 \, (I_{Low}). \tag{4.3}$$

In this view, the best tax rate on High is the one that results in the largest total income for the two groups combined. Whether those in High who earned the income deserve to keep it isn't a factor; the emphasis is on total income rather than its distribution. In the language of Pareto efficiency, a 15 percent tax rate would cause High to be worse off and Low to be better off. The two are collectively better off, however, because total income has been increased by the decision of those in High to work more and thus defend their pretax income position. The fact that income has increased is shown by the fact that A lies outside the dotted NL line, which represents various ways to distribute High's initial earnings.

We can now see that the Kaldor-Hicks compensation test of Chapter 2, the idea of potential Pareto improvement, is clearly based on additive utilitarian philosophy. In this test, total gains are simply compared to total losses without considering who gains and who loses. That is, the total is all that matters—the distribution is irrelevant. More is preferred to less, viewed in an overall sense. The gains and losses to society might be reflected through changes in consumers' surplus and producers' surplus, as discussed in Chapter 2. A new hydroelectric dam, for example, might have an excess of gains (consumers' surplus among power users) over costs (reduced consumers' surplus from other goods and services that are forgone because of building the dam). Society would be acting in a manner consistent with an additive utilitarian philosophy if it built the dam, even though many of those who bear the costs might not benefit from the new hydroelectric power.

The *maximin utility* position, M, is generally attributed to the philosopher John Rawls (1971). Rawls believes that society should attempt to maximize utility for that member who has the lowest (minimum) level of utility. (Hence, the word "maximin.") At M, those in Low are at their highest possible income level given High's willingness to work at the various tax rates. Rawls suggests that the members of a moral society will create ways of moving toward M, and that they will do so behind a *veil of ignorance* with respect to their own future roles in that society. Any advantages due to economic, political, or social position would be ignored by those holding those positions, because fate (or stock market crashes) might cause them to become the least-advantaged members in society. (Remember, Rawls is describing how a moral community would act, not what it actually does.) Rawls's critics claim that a maximin approach is only one of several approaches that moral persons might find acceptable, and that their first choice might depend on their attitudes toward risk. Even behind a veil of ignorance, people might favor rules that would be personally beneficial if they happened to be born into the middle or upper class, which is a statistically likely event, although these same rules would reduce their welfare if they happened to be born into the least-advantaged family, which is a far less likely event in a statistical sense.

According to *egalitarian utility*, all members should have equal utility (G) if society is to be as well off as possible. A proxy is that all members should have equal money incomes.[5] In this view, Equation 4.1 would be reformulated as

$$\frac{I_{High}}{I_{Low}} = 1.0. \tag{4.4}$$

Although this might seem to be an attractive position, there are three major arguments against the egalitarian approach (Buchanan, 1985, p. 58). For one, different individuals may have different capabilities for enjoyment. Some people can be happy on low incomes; others are miserable with great wealth, although it isn't clear whether they would be happier with less money. This is an old idea: Early utilitarians like Jeremy Bentham ([1780] 1948) and John Stuart Mill ([1848] 1871) believed that those with the most wealth would gain little from additional wealth but that those with little wealth would have large utility gains.

Buchanan's second argument, and a very different type of objection to the egalitarian approach, is that unequal incomes may provide incentives for the less well-off to be more productive, take more risks, and expend more effort. The third argument against egalitarianism is that the degree of government action that would be required to enforce equality would infringe greatly on individual civil liberties. Even if it didn't, this approach could be costly if total income fell substantially at high tax levels. At G, higher tax rates and High's decision to work less would cause total income to fall far below the maximum income level reached at A.

What philosophy should an individual or a society adopt with respect to equity and redistribution? Many people reject the endowment approach because it seems unfair to the have-nots, although the libertarian philosophy is popular among those who place a high value on liberty. Many people reject the egalitarian approach because it would be too costly to achieve and too unlikely to be attained. Remember, we saw earlier in this chapter that the top 5 percent of the families in the income distribution have as much money income as the lowest 40 percent, and that the distribution is becoming even more unequal.

Between these extremes, an argument can be made that social policy should reflect two approaches, not just one. The additive utility approach would work toward enhancing the size of the economic pie: the maximin utility approach would work toward greater fairness with respect to distribution. Buchanan makes this summary statement:

> Some utilitarians . . . have concluded that maximizing social utility requires a relatively large role for the market plus a minimal welfare program or "safety net" or "decent minimum" of basic goods and services guaranteed for all who cannot attain them for themselves. The attractions of this approach are considerable. On the one hand, reserving a large role for the market acknowledges the efficiency of that system, including heightened productivity resulting from · unequal distribution and the minimization of government power. On the other hand . . . a safety net or decent minimum system acknowledges that, at least for . . . certain basic goods such as food and shelter, marginal utility is relatively uniform for all individuals. The trick, of course, is to set the level of taxation needed to provide the safety net high enough to reap utilities that would not be obtainable in . . . an unfettered market but low enough to avoid excessive reductions of incentives for productivity. (1985, p. 59)

Again, we can see efficiency and equity as two basic reasons for collective action. The two will often conflict with each other, however, and someone will need to decide which is more important in a particular situation.

4.4 Summary

We might want to reject the use of markets if the outcomes would be "unfair" to certain groups of people. Lack of fairness will depend on the distribution of income, opportunity, consumption, and civil liberties. Among these, the distribution of income is the easiest to measure. The distribution of money income in the United States has changed little in the past half-century; the top 5 percent of families receive as much money income as do the bottom 40 percent of families. The 1980s saw political controversy about incomes, but inequality became even greater during that decade.

Four different philosophic approaches to equity give four very different answers to the question, What is a fair and equitable distribution of income? A tax example helps to clarify the four. The endowment approach to equity, including the modern libertarian view, would approve of only voluntary exchanges based on initial endowments, justly acquired. The additive utilitarian approach to equity, as reflected in the Kaldor-Hicks compensation test of Chapter 2, would favor the tax plan that leads to the largest total income, regardless of its distribution within society. The maximin utility approach would favor making those worst off as well off as possible, and the egalitarian approach would go farther and call for equal incomes among all members of society.

Appendix: Income and Substitution Effects

If those in the High group spent all their time at leisure and didn't work at all, they would be at H with no labor income (Figure 4.2). If they could work at $10 per hour (wage line W_0), they would choose to work L_0 amount of time. This would reduce their leisure from H to L_0, but it would enable them to earn I_0 income and put them on a higher indifference curve (U_0) than if they didn't work at all. If a 15 percent tax were instituted (wage line W_1), the net hourly wage would fall from $10.00 to $8.50. Because the effective wage rate would decline, two related things would happen for those in High. One is that leisure, the amount of time spent *not* working, would become cheaper; less income would be forgone if someone worked an hour less. Because leisure is a consumption good, its use would increase if it was cheaper. This is called the *substitution effect* of a wage change; other things equal, those in High would tend to consume more leisure by reducing the number of hours worked.[6]

But other things aren't equal. Leisure becomes less expensive, but the worker now has less income because of the increased tax. Labor earnings would fall from I_0 to I_1 if the wage rate fell from W_0 to W_1 and if the worker maximized utility by choosing the E_1 combination of labor and leisure. The second effect of the tax is called the *income effect*. The worker would respond to the tax by increasing labor supply in response to the income effect instead of reducing it as with the substitution effect. In this case, the income effect of the wage change is stronger than the substitution effect, so the net effect, the sum of the two, is that the worker works more, not less.[7]

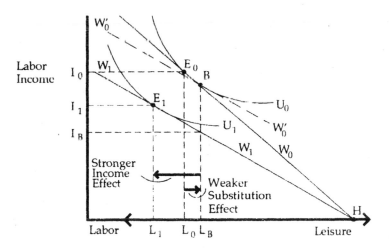

FIGURE 4.2 Allotment of High's Time Between Leisure and Labor in Response to a Tax on Labor Earnings

The reason that line NO in Figure 4.1 has its curved shape, then, is that the net effect of a tax on labor supply may vary depending on the level of the tax, the worker's income, and the rate at which he or she is willing to give up income to obtain leisure. At low levels of the tax, NO is drawn to reflect an increase in labor supply; the income effect dominates the substitution effect, as shown in Figure 4.1. At high tax levels, one might expect the opposite result; the substitution effect would dominate the income effect, and the worker would work less instead of more.

Terms and Concepts for Review

market income
transfer income
imputed or in-kind benefits
money income
Laffer curve
endowment approach to equity
libertarian view of equity
utilitarian approaches to equity
additive utility
maximin utility
egalitarian utility
veil of ignorance
substitution and income effects of a wage change

5

Voluntary Solutions
to Market Failure

5.0   Introduction

We have seen that markets may fail for efficiency reasons if a commodity has public good characteristics that don't allow benefits to be fully captured or costs to be fully borne by decisionmakers. We have also seen that markets may fail for distributional reasons when certain people or groups aren't rewarded by the market to the extent that society might like. Now we need to consider options in a spectrum of choice for deciding how resources should be allocated. The market is at one end of this spectrum, with willing buyers and willing sellers. In spite of the problems of Chapters 3 and 4—public goods, externalities, high transaction costs, and lack of equity—the market still offers some remedies and possibilities that we need to explore. Toward the other end of the spectrum, in varying degrees of complexity, resources are allocated by collective choice.

We begin this chapter by considering voluntary solutions to market failure—how to make markets work better without resorting to coercion by government. Models of direct or participatory government are considered in Chapter 6. There, people are directly involved in group decision-making without elected representatives. Representative government is the subject of Chapters 7 and 8; political demands are channeled through elected representatives or political suppliers. Bureaucratic government is considered in Chapters 9 and 10; goods and services are delivered by nonelected suppliers. Federated government in which several levels of government exist is considered in Chapter 11. Although a single option is seldom, if ever, used alone, it is productive to look at the collective-choice process in a sequential and increasingly complex way. In this manner, we can identify exactly what each option involves, what its limitations might be, and how it relates to the other options.

The question to be addressed in this chapter is whether voluntary action can resolve problems of market failure. For voluntary action to be effective, it would have to lead to a more efficient level of output or to the right people sharing more fully in the rewards. By asking whether voluntary action can bring about either or both of these situations, we are asking whether there are noncoercive solutions—those that do not constrain individual free choice. To start with a voluntary-actions approach is clearly to make a value judgment, but it is one that many would share because of their concern for individual liberties. Voluntarism is, in fact, a recurring theme in society and government. It was widely promoted by the Reagan administration, for example, to reduce budget costs, to involve citizens more fully in civic life, and to reinforce a sense of community and patriotism among citizens.

To understand whether coercive action by government can be avoided, we need to think first about the nature of self-interest among individuals and how this relates to the "collective interest," if, in fact, there is such a thing. To an economist, thinking about *self-interest* starts with the idea of individual utility. Economists say that "people have utility functions," meaning that people assess and define their own needs and preferences. This doesn't mean that they are necessarily selfish or benevolent. A person who donates all his wealth to charity and has few regrets, for example, might be maximizing his self-interest. So too might the miser who never shares with others. Economists would regard both individuals as rational if their actions are consistent with their goals and objectives.

Determining the *collective interest*, however, would involve aggregating the preferences of more than one person. This raises many questions about how such aggregation can or should be done. As we saw in Chapter 2, the Arrow theorem (1951) did severe damage to the assumption that it is possible to aggregate individual preferences in any unambiguous way. (More on this in Chapter 6.) This leaves collective choice analysts (and students) with the unsettling conclusion that the collective interest is something that doesn't really exist, a will-o-the-wisp, or as conservatives see it, an illusion fostered by liberals to evoke the power of the state in the liberals' behalf. As this chapter proceeds, it will be more productive to think of the collective interest as a concept that is helpful in learning the principles of collective choice, not as one that can be readily observed or implemented in the real world.

5.1 Self-Interest and the Collective Interest

The possibility for conflict between self-interest and the collective interest can be illustrated by an experiment conducted by the periodical *Science 84* (Allman, 1984). Readers were encouraged to return a postcard asking for either $20 or $100, but they were told that if more than 20 percent asked for $100, no one would win anything! For several reasons, the offer was hypothetical. The results: Thirty-five percent of the 33,511 readers who returned their cards asked for $100. Therefore, claimed the sponsor, the deal was off; no one got anything (*Science 85*, January/ February, p. 20).

What can we learn from this experiment? The main lesson is that there may be conflicts between individual self-interest and the collective interest. In this case, individual self-interest can be defined as the expected money gain for an individual. Collective interest can be defined as the expected money gain for the group. Asking for $100 would seem the thing for an individual to do. Asking for this larger amount might have involved little personal cost because the chance was extremely small that any one person would affect the outcome, especially if there were a large number of respondents. The collective interest, in this case, lost out because too many people pursued their self-interest. Thirty-five percent of the *Science* respondents asked for $100, thus causing the offer to be withdrawn and the collective gain to be zero. A more favorable collective outcome would have resulted if fewer than 20 percent had asked for $100. Why didn't this happen? Because too many people took advantage of the fact that the outcome of the experiment was a nonexcludable public good. Had the outcome been favorable, anyone who asked for $100 would have received that amount. To reach that outcome, however, no more than 20 percent could ask for the larger amount. The best deal? You ask for $20 and validate the offer; *I'll* ask for $100!

5.11 The Prisoners' Dilemma

Although the respondents in the *Science* experiment failed to take advantage of the magazine's offer, none were worse off than before. At other times, however, the outcome can be less benign; things can get a lot worse. Mueller (1989), drawing on Bush and Meyer (1974), notes that two people may choose whether to be economically self-sufficient or whether to engage in trade with each other. If they trade, it would be a *positive-sum game* because trade would benefit them both. If they don't trade, they would simply forgo this opportunity. But there is another option: They could each steal from the other! One's gain would be the other's loss. This would be a *zero-sum game* if gains simply equaled losses. But if each of them anticipated that the other might steal, care would be taken to prevent losses. Doors would be chained and locks would be purchased. We would then have a *negative-sum game*, because the resources devoted to crime prevention could be used for other things.

The *Prisoners' Dilemma*[1] is a classic illustration of a negative-sum game—how two parties acting independently out of self-interest may be destined not to cooperate, much to their mutual detriment (Figure 5.1). Consider that a crime has been committed by two individuals working together. The two are apprehended and put in separate rooms; neither can communicate with the other. Identical but separate offers are made to each by the authorities: "If you'll confess to the crime you'll be set free, but the other prisoner will serve a 30-year sentence" (Case 2 or Case 3). "If he *too* confesses, you will both serve 15-year sentences" (Case 4). There is one other option: "If you remain silent for one year without implicating yourself or the other, and the other also elects this option, you'll both be given minimal 1-year terms" (Case 1).

Let's assume that the utility of each prisoner depends only on the length of his own sentence and that the collective interest is the total prison time served by the two. Prisoner 1 doesn't know what Prisoner 2 will do, but he'll be better off confessing in any event. If Prisoner 2 happens to remain silent, which can't be known or influenced, Prisoner 1 will go free by confessing. He will serve one year, however, if Prisoner 2 also remains silent; therefore, he would confess. If Prisoner 2 happens to confess, it will still be better for Prisoner 1 to confess because he'll get only 15 years, but he'll serve 30 years if he remains silent. Thus, the nature of the Prisoners' Dilemma: It is clearly in the best interest of each prisoner, but not the two collectively, to confess.

		Prisoner 2	
		Remain Silent	Confess
Prisoner 1	Remain Silent	-1[a], -1[b] (Case 1)	-30, 0 (Case 2)
	Confess	0, -30 (Case 3)	-15, -15 (Case 4)

[a] The first number shows the jail term for Prisoner 1.
[b] The second number shows the jail term for Prisoner 2.

FIGURE 5.1 The Prisoners' Dilemma

Each prisoner is confronted with the same logic and arrives at the same conclusion. By making independent decisions in their own prison cells, they arrive at a solution (Case 4) that is the worst of the four possible outcomes. Both will receive severe sentences. Prisoner 1's self-interest would be best served by Case 3; Prisoner 2's would be best served by Case 2. If they could cooperate, they could work toward Case 1 and maximize their collective interest of serving the least total time in jail. Instead, the incentives are stacked against them. As with the *Science* experiment, the outcome of this "experiment" is a nonexcludable public good. As viewed by each prisoner, the outcome is beyond control; each responds on the basis of apparent private gain by confessing. To gain a favorable outcome, each would have to contribute to that outcome by remaining silent. Neither, however, has the incentive to do so.

5.12 The Collective Action Problem

The likelihood of conflict between self-interest and the collective interest was the central focus of Mancur Olson's classic book *The Logic of Collective Action* (1965). This pathbreaking book challenged the usual assumption made by social scientists that voluntary organizations and associations exist to further the common interests of their members. Olson argued that these organizations exist in spite of the common interest of their members! Several individuals may have a common interest, but they are also likely to have private interests that inhibit the individual's support for the voluntary organization. Even if they might each gain from formation or existence of a group, they might not act to promote their common interest.

The crux of this paradox, as reflected in the *Science 84* experiment and the Prisoners' Dilemma, is the public good nature of the collective outcome. If organizations are effective in promoting the common interest of members, they provide an outcome with public good characteristics. If group action leads to a new law, for example, or to a more favorable profit situation, the outcome is a nonrival and nonexcludable public good. That being the case, individuals may be able to enjoy the benefits of the group without bearing the costs of group membership.

Consider Figure 5.2, for example, which shows a market diagram for an agricultural commodity and a second diagram of costs and revenues for an individual farmer. A major item of collective interest would be the market price of the commodity; all farmers who produce that commodity would be in favor of receiving a higher price. Most agricultural commodities have inelastic demands, meaning that a reduction in output will result in a greater than proportional increase in price; thus, reductions in output will usually cause increases in the total revenue received by all farmers. Partly because of this, voluntary associations such as the National Farmers Organization (NFO) have made several attempts at withholding actions designed to drive up prices, enhance total farm revenues, and thus contribute to the collective interests of farmers. Midwest farmers, for example, were urged during the 1960s to withhold livestock and dairy products from the market until favorable contracts could be signed with local processors.

In Olson's framework, withholding actions are likely to be ineffective because farmers have private interests that may not be compatible with the collective interest. One crucial private interest would be the individual farmer's net profit, or the excess of returns over costs at the output level at which profits are maximized. If the price of his output could be raised from P_0 to P_1 by withholding actions that would shift the market supply schedule from S_0 to S_1, the farmer who sought to maximize net profits would find it in his best interest to *expand* output from q_0 to q_1 rather than reduce it below q_0. (SMC is the farmer's short-run marginal cost of producing additional output; SAC is his short-run average cost of production.) At q_1, the higher marginal cost of production would just equal the higher marginal revenue obtained from the new market price. If the higher price was available as a nonexcludable public good to withholders and nonwithholders alike, an individual who took advantage of it by increasing production could increase net profit to the area efgh, which is larger than the original net profit of area abcd. In other words, a higher price is important, but it isn't the whole story.

Therefore, even though a group has a common interest, its members won't necessarily engage in collective action; the *free-rider* or *collective action problem* has to be resolved. All three major actors above—the farmer, the prisoner, and the *Science* respondent—were free riders on what appeared to be favorable outcomes—a higher price, a shorter sentence, and a larger amount of money. By acting in their private interest, however, individuals failed to do their part to obtain the public good—by withholding the farm commodity, by remaining silent, or by asking for the smaller amount of money. According to Olson, for group action to be effective, either the individual must be provided with some private excludable good in addition to the public good or there must be some form of moral persuasion, compulsion, or coercion. Unfortunately, threats were used to coerce many potential suppliers in the withholding actions. A happier form of solution would be the provision of inducements to members, usually in the form of private, excludable goods. Chapter 7 presents examples of this. National environmental groups, for example, often provide members with attractive magazines that are not available at newsstands. These are provided to members in addition to

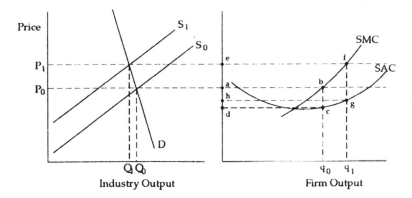

FIGURE 5.2. Individual and Collective Interest in Agricultural
Withholding Actions

providing them with lobbying for environmental action, which is a public
good that provides benefits to members and nonmembers alike.

5.13 The Possibility of Cooperation [2]

Earlier in this chapter, we noted that the self-interest of too many
respondents negated the possibility of an attractive reward in the *Science
84* experiment. The general interpretation was that free-riding will
prevent cooperation in the case of nonexcludable public goods. Another
interpretation, however, is that an overwhelming majority of the
respondents (65 percent) *did* take a group-minded action by asking for
only $20. This may have been due in part to experimental bias; it cost
nothing to be a nice guy and ask for only $20, because the offer itself was
hypothetical. Many scientists, however, feel that much more is involved;
they feel that cooperation is not unexpected, even in a one-time play of
the game and even if real money is involved. According to psychologist
Daniel Kahneman, "There is an assumption that everyone will always
take the free-ride, and it just ain't so." Robyn Dawes said, "The idea that
people will be fair only out of self-interest doesn't really describe their
behavior. There is a value change when people are in a group" (*Science
85*, January/February, p. 20).

Most researchers argue that feedback, learning, and replaying the
game will loosen the shackles of the Prisoners' Dilemma. Realistically,
they say, the major limitation of the dilemma as an analytical generaliza-
tion is the assumption that decisions are one-shot affairs; in fact, we can

learn from repeating the decisions. Robert Axelrod of the University of Michigan conducted a computer tournament for psychologists, political scientists, mathematicians, economists, and sociologists, all of whom had studied the Prisoners' Dilemma in detail (Allman, 1984). Each wrote a computer program for repeated plays of a one-on-one dilemma, using a scoring system that rewarded movements toward maximizing the collective interest. The winner, a simple four-line program called TIT for TAT, was written by Anatol Rapoport of the University of Toronto. Its approach was to always cooperate on the first move, then do whatever the opponent did on the next move.

The evolution of how researchers have viewed the prospects for cooperation in providing public goods is an interesting one. First, there was the conventional wisdom, questioned by Olson, that groups would form to promote their common interest and that larger groups would be more effective groups. Small was not necessarily beautiful if there was a common interest. Olson stood this wisdom on its head, arguing that the larger the group, the greater the disincentive for an individual to provide the good and the greater the potential for free-riding. Would any of the good be provided? In many cases, no. According to Olson, "In a large group in which no single individual's contribution makes a perceptible difference to the group as a whole it is certain that a collective good will *not* be provided unless there is coercion or some outside inducements" (1965, p. 44). And the larger the group, the less potent it would be: "The larger the group is, the farther it will fall short of providing an optimal supply of any collective good, and the less likely that it will act to obtain even a minimal amount of such a good. In short, the larger the group, the less likely it will further its common interests" (1965, p. 36).

After publication of Olson's book, Russell Hardin (1971) showed that the formal logic of the collective action problem was that of the Prisoners' Dilemma for latent groups, those in which individual's contribution will not make a perceptible difference. For groups in which an individual contribution would have a perceptible effect, however, Hardin showed that the outcome would be less clear. Since that time, Olson's portrayal of the negative effects of group size on providing public goods has come under attack (Taylor, 1987; Hardin, 1982). This attack is not based on organizational costs—these are very likely to rise with group size, as we will see in Chapter 6. Instead, the argument with Olson is that increases in group size are usually accompanied by changes in *other* things that also change as group size changes (Hardin, 1982). The benefit to any one individual, for example, may decline in larger groups if the good is not truly a public good. If there is "crowding," less of the good may be available to each member of a larger group. Five people may share a pie, but 100 people probably will not. To current researchers, the efficacy of large groups in voluntarily providing public goods is a complex issue, not the simple matter that Olson described in 1965.

Today's analysts have several reasons for optimism about cooperation. One is that Olson's analysis was static or timeless, but many collective action problems are dynamic. An iterated Prisoners' Dilemma allows players to get feedback from other players and to take action in that light. The TIT for TAT strategy—cooperate first, then do what they do—is a good example of this. Second, coalitions may form within the latent group. If these coalitions are above some minimal size and if the ratio of benefits to costs is attractive, cooperative solutions may occur (Hardin, 1971). As Schofield notes:

> Suppose the coalition to be a town in the wild west, and the defector to be a bank robber. A posse could be formed to hunt down the defector but this could also be very costly (in terms of lives, time, etc.) for the members. But they will calculate that if they don't punish the defector, more defectors will occur. Actually, their best strategy might therefore be to commit themselves to hunting the renegade for some fixed period of time. (1985, p. 210)

A third reason for optimism is *altruism*, or the gaining of utility when another person gains utility from an improved outcome.

The current literature on cooperation is full of interesting variants on these three dimensions and others (Hardin, 1982; Taylor, 1987; Schofield, 1985). Schofield sums up his review of research on cooperation by noting that predictability of response is crucial for cooperation:

> The fundamental theoretical problem underlying the question of cooperation is the manner by which individuals attain knowledge of each others preferences and likely behavior. Moreover, the problem is one of common knowledge, since each individual, *i*, is required not only to have information about others preferences, but also to know that the others have knowledge about *i*'s own preferences and strategies. (Schofield, p. 218)

Whether this knowledge and predictability is most likely to occur through the state or through the emergence of community—through shared norms and voluntary interaction among members—is of central interest to Taylor (1982). It is ironic that coercion by the state may reduce the need for shared beliefs, reciprocity, and the need for trust in judging what others are likely to do. We would like to think that community and the state complement each other, but this may not be the case.

In the rest of this chapter, we will explore the likelihood of cooperative solutions to the free-rider or collective action problem. The first model explores the joint provision of public goods by two parties; a second model looks at market solutions to externalities. In both cases, we ask whether the pursuit of self-interest will lead to maximization of collective interest when the good is a nonrival, nonexcludable public good. We'll then ask why individuals might voluntarily contribute to the supply of certain public goods through private donations or actions when they have the option of free-riding. We'll also discuss some insights into self-interest that are offered by recent experiments in economics and psychology.

Finally, we will consider impure public goods, for which exclusion may be possible. Crowding or congestion may cause these goods to be rival in consumption, thus limiting the number of people who might benefit from their use. We will consider whether voluntary clubs might be able to replace the market in supplying these goods. Several key concepts that relate to incentive frameworks, self-interest, and the collective interest will be discussed. These include free-riding, transactions costs, the Coase theorem, and strategic behavior. Although there is room for optimism about the voluntary approach to resolving market failure, any attempt to reach cooperative and noncoercive solutions has to include consideration of these concepts.

5.2 Joint Provision of Public Goods

5.21 *The Problem*

Two individuals, each attempting to maximize self-interest, may also maximize their collective interest in negotiating the joint provision of public goods. Let's assume that two individuals, A and B, have independent utility functions:

$$U_A = f(X, Y_A) \text{ and } U_B = f(X, Y_B), \tag{5.1}$$

where X is a public good and Y is money as a proxy for access to all other goods. Neither A nor B defines self-interest to include consumption by the other, but each gains utility from additional provision of the public good.[3]

Imagine that the public good in question is a defense capability that is designed to protect this two-person society from external aggression. Defense is made possible by using "defenders" whose services can be purchased in small discrete increments. As a public good, however, any level of defense purchased by either party is equally available to both

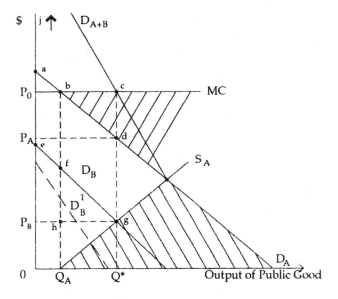

FIGURE 5.3   Joint Supply of a Public Good

parties and can't be withheld. However, it may not be valued equally by both. We'll first assume that any negotiations between A and B are costless, then we'll relax this assumption. The demands by the two individuals are shown in Figure 5.3 as D_A and D_B, respectively. Defense is available at a constant marginal cost of MC; thus, there is no producers' surplus. If we remember that the collective demand for a public good should be summed vertically as D_{A+B}, it can be seen that neither party, acting independently, would purchase a Pareto-efficient quantity of defense (Q^*). At Q^*, the collective marginal benefit of a unit of defense (D_{A+B}) would equal its marginal cost (MC).

This is not a surprise. It simply repeats the contention from Chapter 3 that public goods are not likely to be produced in Pareto-efficient quantities if the matter is left strictly to the market. But it is possible that the two *could* work together, as we will see further on, to voluntarily buy a Pareto-efficient amount and thus reduce or eliminate the need for government intervention.

5.22 *An Efficient Solution*

To see how an efficient voluntary solution might be reached, assume that A, acting strictly from self-interest, decides to buy quantity Q_A. (This avoids the most interesting aspect of the problem, which is the possibility that one or both would engage in strategic action so that the other might supply the public good. We will return to this later.) Even though the good would also be available to B, A makes this purchase because she would gain a consumer's surplus of area abP_0, compared to the alternative of having no defense and no consumer's surplus.

The opportunity for mutual gain comes when A realizes that she could become even better off by arranging to supply B with additional defense beyond the Q_A level. Her supply function, S_A, reflects the difference between what she would have to pay for additional defenders (MC) and the marginal benefit that she derives from these defenders (D_A). This difference is shown as a shaded area. The cost to B at quantity Q^*, for example, would be the difference between MC and D_A, or amount cd, by definition. By construction, the supply price at this point would be P_B because $OP_B = gQ^* = cd$. For simplicity, it is assumed that any payments from B to A would not affect the demand function of either individual even though they would then each have a slightly different amount of money to spend on defense.

In other words, A is saying, "I'll buy more defenders if you'll make up the difference between what they cost me and what they're worth to me." If B accepts the offer, the amount that she would want to buy is $Q^* - Q_A$, because Q^* is the point at which the price that would be paid (P_B) is equal to B's demand for defenders. Q^* would be the quantity that the two would jointly decide to buy; B would pay P_B and A would pay only P_A because she would receive a rebate from B in the amount of cd. These prices, P_A and P_B, are referred to as *Lindahl prices* for a public good; each individual would pay what the good is worth to her, at the margin.

Why would it be in A's best interests to make this offer? Because if it was accepted, A's consumer's surplus would increase from abP_0 to adP_A. (Remember, A would now pay a price of only P_A instead of P_0.) Whether B would accept the offer, however, depends on a self-interested assessment of gains and losses. If A's offer were accepted, B would enjoy a consumer's surplus of egP_B. However, B would have the option of free-riding; she could benefit from A's initial purchase of Q_A without having to pay *any* of the cost. If B acted as a free rider, her consumer's surplus would be efQ_A0 because the price would be zero! As Figure 5.3 is drawn, the consumer's surplus that would be gained by B's acceptance of A's offer (fgh) is greater than the surplus that would be sacrificed by ceasing to free ride (P_BhQ_A0). Area $efhP_B$ remains the same in either case. Thus, B would accept the offer.

If it turns out that A's offer is accepted by B, would this also maximize their collective interest? Let's make a very simple assumption that the collective interest can be found by adding their consumer's surpluses. This is the additive utilitarian approach from Chapter 4, although here it is based on consumer's surplus rather than utility. At the Q^* level of defenders, for example, their collective surplus would be the sum of areas adP_A (for A) and egP_B (for B). Because the demand curves are added vertically, as they should be with public goods, the collective consumers' surplus would be maximized at area jcP_0, which is the sum of the two smaller areas. This would happen only if the output was Q^*, which is, in fact, the equilibrium solution.

In other words, it is possible that two people might negotiate a Pareto-efficient level of the public good and thereby maximize their collective interest as well as their individual self-interest. It is by no means certain that this will happen, however, because free-riding or other strategic behavior may occur. There will likely be problems of preference revelation because of the nonrival and nonexcludable nature of public goods. B would be best off by accepting A's offer, but the fact that defense is nonexcludable would allow her to free ride, if she chose to do so, on A's initial provision of Q_A. In that case, she would still be better off than if no action had been taken by either. A, of course, could look at the situation in exactly the same way; she could sit back and wait for B to provide Q_A and thus generate some consumer's surplus for herself!

One more note: An efficient and voluntary solution to market failure could be reached only if the negotiations between A and B were costless, that is, if transactions costs are zero. This is an important concept and it deserves treatment of its own.

5.23 Transactions Costs

As presented in Section 3.32, transactions costs are those involved in making and carrying out an agreement or contract between two or more parties. These would include the costs of obtaining and evaluating information, establishing a bargaining position, locating someone with whom to bargain, and negotiating and monitoring a contract. These costs could be large if the parties have much to gain or lose in the transaction and if many parties are involved.

If transaction costs exist, there would be less incentive for the two parties to agree on a Pareto-efficient quantity of the public good. Whether A or B would pay these costs would itself be an issue for bargaining, but let's assume that the buyer (B) would bear the costs. The effect would be to shift B's demand curve downward to D_B^1, because part of B's willingness to pay for defense would have to be siphoned off to pay the transactions costs. If A paid the transactions costs, her supply curve would shift upward because of the increased cost of supplying defenders.

In either case, the level of defense would be less than Q* if A and B were to negotiate a solution. The collective interest of A and B, the sum of their consumer's surplus, would still be maximized if transactions costs existed, but at a lower level of utility. This is easiest to see if the buyer paid the transactions costs; this would cause downward shifts in both the buyer's demand function and the collective demand function. It would also lead to a reduction in total consumers' surplus. Clearly, the two would be better off if bargaining was costless.

Costly bargaining may thus inhibit or prevent negotiated solutions. Calabresi (1968) has argued that if transactions costs are high enough to snuff out voluntary solutions altogether, negotiations shouldn't be undertaken because they would reduce efficiency, and the market wouldn't have failed after all. In other words, the absence of a market when all costs are considered would itself be a market solution! The problem with this argument is that other means of reaching an agreement—voting, flipping a coin, following the edicts of a dictator—haven't been considered. Some of these may have lower transactions costs than bargaining, although they may also be less desirable from an equity point of view.

5.3 Market Solutions to Externalities

5.31 *The Problem*

The possibility of market solutions to externalities involves the same basic issue as the previous section. This issue is whether self-interested individuals can get together to change output so that Pareto efficiency is attained. Let's continue to consider pure public goods, those that are nonrival and nonexcludable, because these are the most difficult cases.

First, remember that externalities aren't always bad; education and good health may make others better off. But because many externalities (pollution, for example) are negative, let's consider whether two parties might both benefit from a market that would change the extent of a negative externality. One now benefits from the externality, the other suffers from it.

5.32 *An Efficient Solution*

The horizontal axis in Figure 5.4 shows units of cleaner air as an example of a good or service that might be the focus of a market for externalities. Reductions in air pollution, for example, might improve the air and allow B to see farther and to breathe more easily. The value of these services to B are shown by her demand function for cleaner air, D_B.

Air pollution is caused by A, who uses the atmosphere as a low-cost means of waste disposal in her firm's operations. As the party who causes the externality, however, she has a potential supply function for providing cleaner air. If someone else will pay the costs of installing devices to reduce pollution, A is willing to supply cleaner air if this will increase her net profit. Control measures that would reduce emissions would be progressively more expensive as more pollutants were controlled; thus, A's supply function for cleaner air, S_A, would be upward sloping. A wouldn't supply cleaner air out of the goodness of her heart, remember, or because the law says she has to, but because a market transaction with B might make her better off.

As with the joint provision of a nonexcludable public good (which is still the case here, except one party now views it as a "bad" rather than a "good"), let's assume that transactions costs between A and B are zero. In this case, they could negotiate a market solution where cleaner air would be supplied up to Q^* at a unit price of P^*. If B could pay A a price of P^* for Q^* units of externality reduction, both would feel that their self-interest had been enhanced. The demander, B, would be better off because of her consumer's surplus of abP^*; she would have been willing to pay more than P^* for all except the last unit of cleaner air. The supplier, A, would be better off because of her producer's surplus of

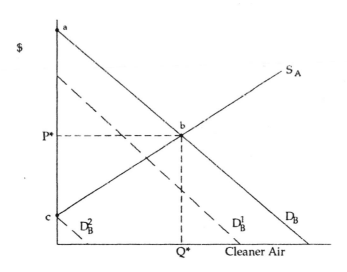

FIGURE 5.4 Market Solution to an Externality Problem

cbP*; she would have been willing to supply cleaner air for less than P* on all except the last unit, which was the most expensive unit of cleaner air to be supplied.

5.33 The Coase Theorem

At this point, you might say, Why should we have to pay for something that's ours, anyway, like clean air? This suggests two things. One, the definition of property rights is at issue. Should the one who caused the externality have the right to pollute, or should she have to acquire that right from those whom she would harm? Second, externalities are reciprocal. The party who is denied the right to pollute has to bear extra costs because of the way property rights are defined. In other words, the question of who should bear the cost of a negative externality is a value judgment that has to be made. Those who want clean air would prefer to have maximum reductions in air pollution. Those who use the assimilative capacity of air as a free input in production would prefer to have no reduction in air pollution.

One might suppose that if markets for cleaner air existed, any reduction in air pollution would depend on how property rights are defined. The essence of the *Coase theorem*, however, was that the definition of property rights would not affect the extent of externality, provided that transactions costs between parties were zero.[4] In his classic 1960 article, Coase assumed that a competitive firm (or an individual) would take opportunity costs into account in making decisions. If a firm had to buy the rights to use the atmosphere for waste disposal, for example, the amount it would pay for these rights would depend on the least-cost nonatmospheric alternative for getting rid of its waste. The more costly the alternative, the more the firm would be willing to pay to use the air for waste disposal. If the firm already had the right to use the air, however, its willingness to give it up (that is, to supply clean air) would still depend on the cost required to dispose of the waste in some other way. The more expensive the alternative treatment, the more the firm would pay for its use of air, and the more it would need to be paid to forgo its use of air.

Much has been written about the Coase theorem, but the role it should play in policy remains unclear. One thing is certain; conservatives like it because it suggests a limited role for government. In effect, it says, Define property rights in some manner (it really doesn't matter who has them), then let a market evolve to decide how much of the externality will remain. To conservatives, this is preferred to regulation by government.

Why, then, do we find that levels of pollution, crime, and health are affected by laws and regulations rather than determined in markets? For one thing, the distribution of income *is* affected by the definition of property rights; people are not indifferent to who has a property right. They will be better off if they own things rather than having to buy them. Second, transactions costs in the real world are not zero. It is usually costly to locate and bargain with an appropriate party and to monitor the bargain. We need to explore this possibility.

5.34 The Coase Theorem with Transactions Costs

Transactions costs may be very different for the various parties who might be involved in a bargaining process. One characteristic that might cause these costs to differ is that the number of parties on either side may differ; it is likely to be more costly for ten firms (or persons) to band together and present a unified front than it would be for two firms (or persons) to do so. A second cost difference might be due to diversity among the parties. Firms that are homogenous with respect to type of product, size, and location, for example, would find it easier to establish a common bargaining position than would dissimilar firms. The degree of previous experience may also matter, especially if this has resulted in an organizational structure for dealing with these issues. Existing trade associations and professional associations would have lower transactions costs than would new groups, who would have to develop staff expertise and a track record. Finally, the legality of the activity might affect transactions costs: Those who venture into illegal activity may find it difficult to enforce contracts except by illegal means.

The size of transaction costs may greatly affect market solutions to externality problems and cause outcomes that are different than shown in Figure 5.4 (Randall, 1972). Consider two possibilities; let's assume that both would require demanders of externality reduction to bear the transactions costs and to buy the rights to pollute from those who hold them. If the transactions costs were small, there might be only a modest downward shift in demand, say, from D_B to D_B^1. This could be the case if the demanders were homogenous, few in number, and had a history of cooperation. If transactions costs were high because of a large number of unorganized and dissimilar parties, however, the costs of developing, making, and monitoring a contract might be so high that all of the willingness to pay for externality reduction would be siphoned off to pay transaction costs. A demand curve such as D_B^2 might result; the outcome would be a zero reduction in externality. This situation—the absence of a market, or a "Calabresi solution"—is not at all uncommon; the costs of a voluntary solution with unorganized and dissimilar groups are often so high that this option goes unexplored.

5.35 Positive Externalities

Our attention so far in this section has been on situations where two or more parties might gain if the level of a negative externality could be altered. There is also a possibility, however, that parties could gain if markets were created to change (increase) the level of positive externalities. Education and good health are examples: Markets might help to expand the output of these goods and services toward Pareto-efficient levels.

Both parties would gain utility from greater amounts of the good; thus, the analysis would be the same as for the joint provision of public goods in Section 5.2. You might be willing to pay a neighbor to help stamp out his noxious weeds; this would benefit both of you. Social customs may work against the formation of a market; you could point out the noxious weed to your neighbor, but he might give you a strange look if you offered to pay him to eradicate it.

5.4 Private Provision of Public Goods

The logic of collective action means that there is a strong tendency for people in large groups to free ride behind cloaks of anonymity. Medical research, according to this logic, would have to be financed solely by government because people wouldn't support it voluntarily when they could have the benefits without incurring the costs. As we noted in Section 5.13 on cooperation, however, this conventional wisdom doesn't always hold true. There is substantial private provision of public goods. The real-world evidence is that billions of dollars are donated every year to charitable, political, religious, and cultural organizations. This money is donated by people who choose not to free ride.

Private giving by living individuals to charitable and religious organizations, for example, was reported in 1989 by the American Association of Fund-Raising Counsel Trust for Philanthropy to be $96.4 billion. Another $18.3 billion was provided by foundations, corporations, and bequests from nonliving individuals (*Chronicle of Higher Education,* June 13, 1990, p. A1). Religious groups received about one-half of all donations.[5] Even if religious contributions aren't considered, this still leaves nearly $50 billion as a rough estimate of voluntary giving to charitable organizations. And a nationwide survey of charitable giving conducted for the Rockefeller Brothers Fund revealed that U.S. households average about $650 per year in donations, or about 2 to 3 percent of household income (*U.S. News and World Report,* April 28, 1986, p. 80).

Many Americans also provide money and time in support of *public interest groups.* These organizations work toward "a collective good, the achievement of which does not selectively and materially benefit the membership or activists of the organization" (Berry, 1989, p. 7). In other words, the goal of a public interest group is the attainment of some nonexcludable public good, where free-riding is possible, rather than the provision of a private good. Membership in public interest groups usually involves annual dues, part of which goes to support lobbying activities. One political scientist, Michael McCann, classifies public interest groups into four general categories: environmental protection, workplace health and safety, consumer interests, and democratic reform of government processes (1986, p. 18). Some of these organizations have overcome the free-rider problem to such an extent that their financial base is quite large. For example, a coalition of fourteen major environmental organizations acts as a "green lobby" in Washington, D.C.; it has over five million members and a collective budget of about $85 million, with annual dues ranging from $7.50 to $20 per member (Smith, 1985). This is a major attempt to overcome the collective action problem.

5.41 *Why Don't People Free Ride?* [6]

Private donations of $96 billion and public interest group budgets of $85 million are not small sums of money. They invite attention to why this money is given, to whom it is given, and to how private and public provision of particular types of public goods are related.[7] With respect to the motives for giving, there are two schools of thought. The first, Mancur Olson's rational choice approach, is that people require some private good or *selective inducement* as a reason for contributing to the public good. Groups that seek to obtain the public interest must recognize that "in the absence of coercion, it is necessary to supply positive incentives or private goods such as insurance policies, group travel discounts, and magazines. These are individual, non-collective goods which the individual can acquire only through membership in the group which lobbies for the collective good" (Mitchell, 1979, p. 90). In this view, any incentive for the individual to contribute toward the public or collective good is undermined by the low probability that one's contribution will affect the outcome and by the lack of exclusion from the benefits of group action. Thus, it is argued that private goods are needed to overcome these negative incentives.

A second motive for giving, and a less-calculating one, is that people practice altruism. Hochman and Rodgers (1969), for example, suggest that many people gain utility when income is voluntarily redistributed by the more well-to-do to the less well-to-do. If both groups feel better off—the poor because they are richer and the rich because they have helped the poor—voluntary giving would be a Pareto improvement. In the rational choice view, however, this task may fall to government because the distribution of income is itself a public good and individual incentives to change it might be lacking. In the altruistic view, the ideology of sharing is a strong common bond, and people will forgo private gain to promote it.

A study of five business interest groups in Minnesota provided one test of the competing explanations of rational choice and altruism (Moe, 1980, pp. 201-218). Each group provided lobbying activities (a public good), as well as member services such as insurance, accounting, and auditing (private goods). Most firms joined the interest groups to obtain member services, but about half of them indicated that they would continue to belong even if member services were discontinued, as long as lobbying was continued. Between 60 and 70 percent of the firms felt that their membership in the interest group made a difference in political outcomes.

Another early test of competing explanations was Mitchell's survey of members in five major environmental groups (1979). The possible costs and benefits that were perceived by individuals in this study are summarized in Table 5.1. Selective inducements weren't particularly important to members, who felt they had a personal responsibility to en-

TABLE 5.1 Benefits and Costs of Interest-Group Membership

I. Costs of Contributing
   A. Money
   B. Time
   C. Loss of social status and reputation

II. Benefits of Contributing
   A. Possible increase in a public good
   B. Receipt of private goods

III. Costs of Not Contributing
   A. Possible continuance of or increase in a public "bad"

---

hance the collective interest. Respondents were much more likely to have joined an environmental group because they sought to enhance public goods rather than obtain private goods. Responses such as "If I don't act now to preserve the environment, things will get much worse" were much more common than other responses such as "I enjoy the magazine and/or benefits of membership, such as outings, very much."

Mitchell concluded that many people join or contribute to environmental lobbies for three reasons. First, the cost is usually small. Second, the potential cost of *not* contributing (especially adverse environmental effects) may be very high if the organization fails. And third, it is not at all certain to members that their individual action will be ineffective. In fact, most people believe that their contributions *will* make a difference, and this is part of why they join.

In reality, there is a large gray area between rational choice and altruism that defies measurement. If I contribute to the poor, am I doing it to better their lot, to make me feel good, or to reduce the chances of social upheaval? What is the nature of my self-interest? In many ways, economists are not yet very adept at dealing with these issues, which are crucial to understanding collective behavior.

5.42 Nonprofit Organizations

To understand why people don't always free ride, it also helps to understand how and why *nonprofit organizations* seek and spend money from donations and memberships. There are two major economic explanations for the existence of the nonprofits. Both explanations have only recently evolved, even though nonprofits are a major force in the economy, employing nearly 12 percent of the nation's full-time labor force as long ago as 1976 (Weisbrod, 1988, pp. 65-66). The first explanation is that nonprofits evolved as a way to tap the demands of those citizens who were not satisfied with existing public-sector output, which may have been zero. To quote Weisbrod:

> It is noteworthy, therefore, that in sixteenth-century England, where governmental provision of any civilian goods or services was very modest, private "philanthropies" (voluntary organizations) were providing funds for such wide-ranging collective activities as schools, hospitals, nontoll roads, fire-fighting apparatus, public parks, bridges, dikes and causeways, digging of drainage canals, waterworks, wharves and docks, harbor cleaning, libraries, care of prisoners in jails, and charity to the poor—in short, for the gamut of nonmilitary goods that we identify today as governmental responsibilities. (1986, pp. 33-34)

In this view, nonprofits arise from market failure and insufficient provision, and they serve as primary suppliers until a political majority assumes the responsibility for provision through the public sector.

The second explanation for the existence of nonprofit institutions is the idea of *contract failure*. In this view, potential donors fear that profit-seeking firms may be unable to guarantee the quality or amount of future output that they, the donors, would desire. Thus, the use of productivity of the donated funds may be too uncertain from the donor's point of view. In view of this uncertainty, the fact that nonprofits must retain and reinvest net profits rather than distribute them to officers, directors, or shareholders is reassuring to donors. According to Hansmann, "Nonprofits tend to produce particular services, these characterized by 'contract failure' because consumers prefer to deal with nonprofits in purchasing those services. This preference . . . is based upon a feeling that the nonprofits can be trusted not to exploit the advantage over the consumer resulting from contract failure" (1986, p. 80). Because of this trust, donors may contribute to nonprofit public radio, overseas relief, medical research, or similar causes with greater assurance that their money will be used as they intend it to be used.

In order for nonprofits to benefit from donations, potential donors must know about and feel comfortable with a particular nonprofit firm.[8] This can often be enhanced by fund-raising. Among others, Weisbrod and Dominguez (1986) argue that the demand for charitable giving by donors depends on much the same factors as the demand for market goods. These factors include price and product quality, as well as advertising and fund-raising. In their study of health, education, welfare, and cultural nonprofits, they concluded that price and advertising were the most important determinants of giving. Fund-raising expenditures by a nonprofit do two things; first, they enhance donations by convincing potential donors about the worthiness of a cause. Second, they reduce the share of each donated dollar that is actually available for the intended purpose. Weisbrod and Dominguez (1986, p. 88) define the price (P) of an organization's output as

$$P = \frac{(1-T)}{1 - (A+F)},\qquad (5.2)$$

where T is the marginal income tax rate of the donor, and A and F are the percentages spent on administration and fund-raising, respectively. If T was 30 percent and (A + F) was 40 percent for a charity, for example,

$$P = \frac{1 - 0.3}{1 - 0.4}\qquad (5.3)$$

$$P = \frac{0.7}{0.6} \qquad (5.4)$$

$$P = 1.17. \qquad (5.5)$$

In this case, a donor would have to pay $1.17 for a dollar's worth of charitable output. If administration and fund-raising were costless, the donor would have to pay only $0.70 to get a dollar's worth of output. These authors concluded that lower prices encouraged donations for the several thousand nonprofits that they studied from 1973-1976. They also found that additional fund-raising expenditures would not have led to any net increase in charitable contributions.

5.43 Crowding Out

Another crucial aspect in the private provision of public goods through nonprofit organizations is the interaction between government support and donor support. Both sources of funds could be used to support medical research, the performing arts, or charity for the indigent. Some people feel that greater government spending will result in *crowding out*, that donor support will fall as government spending increases (e.g., Abrams and Schmitz, 1978). During the 1980s, the nonprofits were alarmed that the reverse might not be true—that increased private donations to the nonprofits would fail to make up for reduced federal spending and the threatened loss of tax deductions for charitable contributions.

Economists have developed several models of charitable giving that are still being tested (Clotfelter, 1985). The key to understanding this aspect of human behavior lies in untangling the donor's utility function. Kingma (1989, p. 1199) summarized the various models by portraying the most general form of the utility function (U) for the ith donor as

$$U_i = U_i(X_i, D_i, R_j, G). \qquad (5.6)$$

That is, the ith donor's utility depends on her personal consumption of private goods (X_i), her own charitable contributions (D_i), charitable contributions by others (R_j), and government support of the charity (G). Whether increased support of a nonprofit by government (or by others) will crowd out private donations depends on how substitutable these sources of support are, at least in the mind of the donor.

If the various sources of support are viewed as perfectly substitutable, charity becomes a pure public good; if any other support is available, the donor will free ride and crowding out will occur on a dollar-for-dollar basis. A second model, the "source of contributions" model, is that the three sources of support generate independent utility for the donor. The donor receives utility from her own contribution, knowing that she has "done her bit," but she also receives utility from government support and from the contributions of others because they increase the overall support for the organization. The three are imperfect substitutes for each other in this second model; the donor may feel that government funds come with strings attached, for example, compared to other private contributions.

Kingma's empirical work on contributions to public radio stations supports a third model of charity, the impure altruist model. In this model, the donor receives utility from her own contribution but views the other two sources (government and others) as perfect substitutes for each other. Some degree of crowding out will occur; Kingma estimated that a $10,000 increase in government support to public radio would reduce private donations by $1,350, leaving $8,650 as the net increase in funding. Increased efforts by public radio to obtain corporate and government support might thus be expected even though there would be some loss of private donations.

5.5 Experiments with Public Goods

5.51 Methods

Another way to learn something about self-interest and the collective interest has been to do experiments with public goods. Economists have usually preferred to work with "real markets" rather than do experimental research, but this is changing, rather rapidly. Charles Plott, one of the leaders in experimental economics, has argued that the distinction between naturally occurring real markets and artificial laboratory markets is greatly overstated. "While laboratory processes are simple in comparison to naturally occurring processes, they are real processes in the sense that real people participate for real and substantial profits and follow real rules in doing so. It is precisely because they are real that they are interesting" (1982, p. 1486). Through experiments, economists are trying to understand how different types of market structure (e.g., monopoly) and different market institutions (e.g., auction markets) will affect market outcomes. Another reason for experiments has been to learn more about how people respond to experiments where the outcomes of the experiments are public goods. In these experiments, subjects (people) are given access to specific resources and allowed to make choices; these choices are observed and recorded. It is crucial that proper experimental methods be followed. The wording and format of the instructions, for example, must be clear to permit others to replicate an experiment. As a result, psychologists and economists have often worked together.

5.52 *Experimental Results*

In one early and widely cited article (Marwell and Ames, 1981), the results are suggested by the title: "Economists Free Ride, Does Anyone Else?" Through twelve carefully designed experiments, they found reason to question the notion that free-riding will be a dominant force in the provision of public goods. Substantial free-riding was observed in only one experiment, and that was among graduate students in economics!

Each person in the Marwell and Ames experiments was given 225 tokens that could be allocated to a private exchange with a guaranteed rate of return to the investor. The alternative was to allocate the tokens to a group exchange, where one's earnings depended on the total investment made by everyone. The private exchange in one experiment paid a one-cent return for each token invested, guaranteeing a profit of $2.25 for each person. If only a few invested, the earnings from the group exchange were less than this, but the earnings could be over $0.05 per token ($11.25) if all tokens were invested in the group exchange. Players could enhance the group outcome by investing heavily in the group exchange, but they could enhance their own outcomes by investing in the private exchange. Despite this opportunity to invest privately while benefiting from the profitable group outcome, between 40 and 60 percent of the tokens were generally invested in the group exchange. This percentage fell only slightly when the stakes were raised to allow earnings up to $33.25 per person.

As an interesting sidelight to the Marvell and Ames research, Carter and Irons (1991) argue that economists may, in fact, *be* different.[9] Using ninety-two students as subjects, they collected experimental data on outcomes of a game called Proposer and Responder, where the task was to divide $10 between two players who alternated roles. A rejected proposal meant that neither player gained, so both had an incentive to agree. The best deal? Propose to keep $9.50, but respond by accepting $0.50; getting *anything* is better than getting nothing! (Only multiples of $0.50 were allowed). As proposers, economics students proposed to keep significantly more than did noneconomists ($6.15 versus $5.44), and as responders, they accepted significantly less ($1.70 versus $2.44). Both of their amounts are closest to the "best deal." Carter and Irons conclude that economics students behaved differently because they self-select themselves into economics as a field of study, not because they change their behavior while in college to become more like the "economic person" that they study.

5.53 Two Incentive Systems

Experimental research and studies of charitable giving both show that some public goods will be provided through voluntary action even though efficient quantities may not be provided. It is also important, however, to know how different incentive systems will affect the extent of private provision. Robyn Dawes and colleagues (1986) experimentally compared two incentive systems: *fair share* and *money back guarantees*. In a fair share system, a subject is assessed if he hasn't already contributed

		Standard Prisoners' Dilemma[a]		Money Back[b]		Fair Share[c]	
		Bonus		Bonus		Bonus	
		No	Yes	No	Yes	No	Yes
Individual Contrib-utes	Y e s	0+0=0	0+10=$10	$5	$10	0	$10
	N o	5+0=$5	5+10=$15	$5	$15	$5	$10

[a] In the standard dilemma, the *first* number in each cell shows the disposition of the $5 gift to each individual. $5 means that he keeps it; $0 means that he contributes it toward the group bonus. The *second* number in each cell shows whether or not he would receive the $10 bonus.

[b] With money back, he would get $5 back if he contributed but the bonus didn't occur.

[c] With fair share, he would pay $5 if he didn't contribute and the bonus did occur.

FIGURE 5.5 The Effects of Two Incentive Systems

to a favorable group outcome; money back guarantees allow a subject to get his money back if a favorable group outcome doesn't occur.

Each of seven subjects in the Dawes experiments was initially given $5. If some minimum number (usually five of the seven) contributed their $5 toward a group bonus amounting to $70, everyone would receive $10 even if they didn't contribute to the group outcome (Figure 5.5). If the group bonus didn't materialize because of insufficient contributions, those who contributed lost their $5. Each subject's one-time decision was made simultaneously and without knowledge of the decisions made by others. This is shown as the standard Prisoners' Dilemma; the deck is stacked, so to speak, in favor of free riding. If an individual chose not to contribute and the group bonus occurred, he would be $15 better off by choosing to free ride; he would have his initial $5 plus the $10 bonus. If the group bonus didn't occur, he would still have $5 because he didn't contribute. In either case, he would be better off by not contributing.

One incentive system was the money back guarantee; those who contributed got their $5 back if the group effort failed (upper-left cell). This system is not uncommon. The authors cite the successful effort by the Association of Oregon Faculties (AOF) in persuading individual faculty members (including this author) to join AOF and help employ a lobbyist at the state legislature. The organizers promised to return all money if a certain amount wasn't reached. It was reached and a lobbyist was employed. In the second incentive system, fair share, if the group effort was successful, anyone who had not contributed was assessed $5 (lower-right cell). The AOF effort had nothing like this; it had no way to collect from nonmembers. In general, according to the Dawes research, paying fair share will remove the possibility of free-riding; a money back guarantee will remove the possibility of being "suckered" by the failure of others to contribute.

Their results were striking; the fair share system clearly brought about more contributions than did the money back guarantees (77 percent with fair share, 43 percent with money back), and far more than the standard Prisoners' Dilemma (23 percent). They feel that money back guarantees may work, but that they may also reduce the incentive to contribute. People may assume that others will be inclined to contribute because of the surety afforded by the guarantee, but there may also be an increased temptation to free ride. Fair share systems, on the other hand, work in the opposite direction by reducing the chances that others will not contribute. But the authors feel that we don't yet have an adequate explanation for why the two systems produce different results.

Much of what social science can demonstrate is already known by evolved social systems, and we speculate that the frequent use of the enforced contribution or 'fair share' device—most notably, of course in labor unions—is a consequence of long experience with alternative ways of trying to persuade the beneficiaries of group efforts to contribute to those efforts. Institutions that work or that add nothing beyond some base tend to be found out, as do institutions that do not work. (p. 1183)

One important difference is that money back guarantees allow a successful outcome to be noncoercive, but fair share systems impose coercion on those who don't contribute. The latter system allowed free-riding by noncontributing faculty members in Oregon (perhaps unwisely). In a labor bargaining unit, however, everyone may be required to pay union dues whether or not they actually hold union membership. There is a fundamental value difference between these two situations in terms of whether coercion is appropriate.

5.54 Contingent Valuation

Another recent type of experimental research has been the use of *contingent valuation* (CV) methods. In controlled experiments, the outcome of the experiment is usually a nonexcludable public good. In contingent valuation studies the object of valuation is usually a nonexcludable public good, often an environmental good faced with an uncertain fate. The purpose of the research is to elicit from respondents a statement of money values associated with the environmental good; these might then be compared with values of a competing use of the resource. A hypothetical market is described for respondents, one in which they could buy or sell access rights to specified activities or services. These experiments are relevant to the public good/free-rider issue because the goods and services are almost always nonexcludable due to physical features (air quality, for example) or the nature of social policy (the tradition of public access to outdoor recreation, for example).

One early concern about contingent valuation research was that respondents might behave strategically, hoping to influence the outcome of the research. They might overstate the value of the environmental good, hoping to influence its availability, or they might understate the value if it appeared that they might have to help pay for providing it. This hasn't generally happened when appropriate experimental procedures have been followed. Instead, the main problem has been to create a hypothetical situation that involves enough realism that respondents can provide monetary values that are reasonable reflections of their preferences and purchasing power.[10] Photographs are often used to provide realism. Other information on the good may also be provided, such as the frequency with which the air quality allows a distant mountain to be seen.[11]

Another problem that researchers are now facing is the frequent large discrepancy between the results derived from two different types of contingent valuation studies (Gregory, 1986; Gregory and Furby, 1987; Gregory and McDaniels, 1987). This problem offers some insight into the key question of the previous section: Why don't people free ride as much as they might? The first type of CV study involves an environmental good that promises to become more abundant or more inexpensive. In the second type of study, the good is likely to become less abundant, more expensive, or nonexistent. Different measures of value are appropriate for each situation. If the respondent expects to gain access to new opportunities, *willingness to pay* (WTP) is considered the appropriate measure of value. This concept was presented in Chapter 2, but by a different name; it is simply the consumer's surplus to be gained from increased availability of a nonmarket good (Figure 2.6). The appropriate measure of value in the second situation is *willingness to accept* (WTA). This reflects a related consumer's surplus, one measured as the minimum amount of money that would be required to compensate a consumer for reduced availability of a nonmarket good.

If the quantity changes are small, researchers have felt that there should be very little difference between these two situations, that WTP and WTA values should be about the same.[12] The empirical differences, however, have often been substantial (Gregory and McDaniels, 1987). In many studies, the WTA values have been three to five times larger than the WTP values. Bishop and Heberlein (1979), for example, found that Wisconsin hunters who didn't have a goose-hunting permit were willing to pay about $20 for one, but those who already had a permit had to be paid nearly $100 to part with it. A variety of explanations have been offered for these differences, including inconsistencies in data collection, strategic bias, and the hypothetical nature of the questions. Coursey, Hovis, and Schultze (1987) found, for example, that the differences were reduced with repeated experimental trials.

A more powerful explanation, however, may be that the large discrepancies between WTP and WTA values are due to fundamental differences in how people view potential gains, on one hand, and how they view potential losses, on the other hand. Economists have usually thought that people maximize their expected utility, but two psychologists think that people make decisions under uncertainty in a very different way than this. This explanation, *prospect theory*, has been developed by Daniel Kahneman and Amos Tversky (1979, 1981, 1984). Prospect theory differs from expected-utility theory in three major ways (Gregory, 1986). First, it says that people perceive and respond to the direction of change rather than to any expected final outcome or position. This suggests that people respond to perceived changes in air quality, for example, rather than to the absolute level of air quality. Prospect theory also proposes that individuals have *asymmetric value functions*, as shown in Figure 5.6. Potential losses elicit larger responses from people than do potential gains. The third difference is that subjective probability plays a much larger role in prospect theory, particularly the idea that people assess losses to be much more likely than warranted by measures of objective probability. Slovic, Fischhoff, and Lichtenstein (1980), for example, found that people greatly overstate the chances that rare events will happen, and that they understate the chances that more common events will happen.

Each of these three dimensions of prospect theory suggests that the "willingness to accept" compensation for those public goods that are expected to become less abundant (0A in Figure 5.6) will be larger than the willingness to pay for public goods that are expected to become more abundant (0P in Figure 5.6). This asymmetry in response may also offer a valuable clue about environmental-group membership. Recall that in Section 5.41, Mitchell noted three such reasons: People may choose not to free ride because of the low cost of participation, because of the potentially high cost of nonparticipation (species extinction, for example), and

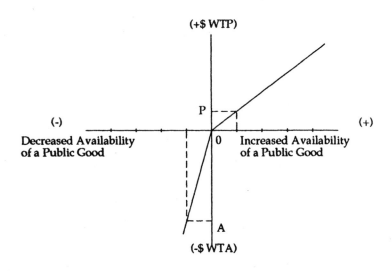

FIGURE 5.6 Asymmetric Value Functions for Expected Gains and Losses

because individual action may be crucial in affecting outcomes. Prospect theory may thus help explain why individuals often provide public goods in spite of the collective action problem.

5.6 Clubs as Voluntary Solutions

We have now considered whether pure public goods would be provided by voluntary action. As we noted in Chapter 3, however, very few goods and services really fit this polar definition. There are, however, many *impure public goods*. These are usually excludable; it is feasible to turn back those who don't pay. They may also be rival in consumption; beyond some point, users may compete for time and space. Some of these goods may be provided by *clubs* as a voluntary solution to market failure. There are many recreational, educational, and cultural clubs, including golf and swim clubs, youth sports programs, civic theaters, and private schools. The providers of these services run the gamut of organizational forms, including not-for-profit groups, profit-seeking firms, and units of government.

5.61 The Basic Model

In 1965, James Buchanan presented an economic theory of clubs for explaining why this type of cooperative arrangement might be an efficient way to organize the production of certain goods. Buchanan recognized that the most efficient consumption unit for a pure private good is the individual; access to the good by one person reduces the quantity available to another person by exactly the same amount. The most efficient consumption unit for a pure public good, however, is infinitely large because use by one member doesn't impinge on the use by another. Buchanan argued that between these two extremes, a variety of clubs could be formed to provide goods that might not be efficiently provided by markets. Different clubs might provide different goods, or perhaps the same club might provide several goods.

Each club would have three characteristics. First, only those who wanted the good and could pay for it would choose to join; it must be possible to exclude others at fairly low cost. Second, impure public goods would be subject to crowding; only a limited number of members would have an incentive to join any one club. Third, beyond some efficient membership size that might vary widely according to the good, it would be efficient to form new clubs.

The incentive for an individual to join would be to maximize utility. The sources of utility could include the use of the good, the sharing of production costs, and sharing of membership characteristics. I might want to join a tennis club in order to play tennis. I might also be prompted to join, however, because others would share the costs with me and because I enjoy their company (most of them). All three sources of utility might not apply in all clubs; the social aspects of a fire-protection club might not be important as long as the fire engine can reach my house in time.

The basic club model for fire-protection services is illustrated in Figure 5.7; dollars are shown on the vertical axis, and membership size (N) is on the horizontal axis. Two initial assumptions are made. The first is that a fixed level of labor and capital resources (fire engines and crews, for example) are available for fire protection. The second is that all club members are alike; all households have identical property wealth, equal chances of a fire breaking out, and equal disutility for personal and property harm. If the members are different, clubs may still be efficient, there may be a need for a differential pricing policy. We'll deal with this in a moment.

Two characteristics of impure public goods such as fire protection would combine to produce an efficient membership size for a club. One characteristic is that the cost per member would fall as fixed labor and capital costs are divided by larger numbers of members. If the costs of maintaining a fire station were $500,000 per year, for example, the average cost to each member at alternative club sizes of 2,000, 5,000, and 10,000 members would be $250, $100, and $50 per year, respectively. These data can be used to derive the *marginal reduction in service costs* per

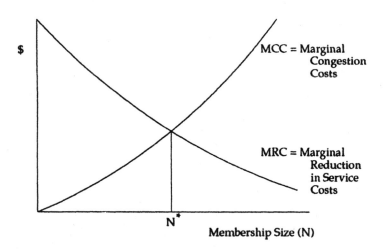

FIGURE 5.7 Efficient Club Membership Size

member, the MRC function. (Note that Figure 5.7 shows continuous rather than discrete functions.) Expanding from 2,000 to 5,000 members would involve a marginal reduction in cost of $150 (from $250 to $100 per member); expanding from 5,000 to 10,000 members would involve a marginal cost reduction of only $50 (from $100 to $50 per member). Hence, the MRC function would slope downward at a diminishing rate as more members were added.

For an impure public good, the advantages of sharing the costs with more people would need to be weighed against the disadvantages of increased crowding, or the *marginal congestion costs* (MCC). Larger memberships would increase the chance that the fire engines would all be busy when you need one; "congestion costs" would take on a whole new meaning if your house happened to catch fire at that time. Congestion costs are less crucial for other impure public goods such as libraries and golf clubs; you might have to wait for a book to be returned or take a later starting time at the golf course. In all three cases, the MCC function is highly subjective, but there could be some monetary costs associated with waiting. The cost of not finding a certain book in the public library, for example, might be its purchase cost at a private bookstore. With fire protection, however, waiting time could easily translate into property loss or even death.

The *efficient club size* would be the level of membership that would equate the (falling) marginal reduction in service cost with the (rising) marginal congestion costs. By assumption, all members are alike; they would each have the same subjective assessment of congestion costs and they would each view N^* as the most efficient size of club. This is only part of the story, however, because there is no assurance that the $500,000 cost level for fire protection is the most efficient level for the N^* members; we just assumed that amount to begin with. An efficient club would thus be defined by two variables, not just one. The first is membership size; the second is the service level, which is represented here by annual costs. Higher service levels (six fire engines, for example, rather than five) would reduce congestion costs, but this would also increase the annual cost for any size of membership, something that could be reduced by adding more members. This would then increase the demand on the system and increase congestion. Buchanan's 1965 paper shows the mechanics of simultaneously solving for the most efficient membership size and service levels.

5.62 Clubs and Society

We now need to ask whether clubs might be good for society as well as for the members. Two related issues need to be addressed. One is whether clubs would be socially desirable; the second is the pricing policy for club services that would be necessary to promote efficiency.

On the first issue, a Ku Klux Klan chapter, a country club, and a Girl Scout troop are all clubs. Even if clubs are efficient ways to organize resources, what they produce and how they produce it may not always be fair, just, and equitable. One of the sources of utility from clubs is the sharing of membership characteristics. This can be done in either a positive manner (a desire for the company of others) or a negative manner (a desire for exclusion of certain others). What is desirable depends on one's sense of fairness; sharing membership characteristics may be wholesome or it may be blatant discrimination, depending on your values.

On the efficiency side, clubs may cause inefficient resource use for several reasons. Like firms or consumers, they can generate externalities of either a positive or negative type. Private security firms, for example, may supplement the efforts of public law enforcement agencies by reducing crime for nonmembers as well as members, *or* they may displace crime toward nonmembers because members are better protected. Duck-hunting clubs may generate positive externalities for an adjacent landowner by attracting ducks through habitat improvement, but they may also divert ducks away from the neighbor's land.

Let's consider how we might go about pricing fire-protection services to club members. Three conditions would have to be met by the policies on pricing, output, and membership if efficiency is to be ensured for others as well as for members (Sandler and Tschirhart, 1980). Each condition can be rather complex mathematically. The first is a "provision" condition; labor and capital resources would need to be provided until the summed marginal benefits to members from reducing the congestion costs were equal to the marginal cost of provision. The second is a "toll" or "utilization" condition; it recognizes that some of the costs are incurred when services are actually used, not just when they are made available for use. An efficient toll would equate a member's marginal benefit from use with the marginal congestion costs that might be imposed on others. If a fire engine is called into duty, it is less available to others. The toll, or charge, for any fire call would be set accordingly; this would encourage members to practice fire prevention. The toll would be the same whether each call was made by a different member or whether all calls were made by one member. Calls of greater lengths or fire intensity would have higher tolls because congestion costs would continue to occur until the engine and crew were available for another call.

The third condition for an efficient club pricing policy is a "membership condition"; new members should be added until the net benefits from membership (through cost reductions to others) equal the congestion costs imposed on others by that member's use of services. To make things a bit more complicated, if members have different preferences and incomes, there are likely to be differences in the amount and value of property to be protected. Some members may also have higher utilization rates than others. In this case the toll might be the same for identical uses of fire-fighting resources, but the membership cost may vary among members depending on their characteristics. Thus, a *two-part pricing* scheme would most likely exist for clubs with heterogeneous memberships.

Finally, a few specific comments about fire-protection clubs. The fact that fires can spread rapidly suggests that voluntary clubs may not be very efficient in providing this service. Externalities would certainly exist if a fire spreads to other property. Someone who preferred to take a financial risk and not join the club could very well endanger the property of members. This helps explain why fire protection has long been provided by mandatory taxes. Without mandatory provision, risk-takers and those who can't afford protection might free ride on members because the fire protection purchased by members would reduce the spread of fire to the property of nonmembers.

5.63 Local Governments as Clubs

One other type of club is worthy of mention, especially in a society where many people have a high degree of geographic mobility. This club-type phenomenon among units of government is called the *Tiebout model* after the late Charles Tiebout (1956). He observed that people can "vote with their feet" for communities of their choice, based on their preferences toward the public services offered by various communities. There are many communities, Tiebout observed, and thus many opportunities for multiple-product packages of public services, each available for "sale" at some tax rate that reflects the cost of production and the number of users. The mobile consumer can choose among packages (communities) based on preferences, costs of production, and population size. The communities themselves are the clubs; consumers enter and exit without coercion, and competition among communities matches users and services at a minimum of cost. An attractive aspect of this model to conservative economists is that it reduces the need for coercion by government. Like-minded people would be attracted to similar communities rather than being coerced to pay taxes for services they may not want.

There is evidence that the quality of public services is important to people, but the actual importance of the Tiebout effect in influencing migration decisions is unclear (Zodrow, 1983). Most economists agree that the assumptions of the model are rather stringent, especially the assumption that household consumption is financed by earnings that are independent of residential location. This isn't true for many people; their earnings might fall too much if they moved to gain a better set of public services. Other people, however, would accept a voluntary reduction in earnings as a price paid for gaining improved access to environmental goods such as outdoor recreation and scenic beauty (Stevens, 1980). There was substantial migration from urban to rural areas within the United States during the 1970s (it has since reverted to the usual rural-to-urban pattern), and there were strong indications that the Tiebout effect was at work (Brown and Wardwell, 1980).

It is unlikely that either voluntary migration by consumers or the offering of a variety of public services by communities could ever eliminate the need for coercive taxing and spending by government. As long as one person doesn't want sidewalks and refuses to move to a small town without sidewalks, we are faced with the likelihood of having to coerce someone through collective choice. Thus it is essential that we begin in Chapter 6 to address two major and related questions of collective choice: how to aggregate individual preferences and how to allow for different intensities of preferences.

5.7 Summary

If there is such a thing as the "collective interest," how can it be ensured if individuals act from self-interest? Adam Smith thought he saw how the invisible guiding hand in competitive markets would translate self-interest into a social virtue by causing consumers to shop for a better deal, thus forcing firms to provide one. Hardin (1982) quips, however, that there is also the *back* of the invisible guiding hand—the very real possibility that self-interest may thwart the collective interest. In the nonexcludable and nonrival public good, we find the main reason for conflict between self-interest and the collective interest—the possibility that an individual might free ride on the provision of the good by others because it cannot be denied him.

Governments, private organizations, and people have to deal with the free-rider or collective-action problem. They may be able to do so in the spirit of cooperation rather than coercion. It is possible to use markets to provide public goods and to resolve externalities, but their usefulness will depend greatly on transaction costs, the assignment of liability, and the possibility for strategic behavior. Some public goods are impure, and clubs may be one option for providing these.

Despite the free-riding possibility, many people choose not to free ride. They voluntarily provide public goods by joining environmental organizations, for example, rather than free-riding on the nonexcludable policy gains made possible by these groups. Selective inducements, social pressure, private goods, altruism, and nonprofit organizations all play a role in determining whether and how the collective action problem may be overcome. Experimental studies of public goods provision are also providing useful information on the preferences and behaviors of individuals. Prospect theory with its very different views about losses and gains may also help explain why people are often motivated to action, usually protective action. Much, however, remains to be learned and understood about individual behavior and collective action.

Terms and Concepts for Review

self-interest
collective interest
positive-sum game
zero-sum game
negative-sum game
the Prisoners' Dilemma
the free-rider problem
the collective action problem
altruism
joint provision of public goods
Lindahl prices
market solutions to externalities
Coase theorem
private provision of public goods
public interest groups
selective inducement
nonprofit organizations
contract failure
crowding out
experiments with public goods
fair share
money back guarantees
contingent valuation
willingness to pay (WTP)
willingness to accept (WTA)
prospect theory
asymmetric value functions
impure public goods

clubs
marginal reduction in service costs (MRC)
marginal congestion costs (MCC)
efficient club size
two-part pricing
Tiebout model

6

Direct (Participatory) Government

6.0 When Some Are Made Worse Off

By their very nature, governments use *coercion*; they are able to bring about departures from the consumption or production pattern that a utility-maximizing individual or profit-maximizing firm would prefer. This suggests a sharp contrast between this chapter and the last, which dealt with voluntary solutions to market failure. We will now recognize that nearly all decisions by government, even the smallest government, make some people worse off.

For example, we dealt earlier (Section 3.41) with the rich family that spends its summers at the beach to avoid the oppressive heat of the city. A city tax for mosquito control is approved with only a few negative votes, including theirs. Are city residents better off as a whole because of the tax? The answer may seem an obvious yes, but this simple example is a reminder that collective choice can be profoundly troublesome. Moral philosophers have struggled for centuries to find ways by which individual self-interest might be subjugated to the collective interest without sacrificing individual freedom, liberty, and dignity. The French philosopher and essayist Rousseau phrased it this way in 1762: "The problem is to find a form of association which will defend and protect with the whole common force the person and goods of each associate, and in which each, while uniting himself with all, may still obey himself alone, and remain as free as before" (p. 391).

The ideal solution, according to Rousseau, is a universally accepted *social contract* by which the rights and duties of the state and the citizens are defined. Imperfect as our attempts to define a social contract might be, they often involve voting as a way to make collective decisions. Thus, it is natural that our focus on direct government and coercion would include voting as a means of aggregating preferences.

Fortunately, voting procedures can be thought of in the Pareto-efficiency terms of Chapter 2. A *unanimity* rule for collective decisions—everyone must agree—would ensure a Pareto improvement in efficiency: A voter wouldn't favor a proposal if it promised to reduce his or her utility. One advantage of the voluntary solutions of Chapter 5, if they are successful, is that they involve unanimity even though voting isn't involved. In each case, anyone who participates is made better off—or else they wouldn't participate—and no one is made worse off.

In many situations, however, unanimity won't occur. In the mosquito example, most city residents would be better off because of the tax, but a few, including the rich family, would be made worse off. Any decision rule of less than unanimity allows for collective action in spite of individual losses. *Majority rule,* the most common rule of this type, would allow a minority to suffer losses if the majority, more than half of those voting, favored a proposal. The efficiency outcome would depend on the extent and the distribution of these gains and losses. The mosquito tax would be a potential Pareto improvement if it passed the Kaldor-Hicks compensation test, that is, if the gainers would be able to compensate the losers and still have something left over. This sounds very plausible in the mosquito case. Other situations might fail the Kaldor-Hicks compensation test, but the proposed action could still pass by majority rule. This would not be a potential Pareto improvement because the gainers couldn't compensate the losers and still have something left over.

Majority-rule voting may thus allow a group verdict to be reached, but it won't necessarily be an efficient verdict. We'll say more about voting rules as the chapter progresses. First, however, we need to consider why a person would ever allow himself or herself to become a "loser" in the first place. That is, why would someone consent to a decision rule of less than unanimity?

6.1 Voluntary Acceptance of Coercion

There are many explanations in the social sciences for the fact that people join groups, but economic models focus on securing gains and avoiding costs. The best-known treatment is by James Buchanan and Gordon Tullock in their influential book *The Calculus of Consent* (1962). They call their model "an economic theory of constitutions." They might have said, "Why I choose to let others decide." It is, in fact, an efficiency explanation for the *voluntary acceptance of coercion,* why self-interested individuals might submit to binding decision rules even though some group decisions may not be in their best interest. The group that an individual might join in the Buchanan and Tullock model could be a club or a government; as we noted in Chapter 5, units of local government might be viewed as a particular type of club.

Let's illustrate their model with what might at first seem farfetched: an individual who is not a part of any political jurisdiction. Although this person enjoys some advantages from his independence, he is also concerned about the danger posed by roving bands of marauders. Let's assume that he could contract with others to protect his person and property for $70 per month. If his expected benefits were only $50 per month, however, it wouldn't pay him to use this option, which is essentially a private market for security services.

Suppose, however, that marauder protection could also be provided through a political jurisdiction that is being formed. The costs of providing protection with this option would decline as more people were protected, allowing his costs to fall below $50 per month. This would appear to make it efficient for him to join the political jurisdiction. There appear to be some advantages to joining with others to produce this service, but our individual is also concerned about what might loosely be called organizational costs—the costs of deciding exactly what type of marauder protection would be provided, how it would be provided, and who would pay for it. Some of these issues are very important, even life-threatening. Who, for example, would determine guilt? Other issues— the type of uniforms that protectors would wear, for example—aren't very important; not everyone needs to spend time and effort on these issues. If organizational costs can be kept low, it might be efficient for the individual to become part of this potentially coercive political jurisdiction.

6.11 Balancing Two Types of Cost

The Buchanan and Tullock model is shown in Figure 6.1; the vertical axis shows expected values of the costs and benefits to the individual. The horizontal axis shows the number of individuals whose agreement is required before collective action can be taken. We'll call the latter the "decision group." The size of the entire group is assumed to be fixed at N^*, but the decision group could range from 1 to N^*, that is, from only one person to everyone. Assume that whether any one individual would be a member of the decision group is a matter of chance. Like Rawls's "veil of ignorance" with respect to a person's position in society in Chapter 4, there is also a veil of ignorance here in terms of any one person's role in group decision-making.

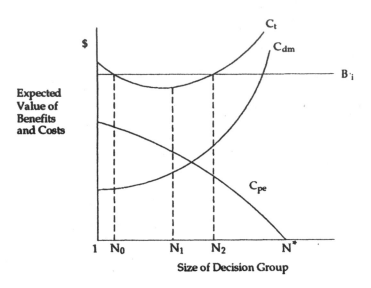

FIGURE 6.1 Voluntary Acceptance of Coercion

The monthly benefit to the individual (B_i = $50) would remain the same regardless of the size of the decision group, but the cost of providing marauder protection might vary greatly with different-sized decision groups. This is because there are two distinctly different costs that could be imposed on an individual. The first are *decision-making costs* (C_{dm}); these are the costs of time and effort that go into making choices if an individual is part of the decision group. These costs would increase with the size of the decision group simply because of the number and complexity of human interactions. They might even rise very sharply as N^* is approached because of potential holdouts who would bargain for a better deal and thus consume the valuable time of group members.

The second cost arises when an individual is *not* part of the decision group. These are *political externality costs* (C_{pe}), a term coined by Buchanan and Tullock to describe how political processes can impose costs on unrepresented individuals, just as imperfect markets impose costs on unrepresented individuals. If you are not in the decision group, for example, the patrols past your house might be less frequent and you might suffer greater losses to marauders. By definition, political externality costs are zero if everyone affected by the decisions is included in the decision group. These costs can be very high, however, if decisions are made in an arbitrary manner by only one person.

The expected total cost of marauder protection would be C_t, which is the vertical summation of decision-making costs (C_{dm}) and political externality costs (C_{pe}). Why are these costs summed? Because for all decision-group sizes except N^* and 1, both costs have nonzero expected values. If one person makes the decision, it is assumed that there are no decision-making costs. If everyone participates in the decision, there are no political extermality costs. Between 1 and N^*, both costs exist.

If N^* was 100 and the decision group size was arbitrarily set at 2, for example, there would be only a 2 percent chance that an individual would be in the decision group. In terms of expected values, there are likely to be substantial political externality costs; any one individual's views are likely to be unrepresented. There are also some expected decision-making costs because this person might be one of the two, but the time and effort required for just two people to make decisions might be minimal. If, however, the decision group is arbitrarily set at $N^* - 1 = 99$, the pattern of costs will be reversed. The expected value of political externality costs will be low because it is almost certain that the individual's views will be represented. The expected value of decision-making costs will be high, however, because it is fairly certain that one can look forward to many meetings and much time spent with the decision group.

If the total cost of marauder prevention could be reduced to less than 50 (his benefit level), the individual's "calculus of consent" would be to

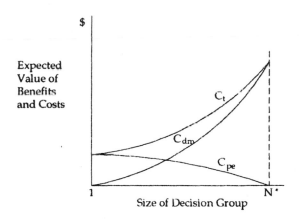

FIGURE 6.2 Efficient Decisions by a Small Decision Group

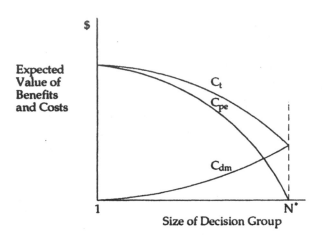

FIGURE 6.3 Efficient Decisions by a Large Decision Group

join the political jurisdiction even though he might be disadvantaged by some specific decisions. But he would only join if the decision group were between N_0 and N_2 in size. Decision groups smaller than N_0 would involve high political externality costs; those larger than N_2 would involve high decision-making costs.

Whether the most efficient decision-group size would be small or large would thus depend on the C_{dm} and C_{pe} functions; this, in turn, would depend on the preferences of individuals and the types and importance of issues. In Figure 6.2, the political externality costs are low relative to decision-making costs; this might happen if the color and style of uniforms for the protectors were at issue. This topic might invite long deliberations within a large group, but it could probably be settled to most members' satisfaction by one person or a small group. In Figure 6.3, the political externality costs are high relative to decision-making costs. In this case, unanimity would be most efficient. This might occur if the issue was how to allocate the protection costs among users. A decision group of $N^* - 1$ might decide that the one remaining individual should pay all the costs!

6.12 Implications for Voting Rules

The Buchanan and Tullock model has several important implications. One is that a person may prefer different voting rules for different situations, depending on an assessment of personal costs. A self-interested individual would lean toward decisions by a few when decision-making costs are high and toward unanimity when political externalities are likely. Guarantees of civil liberties would reduce political externality costs and allow others to make more decisions for us.

The second implication is that unanimity may be very expensive as a general decision rule. The more people who have to agree, the longer the deliberations and the greater the loss of time. Allowing ourselves to be coerced by sometimes "wrong" decisions may be the lesser of two evils. Buchanan and Tullock suggest that unanimity is probably most important for deciding *how* to make group decisions—for selection of voting rules, for example—and that unanimity may be less important for the individual decisions themselves.

Third, the nature of the group may affect total costs and the choice of the most efficient decision rule. People who don't trust each other may prefer unanimity as a decision rule because of high political externality costs; those who trust each other may allow smaller groups to decide. If N^* in Figure 6.1 were a multiethnic community instead of a homogenous group, this might raise both the costs of decision-making and the costs of political externalities.

A fourth implication is that majority rule isn't necessarily an efficient decision rule. There is no apparent reason why C_t in Figure 6.1 would reach its lowest point at exactly one-half the group, plus one. We will say more later about majority rule, but for now recognize that it is deeply rooted in an egalitarian ethic of one person, one vote. Or as a closer reading of history often shows, one adult male, one vote, or one adult male with property, one vote.

Fifth, the voluntary acceptance of coercion by an individual is applicable to both clubs and governments. In fact, some economists argue that clubs and governments really aren't all that different, that governments are basically clubs with geographically defined memberships (Holcombe, 1988). One can exit from either given enough time and dedication. The idea of clubs is a useful analytical construct, but one that is largely devoid of any cultural context. It is a lot easier to say good-bye to your tennis club than to your state or your country. Still, there are similarities between clubs and governments; one of these is that self-interest may dictate that some decisions be delegated to others.

6.2 Voting Without Exit

According to A. O. Hirschman's influential book *Exit, Voice, and Loyalty* (1970), individuals have several options to consider if collective action or market action produces results that are contrary to their preferences. One option is *voice*, a second is *exit*. The option chosen will depend on the situation. If you are dissatisfied with the price or quality of a market good, you can usually exit by switching to another market good. A country club can cancel your membership for nonpayment of the newly approved higher dues, but you don't have to be a member—you can use the exit option. If the city council approves a tax over your objections, however, the exit option requires that you move out of the city to avoid the tax. You can try the voice option by encouraging the city council-members to reverse their decision, but until they do, you'll have to (1) pay the tax, (2) move, or (3) remain, not pay the tax, and face the legal consequences.

Throughout the rest of this chapter, we will assume that coercion by government exists, that the exit option doesn't exist, and that the voice option is limited to voting. In Chapter 7, we will recognize that other forms of voice are possible (lobbying, for example) and that one can usually exit by moving to another political jurisdiction. Throughout the present chapter, it will also be assumed that direct, participatory, or town hall government is practiced—there are no elected representatives. This will enable us to deal with issues one at a time. As a means of aggregating preferences, voting can be done either directly by citizens or by their elected representatives, but representation involves additional issues that are best left until the basic problems of preference aggregation have been discussed.

6.3 Aggregation of Preferences by Voting

6.31 *Majority Rule*

Individual preferences on an issue may be assessed simply by listening to what people say. If we want a more formal assessment, however, we can ask them to vote. And if they vote, they probably expect to vote according to majority rule without considering any other type of voting rule. To most people, voting *is* majority-rule voting.

The tradition of majority rule has deep egalitarian roots that stem from the growth of political democracy. "Although a principle of relatively modern development, it is a product of long evolution, known in rough form in primitive societies, in Greece and Rome, and in the Middle Ages. English adoption into political practice in the 14th and 15th centuries was most influential and led to extensions elsewhere" (*Collier's Encyclopedia*, Vol. 15, 1990, p. 253). There are many aspects of voting other than the choice of decision rule, including the crucial issue of suffrage, or who can vote. The topic of most interest to economists, however, has been the *aggregation of preferences*, or how to add the votes. For several reasons, their conclusions usually don't give majority rule the acceptance that the general population gives it.

There are four pragmatic requirements that any method of aggregating votes might be expected to satisfy.[1] First, it should be operational; voters should understand how the voting will take place and have a reasonable degree of trust in the method of aggregation. Second, the method should be fair to voters and to candidates. Third, the aggregation of votes should be definitive and consistent; repeated circumstances should lead to the same outcome in a predictable manner. A fourth requirement, much more likely to be offered by economists than by citizens generally, is that the aggregation method should lead to efficient outcomes. Majority rule seems to satisfy the first two requirements reasonably well; it works and it usually seems fair. These are two major reasons for its durability. It does not meet the consistency requirement or the efficiency requirement very well, however. We need to address both of these issues, starting with the easier one to deal with—the efficiency requirement.

For an example of how majority rule can lead to inefficient outcomes, imagine an attractive community with tree-lined streets. The citizens have been advised that the spread of Dutch Elm disease is inevitable. Experts say that every other one of the beautiful old elm trees should be removed because the disease spreads through interlocking root systems. A federal grant has been obtained for tree removal; it will cost the community nothing to remove the trees. Because the issue is very controversial, a referendum is held on whether to proceed with the recommendation of the experts.

Assume that the majority of voters (say, 55 of 100) have identical indifference maps as shown in Figure 6.4. They believe that the removal plan will be effective, that it will eventually enhance aesthetic beauty and allow them to increase their utility from U_0 (their anticipated utility level with the spread of the untreated disease) to U_1. Both U_0 and U_1 are below their current utility level, which can't be maintained because of the spread of the disease. In other words, they believe that early treatment will reduce losses. Each majority voter would derive a consumer's surplus of Y_0Y_1 from the experts' plan; this is the maximum amount of money that each would give up to obtain the increase in aesthetic value (see Figure 2.6 for review). Let's say that this amounts to $50 for each majority voter, or an aggregate consumers' surplus of $2,750 if the tree-removal plan is carried out.

Minority voters feel that tree removal will denude the city, that it will do this prematurely, and that it will fail to prevent the spread of disease.

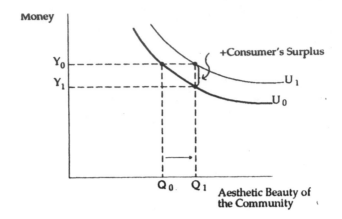

FIGURE 6.4 An Increase in Consumer's Surplus for a Majority Voter

Their utility would fall from U_0 with the untreated disease to U_1 with the experts' plan (Figure 6.5). Their preferences for aesthetic beauty are more "intense" than those of the majority; they would each sacrifice more money (as a proxy for access to other goods) for aesthetic beauty than would any majority voter. Their indifference curves are steeper; thus, the loss of consumer's surplus from the removal plan is Y_1Y_0, say \$100, for each minority voter. Considering all 45 voters, \$4,500 is the minimum amount that the minority would have to be paid to accept the loss of aesthetic beauty.

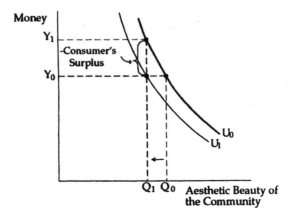

FIGURE 6.5. A Reduction in Consumer's Surplus for a Minority Voter

The tree-removal plan would thus sacrifice $4,500 in minority consumers' surplus to gain $2,750 in majority consumers' surplus, an obviously inefficient outcome. The plan would not be a potential Pareto improvement because the losses would exceed the gains. In this case, the aggregation of preferences through majority rule—one person, one vote—wouldn't help the intense minority, and it would also cause resources to be allocated inefficiently. The efficient outcome would be to listen to the minority and to spare the trees, but this outcome would not be chosen by majority rule.

6.32 *The Arrow Theorem: Aggregation Is Inconclusive*

The third requirement for adding up votes, that a voting method should be definitive and consistent, is concerned with whether that method will have a predictable outcome. If not, the outcome will depend on the starting point, solution path, or some other aspect of voting. The Marquis de Condorcet in 1785 was apparently the first to discover that majority-rule voting may lead to outcomes that are not predictable; even more startling was Arrow's (1951) conclusion that *all* methods of aggregating the votes share this defect, at least in any realistic decision-making circumstances.

For an example of how majority-rule voting can lead to arbitrary results, assume that there are three mutually exclusive uses for a vacant lot that is owned by a city. The first use would be a neighborhood park, the second use would be for a municipal garage, and the third use would be for a teen center. Call these uses X, Y, and Z, respectively. Now, assume that the voters in the community are evenly divided into three groups (V_1, V_2, V_3), and that these groups have the following preferences, in descending order:

V_1	V_2	V_3
X (Park)	Y (Garage)	Z (Teen Center)
Y (Garage)	Z (Teen Center)	X (Park)
Z (Teen Center)	X (Park)	Y (Garage)

At first sight, the outcome would appear to be a standoff; each use would be the favorite of only one-third of the voters. (More on this later.) But let's consider the uses in pair-wise fashion, pitting X against Y, Y against Z, etc., and consider all possible pairs of uses. If we vote by majority rule, X (the park) would defeat Y (the garage) by a two-to-one vote. V_1 and V_3 both favor X over Y; V_2 would be in the minority on this pair. If the vote was then between Y and Z (the teen center), Y would defeat Z, again by a two-to-one vote. V₃ would be in the minority on this pair. One might now suppose that surely X (the park) would defeat Z (the teen center), because X had defeated Y, and Y had defeated Z. Certainly if someone prefers oranges to carrots, and she prefers carrots to zucchini, we might suppose that she would prefer oranges to zucchini. This reasonable expectation is called the *transitivity* assumption. One major problem with majority rule, unfortunately, is that this assumption doesn't always hold. Here, in fact, instead of X defeating Z by majority rule, it would lose to Z!

The collective choice literature calls this the *Arrow problem*, the *voters' paradox*, or *vote cycling* (Figure 6.6). And it is clearly a problem; with three or more alternatives, the winner may be determined by how many times we vote on pairs of alternatives or where we start, rather than any innate or demonstrated superiority. The example comes from the Arrow theorem, a mathematical proof (Arrow, 1951) showing that there is no way to aggregate preferences without violating at least one of these five reasonable axioms or assumptions (Inman, 1987, pp. 682-683):

Pareto optimality: If everyone prefers some alternative x to another alternative, the collective choice process should prefer x to y.

Non-dictatorship: No individual has full control over the collective choice process such that that individual's preferences over alternatives are always decisive, even when everyone else prefers just the opposite.

Unrestricted domain: The collective choice process is capable of reaching collective decision for all possible combinations of individual preference orderings of the alternatives.

Rationality: The collective choice process is rational: first, in the sense that it can *completely* rank all alternatives by stating x is preferred to y, or y is preferred to x, or x and y are equally desirable so we are indifferent; and, second, that all rankings display the property of transitivity.

Independence of irrelevant alternatives: The selection of either of two alternatives must depend on the individual's orderings over only those two alternatives, and not on individual orderings over other alternatives.

The Arrow theorem addressed the question, "Is there a democratic collective choice process capable of allocating societal resources efficiently, even when markets cannot?" (Inman, 1987, p. 681). The key to this question is the reference to two terms—democratic and efficiency. The Arrow theorem and subsequent research, particularly by Gibbard (1973) and Satterthwaite (1975), provide an answer: No. "We stand, therefore,

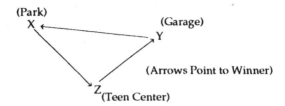

FIGURE 6.6 The Cycling Problem

in the face of a dilemma. Any collective choice mechanism which we might design must be imperfect: either efficient but dictatorial or democratic but inefficient. And we must choose" (Inman, 1987, p. 682).[2] Majority rule may be democratic, but it is also likely to be inefficient in the broadest sense of the word because vote cycling means repetition, inconclusiveness, and waste. By the same token, if choices are efficient, they are likely to be undemocratic—and we don't want that either. Riker notes that "as long as a society preserves democratic institutions embodying Arrow's conditions, it is to be expected that some choices will be unordered and hence inconsistent. If so, then the social outcome is literally without meaning" (1982, p. 44). And to have collective choices that are without meaning implies that we have no way of knowing whether the vacant lot should be used for a park, a teen center, or a municipal garage. We may have processes for making these decisions, but we have no way of knowing whether the right decision has been made. The "public interest" is, in fact, a will-o'-the-wisp.

Research since the Arrow theorem suggests that there are two ways to confront the cycling problem. We need to explore the extent to which they are useful. The first is *agenda control*; some person, group, precedent, or law decides what will be acted on, and by implication, what will not be acted on. For example, if the precedent is to vote only on the first two uses that are proposed at a meeting and this happens to be X and Y, X (the park) will win and the cycling problem will not be observed; Z will never be introduced. Despite its somewhat ominous tone, many collective-choice theorists see agenda control as crucial in restoring stability to a majority-rule system by limiting or defining the alternatives in certain ways. We will say more about this in Chapter 9.

6.33 Single-Peaked Preferences: A Way Out

The second way that cycling may be avoided in majority voting is for *single-peaked preferences* to exist, because dual-peaked preferences are what led us astray above.[3] If we array X, Y, and Z on the horizontal axis in Figure 6.7, the preference patterns of V_1 and V_2 have one "peak" in terms of utility: V_1 peaks at X, and V_2 peaks at Y. V_3 has a dual peak; both X and Z are preferred to Y. The fact that this caused the cycling problem is more than a bit troubling, because all three orderings seem reasonable and defensible. Even though V_3 has a dual peak, this might simply mean that V_3 puts a high priority on developing human and natural resources by her support of the teen center and the park, rather than on promoting downtown business by supporting the parking garage. One doesn't have to agree with V_3's ranking, only admit that it is plausible, to recognize that majority-rule voting can result in cycling and hence, ambiguity.

If V_3's preferences were changed to V_3' by moving Z to the lowest preference, the revised set of preferences (in descending order) would be:

V_1	V_2	V_3
X (Park)	Y (Garage)	X (Park)
Y (Garage)	Z (Teen Center)	Y (Garage)
Z (Teen Center)	X (Park)	Z (Teen Center)

This is shown by the dotted line in Figure 6.7. Now, we have only single-peaked preferences. X would again defeat Y, and Y would defeat Z, but most important, X would now defeat Z (Figure 6.8). No matter where the

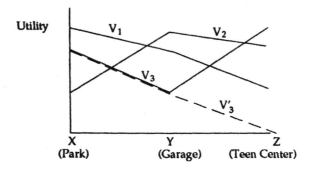

FIGURE 6.7 Dual- and Single-Peaked Preferences

voting starts, with whatever pair, it would stop with X (the park) as the winner.

This example shows that single-peaked preferences can be a stabilizing influence with majority rule, but it does not prove that preferences are, in fact, single-peaked. For single-peaked preferences to occur, there must be *single-dimensioned issues*, that is, the choice among X, Y, and Z must rest on a single underlying evaluative dimension by which all three voters rank various land uses. As we noted earlier, this may not be the case here. In fact, three different dimensions may well exist. One dimension might be one's feeling of support for downtown business. This dimension might be used by V_2, who feels that building a municipal garage to expedite shopping would be the best use for the land. This dimension is not shared by V_1, however, who favors the park and who may be using an environmental dimension to rank the land uses. And V_3, who favored either the park or the teen center in her initial rankings, may be using a human-development dimension to rank the alternatives. All of these are plausible dimensions and each of the three rankings is plausible.

Why and how, then, might issues ever be single-dimensioned? The idea has an interesting history dating back to 1929 when Harold Hotelling asked readers to visualize that competition between business firms might occur spatially, that is, from left to right along a linear scale. Along Main Street, if you will. Even if two firms asked the same price, the buyers (who also live along Main Street) wouldn't be indifferent between firms if transportation costs were a factor. Other things equal, the market would be divided so that buyers would minimize transportation costs. Each firm would sell to those buyers located at their end of the street, and the two firms would share the sales to those buyers who are located between the firms. Competition would cause the two firms to converge at the middle of Main Street; each move in that direction would tap into the other firm's buyers while retaining their own existing buyers.

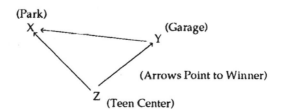

FIGURE 6.8 Resolution of the Cycling Problem

The concept of *spatial voting models* developed from this early idea. These are based on a left-to-right linear scale that represents a single dimension, like Hotelling's Main Street. Hence the analogy to space. Individuals are assumed to evaluate alternatives along this dimension in light of their own self-interest (Enelow and Hinich, 1984). Politicians and political parties are also an active part of this process, but let's save these considerations for Chapter 7 on representative government. Voter i's preferences are represented by her utility function, U_i, so

$$U_i = U_i(X), \qquad (6.1)$$

where X is the single evaluative dimension.[4] In the voter's view, each proposal, whether there are one, two, or many, relates to a particular X value and thus to a particular U_i value. If preferences are single-peaked, X_i^* is the voter's most preferred point along the X dimension; hence

$$U_i(X_i^*) > U_i(X) \qquad (6.2)$$

for all $X \neq X_i^*$.

One situation in which single-peaked preferences have often been assumed to exist is if the amount of public service, the extent of financial resource allocation for that purpose, or more simply, "budget size" is the single evaluative dimension (Figure 6.9). An example would be the budget size for public schools in a community. Assume that a voter is asked to give up income or wealth (access to other goods and services) to provide tax support for local schools. As with other normal goods and services, the voter's marginal rate of substitution (MRS) of income or wealth for public-school services would be expected to decline as more school services are provided and as more tax money is required (Figure 6.10). Y_0 is the amount of money that the voter would have if there were no taxes for schools; U_0 is the corresponding utility level. Assuming that schools are financed solely by local property taxes and that the good is made available at a tax rate of t_0 per unit of schooling, the amount of taxes that the voter would pay depends on how much schooling is provided. If X_1 was provided, the voter's income or wealth would be reduced by Y_0Y_1; it would be reduced by Y_0Y_2 if X_2^* budget size was provided.

If collective choice happened to result in a school budget of X_2^* at a property tax rate of t_0, this fortunate outcome would be exactly the outcome that the voter would have freely chosen. That is, X_2^* is the budget size that would give maximum utility to this voter. If collective choice resulted in too little (X_1) or too much (X_2) of the good, the voter would only be able to reach the U_1 indifference curve. She would have

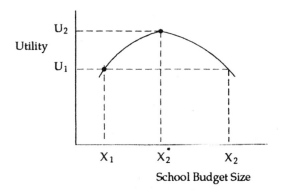

FIGURE 6.9 Single-Peaked Preferences

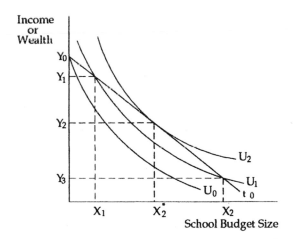

FIGURE 6.10 Voter Choice Between Public Schools and Other Goods

to pay less (Y_0Y_1) or more (Y_0Y_3) taxes than she would prefer to pay. In summary, a single-peaked preference will result if the voter evaluates the issue on only the one dimension of "budget size" if she has a diminishing marginal rate of substitution of money for schools, and if she faces a constant per-unit tax.

6.34 The Median Voter

If voters' preferences are single-peaked, not only is cycling avoided and stability lent to majority-rule voting but a particular type of voter is also identified, one whose preferences will always be favored. In an early and pathbreaking article, Duncan Black (1958) pointed out the importance of the *median voter*, the voter in the middle with as many voters above him (with preferences for more) as there are below him (with preferences for less). Black showed that with single-peaked preferences, the median voter is always a winner under majority rule.

Consider Figure 6.11, for example, where preferences for school budget size—the single evaluative dimension—are shown for three voters. Voter 1 prefers a small budget, Voter 2 a medium budget, and Voter 3 a large budget. The preferences maps are shown as roughly normal distributions; in reality, they may be very skewed toward large or small budgets.

If the vote was between a medium budget, M, or a small budget, S, a majority $(V_2$ and $V_3)$ would favor the medium budget; their utility for budget size would be higher for M than for S. If the decision was between a large (L) or a medium (M) budget, a majority would again favor the medium budget. The majority group this time, however, is V_1 and V_2. Because V_2 is the median voter, she is in the majority in both cases.

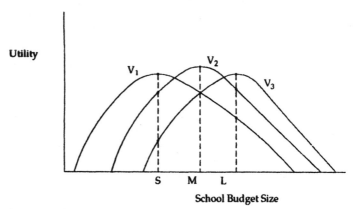

FIGURE 6.11 Preferences of Three Voters for School Budgets of Different Size

Two notes should be added. One, V_2 won't always maximize utility if agenda control is exercised. If some person or rule limits the choice to either a small budget (S) or a large budget (L), V_2 would have a slight preference for a large budget even though she would actually prefer a medium budget to either. Still, V_2 remains the median voter. The second note is an important corollary to the first: only if there is repeated voting, unconstrained by agenda control, will V_2 be able to maximize utility. V_2 might be able to reach her most preferred position if a series of votes are taken, but many votes might be required.

The median voter would thus prevail under majority rule if there was only one dimension, such as budget size. If more than one dimension existed, the same voter would be decisive only if she were the median voter for *each* dimension.[5] If this wasn't the case, cycling would occur under majority rule voting because different voters would be pivotal for different dimensions. This possibility is shown in Figure 6.12, where two evaluative dimensions for schools are assumed to exist. Budget size is one dimension; the second dimension is the nature of the curriculum. This could be reflected in several ways. A progressive curriculum might be more likely to have a higher share of budget allocated to sex education, guidance and counseling, personal awareness, languages, music, art, and drama. A more traditional curriculum would stress the three Rs and vocational courses.

The preferences for these two dimensions among three voters, LOW, PROG, and TRAD, are shown with sets of circular or oval indifference curves; only a portion of these are shown in Figure 6.12.[6] The combination of budget size and curriculum designated as LOW*, for example, is the most preferred position for LOW, a voter who likes a moderate curriculum and small school budgets, and hence, a greater amount of after-tax income available for the consumption of other goods. The closer (from any direction) a point is to LOW*, the more LOW prefers it. He prefers LOW* to A, for example, because the curriculum at A is too progressive and because paying taxes to reach A would cause him to give up too many other goods and services. LOW prefers A to B, however, because the curriculum at B is too traditional and the budget size is even larger.

The second voter, PROG, prefers to be at PROG*, which involves large budgets, a progressive curriculum, and less after-tax income. The most preferred position for the third voter, TRAD, is at TRAD*; he, too, prefers a fairly large budget, but he likes a very traditional curriculum. Note that the median voter is different for each dimension; TRAD is the median voter for budget size, but LOW is the median voter for curriculum. This spells trouble, as we will see

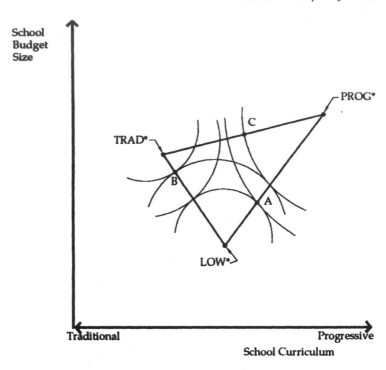

FIGURE 6.12 The Cycling Problem in Two Dimensions

Suppose that the three are asked to vote on the three choices, A, B, and C. Option A has the smallest budget and the most progressive curriculum; B is much more traditional but with a medium budget; C has the largest budget and a curriculum nearly as progressive as A. Assume that the winner is to be selected by majority vote in a pairwise manner. Starting (arbitrarily) with the choice between options A and B, both LOW and PROG prefer A to B because it is closer to their points of maximum utility. PROG likes A because it is more progressive than B; LOW may like it because it will cost less in taxes. TRAD prefers B to A because it is traditional and has a large budget, but A still wins by majority rule. If B and C are then voted on, B wins by majority rule. TRAD prefers B because it is more traditional, LOW prefers it because it costs less. Only PROG, who likes both the larger budget and more progressive curriculum, votes for C.

At this point, A has defeated B, and B has defeated C, in both cases by majority rule. If A and C are then voted on, however, the cycling problem occurs. Transitivity requires A to win over C, but this doesn't happen. Of the three voters, only LOW prefers A to C. PROG and TRAD both vote for C because of the higher budget; TRAD also likes the more traditional curriculum.

This occurrence of cycling, as in the earlier choice among the park, garage, and teen center (Figure 6.6), is no fluke; it can easily happen when different people have different reasons for preferring different outcomes. In fact, research by Kramer (1973), Plott (1967), and McKelvey (1976) has shown that voting cycles are the general case unless voter preferences are essentially identical (Inman, 1987). Unless people are clones of each other, majority rule can be stabilized only by finding a single overarching dimension of ultimate importance to voters in almost all decisions, which seems unlikely, or by finding ways that collective agendas can be controlled.[7] Let's take another look at single dimensions, leaving agenda control until Chapter 9 on administrative government.

6.35 Ideology: A Stabilizing Dimension

One key dimension that may lead to single-peaked preferences—and thus to stability in majority-rule voting—is ideology. This is how Hotelling's "Main Street" analogy was used by Anthony Downs in his book *An Economic Theory of Democracy* (1957): "We assume that political preferences can be ordered from left to right in a manner agreed upon by all voters. They need not agree on which point they personally prefer, only on the ordering of parties from one extreme to the other" (p. 115). Downs thought that a single agreed-upon dimension could exist— political preferences—and that voter preferences for outcomes along this scale would be single-peaked. But how would political preferences be measured?

> These assumptions can perhaps be made more plausible if we reduce all political questions to their bearing upon one crucial issue: how much government intervention in the economy should there be? If we assume that the left end of the scale represents full government control, and the right end means a completely free market we can rank parties by their views on this issue in a way that might be nearly universally recognized as accurate. (p. 116)

Downs defined ideology as "a verbal image of the good society and of the chief means of constructing such a society" (p. 96) and saw it as the way voters make decisions on candidates and parties, especially in light of pervasive uncertainty and minimal incentives on the voter's part to reduce that uncertainty.[8] Subsequent researchers have developed Downs's notion of ideology as a shorthand device by which voters can predict what a candidate or party would do in office, if elected. Hinich and Pollard (1981) developed a predictive dimension for ideology and related it to political issues; Poole, Rosenthal, and Romer have also made extensive use of ideology as a single dimension.[9] They believe that voters consider proposals or candidates

> by gauging how each one fits their basic ideological preference on a liberal-conservative spectrum. Each voter is assumed to have an ideal point on this spectrum with preferences decreasing on either side of the point. . . . Candidates for political office are evaluated according to how their platforms meet with voters' ideological preferences, and each voter is assumed to vote for the candidate whose platform ranks highest according to that voter's preferences. (Romer and Rosenthal, 1984, p. 466)

The preference functions for three voters (V_1, V_2, V_3) along this ideological spectrum are shown in Figure 6.13. As with Figure 6.11 on school budgets, the median voter (V_2) would prevail. To avoid cycling, the policy alternatives have to be viewed in the same manner by all three voters. They have to agree, for example, that a certain trade policy would lie on a certain point on the ideological spectrum, even though their preferences for that point might differ greatly. If P_1 was an existing policy and P_2 was a more conservative alternative, V_2 and V_3 would have higher preferences for the more conservative alternative. P_3 would be an even more conservative alternative, but only V_3 would vote for it over P_2; V_2 would join V_1 in favoring P_2 over P_3. The median voter, V_2, would prevail under majority rule.

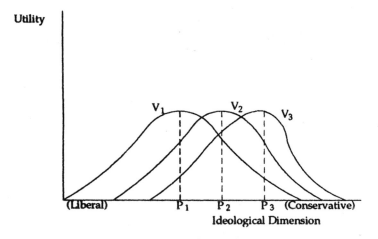

FIGURE 6.13 Voter Preferences Along an Ideological Dimension

The intervals between P_1, P_2, and P_3 are often referred to as *spatial distances* on an ideological spectrum. These distances can be measured in several ways, including the use of interest-group ratings of congressional representatives. These groups typically select a dozen or more issues that are most important to them, then rate each member of Congress in terms of the percentage of "right" votes. Those who have the highest ratings are closest to the position of that particular interest group. Researchers have succeeded in placing all the interest groups and all the individual representatives on the same ideological scale by using a statistical technique called metric unfolding analysis (Poole, 1984). Scale values for U.S. senators, for example, were defined to range from about -1.0 for the very liberal Ted Kennedy to about +1.0 for the very conservative Jesse Helms. Romer and Rosenthal (1984) estimate that about 80 percent of the votes in Congress over the past twenty-five years can be classified along this ideological spectrum; they believe that ideology adds a great deal of stability to the political process.

One may object, however, that even though "liberal" and "conservative" are familiar political terms, they may mean different things to different people. Conover and Feldman (1981) feel that there are two liberal-conservative dimensions, economic and social. Someone might be an economic liberal (approving of government intervention to reduce economic inequality, for example), but a social conservative (disapproving, for example, of government interference with individual decisions such as abortion). Conover and Feldman found that liberalism and conservatism are not simply mirror images along a single dimension. Instead, people who identify themselves as liberals or conservatives stress different things. Liberals tended to identify with social issues (abortion), equality (equal rights), and change (new ideas). Conservatives identified with fiscal policies (particularly the need for free enterprise), New Deal issues (skeptical of minimum wage and social security), and foreign policy (particularly the need for defense).

The Poole, Romer, and Rosenthal team acknowledge that the terms "conservative" and "liberal" don't necessarily indicate that voters or candidates have coherent political philosophies. Instead, Poole argues that the terms "are best understood as *labels* that have become attached to certain consistent patterns of political behavior" (1984, p. 118, emphasis added). If these patterns of behavior are recognizable and predictable across issues, this reduces information costs for voters. Someone might oppose government intervention in the economy, for example, but support government intervention with respect to abortion rights. Is this a conservative or a liberal position? Neither, says Poole, if one insists on a consistent philosophy with respect to government intervention. But, in fact, both of these positions are held by an easily recognized group of congressional conservatives. Hence, Poole and his colleagues would say that this reflects conservative ideology in the minds of voters.

Finally, we can conclude that the median voter will be decisive *if* there is a single unifying dimension such as ideology or budget size, *if* all voters vote, and *if* voting is repeated without limit. It is crucial to remember that these are all properties of a simple theoretical model, not descriptions of reality. In reality, we find that these "ifs" often don't hold. This doesn't mean that the median voter is powerless, but it does mean that he or she becomes less potent if majority rule is used as the voting method.

6.4 Expressing Intensities of Preferences

The limitations of majority rule that have been identified have led people to consider other procedures for aggregating preferences.[10] Several types of nonmajority-rule voting methods are presented through an example. A section is then devoted to a demand-revealing process, which is a voting-like mechanism for allowing intensities of preferences to be expressed. Transaction costs are once again considered, this time in terms of redefining or repackaging individual issues into coalitions of issues to better express preferences. The need to economize on transactions costs then serves as a springboard from direct government to representative government.

6.41 Different Types of Voting[11]

Define V_1, V_2, V_3, V_4, and V_5 as five groups of voters. Within each group, there is an identical set of preferences on four alternatives for solving the Dutch elm disease problem that we discussed in Section 6.31. Let's refer to these alternatives as candidates, which is a more general term from the voting literature. The candidates are as follows:

X = do nothing now and hope the disease doesn't strike
Y = follow the experts' advice to remove every other tree
Z = remove every fourth tree now and perhaps do more later
W = use an untested spraying alternative.

The ordinal preferences (in descending order) of the five groups are as follows; these indicate the order of preference, but not how much one candidate is preferred to another. The underlines indicate an "approval" subset, which we will discuss later.

V$_1$	V$_2$	V$_3$	V$_4$	V$_5$
X	X̲	Y̲	Z	W
Y̲	Y	Z	Y̲	Y̲
Z	W	W	W	Z
W	Z	X	X	X

Recall that a minority of the citizens were dubious about the experts' proposal for early partial removal (Y); this was supposed to save the remaining trees if done before onset of the disease. V$_1$ and V$_2$ make up this minority; both groups favor the passive approach (X), hoping that the problem will go away. There is disagreement within this minority, however, on how to deal with the problem. V$_2$ approves only of waiting; V$_1$ prefers doing nothing with a second preference of adopting the experts' plan. Each of the three majority groups has a very different opinion about the best option. One group favors Y, one favors Z, and one favors W, but they all heartily reject the "do nothing" option (X) favored by the minority.

Unanimity is the one voting procedure that offers a Pareto improvement; someone becomes better off and no one becomes worse off. But in the case of Dutch elm disease, unanimity doesn't happen. These voters simply disagree on the best option.

Majority rule also gets us nowhere with Dutch elm disease. Even if all voters agreed with the one person, one vote idea, majority rule wouldn't produce a winner. About the only course of action that yields three of five votes is to reject X. This may suggest what the group shouldn't do, but it doesn't instruct them on what they should do.

Plurality rule would select that candidate ranked first by the largest number of voters. To its credit, it will always "work"; some candidate will always win or at least tie for first place. This could be a very weak advantage, however, if the outcome was a five-way tie among five candidates, each voting for himself. That isn't very decisive. If you accept the plurality principle, you may have to give up equality among voters. Here, X (no action) would win, but with only two votes out of five. This means that three other voters failed to favor X. To endorse plurality in this case is to say that two is larger than three.

The *Condorcet criterion* is named after the Marquis de Condorcet, a French mathematician and economist of two hundred years ago. This method is one of several that take into account the entire range of voter preferences; each of the three previous methods considers only the most-favored candidate. (We used this method earlier in this chapter in deciding on land use and school issues.) Each candidate is compared with each other candidate in a pairwise manner; the one who defeats all others by majority rule is the winner. The matrix below shows the Condorcet outcomes for the Dutch elm disease alternatives:

X	Y	Z	W	
--	Y	Z	W	X
	--	Y	Y	Y
		--	Z	Z
			--	W

The pairwise winners are shown in the body of the matrix. Y (the experts' advice) defeats all others, Z (removing every fourth tree) defeats each of the remaining two alternatives, and W (spraying) prevails over X (inaction). In contrast with simple majority rule, where there was no winner, and in contrast with plurality rule, where inaction won, the Condorcet criterion identifies a clear pattern of preferences. The entire range of the rankings is considered and the egalitarian basis of majority rule is retained. The disadvantage of the Condorcet criterion is the possibility that no clear winner will emerge. Several top candidates may defeat all others but fail to defeat each other. In fact, we saw this happen in Figure 6.6; each of the three land-use candidates, X, Y, and Z, were able to defeat the other two. Another disadvantage of the Condorcet criterion is that each voter must rank all candidates. This could be gruesome if one was ranking beginning clarinetists.

The *Borda count*, proposed by Jean-Charles de Borda in 1781, allows each voter to assign each of the m candidates a score from 1 to m, with the top candidate receiving m points, the next best $m - 1$, and so forth; the lowest receives one point. Ties can be averaged; the candidate with the most points wins. V_1, for example, gives 4 points to X, 3 points to Y, 2 points to Z, and 1 point to W. Overall, Y wins with 16 points, followed by Z with 12. W and X each have 11 points. Y is thus a clear winner by the Borda count, as it was with the Condorcet criterion. The Borda count has the advantage of allowing voters to express their intensities of preference, but it has the disadvantage of forcing these preference to be in a particular cardinal form. V_1, for example, may prefer X ten times more than W, not just four times more. A *modified Borda count* would remedy this by giving each voter a total of $[m + (m - 1) + (m - 2). . . + 1]$ points, or $4 + 3 + 2 + 1 = 10$ points in this case, to allocate however he or she wishes.

In *exhaustive voting*, the least-preferred candidate is eliminated from all rankings by plurality rule; this process is repeated until a single candidate remains. X is the first to be eliminated; it is the least preferred for all voters except V_1 and V_2. With X deleted from all rankings, W is the next to go; it is the now least preferred by three of five voters. Z falls easily to Y by four of five votes, leaving Y as the overall winner. As with the Condorcet criterion and the Borda count, however, we may not want to identify the least-preferred candidate, especially if the field is large and if there are many obvious nonwinners. In such a case, a modified Borda count would allow us to handle this by simply allocating zero points to candidates who fall below a certain ranking.

The Borda count and exhaustive voting are both subject to strategic manipulation. Entering a new candidate, removing an existing one, switching the rankings, and other strategies can affect the placing of the other candidates. This violates Arrow's fifth axiom on the independence of irrelevant alternatives (see Section 6.32). If W (spraying) is removed from consideration as a Dutch elm disease treatment, for example, Y (the experts' plan) is still the winner with 12 points. Notice that m is now 3 points instead of 4. X (inaction) and Z (every fourth tree) tie for the runner-up spot, each with 9 points. Prior to W's withdrawal, however, Z had defeated X by 12 points to 11 points. Contrary to the fifth axiom, the choice between Z and X *did* depend on the W option. Borda recognized this possibility for strategic voting and is said to have commented that "my scheme is intended only for honest men" (Black, 1958, p. 182; cited by Inman, 1987, p. 690). In fact, voting theorists have proven that a strategy-proof voting procedure cannot exist (Gibbard, 1973), a result that would have been a disappointment to de Borda but not a surprise.

With the last major method, *approval voting,* a voter casts a vote for any and all candidates of whom he or she approves. This may be all of the original candidates, part of them, or none. If the approval subset is empty, one is voting for "none of the above." V_1 would cast one vote each for X (inaction) and Y (experts' plan), for example, but any preference for X over Y would not be recognized. The candidate with the most total votes would win. In this case, Y would win with 4 votes. Approval voting is perhaps best suited to situations where voters can easily discern an approval subset but find it difficult or uncomfortable to discern within that subset or don't wish to do so.

In summary, voting methods may be contradictory because they reflect different considerations. By every voting method except plurality, the tree-removal option (Y) would win. This is so in each determinate case; unanimity and majority rule fail to produce a winner. This situation may sound innocuous, but it is not. For example, the winner of a primary election is usually determined by the plurality method; a majority-rule winner may not be required if there are several candidates. A second election might be required to vote on the top two candidates and thus reach a majority-rule outcome. The problem is that an intense minority can produce a plurality winner, but at the cost of eliminating an eventual Condorcet winner. Whether elections are on candidates or issues, choices rarely come in simple packages of two.

6.42 A Demand-Revealing Process

One voting-like procedure that offers promise for reaching efficient outcomes, but probably not outcomes that would please the majority, is known as a *demand-revealing process*. The origin of the idea can be traced to Vickrey (1961) with major improvements and refinements by Clarke (1971, 1977), Groves (1973), Tideman and Tullock (1976), Groves and Ledyard (1977), and others. With this process, each individual is asked which of two or more options she prefers, and how much she would be willing to pay, in dollar terms, to have her preferred option rather than the other(s). An outcome is then reached by adding up the dollar values for the various options; the one with the most dollars is the winner. A tax is then levied on each voter, based on her impact on the outcome. This tax is referred to as a *Clarke tax*. Consider Table 6.1, for example, where the perceived gains for seven voters are shown for two of the alternatives on the Dutch elm issue. These two are the experts' plan for removal and inaction, at least for the present. The dollar values that are shown are the anticipated gain in consumer's surplus for each of the seven voters should their preferred positions be adopted. Four voters (V_4 to V_7) form the majority. Each would gain a surplus of $25 from tree removal; this would be a $100 net gain if the trees were removed. Three intense voters (V_1 to V_3) form the minority; their anticipated net surplus from inaction relative to tree removal would total $130. On efficiency grounds, inaction would win the vote. On majoritarian grounds, however, the trees would be removed.

The demand-revealing process has three characteristics that make it unique. First, the intensities of voters' preferences as reflected through net gains in consumers' surplus would determine the winner; the number of votes for or against a candidate are irrelevant. (So much for majority rule.) The demand-revealing process, in fact, resembles a modified Borda count, but consumers' surplus gains are aggregated, not some arbitrary point measures. The second characteristic is that voting may not be costless from an individual's point of view. Instead, any imposed tax would reflect the effect that her vote has on others. In effect, Buchanan and Tullock's political externalities (Section 6.1) are taken into account.

And third, the tax is not intended to siphon off the gains of the majority, or to comfort the minority, but to bring about an efficient outcome.

TABLE 6.1 Two Alternatives for Dealing with Dutch Elm Disease

| Voter | Gains in Consumers' Surplus | | |
	Experts' Plan	Inaction	Clarke Tax
V_1	0	+$40	$10
V_2	0	+$50	$20
V_3	0	+$40	$10
V_4	+$25	0	0
V_5	+$25	0	0
V_6	+$25	0	0
V_7	+$25	0	0
Total Value	$100	$130	$40

Specifically, the Clarke tax would impose a tax on each voter equal to that amount needed to balance the total dollar values of the two alternatives, but *only* if that person's vote made a difference in the outcome. Had V_1 not voted, for example, the total value would have been $100 for the experts' plan and only $90 for inaction; thus, her vote clearly did make a difference. Without V_1, her side would have lost. A Clarke tax of $10 would be levied on her; this is the minimum amount needed to balance the dollar values for the two options. Had V_1 understated her preferences and recorded only a $5 value, the Clarke tax would be zero because she would not have affected the outcome. Her side would lose, however, because the total value of inaction would then be only $95; thus, there is little disincentive to understate preferences. Had V_1 overstated her preferences by recording a $100 value, the Clarke tax would still be only $10. As long as her real consumer's surplus ($40) is large enough to pay the $10 tax, any larger bid is redundant.

By similar reasoning, the Clarke tax for V_2 would be $20. Without V_2, the vote would have favored the experts' plan by $20 ($100 - $80); his vote was decisive in the outcome. Like V_1, V_3 would pay a $10 Clarke tax. None of those who favored the experts' plan would be taxed, because their individual votes didn't make a difference in the outcome; they lost.

As Inman (1987) and Mueller (1989) note, the demand-revealing process has a few problems of its own. First, like almost every market arrangement or collective choice device, it can be manipulated by a group of users. In Table 6.1, for example, if the minority (but not the majority) were able to act as a cohesive unit rather than submitting independent bids, the outcome could easily be manipulated. If V_1, V_2, and V_3 each claimed that inaction was worth $100, for example, inaction would win over the expert's plan by $300 to $100. Better yet for the minority, each of them would have a Clarke tax of zero because the "response" of the other two would be sufficient to defeat the other plan. For them, it would pay to plan ahead. A second difficulty with the demand-revealing process is that some people might have to give up all their wealth to pay the tax; this might not be appropriate from an equity point of view. And third, the tax itself would create a budget surplus. The outcome wouldn't be Pareto efficient if the surplus was left unused, because something could have been produced with it. If the surplus was returned to the voters, this would upset the efficiency applecart by changing the distribution of income that gave rise to the responses—and the tax. Groves and Ledyard (1977) have developed a slightly different taxing procedure that would balance the budget, but they still had to assume that all consumers would act independently.

One might object that the will of the majority would be thwarted by this voting process. And indeed, it would be. It is, after all, a "demand-revealing process." Any process that reveals demand is bound to reflect the factors that give rise to demand, particularly the income, tastes, and preferences of the demanders. In this case, inaction would be worth more to a minority than tree removal would be worth to a majority. The distinction between this process and majority rule is straightforward. If you want to live in an efficient world, you would probably like demand-revealing processes and Clarke taxes. If, however, you want to live in an egalitarian world, you probably wouldn't like this approach because it can subvert the will of the majority. To repeat the dilemma stated by Inman, "Any collective choice mechanism . . . must be imperfect: either efficient but dictatorial or democratic but inefficient. And we must choose" (1987, p. 682).

6.43 Coalitions

Although some gains may come through selection of "better" voting methods, the most common and effective action for an intense minority is usually to form a *coalition* with another intense minority. These are explicit or implicit vote-trading arrangements that join different issues to allow for expression of intense preferences. Coalitions are often thought of as different groups of people, each having somewhat different priorities for action. Retired people, farmers, Blacks, Hispanics, or poor people may be likely to form a coalition. In technical terms, however, coalitions are not really the merging of people but rather the merging of issues that are important to these people. When a coalition is formed, issues of different relative importance to two or more groups become coalesced into a smaller group of issues (or even one issue) that becomes important to everyone within the coalition.

Think back again to the Dutch elm disease case (Section 6.31); recall that a fairly passive majority (55 of 100 voters) would approve the experts' plan for tree removal, and an intense minority (the other 45 voters) would suffer a large reduction in consumers' surplus. Regardless of their intensity, they are still a minority; they would lose on the tree-removal issue under majority rule. Their challenge is to find another group of people who are concerned about a related (or even unrelated) issue and to then coalesce or merge these issues for purposes of voting. In this case, the "someone else" would have to come from the other side. The minority would need to attract at least 6 of the old majority to form a new majority while holding firm those already within their own ranks.

One related issue might be what, how, and when to replant the trees, including the question of who would pay the costs (Table 6.2). Assume that there are 10 voters within the tree-removal majority who are also greatly disturbed about the current proposal to replant with very young oak trees. These people would much prefer to use trees that are already fifteen feet tall. Call this group MAJ2. The concerns of these 10 voters needn't be identical; some may think that the young oak trees would grow too slowly; others may feel that a different tree species should be planted. Whatever their reasons for objecting, assume that they would each suffer a $70 reduction in consumer's surplus if young oak trees were replanted. Assume now that those in MIN, the previous minority, would each suffer $50 losses from replanting as well as $100 losses from tree removal, and that those in MAJ1, the remaining 45 members of the old majority, would each have a $20 gain from the replanting alternative.

If the issues were voted on separately, tree removal would pass by 55 to 45 under majority rule, as we have seen, in spite of the large and intense minority. Replanting would fail by a 55 to 45 vote. If the two issues were voted on as one issue, however, the single combined issue would fail by 55 to 45 because of the coalition. Both MIN, the original minority of 45 votes, and MAJ2, the new group of 10 dissatisfied voters, would vote against the single issue—but for different reasons. The swing votes are the 10 voters in MAJ2 who would approve the tree-removal plan but who feel strongly that the replanting plan is flawed. This group

TABLE 6.2 Example of a Coalition

Group	Number of Voters	Change in Consumer's Surplus per Voter		
		Tree Removal	Replanting	Tree Removal and Replanting
MAJ₁	45	+$50	+$20	6 +$70
MAJ₂	10	+$50	-$70	-$20
MIN	45	-$100	-$50	-$150
		Change in Consumers' Surplus		
MAJ₁		+2,250	+900	+3,150
MAJ₂		+500	-700	-200
MIN		-4,500	-2,250	-6,750
Total		-1,750	-2,050	-3,800

would be worse off with removal (+$50) and replanting (-$70) than if nothing was done; they would vote against the combined measure because they would be $20 worse off.

Several other things should be noted about coalitions. One, the parties in an effective coalition don't need to have equal gains, but they all must have *net* gains from the coalition. If the gains happen to be highly unequal, however, the party with the least to gain may be able to extract something extra from the party with the most to gain. Second, coalitions can bring about either a more efficient use of resources or a less efficient use of resources. In this case, efficiency was enhanced, or more exactly, reduced efficiency was prevented. When the two issues are merged, those who would gain from removal and replanting (MAJ1) would have a $3,150 net gain in consumers' surplus. Those who would lose from removal and replanting, the new majority of MIN and MAJ2, would have a net loss of $6,950 ($6,750 for MIN, $200 for MAJ2). By preventing these actions, the coalition prevented a reduction in net economic value. Arguments will be raised in Chapter 7, however, that coalitions often cause efficiency to be reduced rather than enhanced.

Third, the example hints at one of the original theories of coalitions, Riker's (1962) concept of the *minimum winning coalition*. In the example, if MIN had maintained its solidarity, only 6 members of MAJ2—not 10—would have been needed to constitute a new majority of 51 to 49.

This has also been called the size principle: "Minimum winning coalitions are winning coalitions that would cease to be winning if some member were subtracted. Thus the size principle asserts that winning coalitions will not be larger than they need to be" (Riker and Ordeshook, 1973, p. 177). In our example, the extent of gains and losses per voter didn't change as voters switched sides. In other cases, however, dividing a fixed total gain by the smallest-size coalition could maximize the gains per winning member.

Fourth, what we have called a coalition could also be called *logrolling*, but the context is slightly different. Logrolling is a promise between two voters (or more frequently, between their representatives) to exchange votes; A promises to vote to please B on an issue of B's choice if B will do likewise on an issue of A's choice. In the previous case, tree removal and replanting could be voted on separately (or perhaps simultaneously to avoid defections); MAJ2 could agree to join MIN in voting against tree removal if MIN will agree to join MAJ2 in voting against replanting. This agreement comes easily for MIN voters because they planned to vote against replanting in any event, but they are doubly quick to logroll with MAJ2 because they have the most to lose if MAJ2 doesn't vote with them against removal.

Finally, the formation of a coalition can be an expensive proposition, effective though it might be. Transaction costs of time and money would have to be incurred to find out which 10 (or perhaps only 6) of the original majority of 55 voters are sufficiently dissatisfied with the replanting proposal that they would consider forming a coalition of issues. (To find this out might not be too difficult; one could just listen to the testimony at a town hall meeting! The time that it would take to attend the meeting could be used for other purposes, however, so this information isn't costless.) But which one, two, or more of the 45 voters in MIN would be willing to expend resources to try to form a coalition? Out of the goodness of their hearts? Out of self-interest? If a successful coalition would provide a nonexcludable public good to all those in MIN, the incentive for an individual to enhance the coalition would be eroded because each could receive the benefits without bearing the costs. Thus, the collective action problem rears its head once again.

It is possible that a candidate for election to office, a political entrepreneur, could bear the transactions costs of putting coalitions together. This idea, that we may want to have political entrepreneurs facilitate coalitions and seek voter support to gain or remain in elective office, marks the transition to Chapters 7 and 8 on representative government. How efficiently and how equitably the preferences of voters will be relayed through these entrepreneurs are issues that we'll try to assess in those chapters.

6.5 Summary

In spite of the possibilities offered by voluntary action, coercion by government is a reality. In some respects, it is a desirable reality; the decision-making costs of collective choice may be sufficiently high that we wouldn't want to participate in each and every decision that might affect us. If we don't participate, however, we may suffer from political externalities and the outcome may not be in our favor.

How preferences are aggregated in collective choice involves a fundamental dilemma. If we choose majority rule on the basis of egalitarian desires, we run the risk of making inefficient group decisions. An intense minority can easily suffer larger losses than a passive majority might enjoy in gains. But the minority would still lose under majority rule. Intense minority preferences may be expressed through alternative voting methods, although these may lead to contradictory outcomes, and through innovations such as the demand-revealing process. Coalitions are the major practical alternative that minorities use to deal with their minority status; they try to find a related issue and coalesce two or more issues into one that both groups can support.

Majority rule is inherently unstable, as shown forty years ago by the Arrow theorem. Stability can be restored by single-peaked preferences and by the median voter *if* issues are single-dimensioned, that is, if they are arrayed along a spatial plane. Ideology, as manifested through a liberal-conservative political spectrum, offers promise as a single dimension. Agenda control is a second major way to restore stability under majority rule. Both types of stabilizers—ideology and agenda control—are offered by elected representatives who would bear the cost of forming coalitions in exchange for our votes.

Terms and Concepts for Review

coercion
social contract
unanimity
majority rule
voluntary acceptance of coercion
decision-making costs
political externality costs
voice
exit
aggregation of preferences
efficiency outcomes of majority-rule voting

transitivity
Arrow problem/voters' paradox/vote cycling
Pareto optimality
non-dictatorship
unrestricted domain
rationality
independence of irrelevant alternatives
agenda control
single-peaked preferences
single-dimensioned issues
spatial voting models
the median voter
ideology as a dimension
spatial distances
intensities of preferences
plurality rule
Condorcet criterion
Borda count
modified Borda count
exhaustive voting
approval voting
demand-revealing process
Clarke tax
coalition
minimum winning coalition
logrolling

7

Legislative Government: Part 1

*7.0 Why Have Government?

As we begin the next five chapters, perhaps we need to reflect on why we have government. "As a practical necessity," some would say. "To do things that we can't do for ourselves," or "because it's better than the alternative." All of these reasons contain a germ of truth, but they are obviously incomplete. At times in the past, government has been sparse, almost nonexistent.

Government can be "done" in a variety of ways, and government action can range from a little to a lot. We need to develop our thinking about where we want to be along this spectrum. Toward one end, there would be heavy reliance on the market and on voluntary decisions about buying and selling goods and services. It takes a certain type of good, a private good, to make this option work. The existence of public goods, those that are nonexcludable and nonrival in consumption, takes us along the spectrum toward more government and more complex government. Having public goods means that the preferences of those other than the immediate buyers and sellers aren't registered in markets. As a result, too little may be produced (education and income redistribution to the poor, for example) or too much may be produced (pollution and crime, for example).

Various forms of voluntary action may be able to counter the public-goods problem, that is, to bring about more efficient or more equitable outcomes. We may cooperate to build a road, for example, the benefits of which would accrue to several people. We might also cooperate in reducing the level of pollution through a voluntary market for changes in the amount of pollution; those who pollute would be made even better off if they accepted bids to reduce their level of pollution.

---

*Section 7.0 provides a brief overview of Chapters 5 and 6.

But voluntary action as a means of resolving market failure has to contend with two major problems. One is the very nature of a public good. The services of a road, for example, may invite free-riding as a form of strategic behavior. If some cooperators build a road but lack the ability to monitor and control its use, it can be used by others without their having to bear any of the cost. The second problem is that the transaction costs of making and enforcing market bargains may be too high. The two problems are related. Those who get together to build the road may be able to strike a deal among themselves, but if the costs of excluding others are too high, this invites free-riding.

The logic of economic self-interest has been that some, but not enough, roads will be built if free-riding and high transaction costs combine to erode cooperative behavior. The other side of this logic is that a significant number of voluntary solutions do take place in spite of the potential for free-riding. People gave $16 billion in nonreligious charitable contributions in 1985, and many people contribute to nonprofit organizations that provide outcomes that an individual would have access to without contributing. People are able to listen to public broadcasting and benefit from heart research without contributing to either. Many, however, choose to contribute; why they contribute and what this implies about the role of government is still far from clear.

The fact that we have coercive government, empowered to collect taxes and impose sanctions, means that voluntary actions may help resolve market failure but aren't entirely adequate. Those who want to build a road may form a government and force me to pay a tax for my share of the cost. It seems fair that I should pay. But what if the government wants me to pay the entire cost? This suggests that I would want to take part in collective choice in some situations. There are other situations, as we saw in Chapter 6, where we might allow others to make decisions for us.

In spite of the possibility of having different voting methods for different situations, we usually choose majority rule for collective decisions because it embodies a strong egalitarian concept: one person, one vote. Majority-rule decisions may be inefficient decisions, however, because majority rule simply ignores how intense the preferences of the minority might be. If a majority of voters have weak preferences and a minority of voters have intense preferences, an inefficient outcome can easily occur with majority rule.

The other major characteristic of majority-rule voting is that it tends to be unstable. Outcomes may be determined by the order of voting or some other peculiarity, rather than by the merits of the options. This is no fluke; one of the most important findings in economics in the past half-century has been that preferences can't be aggregated except under very limiting circumstances. One of these is the existence of a single evaluative dimension among voters: the amount of expenditures for local schools, for example. In this case, the median voter—the one in the middle in terms of preferences along that single dimension—will determine the outcome if everyone votes.

One way to resolve these majority-rule problems of inefficiency and instability would be to have representatives compete for elected office by forming coalitions or packaging sets of issues that appeal to voters, including minority voters with intense preferences. These elected representatives could also exercise agenda control, something that would restore stability to majority-rule voting. The use of legislative committees to deal with different types of legislation is an example of agenda control; certain committees have substantial power over labor, health, or natural resources, for example.

Aside from any theoretical argument for representative government, it just doesn't make sense for all of us to flock into Washington, D.C., or Sacramento to make collective decisions. For better or worse, we nearly always have representative government rather than direct or participatory government. Is this for the better? Representative government is feasible, it allows intense preferences to be expressed whereas direct voting usually does not, and it can be a stabilizing force when majority rule is the voting procedure. Is it for the worse? Stability may be a pseudonym for allowing those people or groups with intense preferences—large corporations, the gun lobby, or retired people, for example—more influence over legislative outcomes than we may want to allow.

7.1   Representative Government
in Historical Perspective

There are many explanations for the form of representative-democratic government that we have in this country. These explanations are often rich in political, social, and historical detail. In fact, they might seem to intimidate our economic models, which tend to be simple rather than complex, abstract rather than specific, suggestive rather than definitive.

But a story can be told in many ways. For example, the self-interest motivation that plays such a crucial role in economic models also figured prominently in Richard Hofstadter's classic analysis *The American Political Tradition* ([1948] 1974). Conflicts in self-interest show up throughout Hofstadter's interpretation of our political history. He portrays the Founding Fathers, for example, as men of affairs who had considerable distrust of the common man and democratic rule: "Democratic ideas are most likely to take root among discontented and oppressed classes, rising middle classes, or perhaps some sections of an old, alienated, and partially disinherited aristocracy, but they do not appeal to a privileged class that is still amplifying its privileges" ([1948] 1974, p. 5). Hofstadter also argued that the Founding Fathers faced a fundamental dilemma in government; this dilemma was concisely expressed in a personal letter between two influential citizens of the time. In part, it said, "Let it stand as a principle that government originates from the people; but let the people be taught . . . that they are not able to govern themselves" (p. 8). The other side of the dilemma was that the leaders also feared the arbitrary and capricious nature of the sovereign rule they had just escaped, and they feared it even more than they feared the masses and majority rule. According to Hofstadter, the Founding Fathers solved the dilemma with three constitutional devices. The first was a federated government designed to maintain order and stability against scattered majoritarian uprisings. The second was the designation of two legislative bodies—a Senate for the aristocrats and a House for the democrats. The third, of central interest in this chapter and the next, was representation. According to Hofstadter:

> In a small direct democracy the unstable passions of the people would dominate lawmaking; but a representative government, as Madison said, would "refine and enlarge the public views by passing them through the medium of a chosen body of citizens." Representatives chosen by the people were wiser and more deliberate than the people themselves in mass assemblage. Hamilton frankly anticipated (that) the wealthy and dominant members of every trade or industry would represent the others. . . . Merchants, for example, were "the natural representatives" of their employees and of the mechanics and artisans they dealt with. (p. 11)

The Founding Fathers' need for representation to protect against "excesses" of majority rule was recently addressed in an honorary lecture by James Q. Wilson (1990), president-elect of the American Political Science Association. Drawing on James Madison's writings in Numbers 10 and 51 of the Federalist Papers, Wilson argued that the two papers addressed in very different ways how we might strive for justice and protection of essential liberties while still remaining within the context of popular government. According to Wilson, Madison's judgments were conditioned by his views about human nature: "His [Madison's] conclusion was that man is sufficiently self-interested and calculating as to make checks and balances *necessary* but sufficiently virtuous and deliberative as to make it *possible* to design and operate a constitution that supplies and maintains that system of restraints" (1990, p. 562, emphasis added). In more direct language, "To paraphrase a twentieth-century commentator, man is good enough to make republican government possible and bad enough to make it necessary" (p. 562).

With this bit of historical interpretation as backdrop, let's set about developing some basic economic models of legislative government based on the assumption of self-interested behavior among participants. In these models, legislators will be viewed as elected political suppliers. Citizens, firms, and interest groups that make demands on government will be viewed as demanders of political action. Those administrators whose job it is to deliver goods and services to the demanders will be viewed as the appointed political suppliers (Figure 7.1). The focus is first on the demanders, then on the elected suppliers. The two are brought together in Chapter 8. The level of complexity is increased in Chapters 9 and 10 by introducing the appointed political suppliers and how they may or may not be responsive to the demanders and elected political suppliers. Finally, the reality of federated and multilevel government is recognized in Chapter 11.

This may all seem a simple way of viewing a complex world, but it allows us to use the familiar concept of self-interest to analyze collective choice. As most economists see it, governments and markets both involve substantial elements of self-interest. The utility of consumers and the profits of firms are forms of self-interest, a concept that is now extended to a new set of actors. In particular, it is assumed that demanders of political action attempt to maximize utility or profit, that elected political suppliers attempt to maximize the probability of election or reelection,

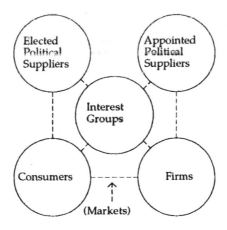

FIGURE 7.1 The Major Actors in Representative Government

and that appointed political suppliers attempt to maximize yet another dimension of self-interest, usually the size of their budgets. An attempt is made to examine each assumption as we go along.

7.2 From the Good Fairy to the Wicked Witch: Four Supply Models

There are four general models about what we might expect from elected political suppliers. These range, one might say, from the whimsical to the cynical. The first is the Good Fairy model, where political suppliers act only to resolve situations where markets have failed or would fail. The suppliers limit their actions to building roads that are needed but not being built, for example. Or suppliers may seek to overcome the collective action problem by transferring income to deserving recipients on the basis of unanimous support among voters. In either case, the elected suppliers would bring about a Pareto improvement; no one would be made worse off. This is the whimsical end of the spectrum; benevolent outcomes like these may happen, but they probably don't happen very often.

The second model is the Semigood Fairy model. Road users, for example, may receive large enough benefits that they would have something left after compensating the losers for their losses—if they had to. In the sense of a potential Pareto improvement, efficiency would be enhanced by building the road. The distributional effects, however, may not be desirable. Those who own the land may feel that they are worse off, even after they are paid full market value for their land. They may feel that compensation doesn't atone for all the damages from road building.

In the third general model of elected suppliers, the Uncertain World model, efficiency may be reduced by collective action, but only because of uncertainty and imperfect knowledge. Due to design problems, the costs of building a road may turn out to exceed the benefits, but this may not have been known when the decision was made to build the road. In this model, elected suppliers want to produce efficient outputs or to benefit certain groups in an efficient manner, but circumstance and limited knowledge may keep these things from happening.

The fourth, the Wicked Witch model, says that elected suppliers are likely to promote whatever issue it takes to hold or gain office. According to this view, if efficiency happens to be enhanced, it will be only a side effect of a successful bid for reelection. In general, self-interested legislators will cause efficiency to be reduced because they promote redistributional programs to gain votes at the expense of economic efficiency. These elected suppliers aren't necessarily bad people, but incentive frameworks within the political process fail to encourage them to be efficient. Mitchell (1983) makes this candid observation about these incentive frameworks:

> In short, the politician is an innovator in redistributive schemes. Public provision of education in the nineteenth century is a fine example; publicly provided medical services is a singularly depressing example of a current effort at redistributive innovation. The first task of the politician is to discover a service in widespread demand which is increasingly burdensome for private persons to finance. Once such a large potential voting group has been located, the politician must devise a scheme that will transfer costs from the intended beneficiaries to third parties. And, ideally the regime's scheme must be such that the beneficiary knows he is a substantial beneficiary while the taxed are left unaware of their increased burden. (p. 94)

Which of these four models is most descriptive of reality? Along with truth and beauty, this is left for the reader to decide.

7.3 Anthony Downs: An Early View of Political Competition

In one of the most influential works of modern political economy, a book titled *An Economic Theory of Democracy* (1957), Anthony Downs gave early support to the Wicked Witch model, although in somewhat benign form. Downs spelled out how political parties or teams of self-interested elected suppliers would seek to rule democratic states by competing for voter approval under a system of majority rule. There are only two main actors in the Downs model: the government or the political party in power and the voters. There are also two secondary actors: an opposition party that reminds voters of promises made by the party in power and interest groups that attempt to influence government on their behalf.[1] The two other major actors in Figure 7.1, firms and appointed suppliers, weren't considered by Downs.

According to Downs, competing parties offer *platforms*, or sets of proposed policies, for voter approval at periodic elections. The basic Downs hypothesis is that "parties formulate policies in order to win elections, rather than win elections in order to formulate policies" (p. 28). This much-quoted distinction neatly captures the central role of party self-interest. The typical voter, a self-interested but largely uninformed utility maximizer, computes an *expected party differential* by comparing the performance of the party in power with the likely performance of the opposition party, had it been in power. If the party in power has promised too much and delivered too little, electoral competition will remove it from office.

The idea of political "firms" responding to all-powerful "consumers" is a very explicit analogy to competitive economic markets in the models by Downs. He recognized, however, that an individual is much less powerful as a voter than as a consumer. Consumers can directly influence market outcomes by buying private goods, but individual voters have little control over voting outcomes, which are usually public goods. There is also a great deal of voter uncertainty about platforms, policies, and about which party would do the best job. In spite of this uncertainty, voters have little incentive to acquire information. The amount of information that one would rationally acquire depends on whether it would be useful in decisions on whether and how to vote. These decisions, as we will see in Section 7.41, depend on whether the outcome will improve the voter's situation and on the likelihood that the individual's vote will affect the outcome. If there are many voters, each will have little effect on the outcome and there will be little incentive to vote. Voting can be encouraged, however, by keeping the costs of voting low. Voters will tend to acquire more information if the acquisition costs can be shifted to third parties, although third-party information may be biased. Various interest groups may help voters evaluate proposed policies, but they will also try to persuade voters.

One way that voters deal with uncertainty, Downs argued, is through ideology. Ideology can be used by voters as a way to reduce the cost of acquiring information about specific issues. As we saw in Sections 6.33 and 6.35, ideology can also act as a single and stabilizing dimension of political preferences among voters. Their preferences for different degrees of government intervention could be arrayed along a Hotelling "Main Street," ranging from strongly liberal or interventionist on the left to strongly conservative or free market on the right. If two competing political firms, Party X and Party Y, were to offer platforms to voters who have preferences as shown in Figure 7.2, Party X would capture all the votes from those with preferences more liberal than the Party X platform (to the left of X); Party Y would capture all the votes from those with preferences more conservative than its platform (to the right of Y). The votes of those with preferences between Parties X and Y would be split between the two; voters would vote for the party that offered a platform closest to their preferences. This would lead to competition for votes. If Party X adopted a slightly more conservative platform (X'), for instance, it would attract new voters (X' - X) at the expense of Party Y while still

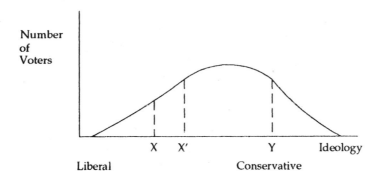

FIGURE 7.2   An Example of Two-Party Competition for Votes

retaining those liberals on the far left. Party Y would then move farther to its left. Electoral competition in a two-party system would thus encourage the parties to converge and have similar platforms; this would favor the median voter under majority rule.

A variety of complications might arise. Voters at the far left or far right might abstain or they might even support a third party (Smithies, 1941). Of particular interest to Downs (in his Chapter 8) was the possibility of a bimodal distribution of voters—one with many votes in each tail of the distribution but few votes in the center. Parties would then diverge rather than converge, and outcomes might be unstable. Skewness of preferences might occur even with a unimodal distribution; the platforms of the two parties might converge with both favoring a conservative (or liberal) ideology.

Although the Downs model of rational choice was a landmark work, several areas of omission and underemphasis have become apparent in the four decades since the book was published. Perhaps the most serious is the overly influential role that Downs assigned to voters and to electoral competition for their votes. Voters may be uninformed and apathetic in the Downs model, but their collective response determines the fate of governments. Elected suppliers who fail to assess voter preferences will be removed by political competition. In this sense, Downs's political systems were very much demand-driven (Mitchell, 1983). The more recent literature, however, has stressed the importance of supply factors, particularly the role of imperfect competition in deciding political outcomes. Downs portrayed government as a single unitary force; Niskanen (1971) and many others have recognized that appointed suppliers can be just as important as elected suppliers in deciding political outcomes. Fiscal federalism adds still another layer of reality and complexity to the Downs model; federal, state, and a variety of local governments exist with their own legislative, administrative, and judicial branches.

A second omission is that Downs made little mention of the role of business firms, even though firms can have a great deal of influence on political outcomes. They can urge their employees to vote and they can make financial contributions to candidates, parties, and issues. Through these actions and through the formation of interest groups, firms can play a key role in the political process.

A third area of underemphasis is the role of nonvoting methods for expressing political preferences. Voting was really the only method of expressing preferences that Downs considered in detail. Once we recognize that business firms are important demanders of political action, alternatives other than voting have to be considered. Firms can't vote, so they have to rely on other means of influencing collective outcomes. Individual citizens may also lobby, carry petitions, and make contributions of time and money in addition to voting.

A fourth area of revisionist thinking has been whether governments tend to enhance or reduce efficiency in the allocation of resources. If market failures occur, competition among political parties and a demand-driven political process like the one that Downs described could lead to increased efficiency.[2] Assuming that the spending purpose and the tax source are both considered at the same time, Downs believed that government would spend and tax until the marginal vote gain would just equal the marginal vote loss (Figure 7.3). Fewer and fewer votes would be gained by additional spending, but more and more taxpayers would become disgruntled and then alienated as spending grew. Thus, the net vote gain would be greatest if an expenditure level of E^* was proposed. This might be close to an efficient level of spending if voter preferences for and against spending were equally intense.

Mitchell (1983, pp. 74-75), however, contends that Downs failed to distinguish the previous case from the situation in which government makes separate decisions on how much to spend and who to tax. In the latter, there is no reason to expect that efficiency will be enhanced. Figures 7.4 and 7.5 show two groups of taxpayers; each group would gain from spending (D_1 and D_2) but suffer from taxation (L_1 and L_2). A government would maximize total votes by allocating a given expenditure level ($E_1 + E_2$) between competing groups so as to equate the marginal vote gain at M_0. The group with the greater demand for spend-

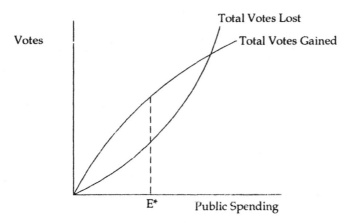

FIGURE 7.3 Spending to Maximize Net Votes

ing (D_1) would receive the most expenditures (E_1). By the same token, the vote loss for the party would be minimized if the tax load was distributed over the two groups so that the marginal vote loss was equal at M_0. The second group (L_2) might be less organized and less aware of the tax than the first group (L_1); they could be taxed more heavily, even though less would be spent on them. One would thus predict that governments

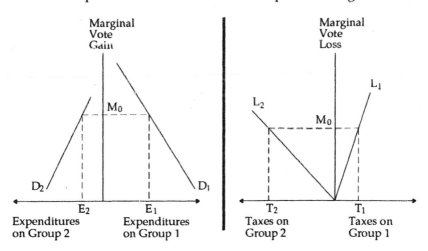

FIGURE 7.4 Marginal Vote Gain from Spending

FIGURE 7.5 Marginal Vote Loss from Taxing

will cause reductions in efficiency if taxing and spending decisions are made separately, as they usually are.

Nevertheless, the Downs model is widely recognized as a classic for its treatment of self-interest among politicians and voters. In Chapters 7 through 10, we will be exploring some of these revisions that have been suggested. Our political system appears to be much more supply-driven and complex than the one Downs described, but his work was original and provocative and it still offers many valuable insights into legislative government.

7.4   The Demands by Citizens for Political Action

Anthony Downs's view of the voter as rationally apathetic was objectionable to many people in 1957. But he did not say that voters should be apathetic. His was a positive model, not a normative one; he tried to understand and predict voter behavior, not prescribe it or justify it. And in order to predict voter behavior and citizen demands for political action, Downs argued, one has to understand the incentives and disincentives to individual action.

Foremost among the disincentives is the opportunity for free-riding, which arises from the collective action problem or public good problem of Chapter 5. Many political outcomes are public goods, as we defined them in Chapter 3; they are available to individuals without action on their part. The outcomes may not always be "good"; some of them may be very undesirable, but they still exist on a nonexcludable basis whether we like it or not. The outcome of a presidential election is a public good, available with or without my vote, and I can free ride on the outcome by not voting. Whether I *should* free ride is important, but that is a different question than whether I *will* free ride.

7.41 Political Participation

If political outcomes are nonexcludable, individuals may be politically inactive. The rational choice model, originating with Downs, asserts that people will assess the marginal gains and marginal costs of political action, however they define these, and take appropriate action. Whether they will be politically active or inactive depends on their assessment of these gains and costs; many will be characterized by *rational apathy*—they will be politically inactive because of "rational" calculations. Yet many people do express themselves politically, and many do more than just vote. Other forms of *political participation* include the following (Breton, 1974):

- joining an interest group
- lobbying and other personal and small group activities
- contributions of money to candidates, parties, or issues
- becoming a candidate for office.

How much do people participate? Alexis de Tocqueville ([1835] 1969), a French diplomat, observed conditions in the United States in the 1830s and concluded that Americans were a "nation of joiners." Despite this much-quoted observation, the extent to which people actually participate in the political process is not clear. One major survey of citizen participation (Verba and Nie, 1972) is more than twenty years old, and there is evidence that some forms of participation have increased greatly since that time. The Verba and Nie data revealed that about half the people vote regularly in local elections and that three-fourths vote in presidential elections, but only one-third have ever worked with others to try to solve community problems.

Some new evidence on political participation comes from a pilot study by Baumgartner and Walker (1988). They found a change in the way Americans participate, one that has led to increased involvement in voluntary associations such as charities or environmental groups. Now, people participate more through national groups than they did twenty years ago. Financial support is often obtained through the mail, although contributors may not see themselves as members of the organization. Baumgartner and Walker also found that many people belong to or contribute to several national organizations of a particular type (environmental groups, for example). This had not been explored in earlier surveys because the focus at that time was on political participation at the local level. Overall, political participation in Baumgartner and Walker's study was nearly twice the level that would have been estimated with the earlier methods of questioning used by Verba and Nie.

Let's consider the various forms of political participation. As Downs recognized, voting is the most common form of participation. It, however, is burdened by a huge disincentive; an individual's expected gain becomes smaller as the number of voters increases, even if he or she regards the election outcome as important. In fact, the effect of one vote on the overall outcome becomes imperceptible as the size of the group grows large. If the voter isn't sure which party or candidate would be best, and especially if he or she is sure that it really doesn't matter which party or candidate wins, the expected gain from voting is further reduced.

The basic self-interest model of voting is the *rational voter hypothesis,* as it was termed by Downs and presented in Mueller (1989, pp. 348-369).[3] A citizen will vote only if

$$P \times B + D > C, \qquad (7.1)$$

where   P =   the subjective probability that one's vote will bring about a difference in policy outcomes

B =   net utility gain from a difference in policy outcomes

D =   private benefits from the act of voting

C =   the costs of voting.

The probability that a single vote will be decisive, P, is itself a function of the number of people voting (N) and the chance (f) that the voter's preferred candidate will win:

$$P = \frac{3e^{-2(N-1)(f-0.5)^2}}{2\sqrt{2\pi(N-1)}} \qquad (7.2)$$

As an example, Mueller shows that P would be .00006 (6 chances in 100,000) if N = 100 million voters and there is a 0.5/0.5 expected outcome. As one might expect, P will fall as N increases, and it will fall on either side of f = 0.5.

If the expected gains from desired policy outcomes are small, voting will occur only if one or more of three circumstances hold: if the cost of voting (C) is very small, if a private or excludable good (D) is produced by voting, or if a private "bad" (-D) is avoided by voting. We try to keep voting costs low by having numerous polling places and by keeping them open for extended hours. Employers are encouraged to allow employees to vote without having to take annual leave or give up income, and the use of mail ballots is on the increase.

Private goods (D) may be obtained by voting, even though one's impact on policy outcomes may be imperceptible. Friends are often seen at the polling place, and community news and gossip can easily be picked up. Private bads (-D) can also be avoided by voting. Those who vote may do so *not* because they think they will affect the outcome but because they will have thus fulfilled their civic duty. By voting, they can avoid the guilt they might feel if they don't vote.

The second and third options for demand expression by citizens, joining an interest group and doing your own lobbying, are defined so that the first invites the free-rider/collective action problem; the second avoids it. Becoming a member of a large interest group such as the Sierra Club, for example, might seem like a good way for me to enhance the quality of our natural environment. But *if* this organization is effective, it will still be effective without my membership fee. Not without *all* our individual membership fees, of course, because this would amount to a substantial revenue loss. But at least without mine. One may object that this is selfish. And it may be. It simply has to be recognized, however, that because of the incentive system, self-interested individuals may choose to free ride rather than join a large interest group, no matter how noble its purpose.

With a local environmental issue the incentives may be different and the options more restrictive. Suppose someone starts a junkyard in my neighborhood. My neighbors will probably expect me to carry petitions and testify before the city council; I would rather be playing golf. Mancur Olson's insights from Chapter 5 apply here; social pressure can be very useful in overcoming the free-riding problem.

As another form of political participation, contributions of money are often tax deductible up to a $50 or $100 limit, thanks to Congress and some state legislatures. If they are fully deductible, the tax cost to a contributor is zero. Even so, there are uncertainties. You might lose the receipt for your contribution, in which case you would not be able to deduct the contribution. You might not owe any taxes at all, in which case tax deductions won't help. You might forget that you made the contribution, and you might even wish you had the money back if you find a better political cause or candidate.

A fifth demand option, becoming a candidate for elective office, invites a huge time cost, as anyone who has served on a local school board or town council can confirm. One general note about political participation is that different people may make different decisions simply because they have different preferences. Some people enjoy the political process and may even run for office; others dislike it intensely. Some might think that a candidate's wine and cheese-tasting party at a beautiful older home is a social bonus; others might find it boring. People often choose to be very different from each other as market consumers, and we really shouldn't expect them to think alike as consumers and producers of public services.

7.42 Market Adaptations

The disincentives for political action stem from many causes: An individual is often one of many, his or her actions usually have little effect on the outcome, the marginal gains from action are often quite uncertain, and gains—if they exist—are often available in any event. The marginal costs of political action, however, are usually fairly certain. If a related good is available through the market, one that would provide excludable and thus certain services, an individual may choose to buy the market good and forgo political action. These *market adaptations to political decisions* include the following:

- the self-supply of public services
- the purchase of market substitutes for public services
- geographic migration
- illegal activities
- joining clubs.

With respect to the self-supply of public services, people may want to supply themselves with additional amounts, but this is often difficult or impossible. The city leaders may not be too happy, for example, if I try to hire additional city police. They might not object, however, if I want to add my money to the police department budget or contribute to the parks department for sports programs in low-income neighborhoods. Even so, this type of adaptation is asymmetric. I may be able to buy more of the public good if I am undersupplied, but it will be very difficult for me to "sell" some of it if I am oversupplied.

The purchase of market substitutes for the public good is usually a more promising option than altering the quantity of the public good itself. Consider, for example, the use of police patrols through neighborhoods to reduce residential theft. If a consumer was to buy this service at a unit price of t_0, her utility would be maximized if $\bar{q}$ was provided (Figure 7.6). Her tax bill for this service would be Y_0Y_2 (point a). If the city council decides to provide only q_p of deterrence, however, and to tax the individual by a smaller amount (Y_0Y_1), this would place her in an undersupplied situation (point b). It may be possible, however, to buy market goods at a higher unit price of p_1, starting from an after-tax position at b. This would allow her an increase in utility from U_0 to U_1 at point c. A simple door lock, for example, is a low-cost market adaptation to an undersupply of police protection. Yard lights, dead-bolt locks, watchdogs, and a variety of other market goods can also make a home more secure from theft. Private security firms can also be hired to reduce this risk.

Another form of a market substitute that can be used by a citizen who is dissatisfied with government, particularly at the local and state level, is geographic migration, or moving to another political jurisdiction. "Voting with your feet" as a way to gain a different set of public services was discussed in Chapter 5. Most geographic migration has little to do

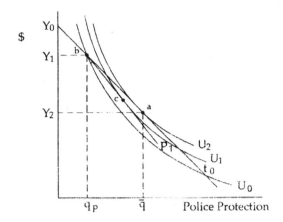

FIGURE 7.6   Augmenting a Public Good with a Market Substitute

with public services; most people move to gain better jobs or for other personal reasons. During the late 1970s, however, a reverse migration occurred; the rural population in the United States grew at a faster rate than did the urban population (Brown and Wardwell, 1980). This was partly because many households moved to obtain a variety of environmental amenities or nonmarket goods. Many in-migrants to southern Oregon, for example, gave up higher-paying jobs in California to gain greater access to environmental amenities and personal safety (Stevens, 1980). The average reduction in household income due to migration was about $10,000 per year, these people were willing to pay a substantial price for goods and services that were undersupplied in their former locations.

Illegal activity, a fourth type of market adjustment, can occur if the consumer is willing to incur a loss of income, time, or personal convenience that may result if the illegal activity is detected and the person is tried and found guilty. The choice among illegal goods and services can run the gamut from prostitution and gambling to newer forms of illegal activity such as the use of marijuana among cancer victims for pain relief.

A fifth type of market adjustment, the use of clubs, was also discussed in Chapter 5 as a form of voluntary action. Goods and services that are excludable to nonmembers lend themselves to this form of provision. Although clubs are likely to be nonprofit, they are marketlike in the sense that consumers are free to join, nonmembers can be excluded, and members are required to pay. A club may be literally that, a country club or a tennis club, it may be a homeowners' association responsible for buildings and grounds, or it may be a group of investors who pool information in making investments.

7.5 The Demands by Firms for Political Action

Anthony Downs made little mention of how business firms might influence political outcomes, although he recognized that interest groups representing firms may be an important factor in the conduct of government. Some would argue that the major historical role of government in the United States has been to protect and enhance business. In any event, we need to recognize how business firms affect the political process and how they adapt to political outcomes. This will be developed in two stages, first by comparing firms and consumers, then by considering rent-seeking.

7.51 General Adaptations

Business firms are actually quite similar to consumers in the types of adaptations that can be made to unsatisfactory political outcomes. They can adapt through the political process, through the market, or both. An obvious difference is that firms aren't flesh and blood—they can't vote—but they can encourage their employees to vote in certain ways. They can also make or withhold contributions to candidates, parties, and issues. And they can become members of large and small interest groups, thereby inviting or avoiding the free-rider problem, just like consumers.

Within the realm of market adaptations, firms can take actions to buy what governments might have provided but didn't provide. They, too, can buy market substitutes such as security services. Firms may be large enough that they will take certain actions without seeking public-sector support. For example, a firm might build a waste-treatment facility or a railroad spur. This firm might be the primary user of these services; to ask government for financial support might not make the voters very happy. If faced with the possibility that the firm might move to another location, however, local and state governments may be persuaded that they should, in fact, build the railroad spur and the waste-treatment plant for the firm. Unless they are highly dependent on natural or human resources that are unique to a geographic area, firms may be able to extract public services from the voters in exchange for a commitment not to leave the community.

Like consumers, firms may also engage in illegal activities if they anticipate large enough gains in profits. These gains would have to be discounted for the adverse consequences of being caught. Tax evasion is a particular temptation for firms, as it is for consumers, and there are other temptations. Employing illegal aliens has taken a sharp upturn in recent years, and not just in agriculture. Prior to the Immigration Control and Reform Act of 1986, most of the penalties for violating the law were imposed on workers, often in the form of deportation. Now, employers who knowingly hire illegal aliens may be subject to fines and other sanctions.

Finally, clubs are as relevant to firms as to consumers as a means of adapting to political outcomes. The local Chamber of Commerce, that venerable business institution for protecting and enhancing the business interests of its members, is nothing more than a voluntary club that provides benefits that are at least partially excludable. Trade associations and other business groups are also clubs that rely on the voluntary membership and self-interest of members in working to enhance a collective interest.

7.52 Rent-Seeking

There is one other form of political adaptation, however, that usually differentiates profit-seeking firms from consumers. This is *rent-seeking*, or the expenditure of scarce resources to capture wealth transfers (Buchanan, Tollison, and Tullock, 1980). As another way of putting it, rent-seeking is attempting to use the political process to allow a firm or group of firms to earn economic returns in excess of their opportunity costs. Every factor of production that a firm uses has an opportunity cost, which is the amount it could earn in its next most profitable use. In a perfectly competitive economy, no factor of production would earn more than its opportunity cost; if it did, the excess return would be competed away by the entry of land, labor, or capital. So a firm may "seek rents," that is, try to earn more through political action than it could earn through market action.

Firms seek rents through markets as well as through the political process. Even textbook authors try to present their offerings in a way that will benefit them the most. The ultimate is to be a monopolist, the only source of supply for a product. This would allow output to be restricted and the price to be set above the marginal costs of production (Figure 3.5). Economic rents can thus be generated. Pure monopolies are hard to come by, but firms and authors generally try to differentiate their products in some way to convince consumers that their products have unique advantages.

As long as the entry of new firms is possible and competitive markets prevail, the tendency to seek rents through markets will be channeled toward the public interest; additional output will be offered if the existence of rents provides an incentive to offer this output. Adam Smith would be pleased with rent-seeking if it took place through markets. The tendency of firms to seek rents through the political process, however, has been criticized by economists as being wasteful rather than productive. In 1967, Tullock focused on use of the political process by firms to gain import restrictions. If competitive markets were free to determine price and output, as in Figure 7.7, an efficient output of Q^* and an efficient price of P^* would prevail. A restriction of output to Q_r because of a tariff or a nonprice barrier to trade would cause the market price to rise to P_r, and the marginal cost to domestic producers would fall to P_c. At the margin, rents or excess returns of $ac = P_r P_c$ per unit of output would be created for producers.

Traditionally, economists have argued that such an output restriction would be wasteful because the net economic value to society could be increased by the triangular area abc if output was increased from Q_r to Q^*. The traditional interpretation of rectangle acP_cP_r has been that this area is simply an income transfer, that domestic producers would be better off by this amount because of the price increase, and that domestic consumers would be worse off by this amount. Tullock (1967), Krueger

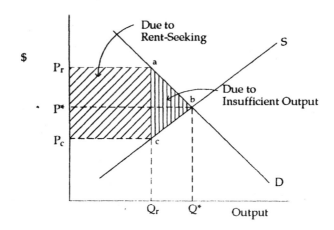

FIGURE 7.7 Two Sources of Efficiency Loss from an Output Restriction

(1974), and Posner (1975) have argued, however, that the triangle greatly understates the real extent of efficiency loss, and that the rectangle represents additional social waste that would result from rent-seeking when a few politically favored firms (or just one) would benefit from an output restriction. Therefore, a net waste, rather than simply an income transfer, would result; each firm would spend money to enhance its chances of being selected as one of the chosen few. Most firms, however, would fail.

City councilors, for example, decide to select one cable television firm to serve local needs. They feel, rightly or wrongly, that allowing more than one firm to offer these services would be duplicative and costly to consumers. Instead of using a bidding system, they announce that they will grant a single franchise, basing their decision on the expected quality of service, the range of programming, the general reputation of the firm, and the proposed charge for cable services. Because the city council would likely be responsive to the quality of the proposals and presentations, each competing firm would have an incentive to spend some fraction of acP_cP_r on preparing a proposal, making a presentation, and lobbying councilors. Only one firm can be awarded the franchise; thus, the costs incurred by unsuccessful firms may be wasted.

The amount that a firm would pay to seek these monopoly rents and whether the area acP_cP_r would be completely dissipated (wasted) by rent-seeking are two topics being debated in the literature. It is a fairly general conclusion, however, that there is substantial waste when scarce resources are devoted to influencing the decision of elected or appointed political suppliers rather than to producing output.[4] It is generally assumed that the maximum rent and the number of competing firms are known by all firms. If ten firms were bidding on rents worth $100,000 to the one winner, for example, and each firm thought it had the same chance of winning as the others, each might pay up to $10,000 to seek the monopoly franchise. In a statistical sense, this amount would be their expected gain. They would pay this much, however, only if they were risk-neutral with respect to money gains and losses. If they tended to avoid risk, if they put great importance on the negative consequences of losing $10,000, they would pay less than this amount. Their responses might also depend on whether there would be any carryover value to future franchise decisions in that city or in other cities. The ease of entry of other firms may also affect the extent of rent dissipation and the amount that competing firms would pay. Higgins, Shughart, and Tollison (1985), for example, argue that free entry will exactly dissipate monopoly rent if firms are risk-neutral.

The social implications of rent-seeking are enormous, because gaining and using political influence is not a cottage industry. As the next section will show, the increase in interest-group activity has been substantial over the past two decades. Many interest groups now exist to protect and enhance the financial position of firms, professions, workers, and regions. Although firms are most often characterized as seeking rents, others do their share in trying to create an artificial scarcity of substitutes to ensure themselves more favorable treatment. Firms seek import restrictions; domestic workers seek restrictions on illegal immigration. Cities or regions want to obtain a linear accelerator facility or a defense plant; professional groups want governments to certify competence and thus limit numbers. Each of these, if effective, tends to create scarcity, drive up the price received by the protected interest, and create rents for those who can influence public decisions.

7.6   The Demands by Interest Groups
for Political Action

The lines in Figure 7.1 indicate that interest groups may be involved in relaying the preferences of firms and citizens to elected and appointed political suppliers. The role of these groups in articulating political preferences and influencing policy has expanded greatly in recent years.[5] Several issues need to be addressed here, including how many interest groups there are (no one really knows), who they represent (nearly everyone, but some more than others), and why so many exist in view of the free-rider/collective action problem. We also need to recognize that interest groups shape the preferences of members as well as relay these preferences, and we need to consider how economic efficiency and equity may be affected by interest groups. An overriding issue, of course, is whether interest groups are good or bad, especially in view of the enormous amount of money they contribute to candidates through political action committees (PACs). We won't be able to resolve all of these issues because, in all honesty, economists are just now beginning to consider many of them. We'll at least cover some of the highlights here and in Chapter 8.

7.61 *Types and Numbers*

First, what exactly is an *interest group?* Jeffrey Berry, a political scientist, defines it as "an organized body of individuals who share some goals and who try to influence public policy" (1989, p. 4). Organization is the key; you may want cleaner air, but you aren't an interest-group member unless you join or contribute to an organization that pursues this goal. The broadest definition of an interest group embraces both voluntary and involuntary memberships, including, for example, workers who belong to closed-shop labor unions and pay dues to support labor union PACs. It also includes a variety of legal and institutional forms. Interest groups can be formed by citizens (Common Cause), by nonprofit organizations (Youth Club of America), by public-sector organizations (National Association of Counties), as well as by profit-seeking firms (Mortgage Bankers Association). There are obviously differences among interest groups in their size, resources, power, and political orientation, but the unifying element is that some degree of shared interest exists among members. Interest groups represent consumers, producers, industries, voters, workers, governments, regions, drainage basins, airsheds, and almost every other category that one can imagine.

Interest groups have a long tradition in the United States. One reason that has been given for their popularity is the weakness of political parties and the general lack of class distinctions (Wilson, 1981, p. 3). James Madison, in Number 10 of the Federalist Papers, foresaw that the new government would have to deal with "factions," as he called them, and that some would be much more powerful than others. As noted earlier, the French observer de Tocqueville (1835), writing forty years after our Constitution was written, noted the extensive use of voluntary associations by people in this country.

The overall number of interest groups has taken a sharp increase in recent years. Schlozman and Tierney (1986) and Walker (1983) found that 30 to 40 percent of the lobbying organizations in their studies were founded after 1960. Berry (1989) reports that the number of lawyers practicing in Washington, D.C., rose from 11,000 in 1972 to 45,000 in 1987. Not all of them are lobbyists, but most are. He also reports that the proportion of national trade associations having their headquarters in Washington, D.C., rose from 21 to 31 percent between 1970 and 1986. Not all the action has been national and corporate; Baumgartner and Walker (1988) found that 90 percent of the citizens in a pilot study of political participation were involved with interest groups. These people averaged over four affiliations per respondent; many of these affiliations were at the local level.

At the national level, there was a surge in numbers and strength of public interest groups and an increase in liberal legislation in the 1960s and 1970s as people learned how to use interest-group concepts. Common Cause and the Ralph Nader organizations, in particular, were highly successful in influencing policy. In turn, these events created a maze of regulations and a related awareness by business and conservative groups that they, too, needed to be better represented in Washington.

Berry argues that the interest-group idea has now been demystified. People and organizations have observed successful interest groups, borrowed ideas from them, learned to raise money, lobbied effectively, and communicated with the folks back home on the prospects for success and the urgency of support.

7.62 Reasons for Membership

Why do interest groups exist, especially when citizens and firms could free ride on the efforts of others? The collective-action problem has reared its head many times in these chapters. According to Berry, there have been three major explanations for interest-group membership. The first, now largely seen as inadequate, was David Truman's (1951) explanation that people who share a common interest will tend to come together to enhance that interest, particularly as society becomes more complex and dynamic and as economic disturbances enhance the need for collective action. This and its historical offspring, Dahl's much-heralded development of pluralism (1961), provided the main rationale for interest groups, which the second explanation, Mancur Olson's *Logic of Collective Action*, confronted head-on in 1965. As we saw in Chapter 5, Olson observed that there are individual interests as well as the common interest and that free-riding rather than group membership may occur if individual interests outweigh the collective interest. Free-riding may be expected, according to Olson, unless a group is small or unless it provides a private or excludable benefit, one that individuals could enjoy only if they belonged to the group.

Olson's explanation for interest-group membership was an improvement over the Truman-Dahl explanation, but it has been roundly criticized within and outside economics for its failure to predict. Simply put, many people do what Olson's model predicts they won't do: they vote, they sacrifice, they join, and they contribute when they could free ride. Understanding this contrary behavior is aided by a third explanation for interest-group membership: the entrepreneurial model of political scientist Robert Salisbury (1969). This model adds several dimensions of realism and humanness. Salisbury stressed the role of the interest group's organizer, the entrepreneur, in explaining how groups form and become effective. This approach stresses the ability of people such as Cesar Chavez, Ralph Nader, and John Gardner to overcome the free-rider problem in creating the United Farm Workers, Public Citizen (among others), and Common Cause, respectively. Charismatic though an entrepreneur might be, something may need to be offered to the prospective member in return for dues or contributions. Salisbury drew on an earlier typology by Clark and Wilson (1961) to identify three types of benefits that help explain interest-group membership and to further understand the inadequacies of the Olson model. Various mixes of the three types of benefits may be available with different interest groups; few groups offer only one type of benefit.

Olson's model stresses the first type, the *material benefit*. An interest group may be able to offer a material benefit, something that is tangible, excludable, and not forthcoming to a prospective member if that person or firm doesn't join the group. Information in the form of a periodical or newsletter is a common material benefit. Environmental interest groups, in particular, have attractive publications. Personal services may be even more important to members. The American Association of Retired Persons (AARP) has a membership of over 28 million members, many of whom join to obtain medical insurance policies, tours and vacation trips, discount pharmacy services by mail, and other commercial discounts (Berry, 1989; Walker, 1983).

The second type of benefit offered by interest groups is a *purposive benefit*, an intangible reward associated with an ideological or value-oriented goal. Saving whales, preventing abortion, and supporting public radio are examples of causes that people support even though they know that their contribution is a pittance and that the benefits of successful group action are nonexcludable. If public radio's pitch for funds is successful, I can free ride by simply tuning to that station. But if I contribute, I will have obtained a purposive benefit or avoided guilt, however one chooses to look at it. And if I can contribute at a low cost, I'll feel even better. Weisbrod and Dominguez (1986) show that the lower the price of obtaining a purposive benefit (the lower the cost of contributing specifically toward the purpose of an interest group) and the higher one's income, the more likely one will join.

The third type of benefit in Salisbury's system is a *solidary benefit*. This type of benefit relates to the social rewards for being part of the process of working toward goals or outcomes. This means the use of one's time, not just money. As Berry points out, "For many Americans . . . mailing a check off to Washington is not enough—they want to get involved" (1989, p. 55). Certain purposive benefits can be obtained by contributing money, but solidary rewards can only be gained by those who invest themselves in a more personal way.

Are interest groups good or bad? This depends, in part, on how effective they are in aggregating the preferences of their members and relaying this information to elected and appointed political suppliers. In a world without interest groups, political suppliers would have a difficult time assessing the preferences of constituents. The economic disincentives for many individuals and small firms to reveal their preferences could be so large that even well-meaning political suppliers would be hard put to decide what the public wants. In this sense, interest groups tend to enhance economic efficiency by revealing and relaying preferences.

Because members of interest groups are nearly always self-selected, however, it may not be clear whose preferences are aggregated or how well the interest group represents some larger segment of society. To what extent does the American Association of University Professors (AAUP) represent the preferences of college teachers? To what extent does the American Farm Bureau (AFB) represent farmers? Berry suggests that pluralism has been an attractive idea to political scientists because it is based on the notion, or more accurately the hope, that interest groups play a countervailing and consensus-building role. This is comforting because it suggests equity and even equality. If, however, the reality is frequent raids on the public treasury, benefiting the few at the expense of the many, then interest groups contribute to inefficiency rather than efficiency. We will return to this issue in the next chapter.

7.7   The Supply of Political Action by Legislators

In developing some basic concepts of legislative government, we started with the demand for political action, looking at the preferences, options, and constraints on citizens, firms, and interest groups. Let's again consider preferences, options, and constraints, but this time for elected political suppliers. In Chapter 8, we'll begin to put demand and supply together; then we'll add complexity in Chapters 9 and 10 by introducing the appointed political suppliers.

7.71   The Desire for Reelection

Before we start thinking about the supply side, remember that it is fundamental to ask exactly what good or service would be supplied, by whom, and why. Governments supply a wide range of goods and services such as postal services and roads, but they also "supply" laws and regulations. These, too, can be viewed as goods and services because they create utility or disutility for people. The passage of a law requiring all auto passengers to use seat belts, for example, is a good or service, although opponents might call it a disservice. The law provides a nonexcludable good if it applies to everyone riding in an auto, although the exemption of certain types of passengers (very small children, for example) would change the nature of the good.

The second question, By whom is the service provided? relates to the identity of the supplier. In contrast to market supply, political supply is defined in terms of promises of future outcomes by elected suppliers, either as individual legislators or as a group. Anthony Downs's observation that parties "formulate platforms to get elected" has an eternal ring of truth. Downs viewed the political party as a team of suppliers, even though he didn't look closely at the interactions and reciprocities among individual legislators. The relationship between the politician and the party is a central issue to most political scientists, but the role of the party is not yet well defined in the economic literature on collective choice. Thus, our focus will be on the individual candidate or officeholder. One reason for this is that political parties aren't very important at some levels of collective choice. They don't exist for country clubs, for example, and they aren't a factor for elected positions in many local governments, particularly school boards and city councils. Political parties can also be viewed, as a first approximation, as a particular type of interest group. Lindsay and Maloney (1988), for example, contend that political parties function as bargaining agents for groups of legislators who want to extract wealth from interest groups in exchange for providing vote support.

The third question is, Why would the service be supplied? The approach here is in terms of self-interest. Instead of assuming that elected suppliers will seek the common good, collective choice analysts assume that there is an *electoral objective*, that elected suppliers will attempt to maximize the probability of their election or reelection. Breton (1974) suggested that an elected political supplier "can be characterized by a utility function defined for a probability of reelection (or election) variable and for variables such as personal pecuniary gains, personal power, his own image in history, the pursuit of lofty personal ideals, his personal view of the common good, and others which are peculiar to each politician" (p. 124). Breton's model is

$$U_p = U_p(\pi, a_m), \tag{7.3}$$

where U_p is the utility of the elected supplier, π is the subjective probability of election or reelection, and the a_m's are the other variables that Breton mentions. The recent collective choice literature is sprinkled with terms that flesh out this formulation. Legislators have *policy preferences*, for example, if they prefer some policies over others rather than simply serve as a vehicle by which constituent demands can be met. It is plausible, then, that legislators, like voters, are really utility maximizers rather than simply vote maximizers.

Equation 7.3 is a very broad and general formulation, of course, and it is consistent with many types of behavior; these range from maximizing legal and illegal wealth, on one hand, to being a sacrificial lamb for a lost political cause, on the other. If either extreme is followed, however, there will be a reduction in the probability of reelection. Most elected suppliers follow a strategy that lies somewhere between the extremes. The pragmatic basis for Equation 7.3 is that to pursue any of the other goals, one has to first be reelected or elected. That is, (re)election is simply a means to power, wealth, fame, service, sacrifice, or duty. If you truly want to serve the people of your district, you have to gain and stay in office to do it. And if you choose to take bribes, you have to gain and stay in office to do that.

7.72 Many Demands, but Only One Quantity

An elected supplier has to attract a majority of the votes if he or she wants to gain or retain office, but there is often a *public good constraint* on how many votes can be attracted; many things that are supplied by collective action, particularly laws and regulations, become public goods once they are supplied. They may not always remain public goods; indeed, converting public goods to private goods for the benefit of selected constituents is a fundamental strategy among legislators.

Once a collective decision has been made and implemented through regulation, one level or one quantity is supplied to all. That is, a public good constraint exists. Unless the law says otherwise, my sixty-mile-per-hour speed limit is your sixty-mile-per-hour speed limit. If preferences and incomes differ among voters, the existence of a nonexcludable and nonrival public good—the speed limit in this case—means that some voters will be undersupplied with the public good and some will be oversupplied (Breton, 1974). A sixty-mile-per-hour highway speed limit is much too slow for some people, much too fast for others. A public school with aging facilities and a 30:1 student-teacher ratio may be viewed by some as "too fancy" even though it may be seen as inadequate by others.

Suppose that two voters have different demands for fire-protection services, D_1 and D_2, because of differences in wealth and property values (Figure 7.8). There is clearly a public good aspect to the city's fire-protection capability; this capability is available to any and all citizens, but a limited number of engines and fire fighters may be available for use at any one time. Call this quantity Q_bQ_b; it isn't a supply function because the output of services doesn't depend on price; rather, it indicates the availability of services to a resident.

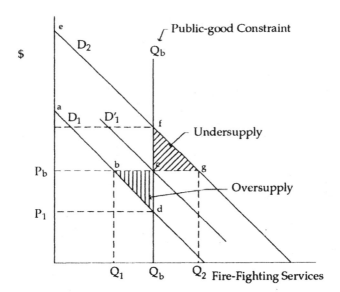

FIGURE 7.8   Undersupply and Oversupply of a Public Service

Assume that the two voters are charged the same unit price, P_b, for fire protection. This would imply equal tax bills for the two because the quantity (availability) is the same for both. At this price, however, the low demander would prefer a lesser quantity, Q_1; he is oversupplied with fire protection at price P_b and quantity Q_b. The consumer's surplus that he would have enjoyed at Q_1, area abP_b, is reduced by what amounts to a negative consumer's surplus of bcd due to the oversupply of fire-fighting services. All units between Q_1 and Q_b cost him more than they are worth. The high demander is coerced by an undersupply of the service. At price P_b, she would be willing to purchase an even larger quantity, Q_2, but she receives only quantity Q_b. She still receives a consumer's surplus, area $efcP_b$, but even more surplus could be added (area fgc) if the city increased the output of services from Q_b to Q_2.

Between quantities Q_1 and Q_2, the elected supplier faces a no-win range of output. Neither consumer is in equilibrium; both are coerced by being unable to have their preferred quantity. Very often there is a real public good dimension to services provided by government. They may be nonexcludable because of cost considerations, as with air quality, or more likely, they are simply defined as nonexcludable because we don't want to exclude anyone. Fire protection, recreation facilities, and libraries are usually available to all, whether they want them or not. Laws, directives, and regulations also have public good dimensions if they apply to everyone; changing them will make some people better off and some worse off. Stricter enforcement of immigration laws, for example, will raise wage rates and create an additional producers' surplus for domestic workers, but it will reduce the producers' surplus for those who hire, transport, and employ the illegal aliens. The creation of a new wilderness area will add consumers' surplus for wilderness users, but it will reduce producers' surplus for workers and owners of lumber mills.

The fact that there is a public good nature to many things that governments do means that no one will get all the votes, and indeed, no one expects to. One view of the dominant electoral objective is to maximize political support as represented by a large vote margin. An alternative view is that under majority rule, a candidate will seek to reduce coercion on only those citizens whose support is crucial to reelection (Breton, 1974, pp. 140-141). If one was to "win big," this might be seen as a mandate for certain policies, but candidates don't necessarily need to win big. They do need to win, however, and one vote over half is still a win under majority rule.

There are several ways that elected suppliers can reduce coercion among voters whose support is needed, but it is important to note that a substantial amount of *electoral slack*, or sluggishness, can exist in the political process (Breton, 1974).[6] Four things contribute to this; each offers some protection to an elected supplier. The first element of slack is majority rule itself. Forty-nine percent of those voting can be highly upset with an incumbent yet unable to remove her through voting. In a close race, coercion need be reduced only on a few voters for an incumbent to win. The second element of slack is that elections are infrequent; few electoral terms at any level of government are less than two years. The length of term could be shorter under a parliamentary system where elections can be called by the ruling party, but in fact, these terms may be longer than under our own system. Third, voter preferences are uncertain and it is time-consuming for a supplier to discover these. Fourth, governments produce a wide variety of goods and services, not just a few, and the level of many of these can be manipulated by incumbents or promised by challengers. Breton calls this last element, *full-line supply*. He summarizes in this manner:[7]

> These three characteristics of the institutional framework share at least one thing: they all have the effect of shielding politicians and political parties from the preferences and the pressures of citizens. The shield is not a perfect one, of course, and the extent of its efficiency depends on the level at which the various characteristics are fixed, but unless unanimity prevails, the length of the election period is zero, and preferences count

for each and every public policy separately, politicians and political parties have a number of degrees of freedom at their disposal which they can use as they please. (p. 43)

The elected supplier's shield is not perfect; something must eventually be done, or promised, to reduce coercion on enough voters in order to be reelected. Because the problem of coercion often arises from the public good constraint shown in Figure 7.8, there are two major types of solutions available to elected suppliers. They can attempt to reduce the differences between the high and low demands, or they can treat the demanders differently. The first solution would alter demand functions, the second would adapt to them as they exist. Let's look at these solutions in turn, recognizing that elected suppliers might try both types of solutions.

Equalizing the Demands. One option for narrowing the differences in demands is *altering the preferences of demanders.* The purpose is to reduce coercion by shrinking the negative consumers' surplus for those who are oversupplied and to shrink the unrealized consumers' surplus for those who are undersupplied (Figure 7.8). This involves convincing the low demanders that they would benefit by a larger amount, that, for example, their demand function should be D_i'. Once convinced, their negative consumers' surplus disappears and the elected supplier has found a friend. Voters can be influenced in a variety of ways. Some public programs and outputs may become more desirable than they had first thought; putting a man on the moon might have some spin-off effect after all. Convincing the oversupplied that their demands should be lessened, however, might involve appeals to patriotism, patience, or concerns about cost.

A second option for narrowing differences in demands is *redefining political issues,* something that elected suppliers do by forming coalitions. The lesser demand function for fire-fighting services might be only D_1 unless an elected supplier can anticipate that it would be even greater (D_i') if emergency medical care and ambulance services were also available through the fire department. This might coalesce two related demands—the demand for fire protection and the demand for emergency medical care—and thus reduce dissatisfaction with the oversupply of fire protection.

Different Treatments for Different Demanders. The second type of solution is to treat the high and low demanders differently, that is, to adapt to voter preferences rather than try to change them. This can involve at least four options. The first is some form of *differential pricing.* If the low demander in Figure 7.8 was charged a price of only P_1 instead of P_b, he would gain a consumer's surplus of P_bbdP_1, as well as escape the negative consumer's surplus triangle, bcd. But this option isn't cost-free; fewer taxes mean fewer services for someone. Fewer services to others may mean the loss of votes, or it may simply mean that additional coercion is imposed on people who would vote against the elected supplier in any event. Majority rule doesn't have to be fair!

The second option for adapting to different voter preferences, *income transfers*, can be used to give low demanders greater access to private goods. The low demander in Figure 7.8, the one who at price P_b would have preferred Q_1 units of fire protection, is effectively put on a lower indifference curve by the oversupply of Q_b (Figure 7.9). He would prefer to pay amount Y_0Y_1, but he finds that taxes have reduced his income by some larger amount, Y_0Y_2. If the low demander's vote was crucial to reelection, an income transfer of $Y_3Y_2 = jc$ would remove this coercion by reducing his tax burden. This could be done, for example, through tax exemptions that would be favorable toward those with low demands. Again, the problem for the political supplier is the vote loss that may be associated with the reduction in public services that would have been provided by the lost tax revenues.

A third option for elected suppliers is *providing other public services* that benefit crucial voters. Use of this option allows those who are coerced by the oversupply or undersupply of one good to gain consumers' surplus by the provision of another good. The problem, again, is how to do this

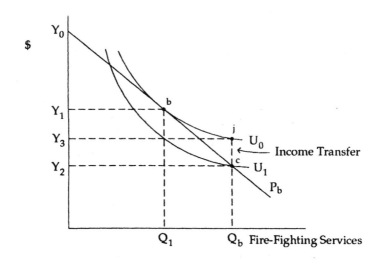

FIGURE 7.9 Reducing Coercion Through Income Transfers

without increasing the coercion on enough other voters that it becomes a self-defeating proposition for the supplier.

A fourth option for adapting to different voter preferences is *selective law enforcement*. For example, legislators could cause administrators to delay or forgo the collection of taxes from the low demander. The law could also be interpreted such that the low demander would not be penalized if he paid a lesser tax than the high demander (P_1 rather than P_b in Figure 7.8). As with the other options, less tax revenue means fewer public services for someone else, which may mean a loss of votes.

There is thus a series of adjustments that can be made to existing demands, all of which revolve around different treatment for different types of people. Each adjustment reduces coercion on some voters at the expense of increasing coercion on others. To gain reelection, an elected supplier has to decide which of these options is most appropriate. A utilitarian supplier, as we noted in Chapter 4, would attempt to balance the utility gained by constituents against the utility lost. The self-interest model, however, says that an elected political supplier will weigh the likely vote gain against the likely vote loss and act accordingly, even if the net utility gains to constituents are negative.

7.73 Tax Policy and Legislative Self-Interest

Although elected suppliers could gain some votes by using the previous options, almost all options involve public spending. Allowing a low demander to pay a lower price, making a direct income grant, and providing an additional public service all involve a cost. The government would then have to print more money, borrow from the existing money supply, or raise taxes to finance this cost of reducing coercion on crucial voters.

Because of this, we need to consider a second major constraint facing elected suppliers: Each of the ways to finance the wooing of voters will make some other voters worse off and more likely to vote against them. Let's briefly consider some options for dealing with this. First, the money supply could be expanded. There are some major consequences, however, in doing this solely to meet short-term contingencies such as reelection instead of letting the money supply grow in an orderly manner dictated by population growth and economic growth. This is a complex question of macroeconomics, one we will bypass here. The size and growth of the national debt is also a major issue in macroeconomics. It is easy to see why elected suppliers might choose this option; future generations, those who can't vote in current elections, are left to pay the debt. For this reason, support for a constitutional amendment to require balancing the federal budget is an article of faith among conservative economists.

The option of raising taxes is the one that we will pursue here. As a matter of perspective, the federal government in 1990 raised \$479.1 billion in revenues from individual income taxes, \$108.5 billion from corporate income taxes, and \$37.3 billion from excise taxes on goods and services. In the same year, state and local governments raised \$181.4 billion from sales taxes, \$150.1 billion from property taxes, and \$106.2 billion in revenues from individual income taxes (*Survey of Current Business*, July 1991, Tables 3.2 and 3.3). There were other sources of tax revenues, including lotteries, but these were minor compared to the ones stated.

Each of these taxes has political and economic consequences, some of which are difficult to discern.[8] Without tackling all of these, which is a major task, let's look at some principles that elected suppliers have to consider in deciding whether and how to raise tax revenues.

The Deadweight Loss of a Commodity Tax. When a commodity tax such as a sales tax or an excise tax is levied, there is another loss over and above the amount of tax that is paid. This is called a *deadweight loss*; it happens because economic efficiency is reduced—the efficiency with which people make choices about consumption goods and labor supply, for instance. For convenience, think of goods and leisure as two commodities; goods are purchased with income, leisure is given up when labor is supplied. An income tax on labor earnings is thus a commodity tax on leisure.

Recall from Chapter 2 that a decline in price makes consumers better off, and that the change in utility can be expressed in dollar terms as an increase in consumers' surplus. For any individual, this is the maximum amount of money that he or she would be willing to give up to buy at the lower price. If the price fell from P_1 to P_0 in Figure 7.10, for example, the gain in consumers' surplus would be area P_1acP_0.[9]

A tax on a commodity has the opposite effect; it reduces consumers' surplus because the price of the commodity has effectively been increased. Suppose that the initial market price is P_0 but the government decides to add a tax of t for each unit of the commodity that is purchased. A consumer might have to pay \$0.25 more, for example, for each gallon of gasoline or each package of cigarettes. This has the effect of raising the price from P_0 to P_1 in Figure 7.10.[10]

Consumers of the good are clearly made worse off by this tax even though the government may put the tax revenue to good use. The extent to which consumers are made worse off by the tax (area P_1acP_0), however, is greater than the amount of tax revenue that the government receives (P_1abP_0). The difference, abc, is the deadweight loss of the tax. At the price of P_0, the net economic value of the good to society would be greatest at Q^*, where the good's marginal benefit to consumers just equals its marginal cost of production. Reducing consumption to Q_1 by

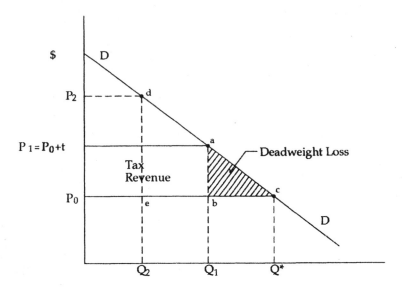

FIGURE 7.10 An Excise Tax on a Consumption Good

imposing a tax interferes with this equality by causing the marginal benefit of the good (*a*) to exceed its marginal cost (*b*).

E. J. Mishan offers this imaginative explanation of deadweight loss:

> The nature of this loss may . . . be better appreciated if you imagine the government, after collecting the tax . . . , allowing consumers to buy additional units . . . free of tax and, therefore, at the old price. . . . Consumers would then buy . . . additional units, and make a consumer surplus on them equal to the shaded triangle. . . . The fact that such a pleasing arrangement would be administratively too difficult and costly to undertake is what prevents consumers from recapturing the shaded triangle of consumer surplus once the tax is imposed. Hence the . . . sacrifice or deadweight loss arising from the . . . tax. (1982, p. 96)

Not only does deadweight loss occur when a commodity tax is imposed, it gets proportionally larger as the tax becomes larger, assuming that the demand function is linear. In Figure 7.10, for example, it can easily be seen that if the tax had doubled, if it had gone up by $0.50 per pack of cigarettes instead of $0.25 (to P_2 instead of P_1), the deadweight loss would have increased from area abc to a much larger amount, area dec.

Deadweight loss is important to the elected supplier because it represents a potential loss of votes. Unless the tax revenue of P_1abP_0 can be put to some use that generates new consumers' surplus or producers' surplus of P_1acP_0 or greater, a net loss will have occurred because of the tax. This may come back to haunt those elected suppliers who are responsible for it. Just creating a new surplus equal to the rectangle P_1abP_0 isn't enough; this makes up for the loss to tax revenue, but it leaves a deadweight loss that could mean defeat for an elected supplier.

The Advantage of a Lump-Sum Tax. In view of the deadweight loss, an elected supplier might wonder whether another type of tax would be better than a commodity tax. The reason that deadweight loss occurs with a commodity tax is that it interferes with individual choice, something that we can see in Figure 7.11. Assume that the initial price of a consumption good is P_0, but that a tax of t per unit effectively raises the price to $P_0 + t$. Instead of reaching A at utility level U_0, the consumer can now only reach B at utility level U_1. She now spends Y_0Y_2 income and consumes Q_1 of the good; a portion of her total expenditures (BC) goes to the government for taxes.

What would happen, however, if this same amount of money (BC) was raised by the government as a *lump-sum tax*? This would allow the consumer to make her consumption decisions on the basis of P_0, the original price. The consumer would be happy to do this, because it would interfere less with consumer choice and allow her to reach a higher utility level than U_1. To see this, draw a new price line (P_0') parallel to the initial

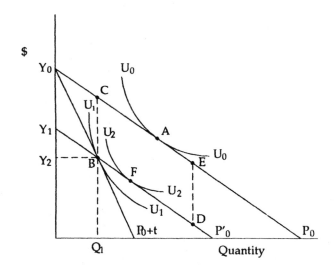

FIGURE 7.11 Consumption: The Advantage of a Lump-Sum Tax

price line (P_0) and below it by an amount equal to BC = Y_1Y_0 = DE. At B, the slope of the (U_1) indifference curve would exceed the slope of the new price line (P_0'). As we saw in Chapter 2, this indicates that the marginal rate of substitution of money for the good is greater than the price of the good, and that the consumer would be better off by consuming more of the good, that associated with F. This would allow her to reach a higher utility level, U_2, than if a commodity tax were levied (U_1).

The idea of a lump-sum tax that doesn't interfere with consumer choice has held the interest of economists for a long time; it could also be of interest to elected suppliers because it is potentially a way out of the deadweight-loss situation. Figure 7.11 seems to suggest that a tax on income, rather than on commodities, might help resolve some reelection problems for elected suppliers. The problem with this idea is that income is an umbrella term; we actually earn income by supplying labor, investing money, clipping dividend coupons, stealing, or whatever. And, unfortunately for the elected supplier, a tax on any of the sources would interfere with individual choice and again lead to deadweight loss.

By far the largest source of personal income is from labor earnings, so let's consider a tax on this source of income. In Figure 7.12, the tax on

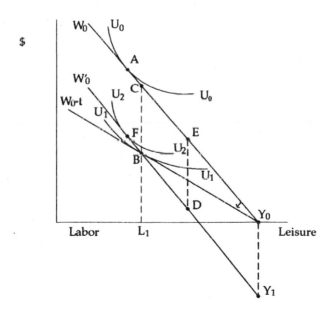

FIGURE 7.12 Labor Supply: The Advantage of a Lump-Sum Tax

labor earnings would shift the net wage rate from W_0 to $(W_0 - t)$, where t is the tax.[11] A worker whose earnings are taxed at the 28 percent marginal tax rate, for example, see his $10.00 hourly wage rate reduced to $7.20 per hour. At the lower wage, the worker might decide to work less and enjoy more leisure (B, compared to A). He would pay a tax of BC; this is the difference between the two wage lines at the L_1 allocation of labor. If, as an alternative to the tax on labor earnings, he could pay BC = ED = Y_0Y_1 as a lump-sum tax, he would choose to work more (F), make more money, and reach a higher utility level (U_2).

Like a tax on consumption goods, a tax on labor earnings would interfere with an individual's choice between income and leisure; thus, it would impose another form of deadweight loss. This suggests that deadweight loss is of general concern to a tax-and-spend motivated legislator, something that we'll return to in the next chapter. Isn't there a tax that doesn't have a deadweight loss? The answer: Only a *head tax* wouldn't distort choice and lead to inefficiency. If everyone could be taxed some specific amount for simply being or existing, inefficiencies would not arise because individual choice (except suicide) wouldn't be distorted by the tax. The problem with a head tax is that it isn't a very fair way to raise tax revenues; people vary greatly in their ability to pay a head tax. Instead, we have chosen to use taxes that are seemingly more related to the ability to pay (the income tax, for example) or to benefits received (the property tax, for example).

The Incidence of a Tax. Elected suppliers might also want to know how the distribution of producers' and consumers' surplus and deadweight losses would be affected by any tax that they might advocate. If suppliers were in good stead with producers but needed consumer support for reelection, they would not want consumers' surplus to fall sharply because of a tax.

The question of who actually pays a tax is one of *tax incidence*. In general, what matters are the price elasticities of supply and demand and the competitiveness of the markets, not what the law says about who should pay the tax or collect the tax. Assume, for example, that a state legislature mandates a new tax of $0.20 on each gallon of gasoline sold at retail. Retailers are obligated to collect the tax and send it to the state treasurer. To stave off irate buyers, retailers make sure that their gas pumps show the amount of the new tax. To satisfy the law, their remittances to the state treasurer would include the $0.20 tax per gallon times the number of gallons sold.

Who actually pays the tax? If the short-run demand for gasoline is highly inelastic, which is quite likely, and if the short-run supply of gasoline is fairly elastic, consumers will bear most of the tax burden in a competitive market (Figure 7.13). The unit tax of t = AB = EF = GH will

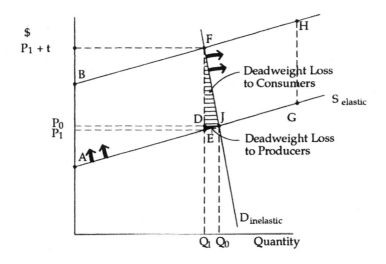

FIGURE 7.13. Tax Incidence: The Consumers Pay

be vertically added to the retailers' supply function; it represents an increase in cost of $0.20 per gallon. The new supply function (BFH) will intersect the demand function at Q_1; consumption will fall, but not by much because of the inelastic demand. At Q_1, the price of gasoline would have risen from P_0 to $P_1 + t$, which is almost the entire amount of the tax (EF). Consumers' surplus will have fallen by $(P_1 + t)FJP_0$; producers' surplus will have declined by a much smaller amount, P_0JEP_1.[12]

The retailer will send tax revenues of $(P_1 + t)FEP_1$ to the state treasurer; almost all of it will have been paid by the consumers. In addition, there will be a deadweight loss absorbed mostly by consumers (FDJ) rather than by producers (DEJ). One month before election is not a good time to propose a new gas tax.

Things can be even worse for consumers. If their demand is perfectly inelastic (vertical) and the dealers' supply function is perfectly elastic (horizontal), as suggested by the arrows in Figure 7.13, the tax will be borne totally by consumers. Consumption will remain unchanged if a tax is instituted; there will be no deadweight loss, just angry consumers who will be likely to vote.

If different supply and demand elasticities exist, the outcome will be quite different (Figure 7.14). Suppose that the demand functions for apple varieties grown in different production regions are highly elastic because consumers tend to substitute freely among them. A tax is imposed on apples from one of the regions to discourage the spread of a certain plant

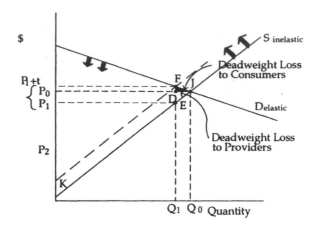

FIGURE 7.14 Tax Incidence: The Producers Pay

disease that exists in that region. Assume that the supply function from each region is inelastic. If the unit tax of $t = EF$ is added to the apple supply function for the region with the disease, the price for those apples will rise only slightly from P_0 to $(P_1 + t)$, and quantity will decline from Q_0 to Q_1. Consumers' surplus will fall by only $(P_1 + t)$ FJP_0, and producers' surplus will plummet by P_0 JEP_1. Producers will pay nearly all the tax; they will suffer from both deadweight loss and the reduction in producers' surplus. If the demand is perfectly elastic and the supply is perfectly inelastic, as suggested by the arrows, the producers will bear the entire tax.

Optimal Taxation. Despite the deadweight losses that are associated with commodity taxes, governments continue to use them to raise revenues. An elected supplier needs to understand, however, that the extent of deadweight losses, consumers' surplus losses, and producers' surplus losses can vary greatly for different commodities because of differences in demand and supply elasticities. For purposes of reelection, the loss of consumers' surplus because of a tax might be offset by gains in consumers' surplus elsewhere. Deadweight losses, however, cannot be offset because of their very nature. They reflect both a reduction in efficiency and a potential vote loss (we'll explore this further in Section 8.13).

Consider Figure 7.15, for example, where a unit tax of t is imposed on two commodities. The initial price for the two is the same (P_0). For convenience, point b lies on both demand functions at the point of initial equilibrium (P_0Q_0). The implicit supply function for either commodity is

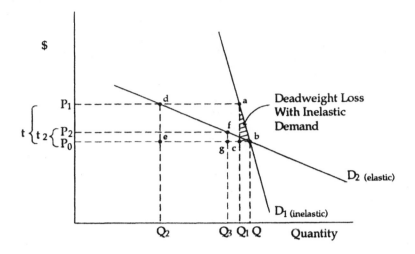

FIGURE 7.15. Optimal Commodity Taxation

P_0b without the tax and P_1a with the unit tax of $t = de = ac$. For the commodity with an inelastic demand, D_1, the tax generates revenues of P_1acP_0 and a deadweight loss of abc. The equilibrium quantity declines, but not by much because the commodity has few substitutes. The same tax, t, applied to the commodity with the more elastic demand, D_2, however, causes a much more radical change. Tax revenues will be only P_1deP_0, and quantity will fall to Q_2 because of the substitution of other products. The deadweight loss, dbe, is much larger in this case because consumers find that the tax has a much greater impact on consumer choice.

Imposing the same unit tax on these two very different commodities would cause very different deadweight losses to occur; the efficiency loss would be much greater for the commodity with the more elastic demand. Moreover, if votes tend to reflect deadweight losses, imposing the same unit tax might not be good strategy for an elected supplier. Both of these considerations point to an old idea called *optimal taxation,* which means to equalize the efficiency losses associated with different commodity taxes. If a lesser tax of $t_2 = fg$ is imposed on the D_2 demand, for example, the deadweight loss (fbg) will be closer in size to abc, the deadweight loss for the D_1 demand.

The mathematical basis for optimal taxation was derived by a British economist, Frank Ramsey (1927). The Ramsey rule is that commodity taxes should be inversely proportional to the demand elasticities if supply is perfectly elastic. If the demand elasticities for D_1 and D_2 are -0.25 and

-1.25, respectively, the tax on D_1 should be five times larger than the tax on D_2. Contrary to intuition, however, the size of the deadweight losses won't necessarily be equal. Instead, think of the rate at which deadweight losses would grow (as the tax increases) relative to the rate at which tax revenues would grow; this rate would be equated for all commodities that are taxed.

Keep in mind that the Ramsey rule is an efficiency rule, not a guide to equity. In fact, those commodities for which sales taxes have been used the most frequently—food, cigarettes, and liquor—are commodities with price inelastic demands, large revenue potentials, and small deadweight losses. Unfortunately, these tend to be commodities that also have income-inelastic demands, those for which consumption changes very little as incomes change due to taxation. This means that following the efficient Ramsey rule will cause us to have *regressive taxation*, that is middle- and upper-income groups will pay disproportionately small percentages of total tax revenues and lower-income groups will pay a disproportionately large percentage of total tax revenues.

7.8 Summary

Most rational choice models of legislative government follow the cue of Anthony Downs (1957), who argued that elected suppliers will formulate policies in order to win elections rather than win elections in order to formulate policies. This portrayal of representatives as self-interested isn't necessarily bad news for voters, however, if electoral competition can force voter preferences to be taken into account. The big question, of course, is the extent to which this happens.

The narrow logic of rational choice suggests that voters are apathetic and uninformed. Many have little incentive to vote or take other political action because they are individually unlikely to affect outcomes. As we saw in Chapter 5, however, many others choose *not* to free ride. Firms may be able to seek and obtain rents through political action, and the political demands of both firms and consumers may be reduced if market substitutes are available. Interest groups seem to be thriving, but they all have to overcome the collective action problem by providing material, purposive, or solidary benefits.

On the supply side, elected representatives have to reconcile diverse demands among the citizens with the fact that most laws, regulations, and funding levels become public goods once they are supplied. As a result, some people will be oversupplied with these goods, and others will be undersupplied. Vote totals can be affected by taxing and spending, and elected suppliers need to consider deadweight losses and the incidence of taxation as well as the extent of benefits from spending.

Terms and Concepts for Review

platform
expected party differential
demands for political action
rational apathy
political participation
rational voter hypothesis
market adaptations to political decisions
rent seeking
interest groups
material benefits
purposive benefits
solidary benefits
electoral objective
policy preferences
public good constraint
electoral slack
full-line supply
altering the preferences of demanders
redefining political issues
differential pricing
income transfers
providing other public services
selective law enforcement
deadweight loss
lump-sum tax
head tax
tax incidence
optimal taxation
regressive taxation

8

Legislative Government: Part 2

8.0 Bringing Supply and Demand Together

Having looked separately at the demand and supply of political action in Chapter 7, we can now bring them together. First, we will assume that legislative decisions are appropriately implemented by appointed political suppliers such as federal and state agency administrators, municipal employees, and school superintendents. In Chapter 9, we'll relax this assumption and recognize that these people may have goals and agendas of their own.

Several theoretical models of legislative government have been prominent in the literature on the economics of collective choice.[1] The first two that we discuss in this chapter deal with whether producers or consumers are favored by elected suppliers, the third model deals with interest groups more generally, the fourth considers the structure of taxes, and the fifth has a geographic focus. Each of these overlapping models has been influential in characterizing political processes, and each lends crucial insights into legislative government; but all need further synthesis and empirical testing.

After considering these models, we'll glance back at Chapter 6 for a refresher on ideology, then use this idea to build a model of economic markets for legislative activities, or for short, *legislative markets*. The demanders and suppliers of political action interact in these markets to create legislative outcomes. One major criticism of the five models has been that they are black boxes devoid of any real-world ways of making political decisions. Critics contend that the models may point to outcomes but do not explain how those outcomes are reached. Our model of legislative markets will need to identify how legislatures organize themselves to reach outcomes that link demanders and suppliers. In particular, we will draw on recent collective choice literature for a focus on the legislative committee system as a means for facilitating exchange.

8.1 Legislative Regulation

8.11 The Stigler Model: Producers Always Win

Elected political suppliers have to resolve conflicting demands within the electorate; this is true whether they are members of Congress, a city council, or a local school board. One common view of the three types of demanders—citizens, firms, and interest groups—however, portrays them in very different ways. According to this view, citizens have weak incentives to become informed and politically active. They may vote if the costs are low and election interest is high, but they will do little more. Free-riding is widespread, especially if clubs and market substitutes are available. Small firms, like citizens, are also politically inactive. Their owners may belong to the Chamber of Commerce for social reasons and to obtain material benefits, but not for political reasons. Large firms, according to this view, have more incentive to play an active political role. They have more at stake financially and they can impose greater threats on others. Because there are fewer firms in an industry, their costs of acting as a group are lower. Firms will not hesitate to seek rents; groups of firms will be able to seek rents even more effectively than individual firms. Citizen-based interest groups may have gained strength in recent years, but those representing business are still far more powerful.

It was from this general view that one of the earliest modern theories of *legislative regulation* arose.[2] It was George Stigler's contention that "regulation is acquired by the industry and is designed and operated primarily for its benefit" (1971, p. 3). Stigler saw two major ways that industry could gain by using the power of the state. The first is a direct money subsidy, an idea doomed to failure unless entry can be limited. As Jimmy Durante said long ago, "Everybody wants to get into the act!" The second and more effective way is to control the entry of new firms, or in more general terms, to limit output.[3] Stigler hypothesized that "every industry or occupation that has enough political power to utilize the state will seek to control entry" (p. 5). Various means could be used to accomplish this, including establishing protective tariffs and nontariff barriers to trade, requiring occupational licensing, making entry more expensive, limiting the creation of new firms, and segmenting markets in which different demands have different degrees of price responsiveness.

Stigler felt that producers have a clear advantage over consumers in affecting the legislative process. For one thing, firms are fewer in number; hence, they are easier and less costly to organize. Firms within any industry are likely to be more homogenous than their consumers, and they may already be organized into trade associations that provide private goods or material benefits to members. Because they are fewer in number than consumers, firms have higher per capita gains than are imposed on consumers as per capita losses. Therefore, there are great differences in the incentive for action. A consumer might grumble about having to pay an extra dollar for shoes because of a tariff on imported hides, but he probably won't fight the tariff politically. Most likely, he won't even be aware of it. A firm, however, might benefit greatly at a dollar more per pair because it will sell many pairs of shoes.

In Stigler's view, elected suppliers are usually ready to cooperate with the producers if it means political support, campaign contributions, future employment, or, for some, bribes. As self-interested individuals, elected suppliers respond to those demands that surface in the strongest and most coherent form. These are the demands of producers because of their small numbers, their superior organization, and their high per capita gains.

8.12 The Peltzman Model:
Either Producers or Consumers Can Win

In many respects, the Stigler model of producer domination of the legislative process simply formalized what a lot of people already "knew," that firms are big, bad, and bold and that consumers are weak and disorganized. This has a familiar ring, one sounded most loudly in this country in the 1890s populist movement, which reflected a feeling that big business is bad and that small business, agrarians, consumers, and workers are good. And there is much evidence in recent times that supports the Stigler model. Robert Crandall of the Brookings Institution (1984), for example, has estimated that voluntary import restraints by Japanese automakers, much encouraged by U.S. carmakers, added nearly $1,000 to the price of an average domestic car in the early 1980s. Americans paid dearly through this loss of consumers' surplus.

For every attractive theory, however, there are counterexamples that cast doubt on whether the theory is right. If producers are always dominant, for example, one wouldn't have expected to see the detailed and controversial regulations that have been generated for the workplace by the Occupational Safety and Health Administration (OSHA). One wouldn't have expected the whole series of business deregulations in the mid- to late 1970s in such areas as brokerage commissions, airlines, cable television, and natural gas and oil pricing, among other things (Magat, 1981). And one wouldn't have expected passage of the Tax Reform Act of 1986, an act that shifted the tax burden from households to business in a substantial way, simplified the tax code, eliminated major tax loopholes, and prompted the book by Birnbaum and Murray (1988) with its classic title *Showdown at Gucci Gulch*.[4]

Each of these examples suggests that individuals rather than firms can sometimes be dominant, whether in the role of workers, consumers, or taxpayers. Because of this, an extension of Stigler's model was proposed by a colleague at the University of Chicago, Sam Peltzman (1976). Equation 8.1 and Figure 8.1 are representations of the Peltzman model. He concluded that legislative regulation can favor producers *or* consumers, depending on the circumstances. The Stigler model had focused on the demand for regulation and on the advantages to firms of limiting entry; Peltzman put equal weight on the supply side, on whether it would be in the self-interest of elected suppliers to provide limitations on entry. If the gains to producers are large and if consumers aren't likely to retaliate at election time, restricted entry may be supplied by legislators. If these conditions aren't met, restricted entry may be denied.

Peltzman claimed that a legislative regulator would seek to maximize a net vote margin or majority (M) in his favor:[5]

$$M = [n \bullet f] - [(N - n) \bullet h], \qquad (8.1)$$

where   n   =   number of potential beneficiaries
           f   =   probability that the beneficiaries will grant financial and political support to the regulator
           N   =   group size
     N - n   =   number of nonbeneficiaries
           h   =   probability that the nonbeneficiaries will actively oppose the regulator.

Both the Stigler and Peltzman models recognize that restrictions on entry are often proposed and that these would transfer wealth from consumers to producers. During the early 1980s, for example, the U.S. Coalition for Fair Canadian Lumber Imports, a group of 650 softwood lumber manufacturers and nine trade associations, asked Congress to impose a tariff on softwood lumber imports from Canada. They argued, with some degree of justification, that federal and provincial governments in Canada had provided large subsidies to Canadian timber companies by selling publicly owned timber at below-market values and by providing industry promotion, low-interest loans, and tax incentives. The U.S. group felt that these subsidies had allowed the Canadian share of the U.S. softwood lumber market to increase from 19 percent in 1975 to about 31 percent in 1982. In view of this, they asked for a whopping 65 percent tariff on Canadian imports of this commodity, an act that the National Association of Home Builders (NAHB) felt would have driven

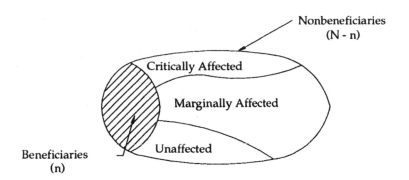

FIGURE 8.1 Peltzman's Theory of Legislative Regulation

up the price of an $80,000 house by $5,000 (Salem, Ore. *Statesman-Journal*, March 9, 1983). This would have been a sizable wealth transfer to U.S. producers.

The effect of the proposed tariff would have been to restrict entry and raise the price of lumber products; this can be shown quite readily (Figure 8.2). Assume that the domestic demand for lumber is shown by DD. The domestic supply function, SS, indicates that at quantities greater than Q_1, it would be cheaper to import Canadian lumber than to use our own. Assume, for simplicity, that the import supply function (S_i) is flat, or perfectly elastic; this means that we could buy any given amount of Canadian lumber without affecting its price. In equilibrium, total domestic consumption would be Q_4, of which $Q_4 - Q_1$ would be imports and $Q_1 - Q_0$ would be from domestic sources.

Now, suppose that a 65 percent tariff is imposed on Canadian imports. This would have several effects. First, it would raise the price of lumber from S_i to S_i'. Second, it would reduce the level of Canadian imports from $Q_4 - Q_1$ to $Q_3 - Q_2$ and it would increase the domestic share of the market from $Q_1 - Q_0$ to $Q_2 - Q_0$. This would put more U.S. mill workers to work, a happy situation for northwestern and southern congressmembers. Third, it would allow the shaded area (fdhg) to be collected as a tax by the U.S. Treasury; this would be equal to the amount of Canadian imports ($Q_3 - Q_2$), multiplied by the tariff ($S_i' - S_i$). Thus, the beneficiaries of the tariff would include domestic mill workers, local communities, and domestic taxpayers.

A fourth effect of the tariff gets more directly to the transfer of wealth that is central to the Peltzman model. With the tariff, the loss of

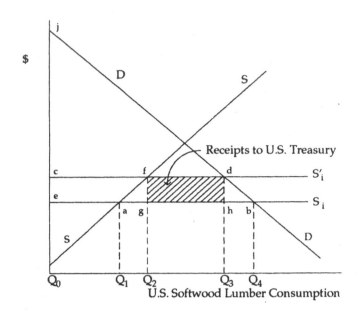

FIGURE 8.2 The Effect of a Tariff on Canadian Lumber Imports

consumers' surplus to domestic users of softwood lumber products would be the area cdbe. Prices would go up and usage would fall; as the NAHB observed, a typical new house would cost $5,000 more. A part of this loss, the shaded area fdhg, would become new U.S. Treasury receipts, but another large part of it (cfae) would be transferred to domestic producers as an increase in producers' surplus.[6] This is the amount that would result from successful rent-seeking by the coalition of producers.

This last effect shows that U.S. lumber producers would have been major beneficiaries of the tariff. It also illustrates the new wrinkle introduced by the Peltzman model, that there are a variety of nonbeneficiaries for any proposed action with the tariff. These range from people who would be critically affected, like young families struggling to buy their first home, to those who would be less affected and those who would be unaffected. Any economist worth his or her salt, of course, could use appropriate supply and demand diagrams to show that very few people would be unaffected by a 65 percent tariff on imports of a basic building material. The critical factor for legislative regulation is whether these effects are perceived by the beneficiaries and nonbeneficiaries, and what actions, if any, are taken as a result. Two actions are suggested by two of the terms on the right-hand side of Equation 8.1; one (f) indicates support by beneficiaries, the other (h) indicates opposition by beneficiaries.

The Support Function. Peltzman shows the support function as

$$f = f(g), \tag{8.2}$$

where g is the per capita net benefit

$$g = \frac{T - K - C(n)}{n} \tag{8.3}$$

and T = total wealth transfer to the beneficiaries
  K = total dollar amount spent by beneficiaries for political support of the regulator
  C(n) = costs of organizing and delivering this support
  n = number of beneficiaries.

The gain to a typical producer would thus equal the wealth transfer minus campaign contributions and organizational costs, divided by the number of producers. The probability of support by beneficiaries would rise with the per capita net benefit, but at a decreasing rate (Figure 8.3). With respect to the lumber example, domestic suppliers would perceive that the tariff would have a favorable effect on them. The greater the increase in producers' surplus (T), the more political contributions (K) they would be willing to make to the regulators. The lumber manufacturers, only 650 in number, wouldn't account for many votes, but their campaign contributions could be effective in influencing other voters.

Organizational costs are also important in determining per capita gains. Established trade associations might have a substantial advantage over fledgling consumer groups in mobilizing support, excluding free riders, and delivering campaign contributions. These costs would probably rise with the size and diversity of any group, whether the beneficiaries were producers or consumers. Increasing the number of beneficiaries (n) has two opposing effects: One would broaden the base of support for delivering campaign contributions (K); the other would reduce per capita gains for any given wealth transfer. In the lumber example, each of the nine trade associations had the option of doing its own political thing; the fact that they formed a coalition suggests that broadening the support base was more important than the dilution of gains.

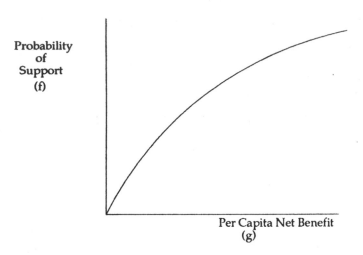

FIGURE 8.3 The Support Function

The Opposition Function. Now, let's consider the probability that nonbeneficiaries would actively oppose a regulator who favored the tariff. The opposition function can be shown as

$$h = h(t,z), \tag{8.4}$$

where

$$t = \frac{T}{B(N - n)} \tag{8.5}$$

and

$$z = \frac{K}{(N - n)} \tag{8.6}$$

with
t = an implicit tax on nonbeneficiaries
B = a typical consumer's surplus
$N - n$ = number of nonbeneficiaries
z = voter-education expenditures per capita.

The implicit tax relationship, Equations 8.4 and 8.5, can be understood with the help of Figure 8.2. The implicit tax (t) on a nonbeneficiary, Equation 8.5, is the percentage reduction in a typical consumer's surplus; or the ratio of area cdbe to area jbe. The reduction in consumers' surplus due to the tariff is area cdbe; this is the approximate amount of Peltzman's variable T, the dollar amount transferred to beneficiaries.[7] The extent of overall consumers' surplus prior to the tariff is area jbe; this, in Peltzman's terms, is the typical consumer's surplus multiplied by the number of nonbeneficiaries (consumers). Thus, the implicit tax imposed by the tariff reflects a percentage reduction in well-being of the non-beneficiaries.

If the implicit tax is viewed as zero, or at least as very small by those consumers who would be unaffected or marginally affected, the probability of their opposition to the tariff is very small (Figure 8.4). Those who would be more critically affected, such as first-time home buyers, would likely be more aware of the tariff and much more likely to vote against the regulator.[8] Voters can sometimes be persuaded, however, that something they're concerned about won't hurt them and perhaps will even be good for them. The idea behind Equation 8.6 and Figure 8.5 is that the probability of opposition by nonbeneficiaries can be reduced by spending money to "educate" them. One can imagine a TV blitz saying that a Canadian lumber tariff would create jobs for U.S. construction workers and mill workers but saying nothing about increased lumber prices and higher costs of home ownership.

Voter-education expenditures, K, would be financed by producers through a portion of the wealth transfer, T. Estimates aren't available for T or K in the lumber import situation. It has been reported in another case, however, that eighteen political action committees (PACs) of U.S. dairy cooperatives contributed $1.8 million to various congressmembers

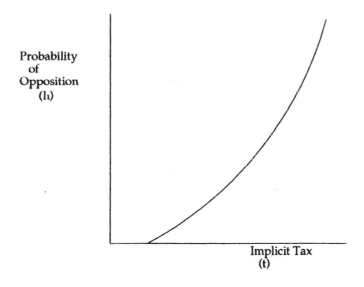

FIGURE 8.4 The Opposition Function (I)

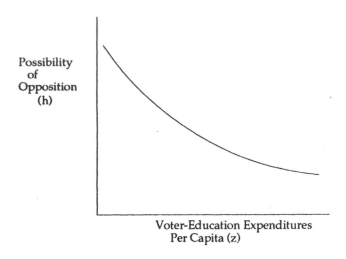

FIGURE 8.5 The Opposition Function (II)

in the 1982 election (Donahue, 1983). This was more than the amount contributed by PACs representing homebuilders, used-car dealers, autoworkers, or physicians, all of whom spent freely in recent elections. The same source reports that about $2.4 billion was spent by the federal government in 1983 to keep dairy product prices above market equilibrium levels and thus benefit dairy producers. Domestic lumber producers may not have faced these particular T and K values, but the crude ratio of $1.8 million in costs to $2.4 billion in gains to dairy producers suggests that the economic returns from rent-seeking may be substantial.

To recap the lumber import example: The Peltzman model suggests that producers may form a coalition to press for import restrictions if they anticipate a net financial gain, even after adding to the campaign coffers of the regulators. The regulators have to make decisions on three variables: the size and composition of the beneficiary group (n), the amount of the wealth transfer (T), and the amount of political support (K). There is an upper limit to what producers can get. If the tariff is set too high, too many nonbeneficiaries will lose, the current losers will become even larger losers, and the regulator will begin to hear the opposition more clearly. It may turn out that the best tariff increase from the regulators' point of view is *no* tariff increase, that any wealth transfer would bring about more opposition than support. An in-between situation might be that certain types of Canadian lumber would be excluded from the proposed tariff. This would reduce the values of all three decision variables. By modifying the price increase, a partial exclusion would reduce the size of wealth transfer, the number and per capita gains of beneficiaries, and thus the extent of political support, but it would also reduce opposition to the measure.

The general conclusions of the Peltzman model are that regulators won't always serve producers, that consumers and other less-organized interests may prevail if regulatory effects are perceived in certain ways. In fact, neither producers nor consumers will usually get all they want. This is shown in Figure 8.6, which shows that increasing the implicit tax rate through a higher lumber tariff causes increasing marginal political costs (C_0) and decreasing marginal political gains (G_0) for the regulator. (Peltzman derives these two functions mathematically from the relationships shown in Figures 8.3 through 8.5.) *Political equilibrium for a regulator* is reached at t_0, where some marginal costs are indeed imposed on nonbeneficiaries through loss of consumers' surplus. At t_0, however, the regulator's marginal political gains are still positive even though the producers would rather be at t_m, which is an even higher tariff. Figure 8.6 also allows us to see that a self-interested regulator could refuse to implement a tariff if the marginal political costs (C_1) were higher than the marginal political gains at all tax rates. In other words, if the two functions never cross, nothing will happen.

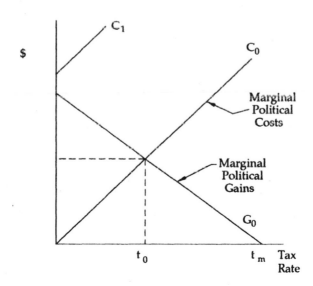

FIGURE 8.6 Political Equilibrium for the Regulator

8.13 The Becker Model:
Pressure Groups and Efficient Wealth Transfers

The third model of legislative regulation, this one by Gary Becker (1983, 1985), is more general in its application, more sweeping in its conclusions, and more controversial than the two preceding models. Rather than dealing just with producers and consumers, Becker recognizes that a variety of what he calls "pressure groups" (we have called them interest groups) can exert influence on legislators in attempting to gain or avoid regulation. Although regulation can occur in a variety of forms, the outcome usually boils down to either granting an indirect subsidy or imposing an indirect tax on members of an affected pressure group. Limiting imports of Canadian lumber, for example, would provide a subsidy to U.S. lumber producers; the accompanying loss of consumers' surplus would, in effect, be a tax on consumers.

Political Pressure. The heart of the Becker model is on competition for political influence, or who gets the subsidies and how much, and who will bear the tax. Denoting subsidies and taxes by S and T, Becker defines an *influence function* (I) as

$$S = T = I\left(p_s, \ p_t, \ \frac{n_s}{n_t}\right),\tag{8.7}$$

where p_s and p_t are amounts of political pressures exerted by those receiving the subsidies and those bearing the taxes, respectively, and (n_s/n_t) is the relative number in each group (1988, p. 331). If two groups have conflicting interests, each will apply political pressure through the lobbying of legislators; this will affect the amount of pressure applied by the other interest group. Equilibrium levels of pressure will be reached, with each group applying an amount that is efficient from its own point of view.

For example, a proposal by producers to limit imports of a competing product would create a subsidy for these producers and give them an incentive to apply political pressure. This would create an indirect tax on users of the product, however, and thus an incentive for them to apply pressure to resist the import limitation. Each group has a production function for political pressure through campaign contributions, lobbying, and other expenditures of time and money (m_i). That is,

$$p_i = p_i\ (m_i, \ n_i), \text{ and } i = S,T\tag{8.8}$$

where $m_i = a_i\ n_i$, with a_i representing per capita contributions.

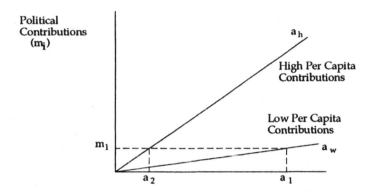

FIGURE 8.7. Two Sources of Political Pressure

The effectiveness with which an interest group can marshal and exert political pressure depends on the prospective gain to members of that group, but it also depends on whether the group can control free riding by its own members. Two groups with different levels of control over members are shown in Figure 8.7. The a_h function shows high per capita contributions; this would tend to occur if the outcome was a private good and benefits could be denied unless a member actually contributed. Lower per capita contributions, the a_w function, would be expected if the outcome had public good characteristics and if members could enjoy the benefits even though they didn't contribute to political pressure. In the public good case, it might take many consumers (a_1, for example) to generate the same level of political contributions (m_1) that could be obtained from a tightly knit but much smaller group of producers (a_2).

Efficient Transfers. To this point, we appear to have old wine in new bottles; the Becker model seems very much like the Peltzman model of legislative regulation. Instead of support functions and opposition functions, we now have production functions for political pressure. The Becker model breaks sharply with tradition, however, with its startling conclusion of *efficient transfers*—that government will tend to choose efficient rather than less efficient ways of redistributing income via taxes and subsidies.[9] Becker argues that just as competition among firms will enhance market efficiency, competition among interest groups will enhance the efficiency with which government works.

It is crucial that we recall the notion of deadweight loss with respect to taxation (Section 7.73) in order to understand this model. Levying a commodity tax through an import restriction, for example, will reduce consumers' surplus. What is most important for Becker's argument, however, is that a commodity tax will reduce consumers' surplus by *more* than the amount raised in tax revenue. The potential for tax revenue is area P_1abP_0 in Figure 7.10, yet consumers are made worse off by area P_1acP_0, which is greater than the amount of tax revenue. The difference is area abc, the deadweight loss.

Becker's claim is that someone will bear this deadweight loss, and that this gives legislatures an incentive to consider both who and how much to tax and who and how much to subsidize. He explicitly assumes that deadweight loss is perceived by taxpayers and that these perceptions are translated into political pressure to reduce the loss. Because deadweight loss rises more than proportionately as the level of the tax rises (Figure 7.10), and because it seems safe to assume that the marginal gain to spending beneficiaries falls as subsidies rise, Becker concludes that "higher subsidies and taxes tend to raise the 'countervailing political power' of taxpayers" (1985, p. 334).

Becker's general hypothesis is that when legislatures are persuaded to transfer income to a particular group, they have an incentive to select an efficient transfer scheme. Otherwise, the deadweight costs will prod losers into organizing and overturning the scheme. Becker goes even farther by suggesting that if those who would gain from a proposal can exert more pressure than those who would be harmed, and if access to political influence is equal for the two groups, a potential Pareto-improvement in social well-being will occur if the legislature approves the gainer's request. That is, the gainers would have the potential to compensate the losers (pay Kaldor-Hicks compensation) and still have something left over.[10]

An Empirical Test. One source of data with which to test the Becker model is the U.S. agricultural sector, where there are many farm commodities and many ways to transfer income to producers. Let's compare two of these: production controls and price subsidies. If the demand for a commodity is highly inelastic (D_i) and the supply is highly elastic (S_e), as in Figure 8.8, then production controls that would reduce the supply from Q_0 to Q_1 would be the most efficient means of obtaining a higher price (p_1). (The second supply function is not shown in order to simplify the diagram.) Production controls could take the form of acreage allotments, production quotas, marketing orders, quality standards, or other supply-control devices. A deadweight loss of abc would occur because of the restricted supply. This amount, however, would be much smaller than the deadweight loss of bde that would occur if price p_1 was obtained as a guaranteed price subsidy to producers. The latter would cause producers to produce Q_2; the marginal value of the commodity to consumers (*e*) would then be much less than the marginal cost to producers (*d*). Consumers would buy only Q_1 at the higher price; thus Q_2Q_1 of the commodity would have to be put into storage at a cost to the Treasury.

If the demand for the commodity is elastic (D_e), however, and the supply is inelastic (S_i), it is more efficient to transfer income through price subsidies (Figure 8.9).   Production controls would impose large dead-weight losses (abc), largely on producers. The deadweight losses due to excess production brought about by price subsidies, however, would be small (bde) because of the lack of responsiveness of supply.

Two recent research efforts have tested the Becker hypothesis that an efficient method of income transfer will be used. The first, Gardner (1987), found that those agricultural commodities with either an inelastic supply (Figure 8.9) or an inelastic demand (Figure 8.8) had the largest price gains from the various forms of agricultural market intervention. This is consistent with Becker's model; at least one form of intervention should have small deadweight losses and thus be attractive to political suppliers. Another research effort, however, found that differences in political pressures are quite capable of overriding any efficiency advantages offered by the two alternatives, so that redistribution won't necessarily be efficient. Babcock, Carter, and Schmitz (1990) studied the five-year cycles of farm commodity legislation and found that by 1985, falling exports, rising storage costs, and larger support payments to wheat producers had brought about a situation resembling the dark side of Figure 8.8. Large deadweight losses of bde *were*, in fact, being incurred through high storage costs, and many observers agreed that a change in policy was needed.

Two political sides formed. One wanted to use production controls to reduce supply to Q_1, that is, to use markets and the inelastic demand for wheat to transfer income to producers at the lower deadweight loss of abc (Figure 8.8). The other side, however, ably abetted by grain marketers and input suppliers, those who would benefit by high levels of wheat production, wanted to continue the high support prices, even at a deadweight cost of bde. The advocates of plenty won despite the Becker hypothesis that an efficient means of redistributing income would be chosen. The tax savings from using production controls would have been about $15 per capita per year, which is not a small sum taken over the entire national population.

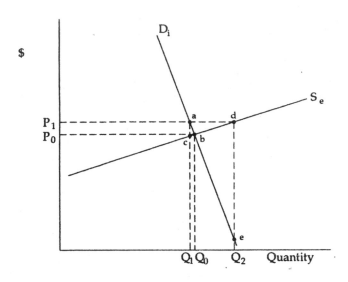

FIGURE 8.8 Production Controls

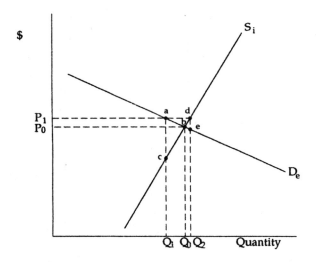

FIGURE 8.9 Price Subsidies

Why didn't Becker's model predict this outcome? As Babcock, Carter, and Schmitz note, the Becker model implies that "the outcome of a struggle among farmers, taxpayers, agribusiness firms and consumers will depend on the deadweight losses of the groups' preferred policies *and on the relative ability of each group to produce political pressure*" (1990, p. 349, emphasis added). These authors argue that related firms that would benefit by abundant wheat production—the agricultural input suppliers, the grain handlers, the food manufacturers, and the grain exporters—are a small, homogenous, and powerful group compared to taxpayers and consumers, and that their influence on the 1985 Farm Bill has been amply documented (Guither, 1986). In language that favors the Peltzman model over the Becker model, the authors state, "The choice of policies in the 1985 Farm Bill demonstrates that interest groups having potentially large per capita, clearly identifiable gains (or losses) have the lobbying advantage. Even with the extra push from low deadweight losses, advocates of supply controls were unable to overcome their inherent limitations in producing political influence" (1990, p. 350). In summary, equal access to political influence may, in fact, *not* exist, and *in*efficient outcomes may well be selected by vote-maximizing legislators in spite of Becker's model.

8.14 The Tax Structure as a Political Outcome

In an extension of the Stigler-Peltzman-Becker tradition, Hettich and Winer (1988) developed a model to explain the various tax systems that may be determined by vote-maximizing legislatures. The previous models dealt with indirect taxes and subsidies, usually those created by restrictions on entry, but the Hettich and Winer model deals with direct taxation in a manner resembling the Downs models of Section 7.3.

Any tax system has three elements: the tax base (those activities that are pooled for taxation), the rate structure (the rate at which income from these activities are taxed), and special provisions (exemptions and deductions). The labor earnings of a construction worker and a factory worker, for example, are usually part of a common tax base. Both are regarded as labor income and both are taxed at the same rate if the two workers have the same amount of taxable income. Doctors also earn labor income; they may face a higher tax rate than either of the two workers, but this is because they have higher incomes, not because they have a different tax base. Labor income and long-term capital gains, however, have usually been treated as two separate tax bases. A lower tax rate has usually been applied to income from capital gains, ostensibly to promote investment and productivity.

Hettich and Winer contend that tax outcomes in legislatures can be explained by the incentive systems of those who benefit from tax-provided services, those who pay taxes, and those who decide on taxes. Many of these incentives—political pressure and deadweight losses, for example—are also found in the previous models. One unique aspect of the Hettich and Winer model, however, is the administrative cost of a tax system. These include the costs of processing tax payments, particularly the costs of monitoring compliance with tax laws. The simplest system might tax all income at the same rate regardless of source; the rate would be one that would maximize political support based on benefits received and taxes paid by individual citizens. Some income sources are more difficult (costly) to tax than others; labor income, in particular, has traditionally had better "tax handles" than capital income because of the tax-withholding system.

The Hettich and Winer model can be illustrated with Figure 8.10, which shows how a vote-maximizing legislature would decide on the number of tax bases and tax brackets. In either decision, the *marginal tax administration costs* (BB) are pertinent. More tax bases and more rate brackets would involve larger administrative costs, particularly for monitoring compliance. Going from one tax base (all income) to two tax bases (labor income and capital income) to three tax bases (labor income from gambling, labor income from all other sources, and capital income, for example) would be increasingly costly to administer. Moreover, the money used for monitoring compliance might be used more productively by legislators in producing public services and thus gaining votes.

By the same token, the *marginal tax discrimination benefits* (AA) are also pertinent. Many voters might prefer to have labor and capital income

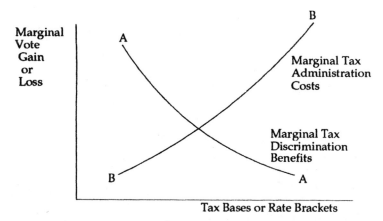

FIGURE 8.10 The Politically Optimal Number of Tax Bases or Tax-Rate Brackets

kept separate for tax purposes, but few would care whether labor income from construction and that from manufacturing were kept separate. Having only one tax bracket (a 25 percent rate, for example) might leave many taxpayers far from their preferred rate. Progressive taxation with six rate brackets based on the level of taxable income might reduce some of this dissatisfaction. If one's preferred tax rate was 15 percent, being taxed in the 16 to 18 percent bracket would be better than being taxed at a uniform rate of 25 percent.

8.15 Voting Your District: Bringing Home the Bacon

A quite different view of legislative regulation centers around the implications of having political representation by geographic region, a system that we tend to take for granted. The particular model shown here was formalized by Shepsle and Weingast (1984), but it draws heavily on the earlier work of Mayhew (1974), Fiorina (1974 and 1989), Fenno (1978), and many others. The basic idea of *voting your district* is that a legislator will consider the effects of policies only insofar as they are felt by his or her constituents within a geographically based legislative district. The policy may be a loser from a national point of view, but if it is looked on favorably within the district, a reelection-seeking legislator will vote for it. Voting your district is a very narrow and provincial outlook in many ways. In other respects, it is regarded as the way the democratic process should work; we want our representatives to represent *us*, not the people in the next district.

In the Shepsle and Weingast version of the model, an elected representative from the jth district has a political support function that will determine how he or she would assess a proposed public policy or project (x). The political support function can be represented as

$$N_j(x) = b_j(x) + f[c_{1j}(x)] - c_{2j}(x) - t_j T(x), \tag{8.9}$$

where $N_j(x) =$ political support within district j for the representative because of position or actions on the proposed policy or project (x)

$b_j(x) =$ social and economic benefits to constituents within district j

$f([c_{1j}(x)] =$ the economic impact of public expenditures made within district j

$c_{2j}(x) =$ negative externalities that are imposed on constituents in district j

$t_j T(x)$ = the district's share (t) of the total tax bill (T) for the policy or project.

Political support for a representative would be increased by consumer benefits and public spending in the district, but it would be decreased by negative externalities and taxes. The idea is very plausible; representatives usually want such things as military bases and water resource projects in their district unless the expected externality costs are too high or the tax costs to constituents are too high. A military base would defend constituents, largely at the expense of other taxpayers, but more importantly, it would provide jobs, increase business output, enhance land values, and strengthen tax revenues to local government. A representative can claim political credit by securing this type of activity.

According to Shepsle and Weingast (1984), Ferejohn (1974), and many others, however, it is very unlikely that the narrow incentive structure in voting your district will result in economic efficiency. The benefits of a project are often geographically concentrated, but the costs are often widely dispersed, even across the entire nation. If a project will create new construction jobs and higher payrolls in one district, political pressures will be created to obtain or maintain that type of public spending. There is often little political incentive elsewhere, however, to protect against incurring the costs imposed on each of the other districts, because these costs are small. Coalitions of gainers against under-represented losers can further reduce economic efficiency. Many military bases have become redundant in light of current defense needs, but the pressures to maintain these bases suggests that political gainers have more incentive for cooperation action than do political losers, even though the latter are more numerous. By the same token, it may be more efficient for the nation to have certain externality costs imposed on particular districts. Not surprisingly, these districts often vigorously oppose these actions. LULUs, or locally unwanted land uses such as prisons and nuclear waste repositories, are classic examples.

A second reason to expect inefficient outcomes is that the $f[c_{1j}(x)]$ term, the local impact of public expenditures, will often be offset by reduced business activity elsewhere in the economy even though the gains within the representative's district may be significant and visible. Other private and public spending will usually have to shrink so that taxes can be paid to finance the project. The local economy may glitter *because* the lights have dimmed somewhere else. Again, these costs are usually dispersed fairly widely across the economy rather than concentrated in a few districts. If economic markets work well, all resources should be able to earn their opportunity cost, or what they could earn in other uses. If construction workers aren't building an airstrip at a military base, for example, they should be able to earn as much by building apartments or houses. But markets aren't always perfectly competitive; Haveman and Krutilla (1968) have shown that some unemployed resources can be returned to work at zero cost through public spending. In general, however, economists tend to see the $f[c_{1j}(x)]$ effects as being offset elsewhere in the economy.

Shepsle and Weingast (1984) offer a simple but very important extension of the voting-your-district model. That is, a representative's real constituency may be smaller than the geographic district, but it also may be much larger than the district. The first such group is a *subdistrict constituency*. Political science texts are loaded with examples describing the people within a district who have more political power than others, those to whom vote-seeking representatives tend to listen. People without power and organization are slighted, but those with power and organization are rewarded.

There are also subdistrict constituencies, however, that might seem to be powerful but aren't. In particular, think back to Section 7.7 and the various vote-getting options that are available to an elected supplier. Each might be used to enhance reelection, but slack may exist in supply responsiveness. Because of majority rule and infrequent elections, an elected supplier doesn't have to please everyone all the time (Breton, 1974). Instead, he or she needs only to reduce coercion on those voters whose support is needed for reelection under majority rule. In a traditional model based on political power, one needn't cater to subdistrict constituencies that have little or no political power. If slack exists, however, even some powerful groups might safely be ignored, in the short run at least, because their support isn't crucial to reelection. Some of these groups may be disgruntled, but not enough to warrant the costs of attention.

From the representative's point of view, the cost of gaining political support may differ greatly among various subdistrict constituencies. Those who are already supportive may be virtually costless to maintain; those who are solidly in another political camp may be infinitely costly to convert. In between, the cost of gaining enough votes for reelection depends on the extent of coercion and the effectiveness of various supply options. This brings in Shepsle and Weingast's second constituency, a *supradistrict constituency*, an important portion of a representative's constituency that lies outside the district. At first, it might seem puzzling that people or groups from outside the district would offer political support. They obviously can't vote. But they can be helpful by participating in legislative markets, that is, by providing campaign contributions, in this case from outside the district, in exchange for future legislative consideration. As a substitute for more substantive action, campaign funds can be very useful for "informing" district voters and for altering their preferences. Name familiarity can solidify preferences of less-committed voters. There is little doubt that sophisticated media messages can be effective in providing name familiarity; whether these add to substantive knowledge among voters is much less clear. By the end of the 1988 presidential campaign, for example, voters knew much more about "twenty-second sound bites" than they did about the issues.[11]

Political campaigns at all levels have become more expensive, and many representatives feel they need more money to wage these campaigns. For better or worse, many interest groups have been formed to channel that money into the electoral process, largely through *political action committees*, PACs, which are organizations that have been formed to raise and distribute money for political purposes. We'll discuss these in more detail in Section 8.2. Many of these interest groups span a number of geographic districts and offer potential supradistrict constituencies for elected suppliers who vote their district.[12] Interest groups need access to elected suppliers, and elected suppliers need media time to assure district voters that the things promised in Equation 8.9—social and economic benefits, local public expenditures, minimal externalities, and low tax bills—either have happened or soon will happen.

As evidence that supradistrict constituencies are important, Janet Grenzke (1988) found that incumbent House members depend heavily on campaign contributions from outside their district. In the 1982 election, for example, about 98 percent of the PAC contributions to incumbents came from outside their district. Only 2 percent came from subdistrict constituencies. This figure held true for all types of PACs—labor, corporate, trade association, and independent. Moreover, at least 80 percent of this money came from outside the state as well as outside the district.

In an important article on how supradistrict constituencies function in legislative markets, Denzau and Munger (1986) picture an interest group (I_i) that views different legislators as alternative providers of legislative action that is sought by an interest group. The interest group may be willing to make campaign contributions in exchange for legislative consideration; these contributions can help sway unorganized voters. Voters have opinions and voting preferences of their own, but some of them can be swayed by new information provided through the media and financed by campaign contributions. The willingness of a legislator to adopt the interest group as a supradistrict constituency will depend on the preferences of geographic constituents and on the extent to which these preferences can be modified by political advertising. If the constituents of some of the legislators have strong preferences against the policies that the interest group desires and if these preferences can't be modified with a media blitz, then the interest group will need to look toward other legislators as alternative suppliers.

If an interest group wants to promote handgun control, for example, it probably shouldn't expect much help from representatives in the rural West. Most voters in these districts will probably have strong preferences against gun control even if the airways are filled with gun-control ads. These strong preferences will usually surface in the next election if a representative votes for gun-control legislation. A legislator from a high-crime urban district, however, might be able to accept campaign contributions from the gun-control group without alienating constituents and might even be encouraged to accept them. More media money could then be spent by the urban legislator, not necessarily to promote gun control but to tell the voters how effective he or she has been in voting the district.

This idea of legislative markets based on campaign contributions from potential gainers needs to be more formally developed, something we will do in Section 8.2. We need to approach this topic by way of what might seem to be a detour on ideology; this turns out not to be a detour at all but rather a key to understanding how legislative markets work.

8.16 *Ideology and Political Support: Listening to Polarized Preferences*

One of the most fundamental issues in collective choice is how electoral competition and the median voter are related to the aggregation of preferences. Anthony Downs's (1957) models, for example, were highly competitive and demand-driven; a governing party that fails to assess the preferences of the voters is likely to become the party out of power. In most cases, Downs's models predicted that competing parties would converge around the preferences of the median voter.

A dissenting view was heard in 1974 when Fiorina argued that it wasn't clear how voter preferences are related to electoral outcomes. In marginal congressional districts, those that tend to have close elections, electoral competition should force candidates to discover and heed the preferences of the median voter. Conversely, in districts that are electorally "safe," candidates might have more room for discretionary behavior. But Fiorina found significant exceptions to this, particularly in an early study by Miller and Stokes (1969). They found that congressmembers in marginal districts were likely to vote their *own* preferences rather than their constituents' preferences and that congressmembers from safe districts actually had the most accurate assessment of constituent preferences. Fiorina concluded that candidates won't usually go after the middle-of-the-road median voter, as Downs had predicted, but that they will align themselves with one major constituency or another.

The size and technology of political campaigns have changed greatly since Fiorina's influential work in 1974, but the unexpected behavior of listening to the extremes rather than the center seems to persist. In Chapter 6, for example, we noted the research of Hinich and Pollard (1981), Romer and Rosenthal (1984), and Poole and Rosenthal (1984); this work shows that noncentrist preferences have been very important in congressional voting patterns. These researchers feel that voters and representatives use an *ideological dimension* that ranges from liberal to conservative in evaluating, ranking, and voting on candidates and policies. Each person has an ideal point somewhere along this ideological spectrum, and preferences for candidates or policies decline on either side of this point. Moreover, it is assumed that a voter can place any candidate or policy somewhere along the ideological spectrum. Most candidates might be viewed as too liberal for a very conservative voter, for example, but there could even be a few candidates who would be viewed as too conservative. Using sophisticated statistical analyses of interest-group ratings and roll-call votes, Poole and Rosenthal (1984) were able to correctly classify about 80 percent of the votes in Congress over the past twenty-five years.

When we discussed this research in Chapter 6, our focus was on stability and whether a single evaluative dimension of preferences actually exists in individual and group decisions. Poole and Rosenthal (1984) argued that this single dimension does exist—and that ideology is that one dimension. They asked whether this dimension helps stabilize group decisions in view of the cycling phenomenon—and they argued that it does. Now, however, we want to look at their work in a slightly different context; that is, how well are the preferences of constituents represented by elected suppliers? These researchers, like Fiorina, have found that elected suppliers respond to polarized preferences rather than central preferences. Their research shows that voters are mainly moderates but that elected suppliers are much more polarized. Figure 8.11 shows the distribution along the ideological spectrum of 1,271 voters who were sampled in 1976 by the Center for Political Studies at the University of Michigan. This normal distribution indicates the centrist preferences of most voters. (Romer and Rosenthal note that the French have a word for this middle-of-the-road tendency—the marais, or the swamp.) The ideological distribution for members of Congress in 1980, however, shows a cluster of liberals on the left and a cluster of conservatives on the right, with only a few centrists (Figure 8.12).

At this point, it seems logical to ask why the distributions of preferences for the electorate and the elected are so very different. Part of the

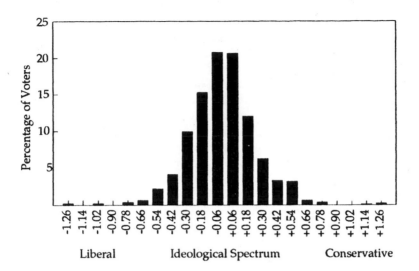

FIGURE 8.11 Ideological Positions of Voters, 1976

Source: Thomas Romer and Howard Rosenthal, "Voting Models and Empirical Evidence," *American Scientist* 72 (September-October, 1984): p. 469. Reprinted by permission.

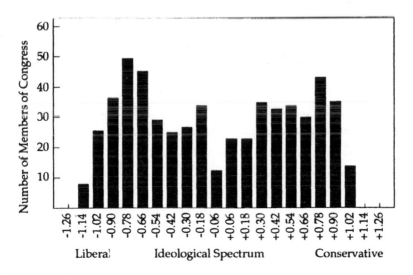

FIGURE 8.12 Ideological Positions of Members of Congress, 1980

Source: Thomas Romer and Howard Rosenthal, "Voting Models and Empirical Evidence," *American Scientist* 72 (September-October, 1984): p. 468. Reprinted by permission.

answer is that participation in the political process is highly self-selective. Consumers, workers, voters, and firms who have the largest net gains from action (or the largest net losses from inaction) will tend to participate. This is consistent with economic reasoning; participation is costly, so only those with the most to gain or lose will participate. And because the ideological spectrum reflects peoples' opinions about the role of government, self-selected liberals will cluster on the left, wanting more government intervention in markets, and self-selected conservatives will cluster on the right, wanting less government intervention. This clustering is true of both individuals and groups, but it may be most true of interest groups because they are self-selected groups with self-selected members—a double whammy. Table 8.1 shows the ideological positions of a variety of liberal and conservative interest groups; these groups are far more polarized than either voters or congressmembers. Because the members of these polarized interest groups are largely self-selected, and

TABLE 8.1. The Polarized Ideological Positions of Selected Interest Groups, 1980[a]

American Civil Liberties Union	-1.06
Americans for Democratic Action	-1.03
American Federation of Teachers	-1.01
Committee on Political Education	-1.00
League of Conservation Voters	-1.00
American Federation of State, County, and Municipal Employees	-0.98
National Council of Senior Citizens	-0.97
United Auto Workers	-0.96
League of Women Voters	-0.88
National Farmers Organization	-0.35
U.S. Chamber of Commerce	+0.57
National Federation of Independent Business	+0.79
Conservation Coalition	+0.91
National Alliance of Senior Citizens	+1.05
Americans for Constitutional Action	+1.09
American Conservative Union	+1.17
National Taxpayers Union	+1.29

[a] The computed ideological spectrum ranges from highly liberal (-) to highly conservative (+). A zero value would be neutral.

Source: Keith T. Poole, "Least Squares Metric, Unidimensional Unfolding," *Psychometrika* 49 (September 1984): p. 322.

because they often stand to gain or lose significantly because of government action, they play a very important role in the electoral process. According to Romer and Rosenthal, "Presumably it is the need to appeal to the support and resources of these groups, and the need for candidates to distinguish themselves from their opponents, that pulls politicians away from the moderate center and to the highly liberal or highly conservative positions that most of them hold" (1984, p. 469).

Romer and Rosenthal found that candidates don't generally change their ideological position once elected. They also found that ideological changes tend to occur only when a legislative seat changes hands, and that polarization in U.S. politics has increased over the past twenty-five years. From an interest-group standpoint, one lesson is fairly clear; if you can't change the way an elected supplier thinks and votes, change the elected supplier! To do this, however, takes time and costs money. With these views about the role of ideology in mind, we now need to look at legislative markets, campaign finance, and in particular, that moneyed offspring of the interest group, the political action committee.

8.2 Markets for Legislative Activities

8.21 *Political Action Committees (PACs)*

A political action committee is a legal entity of a labor union, corporation, professional association, trade association, or some other interest group.[13] Its primary purpose is to raise money and distribute it to multiple candidates for political purposes. Although individuals can support candidates through direct giving or through contributions to political parties, PACs have become the dominant form of campaign finance—and the form that worries people the most. In terms of Equation 8.3 of the Peltzman model, they have become the main way for interest groups to seek wealth transfers (T) by channeling funds toward candidates (K). They can also be used to promote ideological causes such as school prayer, abortion, and gun control, but their bread-and-butter use is to gain or resist changes in the economic environment.

Four issues about PACs are of interest here: their rapid growth, the fear that they exercise undue influence in political life, the constitutional questions raised by spending limits on individuals, and the question of cause and effect. We will look at the first three through a brief history of the PACs, then turn to an economic model of legislative markets. In considering that model, we will explore the evidence on whether PACs influence legislative suppliers, whether they help in changing these suppliers, and whether the interest groups themselves are exploited for financial advantage by rent-seeking legislative incumbents.

As a side-note, one of the apparent ironies in our political evolution is that we have historically espoused free enterprise but we have distrusted business, especially big business. In particular, we have feared that big business may be able to avoid the discipline of competition by gaining political control over its economic environment. The Tillman Act of 1907 and the Corrupt Practices Act of 1925 arose out of this concern; the latter explicitly forbade corporations to contribute money to candidates.[14] Labor unions, however, were allowed to make contributions, at least until the Taft-Hartley Act of 1947 leveled the playing field by forbidding either side to do so.

Twenty-five years later the U.S. Supreme Court ruled that a campaign fund created by a union was not in violation of the Taft-Hartley Act (*Pipefitters Local No. 52 vs. United States*, 1972). This opened the door for interest-group contributions, including those by corporations and unions. The Federal Elections Commission (FEC) was created in 1974 to set and enforce regulations on contributions and spending. Limits were set on individual contributions, but some of these were later ruled unconstitutional by the Supreme Court (*Buckley vs. Valeo*, 1976) when it interpreted certain types of campaign giving and spending as a freedom of speech issue (Alexander, 1984, pp. 38-42). Although there are still limits of $1,000 per individual and $5,000 per PAC for a candidate in any one election, new PACs can be formed to support that candidate and others. In addition, PACs can also "bundle" contributions by soliciting money from organizations and individuals and sending it directly to a candidate. In the absence of substantive ability to control the amount of contributions, the FEC has focused on accounting, disclosures, and other regulatory issues.

The number and importance of PACs has grown rapidly since the mid-1970s. Corporate PACs have grown the most rapidly, increasing from about 700 in 1978 to over 1,600 in 1986; labor union PACs stayed at about 400 throughout this period (Berry, 1989, p. 121). Total PAC contributions to House and Senate candidates rose sharply, going from $34 million in the 1978 election to $132 million in 1986 to $159 million in 1990 (Federal Elections Commission, 1991). Corporate PACs gave $36.2 million to House candidates alone in the 1990 elections, labor unions gave $27.9 million, and trade, membership, and health PACs gave $32.6 million (Federal Elections Commission, 1991). Probably the most striking indicator of PAC importance, however, is the share of total campaign

TABLE 8.2 Number of U.S. House Members Receiving 50 Percent or More of Total Campaign Funds from PACs.

Year	Number
1988	205
1986	194
1984	164
1982	94
1980	85
1978	63

Source: Jeffrey Berry, *The Interest Group Society*, 2nd ed. (Glenview, Ill.: Scott, Foresman, 1989), p. 122; Common Cause, "Congressional Campaign Financing: The Case for Reform" (Washington, D.C.: January 1989), p. 2.

finance that they provide (Table 8.2). In the House, 63 of the 435 members received half or more of their total campaign funds from PACs in 1978; This number had tripled by 1986 and is still rising.

Whether these sums of money have been accompanied by the outcomes that the PACs seek is an issue that we'll examine in the next section. Regardless of the evidence, it is generally thought—or feared—that they *are* effective. Their growth, their press coverage, and the magnitude of bad things that may happen if your trade group, union, or professional association doesn't have one—all of these suggest that PACs are valuable on offense and indispensable on defense. Berry captures this view very well:

Because PACs can gain the gratitude of members of Congress and presumably more access to them, we see why so many have been formed in recent years. They have been started in just about every sector of American society. It is not only PACs such as the United Steelworkers of America Political Action Fund and the Realtors Political Action Committee, which represent large political constituencies, but also EggPAC, FishPAC, FurPAC, and LardPAC. The Dr. Pepper PAC is matched by the Coca-Cola PAC. The brokerage house of Merrill, Lynch, Pierce, Fenner & Smith has a PAC, as does the law firm of Dickstein, Shapiro & Morin. Inevitably, beer distributors are represented by SixPAC.[15] Although not every one of these and other PACs is of great significance, what is important is that so many constituencies feel they must contribute money if they are going to be paid attention to on Capitol Hill. (1989, p. 123)

In spite of the explosion in PAC numbers and contributions, their impact on legislative outcomes is a matter of debate. Journalists generally have no trouble in establishing cause-and-effect relationships; that is, legislators wouldn't take large sums of PAC money if they weren't expected to do something in return. Mark Green, a leading critic of PACs, put it this way a decade ago: "For in Washington today, PacMan is not a video game for kids. It is a cynical business affecting the behavior of adults who govern us, and it takes, not quarters, but $5,000 checks to play. This is not a game that democracy can win" (1982, p. 25). Those political scientists and economists who have researched the matter, however, are more cautious. They usually argue that legislators will accept PAC support from an interest group if their own views and voting records generally coincide with the needs of that interest group.

There is thus a critical issue of causality: Does PAC money affect outcomes or does it go to legislators for services that would have been rendered in any event? Fiorina puts it succinctly: "In a nutshell, does money buy new friends, or does money reward existing friends?" (1989, p. 127); two economic researchers put it their way: "PAC contributions . . . may be more like protection money than attempts to buy votes or access" (Keim and Zardkoohi, 1988, p. 21). Fiorina is also skeptical that legislative behavior is changed by PAC money. He portrays the enthusiasm of Senator Hubert Humphrey (D., Minn.) and other dairy state senators for higher dairy price supports in the early 1970s this way:

Rather than believe that Hubert Humphrey was bought for $10,625, I find it easier to believe that Humphrey did what he did for the sake of Minnesota dairy farmers, who had been an important part of his coalition from the beginning. Did he and Senator William Proxmire (D., Wisconsin) and Senator Harold Hughes (D., Iowa) advance a special interest? Absolutely. Did they do it for money? Probably not. (1989, p. 128)

8.22 Legislative Markets: The Theory

Markets for legislative activities work for the same reason that conventional markets work—the opportunity for mutual gain. Based on the demand for legislative activities by interest groups and others and on the supply of these activities by self-interested representatives, these markets would have several characteristics. First, the outcomes are anticipated rather than actual; all parties look to the future, guided by past experience. Second, the expected outcomes are favorable for both demanders and suppliers; otherwise, they wouldn't be sought. Interest groups expect to gain something, perhaps profit, perhaps consumer protection; legislators also expect to gain through tilting the election odds, serving the public, or increasing personal wealth. The third characteristic of legislative markets is that outcomes are uncertain. By definition, collective choices are made by more than one person; any one legislator can only try to affect outcomes. Some, however, will have more success than others. Fourth, the outcomes may be short-lived; the very next legislature or city council may reverse today's decision. Fifth, legislative activities vary greatly in type and importance. Having a legislator hear your plea for an import-restriction bill and having her work hard for that bill are both favorable outcomes, but the latter is more important than the former.

Legislative Activities. To think about legislative markets, one has to first define legislative activities, a task that is inherently subjective and arbitrary. One type of activity that elected suppliers provide is *access*, or simply agreeing to hear someone's view or position. According to Berry,

> PAC directors freely acknowledge that money buys access while categorically denying that it buys influence. Dividing access and buying influence into two entirely separate phenomena is a convenient rationalization for PAC officials that absolves them from any impropriety. But access *is* a form of influence. If congressmen and their staffs favor those who contribute with greater access, that cannot help but influence their perceptions of the public policy issues before them. The conversations that legislators and staffers have with a group's lobbyists and the documents they read prepared by that organization all work to reinforce the group's message about what needs to be done. The more access a lobbyist has, the more chance he or she has to define what the policy problems are. (1989, pp. 134-135)

Even though access may not secure a favorable vote from a representative, it can lead to a second activity that might, for want of a better word, be called *consideration*. This can take a variety of forms. Legislators can lobby for or against bills that are important to a demander, they can introduce bills and hold hearings, and they can work against bills that are opposed by a demander. Any of these might be done by an individual legislator or by a coalition of legislators. These actions all go beyond access, but they stop short of casting a ballot. A third type of activity by a legislator is *voting*; this can be done in a subcommittee, committee, or on the chamber floor. It is possible, of course, that voting could take place without access or consideration; a representative could simply vote on a measure. In many cases, however, there will probably be some form of interaction with demanders prior to a vote.

The demand and supply for each of these three activities is shown in Figure 8.13. The horizontal axis shows the amount of each activity; because the three are qualitatively different from each other and because they are difficult to quantify, the scales for the three are not comparable. Still, one can think of more or less of each activity, even voting; votes can often be cast on amendments and related issues as well as on the main issue. The market price of each activity is shown on the vertical axis; these are the contributions of PAC money and other campaign resources that flow from demanders to legislative suppliers.

One of the basic ideas in economic theory is that a market equilibrium with respect to price and quantity is determined by the interaction of demand and supply. The market for shoes, for example, is based on intermediate markets for factors of production, including leather, assemblers, and shoe-manufacturing equipment. The interaction among willing buyers and sellers and the existence of competition should produce an equilibrium price and quantity in each of these markets.

In this respect, legislative markets are best thought of as intermediate markets rather than consumer-goods markets. The most basic resources or factors of production that go into producing legislative activities are the time, expertise, and influence of the representative and staff. The deployment of these resources is the stuff of which many political science books are made, and much of it is useful and enlightening for learning

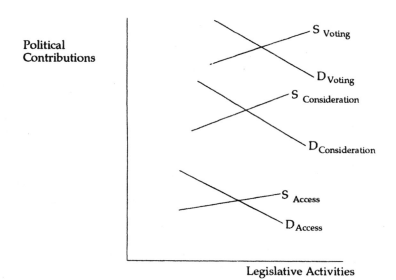

FIGURE 8.13 Demand for and Supply of Three Legislative Activities

about legislative markets (for example, Fenno, 1978, especially Chapter 2). In 1989, for instance, members of the U.S. House of Representatives received an annual clerk-hire allowance of $379,480, not to exceed more than eighteen full-time and four part-time employees, plus about $200,000 for office expenses, including 15,000 minutes of long distance calls to the district (Davidson and Oleszek, 1990, p. 140).

From the House member's point of view, the challenge is to channel these resources into their most valuable uses in serving the nation, the district, and the prospects of reelection, although not necessarily in that order. The demand for these legislative resources will depend on the same basic factors that determine the demand for cobblers or the demand for shoe leather, in particular, the marginal productivity of the resource in producing output and the value of that output to the consumer. In these terms, a good cobbler is one who can make many pairs of shoes each day and, more specifically, many valuable pairs of shoes.

The Legislative Committee System. The *legislative committee system* is an important institution that greatly enhances the productivity and thus the demand for committee member services because it bestows responsibility to committees for certain subsets of policy issues (Shepsle, 1979; Shepsle and Weingast, 1981 and 1984; Weingast, 1981; Weingast and Marshall, 1988; Denzau and Munger, 1986; Grier and Munger, 1991). Committee members have disproportionate power over policy for several reasons. One is that the committee system creates monopoly rights to the introduction of policy proposals in that jurisdiction. Banking proposals must be introduced in the banking committee; trade proposals must be introduced in the trade committee. Along with this monopoly come gate-keeping rights; a contrary-minded committee can usually keep a bill bottled up in committee even if it would be favored by a majority of Congress. Committees thus have broad agenda-setting prerogatives in determining the content and timing of legislation to be submitted to the entire legislature. Along with this comes oversight responsibilities for how legislation is carried out. Committees have the right to hold hearings, recommend budget, earmark certain budget items, forbid certain expenditures, and recommend appointments in the administrative agencies within their policy jurisdictions.

Going back to Figure 8.13, let's assume that the demand for each of the three types of legislative activities would be downward sloping. Voting and consideration will be worth more to demanders than simple access, because they are based on a foundation of access. Voting won't necessarily be the most valuable activity; in fact, consideration may be far more valuable at times because of the committee system. A committee member may be extremely useful to a demander in introducing legislation and guiding it through committee, for example, although his vote would be only one of many. In other cases a single vote can be crucial, especially in subcommittees with small memberships. These considerations suggest that larger PAC contributions will be made to legislators who are more productive because they serve on key committees or subcommittees. In terms of the value of outputs, larger contributions will be made to those members who support legislation that the demanders deem important, especially if the demanders are well organized and the per capita benefits are large.

Now, let's turn to the supply side of legislative markets. The cost to a legislator of supplying a certain legislative activity depends on what has to be given up. One cost is time. The cost of providing access to a new interest group, for example, is largely a matter of time. Its use for one group precludes its use for another. Time spent on providing access may also reduce *casework*, the number of constituent requests for information and assistance that the representative's staff is able to respond to. Doing casework is, in fact, a central part of the electoral strategy of many representatives (Fiorina, 1974, 1989).

Time is also required for the other legislative activities—to provide consideration and to vote. These can result in a more direct cost in the form of vote loss, especially if voting clearly identifies and affirms the ideology of the legislator. One way to portray this is with an upward-sloping supply function for an activity (Figure 8.13).[16] The use of time for any activity implies a forgone opportunity, a cost that may rise with the extent of that activity. A legislator's supply function will also be shifted upward at *all* levels of an activity, however, if voting in a particular way will displease some, even though others may be pleased.

A legislator may engage in many activities—listening to interest groups, initiating legislation, and voting on bills—but separate markets don't exist for each of these activities. Instead, there is only one market for the services of any legislator. And with legislative markets, as with conventional markets, price and quantity tend to reflect the expectation of future demand and future supply costs. The uncertainty about these demands and costs can be greatly reduced by the committee system, however, and by the composition of those committees.

For example, let's assume that a labor union would like to secure passage of stronger workplace safety laws (Figure 8.14). The labor union is national in scope, representing members in a variety of locations and employments, and it spans many legislative districts. Because of this, the union's PAC has flexibility in choosing among legislators who might support its workplace safety bill. These legislators, however, will be able to choose among various sources of campaign support, not just that of the labor union. There is thus a potential market for support of the workplace safety bill.

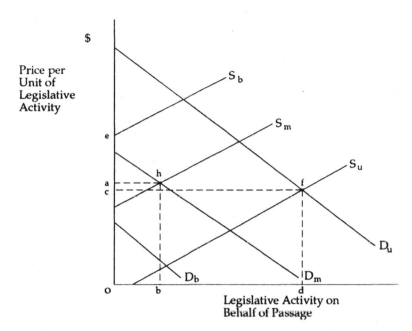

FIGURE 8.14 The Market for Legislative Services: A Workplace Safety Bill

Three sets of demand and supply functions for legislative activity can be imagined. Each set is associated with the services of a particular legislator. From the union's viewpoint, one legislative prospect (*u*) is promising, the second (*b*) is very unpromising, and the third (*m*) is somewhere in between. Each demand function reflects both the value of the workplace safety bill to the union and the expected productivity of that legislator in securing passage of the bill. The D_u demand function is for legislative activities by the promising prospect—a legislator who is a friend of union efforts, an effective organizer, and most important a member of the House Education and Labor Committee. By virtue of the committee system, this legislator is well placed to hear the union proposal, to introduce it as a bill, to work for its passage, and to make it part of the coalition of labor issues.

The D_m demand function, however, lies to the left of D_u. The in-between legislator is an effective moderate with a voting record that has sometimes been favorable to unions. She is not, however, a member of the labor committee. This reduces her productivity. For example, there will be no opportunity for her to alter the workplace safety bill in its formative stage. The third demand function, D_b, is for activities by a probusiness opponent of the bill. It lies to the left of the other two demand functions. At any level of activity, this person's effort would be the least productive of the three. Not only is he not a member of the appropriate committee, any activities that he might undertake in support of the bill might lack credibility because of the contrary ideology that is reflected in his past voting record.

The three supply functions in Figure 8.14 represent the costs of the various types and amounts of legislative activities by the three reelection-seeking legislators. These costs have two components—the opportunity cost of time and other resources and the vote loss from activity on behalf of the workplace safety bill. The time costs are assumed to be the same for the three legislators in order to simplify matters. The vote losses, however, are likely to be very different. For the probusiness legislator, the vote loss is shown by the high vertical intercept (oe) of his supply function (S_b). His vote loss for supporting the bill would be the highest of the three legislators because his key constituents are largely business people, many of whom might suffer reduced profits because of the bill. The supply function of the in-between legislator, S_m, would show a lesser vote loss at any level of legislative activity. The supply function S_u might even be negative for the prounion legislator over some range of legislative activity if his constituents expect him to support the bill.

The amount of campaign contributions to each of the three legislators would thus depend on the price per unit of legislative activity and the amount of legislative activity. We would expect to observe larger PAC contributions to those legislators who are members of the relevant legislative committee and have constituencies that are favorably disposed toward the action being sought. Campaign contributions to the prounion legislator would be the area cfdo; this would be a larger dollar amount than ahbo, that received by the in-between legislator.[17] The supply cost of the probusiness legislator would exceed his expected productivity; the supply function would be above the demand function at all levels of activity. He would neither receive nor ask for political contributions from the labor group.

In conventional markets, the supply and demand for output are usually influenced by different factors. Legislative markets tend to be implemented through committee systems that *link* demand and supply. Legislators with well-defined constituencies such as Kansas wheat farmers, Cleveland steelworkers, or senior citizens in Florida are attracted to those committees that are most crucial to these constituents. If a legislator can gain a seat on a relevant committee, this shifts the demand function for her legislative activities to the right—she becomes more productive; it also shifts the supply function for her legislative services downward—the costs of serving her constituents are reduced. Both of these tend to increase campaign contributions on her behalf.

This leads us to explore why legislative markets might operate in the manner described. First, a cynical view: Legislators created the committee system to enhance their own earnings. A plausible view perhaps, but how could those who created the system make sure *they* would be the ones who would benefit by it? After all, the committee system has been evolving for many years, starting long before the days of expensive campaigns.

Weingast and Marshall (1988) make a very plausible argument that the committee system has evolved to reduce the instability and uncertainty that would be inherent in legislatures that have no committees. Much of this instability and uncertainty, they believe, would come from impediments to bargaining and exchange among legislators. Binding contracts that exist in private markets don't fit very well in a legislative setting; one legislator can't sue another legislator for changing his mind on a crucial vote. Another major means for expressing intense preferences in collective choice, as we saw in Chapter 6, is to form coalitions of issues, something that legislators have always done. Logrolling is one way to express these coalitions; "I'll vote for your bill if you'll vote for mine."

But logrolling and coalitions also have some real limitations in a legislative setting, according to Weingast and Marshall. One limitation is that bargains between legislators might expire after a two-, four-, or six-year term. And an even shorter bargain lifetime might exist because the timing of different decisions might change the incentives for logrolling. For example, two groups might logroll to get water resource development projects for A and restrictive trade policies enacted for B. Once A has her dams built and in operation, however, she may find it advantageous to logroll with C on another issue, perhaps at the expense of undoing B's trade benefits.[18]

Because of these types of limitations, legislative bodies have had to develop better ways of facilitating exchange. The particular institution that has been developed, according to Weingast and Marshall, is a system in which certain committees have sole jurisdiction for initiating action in designated policy areas. Representatives bid for seats on these committees and successful bidders acquire seniority and additional productivity.

The committee system institutionalizes . . . trade among all the legislators, policy area by policy area, for the right to . . . replace the status quo. But this is neither accomplished nor enforced by an explicit market exchange. Rather, a legislator on committee i gives up influence over the selection of proposals in the area of committee j in exchange for members of committee j's giving up their rights to influence proposals in area i. Institutionalizing rights over agenda power—that is, control over the design and selection of proposals that arise for a vote—substitutes for purchasing the votes of others in an explicit market. (1988, p. 145)

Their argument is that the committee system adds durability and enforceability to legislative bargains and allows a legislature to work more like a market. Instead of exchanging votes through logrolling, legislators acquire property rights in certain jurisdictions and give up their rights in other jurisdictions. Not coincidentally, these rights are also of special concern to legislative constituents, whether they are wheat farmers in Kansas or autoworkers in Detroit.

8.23 Legislative Markets: The Evidence

The previous section may be an apt description of how representative government tends to work, especially at the federal level, but it is also disturbing if one thinks that Congress already works too much like a market. Before drawing this conclusion, however, we may want to look at the empirical evidence to see whether the facts are consistent with the theories.

The primary hypotheses about legislative markets are that campaign contributions and the extent of legislative activity by legislators are determined by committee membership and other sources of productivity and to vote loss among constituents because of support for certain issues. One obvious problem with testing these hypotheses is that the extent of various political activities is difficult to compare. The assistance that a legislator may give an interest group comes in many forms: meetings, letters, phone calls, introducing or cosponsoring bills, attending hearings, and voting. Some of these activities are time-intensive. Others require little time, but they may be costly in terms of vote loss. Voting the wrong way on gun control or abortion legislation may be political suicide with certain constituencies.

Voting. In spite of this measurement difficulty, the effect of PAC and other campaign contributions on the extent of legislative activities has been investigated in several ways. The most common measure of alleged PAC influence has been its effect on how legislators vote. A common procedure has been to associate PAC contributions with roll-call votes on specific issues, followed by the explicit or implicit conclusion that "money bought votes." Berry, for example, cites the case where the House approved a resolution that overturned a Federal Trade Commission regulation requiring used-car dealers to list any defects of a car on a window sticker—the so-called lemon law (1989, p. 132). Of the 216 House members who cosponsored the resolution, 186 received an average PAC contribution of $2,300 from the National Association of Automobile Dealers. This included sixteen members who signed on as cosponsors within ten days after receiving the PAC money. Berry asks a crucial question: Did money buy votes or would the House members have voted much the same way in any event?

> In sum, analyses of the relationship between PAC contributions and voting on the floor of the House and Senate do not show that PACs are consistently or even usually effective in changing the way legislators would have voted in the absence of PAC gifts. At the same time, credible cases can be cited where PACs did seem to influence the outcome. It is interesting to note, however, that although the primary focus of lobbyists is on committee work, journalists and political scientists trying to trace the effects of PAC money look more toward floor votes. The reason for this is that the relationship between money and floor votes can be quantified, offering analysts a rigorous means of evaluating the impact of PAC money. Even though such efforts are not a precise measure of influence, they are more feasible to do than assessments of long-term committee lobbying, which is less visible and less quantifiable. (1989, p. 133)

As we noted, voting is only one form of political activity, and it may not always be the most important form. Berry notes that PAC money may be even more influential in gaining what we have called access and consideration. Cosponsoring friendly amendments, turning a cold shoulder to unfriendly ones, lobbying colleagues—all of these may be influenced by PAC support. To cite Berry:

> Take, for example, banking legislation. During the 1985-86 election cycle, the members of the House and Senate banking committees received $3.5 million in contributions from PACs with a direct interest in banking legislation. How did this enormous sum of money shape the alternatives considered by the banking panels in the sessions that followed? . . . No real measure of how contributions shape agendas and alternatives in committees exists, but it is foolish to think that examining floor votes on banking legislation is an accurate measure of PAC influence. (1989, pp. 133-134)

Campaign Spending. A second measure of alleged PAC influence is its effect on campaign spending by candidates. This focus is on how much candidates spend on campaigns rather than on how much is contributed. If contributions exceed spending, a "war chest" can be accumulated to discourage future opponents. This research has been plagued by the problem of causation: Do dollars produce outcomes or do expected outcomes produce dollars? Research on congressional elections by Gary Jacobson (1980, 1985), for example, apparently shows that greater spending by challengers leads to more votes cast for them, but that greater spending by incumbents has little effect. Rather than proving to incumbents that they shouldn't spend more money in a close race, Jacobson argues that incumbents increase their spending *because* they anticipate a close race. Figure 8.15 shows the vote response along the C_1

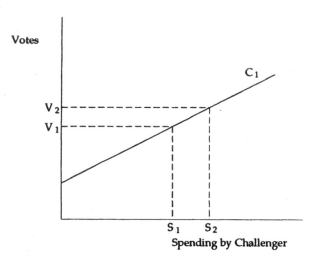

FIGURE 8.15 Vote Response for Challenger Spending

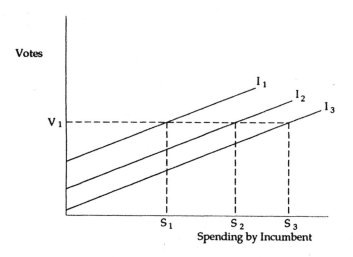

FIGURE 8.16 Vote Response for Incumbent Spending

function for a challenger: More spending (S_1 to S_2) brings more votes (V_1 to V_2). Increased spending by an incumbent might also have a positive effect except that some of these votes have been lost to the challenger (Figure 8.16). The vote function for the incumbent thus shifts down from I_1 to I_2 to I_3 because of increased spending by the challenger; it now takes more incumbent money just to maintain the same vote total (V_1).

Part of this puzzle may have been resolved by Green and Krasno (1988), who included measures of the quality of the challenger in their statistical analyses of the 1978 House elections. With this twist added, they found that the effect of challenger spending on vote share was positive, as others had found, but more important, that spending by an incumbent did add to the incumbent vote share. This result had not been established by previous research.

Incumbency and Committee Assignments. The prospects for many challengers are limited by the amount of campaign contributions they can raise; these amounts depend on whether potential supporters think they can win (Berry, 1989; Jacobson, 1985). This brings us to the advantages of incumbency, a matter that links many of the previous issues. The one main advantage of congressional incumbents is that they usually win! Most Senate races have been won with less than 60 percent (Jacobson, 1980, p. 4). Reelection rates for House incumbents, however, have generally been over 90 percent in every general election since 1974 (*Congressional Quarterly Weekly Report*, November 10, 1990, p. 3796). Another advantage of incumbents is that they usually win by large margins, especially in the House. It is not unusual for 10 to 15 percent of the House seats to be uncontested and for most of the incumbents who face challengers to win with more than 60 percent of the vote. In fact, the average vote percentage among House incumbents in 1990 was "only" 63.5 percent. This was the lowest average in any general election since Watergate in 1974 (*Congressional Quarterly Weekly Report*, November 10, 1990, p. 3800). Name recognition, constituency service, committee memberships, franking privileges, and other perquisites all contribute to the advantage of incumbents.

To no one's surprise, the lion's share of PAC money in the House goes to incumbents. For those House seats where an incumbent was running for reelection in 1980 and 1982, 70 and 77 percent of PAC contributions went to incumbents rather than challengers (Jacobson, 1985, p. 14). By 1986, this percentage had increased to 82 percent (Berry, 1989, p. 129). In 1990, $74.7 million in PAC money went to incumbents, and only $4.7 million went to challengers (*Congressional Quarterly Weekly Report*, November 3, 1990, pp. 3756-3759). Now, 95 percent of the House PAC money goes to incumbents—the same percentage as their reelection rate. These contributions are generally viewed as pragmatic investments based on the expectation that money gains will be enhanced and money losses will be avoided: "Incumbents of both parties have benefitted most from growing PAC largess, further evidence that PACs are usually more interested in having access to winners than they are in affecting election results. Only PACs with a strong ideological bent give more to non-incumbents than to incumbents, and less than 10 percent of PAC money comes from them" (Jacobson, 1985, p. 13).

Not all incumbents receive equal amounts of PAC money. Several researchers have tried to understand the reasons for this. One major decision that researchers have faced is whether to try to explain only the extent of PAC contributions—a single-equation approach—or whether to try to explain the extent of several variables as a system of equations. At least one major study has taken the latter route. Kau and Rubin (1981) and Kau, Keenan, and Rubin (1982) argued that three variables are closely related: the voting behavior of congressional representatives, the voting behavior of their constituents (expressed as the vote share or electoral margin), and the extent of campaign contributions. The vote share was expected to depend on the extent and source of campaign contributions, which in turn depended on the voting records of congressional representatives. In general, their findings were not surprising. Labor unions, for example, tended to give more money to representatives who voted according to union preferences, especially in liberal districts.

Poole and Romer (1985) analyzed the determinants of campaign contributions by the top 500 PACs in the 1980 House elections. PAC contributions were treated as the single dependent variable, based on the assumption that the voting records of incumbents are not swayed by campaign contributions. The researchers developed a huge matrix with 389 rows, one for each House seat with an incumbent running in 1980, and 407 columns, one for each PAC that contributed in any of these races. Most PACs gave nothing to most candidates: A zero contribution was far more common than either a contribution to an incumbent or a "negative" contribution to a challenger. Contributions were highly related to whether a candidate and a PAC were close together on the ideological spectrum ranging from highly liberal to highly conservative (Table 8.1, Figures 8.11 and 8.12). A contribution from a conservative corporate PAC, for example, was much more likely if the candidate was also a conservative. There were very few instances of a PAC giving to a candidate at the opposite end of the spectrum. Relatively few PACs other than the National Rifle Association gave to both incumbent and challenger in any one race. Only milk-producer PACs were opportunistic in the sense of contributing to candidates all across the ideological spectrum.

One of the limitations of the Poole and Romer research was that they didn't explain why different types of PACs might have different contributing behaviors. Labor PACs were fairly homogenous in giving, for example, but there was a great deal of diversity among trade association and corporate PACs. Keim and Zardkoohi (1988) have argued that because labor PACs are fewer in number, more homogenous, and better able to concentrate their contributions, they are better able than corporate PACs to negotiate with elected legislators. These authors conclude that political markets are more nearly sellers' (legislators') markets than buyers' (interest-group) markets and that labor PACs are more likely than corporate PACs to unite successfully and gain political leverage.

One factor that seems crucial to whether firms will form PACs and take other political action is industry structure and the concentration of sales among firms. Grier, Munger, and Roberts (1991) examine a variety of conflicting theoretical arguments about why firms in more concentrated industries would take more (or less) political action, either on their own or collectively, than would firms in less-concentrated industries. Empirically, they found that firms in industries that have either a very high or very low concentration of sales are less likely to form their own PACs than are firms in the middle. Much remains in putting together the puzzle of corporate and union political participation.

Evidence can also be cited that PACs have less influence than most people think. Wright (1985) points out that PACs are usually affiliated with existing organizations such as a corporation, labor union, or trade association and that the parent organization usually handles the lobbying while the PAC raises the money. This often puts the PAC at a disadvantage, because the parent organization may already be providing members with private goods or material benefits. The American Medical Association (AMA), for example, tries to discourage free-riding with offers of continuing education and liability insurance, but for members only. Wright believes that this leaves providing solidary benefits, that is, selling ideology to raise funds, to its AMPAC (American Medical Political Action Committee). Moreover, because many of the larger PACs have decentralized organizations, the decisions on how to spend the PAC money are usually made at the local level. This further reduces the ability to concentrate money on a few specific candidates. To cite Wright, "An official from still a different PAC summed it up this way: They [the local officials] raise the money; they ought to be the ones who spend it" (1985, p. 405).

A recent study by Grier and Munger (1991), however, shows that committee assignments and potential vote loss clearly did affect the pattern of PAC contributions to House incumbents between 1978 and 1984. Committee assignments and the prospects of vote loss, it should be recalled, were the primary determinants of demand and supply in our

TABLE 8.3 Estimated Relationships Between Corporate PAC Contributions and Characteristics of House Incumbents

Characteristic of Incumbent	1978/1980		1982/1984	
	Coefficient	t-Statistic[a]	Coefficient	t-Statistic[a]
Constant term	6087.8	(1.53)	3176.6	(0.56)
Freshman	4658.7	(3.26)	3437.5	(1.77)
Seniority	258.4	(3.28)	361.0	(3.44)
Margin	-128.5	(3.60)	-179.4	(3.45)
Democrat	-2237.7	(1.81)	-4922.9	(2.45)
Chamber of Commerce vote score	289.6	(2.72)	900.3	(5.83)
Chamber of Commerce vote score (squared)	-1.1	(1.53)	-6.2	(4.40)
Committee Dummy Variables:				
Agriculture	346.9	(0.19)	3527.7	(1.65)
Appropriations	-125.6	(0.07)	6665.9	(3.02)
Armed Services	730.7	(0.43)	2887.3	(1.35)
Banking	2649.5	(1.64)	2174.6	(1.46)
Budget	-275.5	(0.13)	5101.5	(3.34)
District of Columbia	-1863.1	(0.80)	1408.9	(0.53)
Education and Labor	-3133.0	(1.88)	-3521.3	(1.75)
Energy and Commerce	6709.5	(3.57)	15963.1	(6.25)
Foreign Affairs	-2701.1	(1.65)	-3808.9	(1.46)
Government Operations	-56.3	(0.05)	794.2	(0.40)
House Administration	-2570.3	(1.21)	1311.0	(0.48)
Interior	2747.6	(1.47)	5777.3	(1.85)
Judiciary	-2110.7	(1.05)	-3808.9	(1.44)
Merchant Marine	278.7	(0.17)	3019.8	(1.20)
Post Office	579.9	(0.36)	-3392.9	(2.03)
Public Works/ Transportation	5451.7	(2.91)	6111.4	(2.52)
Rules	3994.0	(1.34)	7211.6	(1.65)
Science and Technology	719.9	(0.40)	1788.1	(0.89)
Small Business	-525.8	(0.33)	2211.8	(1.17)
Standards of Conduct	-229.3	(0.07)	-3150.2	(0.87)
Veteran's Affairs	56.5	(0.04)	2062.6	(0.95)
Ways and Means	7825.9	(4.40)	20130.3	(7.11)
Number of observations	753		776	
pseudo R^2	.232		.272	

Table 8.3 (*continued*)

Dependent variable: Real (1978 $) total contributions by nonparty political action committees to incumbent candidates in the U.S. House.

ᵃ Values of about 2.0 or larger indicate that the coefficient is statistically different from zero at a high level of probability ($\alpha < 0.5$).

Source: Kevin B. Grier and Michael C. Munger, "Committee Assignments, Constituent Preferences, and Campaign Contributions," *Economic Inquiry* 29 (January 1991): p. 34. Reprinted by permission.

earlier model of legislative markets. The Grier and Munger estimates of the determinants of contributions from corporate PACs are shown in Table 8.3. (Three other types of PACs—labor unions, trade associations, and cooperatives—were also analyzed.) On the demand side, they found that most corporate PAC dollars were spent on incumbents who had committee assignments involving legislative and regulatory jurisdictions affecting business firms. After membership on the Ways and Means Committee ($20,130), membership on the Energy and Commerce Committee ($15,963) was valued more highly than membership on other committees in the 1984 elections. Corporate PACs also gave more to Republican incumbents ($4,923) and to those who had a high probusiness rating by the U.S. Chamber of Commerce. House seniority was moderately rewarded, and PACs also gave more to incumbents with narrow margins of victory in the previous election.

The value of most committee memberships in the Grier and Munger study rose sharply between the 1978 and 1980 elections and the 1982 and 1984 elections. The value of a seat on the Energy and Commerce Committee, for example, rose from $6,709 to $15,963 in deflated dollars. Overall, a five-term Republican with a probusiness Chamber of Commerce rating of 70 and a seat on the Energy and Commerce Committee would have received $120,515 in PAC contributions, with only 12.8 percent coming from union PACs. This is the most definitive evidence to date that legislative markets are indeed alive and well, especially in Washington, D.C.

8.24 Policy Implications

One might ask, Whatever happened to the old-fashioned idea that elected representatives should represent the people rather than serving organized interest groups? The very idea of buying and selling political influence is repugnant to many people. Remember, though, that our model of legislative markets is a positive model of how political markets work, not a normative model of how they should work. But because normative issues can't and shouldn't be ignored, let's consider them in more depth.

First, both the economic markets and legislative markets are based in large part on self-interest. This may be good or bad. Self-interest will involve trying to please constituents. As we saw in Chapter 2, self-interest can lead to efficient market outcomes under certain conditions, in theory at least. Adam Smith ([1776] 1937) sagely observed that what concerns the baker isn't necessarily the well-being of the consumer, but his own profit. If things go right, good bread will be supplied at the right time and at the lowest cost, not from the goodness of the baker's heart, but because if he doesn't do it, someone else will. It also seems realistic to assume that self-interested legislators will try to maximize the prospects of reelection, just as self-interested firms try to maximize profits. But the right incentives and circumstances have to exist in either type of market. One of these circumstances is competition—the presence of others who could serve as suppliers of market goods or political services.

A second thought is that legislative markets and economic markets will generally respond not to preachments but to purchasing power. For better or worse, purchasing power is important in both types of markets. If we get unfair outcomes in legislative markets because of the distribution of purchasing power, there is no assurance that things would be any better in economic markets. And vice versa.

Third, current trends will likely continue. The public will be concerned about PAC influence, and there will be heavy PAC support of incumbents; this means large war chests to discourage challengers and reduce electoral competition. In the 1988 elections, when a record 98 percent of the House incumbents who sought reelection won, more incumbents died in office than were defeated. Seven incumbents died in office in the 1987-1988 House, but only six were defeated in their bids for reelection.

Moreover, most House elections are very one-sided; a record 88 percent of those incumbents who won in 1988 did so with more than 60 percent of the vote. Ironically, even with low levels of electoral competition, the average House and Senate winners spent about $370,000 and $3.7 million, respectively, in the 1990 elections (*Congressional Quarterly Weekly Report*, June 29, 1991, p. 1727). Surplus campaign contributions can now be retained as cash on hand for the next election and used, not coincidentally, to scare off potential challengers.[19] Thus, the ability of challengers to compete effectively gets caught up in the negative dynamics of large money needs and poor prospects of winning. To cite Berry:

> Beyond the incumbent's inherent advantage, the behavior of PACs can make the incumbent's victory a self-fulfilling prophecy. By determining that

specific candidates are likely to win and thereby withholding support from challengers, PACs further undermine the challengers' chances. Once deemed unlikely to win, a challenger's chances are worsened because of the critical need for contributions to make the campaign viable. (Berry, 1989, p. 130)

This usually means reduced electoral competition, as captured in this wry note from the 1986 House elections:

> Rep. David Dreier, a Republican incumbent from a strong Republican district in suburban Los Angeles, emerged from the 1986 campaign with more cash on hand—$949,829—than any other House member. A spokesman for Rep. Dreier said the money, which accumulated during the past four years, came mainly from individual donors. "The representative has been fortunate not to have had the strong races that had been anticipated," the spokesman said. (*Wall Street Journal*, April 8, 1987)

As a fourth thought, the lack of electoral competition has been the topic of a timely editorial on ethics in government by one of the market economy's leading publications. Specifically, the editorial comments were addressed to the clamor for action for new ethics laws following the sixty-nine alleged violations of House rules by House Speaker Jim Wright (D., Tex.). Wright subsequently resigned. The editorial concluded:

> Washington doesn't need more ethics. What it needs is more *politics*. Washington has become ethically loose because it has become so politically flabby. The incumbency rate in the House is now 99%. Real politics, unlike Washington's, includes real competition for an institution's seats of power. It includes accountability, so that challengers can criticize their opponent's votes. The current Washington system is designed to minimize these forces. No corporation or any other private institution could remain vibrant or viable for long without competition or accountability. Congress can't either. (*Wall Street Journal*, April 18, 1989)

The obvious implication is that if government was just more competitive, we could vote the bad guys (or women) out and the good guys (or women) in. In this way, the appearance—if not the fact of—impropriety and undue influence now generated by PAC money would be reduced, because PAC money would itself be reduced. As in markets, it would be competed away by the entry of new suppliers who would work for less, regardless of whether ethics, defense, or deregulation were the legislative issue of the moment.

8.3 Summary

Several theoretical models of legislative government have been prominent in the literature. Each features reelection-minded legislators who make proposals to self-interested voters, firms, and interest groups. The Stigler model features firms that seek government regulation for their own benefit, usually through limiting entry by competitors. Legislators in the Peltzman model, however, see warning flags raised by non-beneficiary voters, who despite Downs's image of them as rationally apathetic, might cringe at price increases and associated wealth transfers to producers. In classic Chicago style, the Becker model recognizes that government will engage in wealth transfers but argues that it will likely do so in—no surprise—efficient ways. A variant of these three models, a tax model by Hettich and Winer, sees legislators as setting tax rates, tax bases, and tax exemptions in ways that will enhance their reelection. And a fifth model says that legislators will vote their district by paying attention only to local benefits and costs. In general, these models will not comfort those who are efficiency-minded.

The second half of the chapter focused on markets for legislative activities—a concept that was implicit in the previous models. PAC money is the main currency in these markets. It is not clear whether money buys new friends or rewards existing friends, but most collective choice analysts would probably argue for the latter interpretation.

On a liberal to conservative spectrum, ideology turns out to be a fairly powerful predictor of PAC contributions. Highly polarized interest groups compete for economic favor by funding legislative campaigns, thus giving candidates the media time to compete for votes from the moderate center. The committee system has evolved within Congress as a major way for self-interested legislators to affect legislative outcomes. This and a general lack of electoral competition due to high entry costs have led to high incumbency rates and one-sided elections in the U.S. House of Representatives, in particular.

Terms and Concepts for Review

legislative markets
legislative regulation
Stigler model of regulation
Peltzman model of regulation
wealth transfers and the support function
the opposition function

political equilibrium for a regulator
Becker model of regulation
influence function
efficient transfers
marginal tax administration costs
marginal tax discrimination benefits
voting your district
subdistrict constituency
supradistrict constituency
political action committees (PACs)
ideological dimension
access, consideration, and voting as legislative activities
the demand for legislative activities
legislative committee system
the supply of legislative activities
casework
incumbency and political competition

9

Administrative Government:
Part 1

9.0 Introduction

In the previous two chapters, we have assumed that appointed political suppliers—the bureaucrats—simply do what elected political suppliers tell them to do. A much more common view is that government agencies are hydra-headed monsters that are able to grow back two departments for every one lopped off by tax-conscious legislators.

In this chapter, economic concepts of collective choice will be used to address this crucial disagreement between the common view and the assumption of obedience. We will assume that administrators, like voters, firms, and legislators, are motivated by self-interest. We will continue to note, however, that self-interest isn't always selfish. School superintendents may press for greater spending, for example, not because they want larger salaries but because they believe it is needed to provide a better education for students.

The chapter starts with a brief historical review of public administration. It then considers the venerable notion of iron triangles, or subgovernments within government, followed by the first major economic model of bureaucratic government, Niskanen's budget maximization model. After this we'll look in depth at two ways that legislators might exercise control over appointed suppliers. The first involves the economics of organization or hierarchy. It offers a promising approach to a very general question: How can a "principal" (a legislature, a firm, or an investor, for example) maintain control over an "agent" (an administrative agency, an employee, or a stockbroker) when their interests are likely to conflict, when they have different types and amounts of information, and when they have different incentives to reveal that information?

The second concept deals with agenda control for stabilizing and directing outcomes. In Chapter 6, we found that having stable outcomes might be regarded as a good thing; the Arrow theorem has shown that decision-making with majority rule is an indeterminate process unless vote cycling can be avoided. Instead of just stabilizing outcomes, however, agenda control can also dictate outcomes; this may be either good or bad depending on your point of view. Two examples of agenda control are discussed. The first, congressional dominance, features the oversight role of congressional committees with respect to the activities of administrative agencies. The second—this one at the local level—is the use of reversion budgets to augment school spending.

In general, there is a great deal of disagreement in the economic literature on collective choice about who's running the show. The Niskanen model said that the agencies almost always do, but the more recent congressional dominance approach says that legislatures usually prevail. A third point of view is that the truth lies somewhere in between. This isn't a very definitive conclusion to look forward to, but let's examine the issues.

9.1 Public Administration

Until now, nearly all economic models of administrative government have been normative rather than positive, saying how government should work rather than describing how it works. Economists have developed benefit-cost analysis as a powerful means of evaluating efficiency in government programs (Section 10.1), but they have done little to understand the processes by which appointed political suppliers actually deliver goods and services to clientele. Only Niskanen's (1971) hypothesis that bureaus try to maximize budgets (Section 9.3) has been a major step toward understanding how administrative government works; even so, his model remains largely untested. Nevertheless, the growth of administrative government and the delivery of public services by bureaucratic organizations are facts of life in this nation and throughout the world.

Another group of academics and practitioners, including some economists, has, through the field of *public administration*, made the study of supply by appointed political suppliers its central concern. The models of this group have been both positive and normative. Moreover, an increased recognition of the interaction between elected and appointed suppliers has evolved over time. One textbook gives the traditional view:

> Public administration may be defined as all processes, organizations
> and individuals . . . associated with carrying out laws and other rules
> adopted and issued by legislators, executives and courts. . . . Public
> administration is simultaneously a field of academic study and . . .
> professional training, from which substantial numbers of government
> employees . . . are drawn. (Gordon, 1982, p. 6)

An alternative view is that administrative government plays a far more
active role than this:

> For many years American politics could have been studied with little
> or no attention to bureaucracy. A long intellectual tradition in political
> science separated politics from bureaucracy (administration). Politi-
> cians were supposed to make public policies . . . ; administrators were
> supposed to implement those policies. . . . However, as the roles of
> government increased and expanded and public policies grew more
> complex, politics and administration became thoroughly intertwined.
> (Nachmias and Rosenbloom, 1980, p. 2)

In this view, appointed political suppliers not only implement public
policies, they also play a major role in policy-making.

The first view comes from a view of administrative government that
was heavily influenced by the writings of prominent German sociologist
Max Weber (1946). Like others who have stressed authority and
organization as the keys to getting things done in large governments or
businesses (e.g., Gulick, 1937), Weber believed that what matters in
bureaucratic government is how authority is structured and how tasks
are carried out. In Weber's terms, authority in a modern society is legal
and rational rather than charismatic or based on tradition; this legal and
rational authority allows for rule-based, rather than people-based, government. According to Weber, several elements need to exist to have good
bureaucratic government. These include the following (Gordon, 1982, p.
178):

- a clear division of jurisdiction or duties
- a vertical hierarchy or chain of command
- a formal set of rules and procedures
- maintenance of files and other records
- professionalization of employees.

With these elements, professional employees could "apply general rules
to specific cases"—a hallmark phrase of Weberian logic. The bureaucratic
process might be impersonal, but the rules would provide for efficiency
and equal treatment for all who deal with the bureaucracy.[1]

Management would be from the top down, based on laws or decisions by duly constituted (usually elected) authorities.

These views of Max Weber's, along with those of Woodrow Wilson (1885), who is often called the father of public administration, are still much in evidence in the teachings and writings of many in public administration. They have been softened and shaped over time, however, by the criticisms and insights of such authors as Herbert Simon (1946, 1947), who showed how the "proverbs of public administration" were often logically contradictory, and Vincent Ostrom (1989), who argued that overlapping jurisdictions and fragmentation of authority could often lead to improved outcomes. A new challenge to the conventional wisdom is now offered by James Q. Wilson (1980, 1989) and his "bottom up" approach to understanding agency behavior. In his recent landmark book *Bureaucracy: What Government Agencies Do, and Why They Do It*, Wilson writes:

> There are two ways to look at government agencies: from the top down and from the bottom up. Most books, and almost all elected officials, tend to take the first view. The academic perspective, much influenced by Max Weber (and lately by economic theories of the firm), typically centers on the structure, purposes, and resources of the organization. . . . These are important matters, but the emphasis . . . has caused us to lose sight of what government agencies *do* and how the doing of it is related to attaining goals or satisfying clients. (1989, p. 11)

Wilson's bottom-up approach uses a three-pronged people scheme: Operators perform the central tasks of the organization, managers supervise and coordinate activities within the organization, and executives ensure the flow of resources to the organization. One of Wilson's former students, John J. DiIulio, offers this comment on the importance of that topology:

> In *Bureaucracy*, Wilson treats operators, managers, and executives in that order, and the order is not incidental. Rather, the order reflects one of his most fundamental and persistent ideas about the determinants of agency performance; namely, that it is . . . the nature of operators' tasks—as opposed to the styles of the agency's managers, the behavior and preferences of its executives, and the goals carved into statutes by those who legislate and lobby over its existence—that ultimately determines "what government agencies do and why they do it." (1991, p. 194)

9.2 Iron Triangles and Subgovernments:
A Consensus Model

One representative of an active role by appointed suppliers is the *iron triangle*, or *subgovernment* concept; this simply adds an administrative agency as a third party to the Chapter 8 alliance between interest groups and legislators.[2] According to Berry, "a subgovernment consists primarily of interest groups advocates, legislators and their aides, and key agency administrators who interact on an on-going basis and control policy making in a particular area" (1989, p. 172). One can think, for example, of a water subgovernment, a health subgovernment, or a defense subgovernment, the latter manifested in President Eisenhower's farewell warning about a military-industrial complex involving the defense industry, the Department of Defense, and those legislators who want to gain or protect military bases in their districts.

9.21 Origins

According to Berry (1989), the iron triangle, or subgovernment, concept can be traced to Ernest Griffith's *Impasse of Democracy* (1939). It has long been a staple in political science and public administration. One reason for its longevity has been that it offers a challenge to the pluralist point of view that policy-making is open, responsive, and not dominated by just a few groups (Truman, 1951; Dahl, 1961). Berry portrays the persistence of the idea in this way: "Subgovernments offer an image of agency capture by clientele groups, highly restricted participation, stability that preserves the status quo, and centralized decision making. Subgovernments are thus evidence that our group-based policy-making system is deeply flawed and does not promote democratic government" (1989, p. 195).

There seems to be general agreement among political scientists that iron triangles have had great influences in some policy areas in the past. In few areas has this influence been as strong as in water resource development. Starting in the 1950s, there was a great deal of federal investment in water resource development, much of it involving river and harbor improvements and multiple-purpose reservoirs for flood control, power generation, and other uses. Many of the benefits were either nonexcludable (flood protection, for example) or socially desirable (water-based recreation, for example), so the federal government paid most of the bill. The construction projects gave local economies a boost, making them attractive to local politicians, and the Army Corps of

Engineers and the Bureau of Reclamation were not at all reluctant to build dams.

The power of the water triangle can be illustrated by President Carter's ill-fated proposal to eliminate thirty-two major water resource projects; this "hit list" proposal was made soon after he took office in 1977. Some of the projects were already well under way, and some were in key legislative districts (Schooler and Ingram, 1981-1982). Tim R. Miller interviewed thirty experts on water policy in 1983 and found that the following statement about an iron triangle, along with one on ineffective presidential leadership, best described why the experts thought Carter's proposal was doomed from the start: "President Carter's hit-list water policy failed . . . because federal water policy making is dominated by . . . *congressional water committees* and/or subcommittees, top officials of the *water agencies,* . . . and various pro-development *interest groups*" (1985, p. 398, italics added).

9.22 Criticisms

The importance and even the existence of subgovernments has come under scrutiny in recent years. Two broad types of criticism have been raised. The first is the lack of a strong theoretical basis; the concept is a snapshot of the main actors at a point in time, rather than an explanation of how the system came to be or how it might change over time. To most economists, iron triangle is an archaic term with little analytical content. Political scientist Hugh Heclo comments that the concept "is not so much wrong as it is disastrously incomplete" (1978, p. 88, quoted by Berry, 1989, p. 174). Heclo and many other political scientists see the idea of issue networks as a vast improvement over iron triangles; these are groups of people and organizations who share technical expertise and information in certain areas of policy (Berry, 1989, Chapter 8).

The second type of criticism is that although subgovernments are portrayed as consensual or harmonious, the real world is often filled with conflict. Berry cites several studies in which a high percentage of interest groups felt that they faced strong adversary interest groups. Salisbury and others (1987), for example, found that the number of interest groups that were actively involved in different stages of policy formation and execution ranged from twenty-four to twenty-eight in various areas of public policy. This is not quiet, consensual government.

Berry attributes most of the weakening of subgovernments to the proliferation of interest groups, each having a voting constituency and a claim to legislative attention. In the water resource area, for example, the strong prodevelopment bias of the 1950s and early 1960s was reduced by a variety of factors. Each of these opened up the political process. One key factor, somewhat unique to the water policy area, was that most of the best dam sites had been used by about 1970—the remaining projects involved much higher economic and environmental costs. Increased awareness of environmental issues after Earth Day in 1969 led to protests, new alternatives, greater citizen activism, and the passage of legislation such as the National Environmental Policy Act (NEPA). In Miller's (1985) study, the thirty national water authorities agreed that even though the water subgovernment was still strong enough to clobber Carter's "hit list" in 1977, it had been in a state of decline since the mid-1970s. Most of them attribute this decline to environmental opposition and to changes in membership and attitudes in Congress.

The growth of competing interest groups can also be documented in many other areas of policy. Many of these are citizen-based, and without doubt, they have made life much less comfortable for entrenched, prodevelopment producer groups. A recurring puzzle, of course, is why citizen-based interest groups have been able to grow in numbers and strength in view of the ample opportunities for free-riding by individual citizens.

9.3 Niskanen and Bureaucratic Government: A Conflict Model

The subgovernment concept can be criticized because it is theoretically fuzzy and too attuned to consensus. The Niskanen (1971) model of bureaucracy met both of these criticisms. It was the first major deductive model of bureaucracy in representative government, and it was based explicitly on conflict between legislative and administrative branches of government.[3] The model has now been eclipsed to some extent by more formal successors, but it made a long-lasting contribution by focusing on three crucial elements of the relationship between elected and appointed suppliers. These three elements are bilateral monopoly, asymmetric information, and budget maximization.

9.31 Bilateral Monopoly and Asymmetric Information

As far back as Woodrow Wilson and the early days of public administration, that profession claimed that the best way to organize administrative government is to make it hierarchical and noncompetitive (Ostrom, 1989). That is, government agencies should be in layers, with different levels of responsibility and different scopes of activity. It would be appropriate, for example, that the Parks and Recreation Division of city government consist of a Parks Branch and a Recreation Branch. This would invite specialization of tasks and skills, avoid duplication of effort, and allow the division chief to parcel out blame for things not done and for things done poorly. The chain of command would be well specified and the organizational chart would glimmer with an air of order.

Niskanen observed, however, that this is exactly how one would *not* want to structure a market economy. If one firm produced all the clothing and another firm produced all the furniture, this would create two monopolies—each free to gouge the consumers. And a bureau that was set up in this manner would also be an invitation to exploitative behavior. If it was the sole source of a particular service, and especially if it was the only provider of a range of services that could substitute for each other, an agency could exact a higher "price" than if there were other sources of supply.

This way of looking at the world invokes agencies as taking an active role, and this is exactly how Niskanen thought they should be viewed because their administrators are motivated by self-interest. The degree to which the agencies are successful, however, is constrained by the fact that most legislatures are arranged in a similar manner. Rather than being vertical structures with different levels of authority, legislatures are usually organized into committees with different types of authority. Legislative structure tends to be horizontal rather then vertical, but as with the agencies, there is still specialization of duties and skills.

These structures create a *bilateral monopoly* situation; there is often only one seller of a particular service—an administrative agency—and one buyer of that service—a legislative committee. For example, the National Park Service (NPS) is one of five major administrative units within the Department of Interior. It is responsible for the administration of national parks, monuments, historical sites, and recreation areas. According to the Niskanen model, organizations like the National Park Service can be defined as bureaus because they are "nonprofit organizations which are financed, at least in part, by a periodic appropriation or grant" (1971, p. 15). They may sell some goods and services, which the National Park Service does by charging admission to certain areas and facilities and by granting leases to park concessionaires for food and lodging. But the agency must also seek periodic appropriations of money from the public treasury, because it "specialize[s] in providing these goods and services that some people prefer to be supplied in larger amounts than would be supplied by their sale at a per unit rate" (1971, p. 18). Most people would probably agree that markets alone wouldn't provide an appropriate amount of historical, cultural, and natural preservation; thus, periodic appropriations to the National Park Service would be in the public interest.

To gain these appropriations, however, means that at least two appropriate congressional subcommittees must support the budget request of the National Park Service. In the 102nd Congress (1991-1992), one subcommittee is the House Subcommittee on National Parks and Public Lands, which is one of six standing subcommittees of the House Interior and Insular Affairs Committee. The other is the Senate Subcommittee on Public Lands, National Parks and Forests, which is one of five standing subcommittees of the Senate Energy and Natural Resources Committee.[4] These two subcommittees from their respective chambers have jurisdiction over legislation in three areas: recreation, the national park system, and the Bureau of Land Management. Jurisdiction for funding levels and revenue sources belongs to the appropriations and revenue committees in each chamber, but these two subcommittees are charged with oversight functions, including recommendations on funding levels. Each of these is what Niskanen called a "sponsor"; each bargains with the bureau in a bilateral monopoly context through subcommittee hearings on program, timing, geographic location, and other dimensions, all of which are ultimately translated into an appropriations request.[5]

In market terms, the outcome of a bilateral monopoly is usually indeterminate. Whether the buyer or seller comes out ahead depends on many things, including strategy, information, circumstances, and luck. Not coincidentally, bilateral monopoly is a topic in economics where decision making under uncertainty and the theory of games reign supreme as analytical tools. The one element of uncertainty that Niskanen stressed most heavily in applying it to bureaucracy was *asymmetric information*—the fact that an agency, as supplier, usually has much more information about its activities than does the sponsor. This is greatly complicated, Niskanen argued, by the fact that most of the data and statistics that agencies present in defense of budget requests are measures of inputs rather than measures of outputs. They reflect the things that the agency does, uses, or buys rather than what it produces with these actions or purchases.

For example, one major statistic that the National Park Service would surely present to its sponsor would be data on the numbers of people who have visited national parks in recent years. If the very reason for having the agency, however, is to protect certain areas of natural and historical significance and to enhance public understanding, enjoyment, and appreciation of these areas, attendance at the parks is simply a way of allowing this to happen; it is not the final product. The final product is the extent of public understanding, enjoyment, and appreciation—these are very difficult things to measure.

The difficulty of measuring outcomes, according to Niskanen, is the crux of the bureaucratic problem. Agency output is usually vague and highly subjective, and it is costly for a sponsor to determine how inputs are translated into outputs and to monitor the delivery system. The National Park Service hires people to lead nature hikes, maintain campgrounds, restore historic buildings, and many other things. Each of these is an input into the agency's output of enhancing understanding, enjoyment, and appreciation. In economic terms, each is a part of the agency's production function. It would be helpful if the agency and its sponsor knew, for example, that it takes six hours of campground maintenance to produce one unit of final output but only two hours of nature hikes to do the same thing. These facts aren't usually known, however, and the agency and sponsor must bargain over the extent of inputs or activities, rather than over outputs.

Government agencies, according to Niskanen, almost always have better information on the cost and productivity of inputs than do their legislative sponsors. Based on past experience, the National Park Service will know with reasonable certainty how many nature hikes can be led and how many historic buildings can be restored with a budget of a given size. Knowing this, the agency will offer the sponsor a particular set of activities in exchange for an appropriation or budget of a certain size. The activities will certainly have something to do with output, but the relationship will necessarily be vague. The level of overall activity that the agency will offer, however, will depend on the consequences of different-sized budgets.

In most cases, the total cost of the activities will rise as shown by the TC function in Figure 9.1; this reflects the *minimum* budget that the agency would need to deliver a range of possible outputs. To deliver Q^* output through a set of activities, for example, would cost at least C^*; the agency couldn't do it for less. The marginal cost of additional output (MC) might be constant over some range of output, but for realism, it is shown as increasing throughout the range of output in Figure 9.2. If more output was produced, higher prices would have to be paid for some inputs, especially those that are specialized to the types of things that the National Park Service does. More aggressive plans for land acquisition might drive up the price of land, for example, and specialized labor for historic restoration might also be in short supply.

The set of activities that the agency will promise and the budget amount that it will request depends on how the agency views the demand by the legislative sponsor for different levels of output. Because the sponsor represents a constituency that values these services, and because the sponsor wants to be reelected, the sponsor will offer a budget in exchange for the agency's set of activities. More activities by the

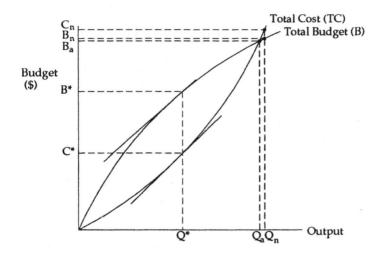

FIGURE 9.1 The Output of a Public Agency

National Park Service will usually require more tax dollars, however, and this will mean fewer public goods and fewer after-tax private goods for constituents. And the legislative sponsor also has jurisdiction for recreation and for the Bureau of Land Management as well as for the National Park Service; each of these may be another option for keeping constituents happy. Thus, the total budget (TB) function in Figure 9.1 reflects the *maximum* budget that the sponsor will grant (B^*, for example) in exchange for a certain level of activities and expected output (Q^*, for example). The maximum budget will probably increase over some range of proposed outputs, but at a diminishing rate because the marginal benefits to constituents will be declining. Thus, the sponsor's marginal benefit (MB) function in Figure 9.2 will be downward sloping, much like a consumer's demand for a market good.

Three questions might be asked about Niskanen's model. One is whether the preferences of constituents are accurately reflected in the marginal-benefit function. To simplify his analysis, Niskanen swept this key issue aside by assumption: Constituent preferences were assumed to be accurately reflected through the legislative process. A very different argument could be made, of course, that certain preferences are over-represented in the legislative process because the sponsors that deal with specific jurisdictions such as the National Park Service have strong vested interests in those particular goods and services. We need to return to this issue later in the chapter.

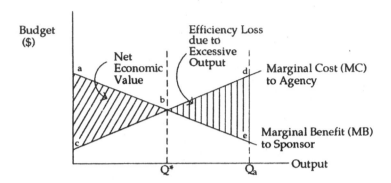

FIGURE 9.2 Marginal Costs and Benefits of Agency Output

A second question is whether the marginal benefit and marginal cost functions are accurately perceived by the agency. Niskanen believed that agencies usually have a good idea of costs, and indeed, there is an incentive for this—the agency head doesn't want to be embarrassed by promising an output that cannot be delivered with an assigned budget. Agency personnel have more frequent and direct contacts with users than does the sponsor; thus, the agency may have the better knowledge of benefits as well as costs.

A third question, however, is the key to the Niskanen model. Among the different outputs that the agency could promise and the different budgets that they could propose, which one *will* they propose, and why?

9.32 Budget Maximization

Niskanen's response to this question was direct and simple: An agency will try to maximize its budget.[6] Although Niskanen stated this as a hypothesis for others to test, his own recounting of personal experiences in government left little doubt that he viewed it as fact waiting to be confirmed. One often-quoted assertion is the following:

> The rationality of budget maximization by bureaucrats may best be illustrated by considering the consequences of contrary behavior. Consider the probable consequences for a subordinate manager who

proves without question that the same output could be produced at, say, one-half the present expenditures. In a profit-seeking firm this manager would probably receive a bonus, a promotion, and an opportunity to find another such economy; if such rewards are not forthcoming in a specific firm, this manager usually has the opportunity to market his skills in another firm. In a bureau, at best, this manager might receive a citation and a savings bond, a lateral transfer, the enmity of his former colleagues, and the suspicion of his new colleagues. Those bureaucrats who doubt this proposition and who have good private employment alternatives should test it . . . once. (1971, p. 38)

An alternative and, in Niskanen's view, more naive model of agency behavior is that an agency would offer an output level (Q^*) and request a budget level (B^*) that would maximize the net economic value from the agency's activities ($B^* - C^*$, Figure 9.1). At output Q^*, the marginal budget received from the sponsor (and by assumption, the marginal benefits of agency output to the sponsor's constituents) would equal the marginal cost to the agency (Figure 9.2). This, it should be noted, could be consistent with either the Good Fairy model (no losers) or the Semigood Fairy model (the losers might or might not be compensated) of Chapter 7. That is, government would intervene to produce what the market would not produce. Not only would it produce the good, it would produce an efficient amount of it, restricting output to Q^* because the net economic value (consumers' surplus plus producers' surplus) would be the greatest at that point. The Uncertain World model, however, recognizes that agencies may seek an output other than Q^* because of uncertainty about agency costs or sponsor (constituent) demands.

The Niskanen approach is definitely of the Wicked Witch genre; it says that self-interested agency heads will seek budgets that are inefficiently large. If they emerge victorious from bilateral monopoly at bargaining with their less-informed sponsor, as one would expect, they will have promised an output level of Q_a and obtained a budget of B_a. Not only will they fail to capture the net gains that Q^* could have produced (area abc in Figure 9.2), they will cause additional output to be produced so that an equal amount of negative net economic value (area bde) will result.[7] At Q_a output, nothing is really produced except a larger agency. By expanding, the agency absorbs any possible gain to constituents and negates its reason for being. The Niskanen model was powerful stuff indeed.

Niskanen explored various reasons for an agency's trying to maximize its budget. He concluded that it probably doesn't matter; all the major contenders are positively related to budget size. Included among the reasons are the agency head's salary, the salaries of his key subordinates, their perquisites in office—power, prestige, patronage—and the reputation of the agency head and of the agency itself. Just as a (successful) self-interested legislator can do good or evil in office, a (successful) self-interested bureaucrat can also do good or evil. And the larger the budget, the more good or evil he or she can do.

9.33 Criticisms of the Model

Because of its simplicity and powerful conclusions, the Niskanen model quickly became a major part of collective choice lore. As the first real supply-side theory in what had been a demand-driven Downsian world (Section 7.3), the idea of budget-maximizing bureaucrats caught on fast among collective choice analysts. Agencies would produce too much, even without friendly faces among the legislative sponsors, and they would produce far too much if those faces were friendly, which would usually be the case.

But there were criticisms of the Niskanen model. To some, the idea of budget-maximizing was ideologically slanted; they charged that conservatives such as Niskanen simply don't like big government and that his model was a pseudoscientific way to bash government. Others were offended because their view of agencies was that of people trying to help people, not of people possessed by self-interest. Hiemstra's (1973) and Breimyer's (1973) vehement rejections of Bryant's (1972) portrayal of the federal food stamp program along budget-maximizing lines was an early case in point.

Other social scientists criticized the model because it was not consistent with fact. Ruttan (1980), for example, wondered why the rate of return to public investment in agricultural research was still in the 30 to 60 percent range, far above what might be expected from a private firm. To him, this indicated underinvestment and too little public output, rather than overinvestment and too much public output. He concluded that "There is little doubt that a level of expenditure that would push rates of return to below 20 percent would be in the public interest" (p. 531). Other critics have focused on the cost of agency output, that is, the location of TC in Figure 9.1. Clearly, the public's perception of agencies as suppliers includes such needless expenses as $400 hammers and $600 toilet seats. There is a body of research that compares the costs of agency and private-sector output, with the agencies usually looking bad, but that literature is not yet very extensive because of problems with comparing the quality of outputs.

One of the major criticisms of the Niskanen model, however, is the limited extent to which it can be tested with scientific methods. The model describes relationships that may exist in people's minds, but if these relationships can't be objectively measured, it may be difficult to know whether people are talking about the same thing. Assume, for example, that MB_{true} in Figure 9.3 represents the true preferences of constituents for National Park Service output. If the costs of providing this output were MC, output Q^* would maximize the net economic value of the park system's activities. If the National Park Service acted as a successful budget maximizer in bilateral bargaining with its legislative sponsor, however, output Q_a would occur. The net economic value of the agency's output would be zero; area abc would be matched and negated by area bde.

But we may never know what MB_{true} is, for several reasons. By its nature, a considerable portion of National Park Service output is provided as nonexcludable public goods (scenic views and historical restorations, for example). Even if users had to reveal their preferences for these goods, we might not know whether these preferences were accurately transmitted through the political process by elected suppliers. Because of these factors, agency personnel may honestly feel that the constituents' true preference for agency output is MB_{agency}. If this is true,

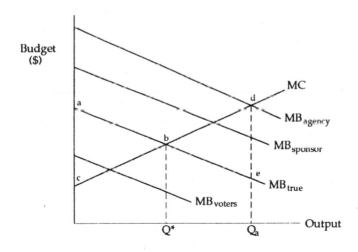

FIGURE 9.3 Different Perceptions of National Park Service Output

output Q^* will be inefficiently small and agency people may rightly claim that output Q_a will maximize net economic value.

By the same token, the sponsor may see the value of National Park Service output as $MB_{sponsor}$. From the voting-your-district model of Chapter 8, it seems likely that sponsoring legislators would tend to be from districts where the parks, historic sites, and recreation areas are located or from urban districts that have high percentages of park users. These legislators would thus have a greater-than-average interest in the National Park Service. Even so, they might have a lesser estimate of value than would agency employees, who tend to be strong advocates of their own programs. Quite likely, all three of these functions will exceed MB_{voters} because many voters may not be aware of the historic and natural values that the agency is trying to preserve and enhance.

Budget maximization is posed by Niskanen as a goal that is likely to be achieved because the agency knows more about its activities than does the sponsor. Because we lack knowledge of the marginal benefit function, however, it is not clear what conclusion should be drawn even if we could, in fact, establish that Q^* was the output level. One conclusion might be that the agency had tried to maximize the budget by offering output Q_a but had succumbed to the bargaining power of the sponsor and wound up producing only Q^*. A second and very different conclusion is that agencies really do try to produce Q^* and thus maximize net economic value rather than maximizing their own budget size. The two conclusions are miles apart, yet both are consistent with the existence of Q^* output.

Despite these objections, the Niskanen budget-maximization hypothesis has won a permanent spot in the collective choice hall of fame because it is a plausible explanation, one that is consistent with the reality of excessive government size that many people claim to observe. Regardless of how "right" the model turns out to be, its focus on conflict between the legislators who make the rules and the agencies that administer them is a lasting contribution.

9.4 The Economics of Organization

The main question in this chapter is, Who's in charge—the elected suppliers who make policy decisions or the appointed suppliers who administer these decisions? The idea of iron triangles seems too mushy, but Niskanen's model of a budget-maximizing bureaucrat is a step in the right direction. In the rest of this chapter, we'll look at several newer insights that aid in understanding legislative-administrative interactions.

Many of these insights have to do with the economics of organiza-tion.[8] In the past, economists have generally ignored *organizations*, which might be defined as groups of persons organized for some end. Instead, they have preferred to use more vague and formless concepts on the grounds that they didn't need to study real-life organizations. Markets, for example, are assumed to be made by willing buyers and willing sellers. Firms produce goods and services. Even though this high degree of abstraction puzzles some, economists have justified it on grounds of simplicity. They argue that if simple assumptions help generate testable propositions, why use more complex assumptions even though they may be more realistic? Every budding economist is given Milton Friedman's (1953) advice that one should not judge assumptions by their realism but by the validity of the predictions that they allow.

In spite of this tradition, economists have now become more interested in organizations, and in particular in how incentives help determine economic outcomes. Moe (1984) characterizes this new interest in the economics of organizations as having three elements. The first is a contractual perspective, the second is the focus on hierarchical control, and the third is the use of principal-agent models.

9.41 The Shoemaker's Shop

Although a few economists took a behavioral approach to under-standing the economics of organization (Simon, 1947, 1957; March and Simon, 1958; Cyert and March, 1963), a contractual approach has been more common. In 1937, a focus on contracts led Ronald Coase to the first major explanation for the existence of firms. That is, firms emerge as units of social organization when transactions costs can be reduced and profits enhanced by contracting; authority is thereby substituted for markets as a control mechanism. To illustrate Coase's argument, let's suppose that a shoemaker has two options in deciding how to operate his shop. The first is to remain a one-operator show and to use markets for every transaction that might be needed in making and selling shoes. As we noted in Chapter 3, transactions costs would have to be incurred in acquiring and evaluating information and in making and monitoring agreements. For example, a contract would have to be made each time leather is purchased and each time labor is hired. These costs would have to be incurred for each separate use of the market, although some of the contracting procedures could no doubt be simplified.

The second option would be for the shoemaker to substitute hierarchy for markets as a means of operating his shop. Oliver William-son, a leader in the field of organization, contrasts the two options as follows: "Market transactions involve exchange between autonomous economic entities . . . hierarchical transactions are ones for which a single administrative entity spans both sides of the transaction, some form of subordination prevails, and typically, consolidated ownership obtains" (1975, p. xi).

Instead of using the market for each transaction, the shoemaker could hire a helper to tan and cut the leather, to make the shoes, and perhaps even to sell them. The shoemaker would still have to use markets for some things—buying the untanned leather, for example—but the transaction costs of hiring a subordinate as a versatile factor of production might be less than the transactions costs of a series of market contracts. "In other words: For this series of contracts is substituted one . . . whereby the factor, for a certain remuneration . . . agrees to obey the directions of an entrepreneur within certain limits. The essence of the contract is that it should state only the limits to the power of the entrepreneur" (Coase, 1937, p. 391).

Although the shoemaker's simple shop may seem like a homely example, it contains, in microcosm, most of the major concepts that can help us understand the interactions between Congress or other legislatures and the bureaucracies they are supposed to govern.

9.42 Hierarchy and Conflicts of Interest

The shoemaker example introduces hierarchy and subordination, and in so doing, it introduces two major problems that beset any hierarchical firm or government agency. One is the potential for conflict of interest, the other is the problem of asymmetric information. Both involve incentives, and both affect outcomes. A conflict of interest may exist, for example, between an agency head who wants to maximize budget size and workers who want to maximize some combination of earnings, leisure, and job satisfaction. This type of conflict may also exist, of course, between profit-seeking entrepreneurs and their employees.

Let's look, then, at self-interest and conflict of interest in the shoemaker's shop. The shoemaker's helper may engage in what the literature calls *shirking*: He may doze off, for example, and this would generate a cost for the shoemaker—profits would be reduced. For the shoemaker to constantly monitor the helper would also involve a cost, and perhaps a large cost, on the shoemaker's part. An appropriate incentive system needs to be created to solve this problem. Coase thought that the shoemaking firm would exist because of reduced transactions costs, but Alchian and Demsetz (1972) based their explanation for the firm's existence on reduction in shirking. The shoemaker and his helper are both *team members*, they argued, and the productivities of the two are interrelated. There is thus an incentive for both to free ride on the productivity of the other, especially if there happen to be many team members and if the costs of monitoring are high. Alchian and Demsetz argued that the firm evolves as a social unit when society allows one team member, the shoemaker in this case, to claim marketable title to the output of the team. The shoemaker has to pay the helper for the share of the output that the helper has created, but beyond that, the shoemaker can pocket the rest as profit. Therefore, the shoemaker/entrepreneur has an incentive to monitor performance, an incentive that would be lacking if no team member could claim the residual.

9.43 Principals and Agents

A subsequent approach has been to look more closely at the causes of shirking, not just at the effects. This approach stems from a variety of intellectual sources, but they all point to an inherent problem with hierarchies—the asymmetry of information among contracting parties. These sources include work on incomplete information and risk-sharing (Ross, 1973; Spence and Zeckhauser, 1971; Spence, 1974; Shavell, 1979), markets and hierarchies (Williamson, 1975), and organizations (Mitnick, 1980; Fama, 1980; Jensen, 1983). The sources agree that some parties have more and different information than do other parties. This, together with the likelihood of conflicts of interests, is often modeled as a *principal-agent relationship*. Moe expresses it this way:

> The principal-agent model is an analytic expression of the agency relationship, in which one party, the principal, considers entering into a contractual agreement with another, the agent, in the expectation that the agent will subsequently choose actions that produce outcomes desired by the principal. Examples of agency relationships are legion; lawyer-client, doctor-patient, broker-investor, politician-citizen, and, most generally, employee-employer. As these examples tend to suggest, a principal may seek out an agent for various reasons. Often he may lack specialized knowledge or legal certification that the agent possesses, and sometimes the size or complexity of the task simply requires coordinated action by persons other than himself. But . . . the principal's decision problem is far more involved than simply locating a qualified person—for there is no guarantee that the agent, once hired, will . . . choose to pursue the principal's best interests. . . . The agent has his own interests at heart, and is induced to pursue the principal's objectives only to the extent that the incentive structure imposed in their contract renders such behavior advantageous.

> The essence of the principal's problem is the design of just such an incentive structure. The difficulty, of course, is that information about the agent's actions . . . is not only imperfect but skewed in favor of the agent. (Moe, 1984, p. 756)

As an alternative view, Kiewiet and McCubbins stress the role of authority rather than contract. In their definition: "An agency relationship is established when an agent is delegated . . . the authority to take action on behalf of . . . the principal" (1991, pp. 239-240).

The two general types of problems that plague principal-agent relationships are known as *adverse selection* and *moral hazard*.[9] These two concepts (and the particular terms used to describe them) emerged from the early insurance literature, where they were used to describe different types of risks that are faced by insurance companies as principals. The problem of adverse selection is due to unobservability of the information, benefits, and values on which the decisions of others are based. Moral hazard arises from unobservability of the actual behavior of an agent (Moe, 1984, pp. 754-755). The first problem is ex ante, or prior to the making of a contract; the second is ex post, after a contract has been made. In simple terms, the risk of adverse selection is that the principal may not know which agent would be best to hire or how to define the terms of a contract or the scope of authority. The risk of moral hazard arises when an agent, once hired, changes his behavior to the detriment of the principal. In either case, an *agency problem* may exist for the principal.

Now, let's go back to the shoemaker's shop. The shoemaker needs a helper, but there is unavoidable uncertainty about which job applicant he should hire. The shoemaker has in mind a set of criteria: experience, intelligence, work habits, attitude, maybe even subservience. But he has only crude proxies about how each candidate or agent would stack up. Have they worked as helpers? Do they know what the various shoe-making tools are for? Have they ever been fired? (Do they always tell the truth?) The ironic reality of adverse selection is this: At the offered wage, those applicants who are most qualified for the job are the least interested because they have better options! Those applicants who are least qualified are the most interested in the job because it's the best one they can find.[10] The shoemaker, like any principal, is faced with an adverse selection problem that arises because the applicants know more about themselves and their capabilities than he, the principal, does.

Once a helper is hired, the moral hazard problem arises. The agent, having landed the job, may change his behavior to enhance his self-interest. Getting fired won't help, but there may be opportunities to enjoy more leisure than is intended by the principal. To quote Moe:

Shirking behavior, therefore, is an aspect of moral hazard, with the incentive to shirk deriving from underlying information asymmetries. . . . Moral hazard and adverse selection are general problems whose potential is inherent in all contracting and hierarchical relationships. As theoretical concepts, they are particularly valuable for understanding situations in which one party seeks to control the behavior of another, or more generally, to achieve certain outcomes (such as profits) by relying on and structuring the behavior of various other actors. (1984, p. 755)

The shoemaker, the chief executive officer of a large corporation, or a Congress will thus succeed as principals only if they understand that:

The design of an efficient incentive structure is thus bound up with the development of monitoring systems as well as mechanisms for inducing the agent to reveal as much of his privately held information as possible. The principal must weave these interrelated components into a contractual framework that . . . prompts the agent to behave as the principal himself would under whatever conditions might prevail. (Moe, 1984, pp. 756-757)

An auto insurance company, for example, faces an adverse selection problem; the drivers it would like to insure—the truly low-risk drivers—are those who are least likely to need or buy the insurance. Instead, the company will receive too many applications from high-risk drivers, so they will need to address this problem by setting up a premium structure that reflects actuarial risk. The company also faces a moral hazard problem; even low-risk drivers may become careless about locking their car, for example, after they purchase an insurance policy. A common way for the company to address this risk is through a deductible clause in which drivers must pay the first amount of any loss from theft (usually $100 or $500). The intent is that drivers will be more likely to remember to lock their cars.

9.5 Principals and Agents in Government

This chapter is not about shoemakers and auto insurance but about whether elected legislatures or nonelected agencies tend to dominate the other. An iron triangle advocate would claim that the two sides usually join forces to do so; Niskanen would say that bureaus, by their nature, have the most information and thus the most leverage in bargaining with legislatures. A third and more recent approach, congressional dominance, takes the opposite point of view—that Congress as principal effectively controls the bureaus as agents. So, who really controls whom?

9.51 Adverse Selection and Moral Hazard

Before we go further, we need to consider the question of whether the ideas of organization and hierarchy apply to governments as well as business. The shoemaker's helper may shirk and insurance premiums may reflect risk, but how do these concepts apply to legislatures and agencies? How well does the new economics of organization fit the public sector, where the profit motive doesn't apply?

Three points seem appropriate in arguing that the analogies are, in fact, useful. First, the principal-agent analogy is valid because the law says it is valid. That is, "Congress is the bureau's superior in the hierarchy of governmental authority—it is the principal (or, in practice, its committees are) and the bureau its agent. As a principal, Congress therefore has the authority to issue orders, adopt incentive systems, control the bureaucratic agenda, and otherwise structure the principal-agent relationship as it sees fit" (Moe, 1984, p. 778).

The principal-agent relationship is likely to be plagued, of course, by conflict of interest and asymmetric information. Conflict of interest will occur if legislatures try to maximize the chance of reelection and if bureaus try to maximize budget size or some other dimension of self-interest. The iron triangle approach suggests that there are ranges of compatibility, that legislative high-demanders and certain agency administrators can find areas of consensus that will benefit both groups as well as key interest groups. This, of course, simply highlights the fact that in government, there are bound to be multiple principals; a legislature is likely to have a divided opinion about what it wants an agency to do. Some legislators may want more flood-control dams built, for example, but others may fight these projects tooth and nail on environmental grounds. Which side will win depends on relative numbers, intensities of preferences, the costs of forming coalitions, and whether agenda control can be exercised.

A second reason for arguing that ideas of organization and hierarchy apply to agencies and legislatures is that they have different types and amounts of information. In most cases, it seems unlikely that it could be any other way. This doesn't mean that all information is equally valuable; legislative committees simply don't need or want all the information that agencies possess. The more pertinent question is whether the committees know what information they need and whether they can gain access to it in a timely manner.

A third reason to believe that the ideas of organization and hierarchy apply to governments is that there are, in fact, significant problems of adverse selection and moral hazard in the implicit contracts between legislative committees, as principals, and bureaus, as agents. Kiewiet and McCubbins (1991, Chapter 2) discuss four general types of measures that principals can use in attempting to overcome the general agency problem. The first is *screening and selection* of agents. If there is a choice of government agency to which a task can be delegated, a legislative committee can reduce the problem of adverse selection by using proxies about the likely behavior of the multiple agents. The previous performance of an agency is one such proxy.

A second way to deal with the agency problem is through *contract design.* If there is only one possible agent, the magnitude of the agency problem may depend on how administrative responsibility is assigned to the agents rather than to whom it is assigned. Some types of contract design may be more attractive than others to a legislature. One element of design is the choice of regulatory method. McCubbins (1985) suggests two methods that a legislature might use in countering the risk of adverse selection and particularly moral hazard. The first is for a legislature to explicitly define the regulatory scope of a legislative act; the second is for it to define procedural requirements for administering the act. Each of these is an element of the contract with an agency. In the Toxic Substances Control Act, for example, the regulatory scope was defined to include one class of chemicals that the Environmental Protection Agency had authority to regulate and another class (pesticides, drugs, food additives) that it did not have authority to regulate. According to McCubbins, "By constraining the range of alternative regulatory targets, Congress can reinforce its control over the decision making. By constraining the range of potential regulatory targets, Congress also limits the administrator's substantive discretion and protects itself against manipulation and exploitation by agents" (1985, p. 726). The definition of procedural requirements for administering this act could involve specifying the hearing process, the burden of proof, and the standards and evidence for review. More rigid sets of procedural requirements would limit agency discretion more than less rigid sets.

A third way for principals to deal with the agency problem is through *monitoring and reporting.* As we know, the risk of moral hazard exists for the principal because an agency may change its behavior after a contract is made, especially if the agency is allowed substantial discretion by the legislature. As we saw with the National Park Service example (Section 9.31), monitoring an agency to reduce moral hazard is often difficult and costly, especially if output is hard to define.[11] Monitoring may be costly, but allowing the agency to set its own course may also be costly for a legislature facing reelection. Two issues are raised; one is how to monitor, the second is how much to monitor, and conversely, how much risk might rationally be incurred by a principal.

On the issue of how to monitor, the McCubbins and Schwartz (1984) distinction between *police patrol oversight* and *fire alarm oversight* is highly instructive. Police patrols, so to speak, involve audits, investigations, and other direct methods of monitoring and reporting. These can be most effective if an element of surprise is preserved, but they may be costly in time and effort and may reduce morale and agency effectiveness. Fire alarms go off when third parties—primarily interest-group beneficiaries—become dissatisfied with agency performance. This reduces the principal's monitoring costs because the third parties have an incentive to shoulder those costs; they want to keep the benefits coming their way. Serious violations are more likely to be brought to the principal's attention than less serious violations, which is an efficiency advantage. A muddling-through advantage of fire alarms is also noted by Kiewiet and McCubbins: "It is usually difficult to specify . . . a contract with the agent that unambiguously covers all contingencies, and consequently it is hard to tell whether an agency has violated the contract. In this situation, complaints by the affected third parties give principals the opportunities to spell out their goals more clearly" (1991, p. 32).

An extension of the fire alarm method is that principals can require agencies to notify third parties of future actions that might affect them. This is a key part of the recent emphasis on *administrative procedures* as instruments of political control (McCubbins, Noll, and Weingast, 1989). These procedures cause an agency to announce in advance its intention of taking an action; it nearly always solicits comments on that action and thus causes evidence to be brought to bear on the issues. In effect, the agency creates an early warning system that alerts third parties to the possibility that it may change course. Administrative procedures also create a time delay, allowing the principal to explore options, including the generation of more pressure (or less pressure) on the agency from interest-group constituents (McCubbins, Noll, and Weingast, 1989).

Now, the second issue with respect to monitoring: How much risk should a legislature tolerate? One might think that agencies would be kept on a tight rein by exactly specifying the regulatory scope of an act, the procedural requirements for implementing it, and other features as well. There are many instances, however, where these are left very vague by legislators. This may appear irrational because it gives great discretion to an agency. One common explanation for this is complexity: the idea that many issues are complicated, time consuming, and require technical expertise as well as political judgment. But complexity by itself is not a sufficient explanation for delegation of authority by legislatures to agencies:

> Delegation of legislative authority to administrative agencies . . . is not universal; Congress has itself dealt in detail with a number of regulatory problems. Congress prescribed . . . auto emission levels in the Clean Air Act instead of delegating the choice to the EPA; Congress banned PCB's explicitly in writing the Toxic Substances Control Act (TSCA); in reorganizing Amtrak in 1979 Congress got down to determining routes and rates for passenger rail service. (McCubbins, 1985, p. 722)

Why would a legislature delegate substantial authority to an agency in some cases, thus running the risks of adverse selection and moral hazard, yet choose in other cases to make major regulatory decisions itself? A rational choice explanation, particularly as advanced by Fiorina, is that self-interested legislators will shift responsibility to agencies by delegating authority when the political costs of regulation are high, but that they will themselves decide if the benefits from so doing are high. According to Fiorina, "Where politicians have the incentive, they manage to deal with complexity, and they find the time to do it" (1982, pp. 60-61). That is, if direct action can generate personal benefits, legislators will take direct action and claim those benefits. If the political costs of regulation are highly visible, however, legislators will be less aggressive and allow the agencies more discretion. McCubbins says, "The legislative choice to delegate authority to an administrative agency . . . follows when the act of delegating disguises the cost of regulation to a larger extent than it disguises the benefits" (McCubbins, 1985, p. 723).

Finally, the fourth measure for dealing with the agency problem is that of *institutional checks*. These usually call for action by alternative agents who have authority to veto or block the actions of a designated agent. Institutional checks may protect the principal, but they may also block desirable action. In other words, the security offered by checks and balances within government may come at the price of flexibility and efficiency.

9.52 Congressional Dominance

The concepts of organization and hierarchy thus seem to allow insights that are useful in assessing the extent of control by elected legislatures, on one hand, and by appointed agencies, on the other hand. The principal-agent analogy seems legally appropriate, asymmetric information seems quite likely, and there are risks of adverse selection and moral hazard even though legislatures may rationally choose to delegate authority in spite of those risks.

Although the concepts of organization and hierarchy are useful, they still don't tell us whether legislatures or agencies generally have the upper hand in their principal-agent relationships. One major thrust in the collective choice literature of the 1980s was *congressional dominance,* the idea that Congress does, in fact, dominate the principal-agent relationships with its administrative agencies. The approach has been contested, like most academic claims, but it deserves our attention.

The congressional dominance approach began with highly mathematical explanations of how real-world institutions, particularly the congressional committee system, have been structured to stabilize and direct political outcomes. The idea behind this approach, largely associated with Shepsle (1979) and Shepsle and Weingast (1981), is *structure-induced equilibrium:* Through agenda control, a committee system will reduce instability and generate predictable and stable outcomes. Weingast (1981) gives an example of a three-person legislature considering various subsidy levels to two different industries (Figure 9.4). The three legislators have different preferences for subsidy levels. Legislator 1 is the least prone to grant subsidies; she prefers to use public resources for other purposes. Her ideal combination of subsidies, using circular indifference curves like those in Section 6.34, is for low subsidy levels to both industries. This is shown as 1 in Figure 9.4; points farther from 1 in any direction are less preferred by Legislator 1 than are closer points. The other two legislators are bigger spenders, at least for these purposes. Legislator 2 would favor spending for Industry Y; Legislator 3 would favor spending for Industry X.

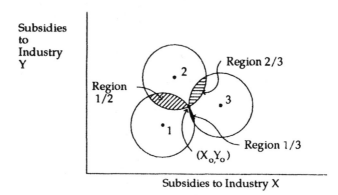

FIGURE 9.4 Structure-Induced Equilibrium for Two Types of Subsidies

If the three-person legislature was to decide on this issue, instability could occur under majority rule. This is because Legislator 3 is the median voter on subsidies to Industry Y, but Legislator 2 is the median voter on subsidies to Industry X. Any of three types of proposals could win a majority vote, but cycling could occur among the three and a true winner might not emerge. Any combination of subsidies within the shaded area denoted as Region 1/2 would be favored by both Legislators 1 and 2 over combination (X_o, Y_o), which is the status quo point, or the current subsidy levels to the two industries. By the same token, any combination within Region 1/3 would also defeat (X_o, Y_o) under majority rule because Legislators 1 and 3 would both be better off within this area than at (X_o, Y_o). By the same reasoning, a subsidy combination within Region 2/3 would win the votes of Legislators 2 and 3. Thus, the outcome would depend on which alternative to the status quo is proposed; each of three types of proposals could defeat the status quo.

The committee system comes to the rescue of stability, however, with a device that we identified in Chapter 6 as agenda control. Whether a proposal from Region 1/2, from Region 1/3, or from Region 2/3 will be made depends on how the legislature makes decisions. Congress and many other legislatures rely on a committee system with limited memberships and specified policy jurisdictions in the various committees. Legislators tend to self-select themselves for specific committees, based on their desire for reelection. They have *electorally induced preferences*, that is, the legislators enhance their self-interest by promoting policies that benefit their district constituency (Weingast, 1981). The committees that provide those benefits have agenda power within a policy jurisdiction. They alone, not the entire legislature, have agenda power—and hence veto power—to make proposals within the health or natural resources jurisdiction, for example.

This solves the potential instability in Figure 9.4; the committee system might vest Legislator 2, Legislator 3, or both with the right to propose a subsidy level as an alternative to the status quo (X_o, Y_o). If both legislators were on the committee, both would favor larger subsidies than the status quo, and a proposal from within Region 2/3 would be approved. Larger subsidies would be granted to both Industry X and Industry Y. The composition of the committee thus determines the outcome; a change in policy would be expected only if the composition of the committee changed, other things equal. As stated by Weingast:

> The main implication . . . is that policy remains stable and beneficial to congressional-agency clientele as long as the relevant variables of public opinion, balance of power of interest groups, presidential initiative, and precedential legal decisions are stable. As long as these

variables remain constant, the political rewards from various alternatives remain constant. . . . Stability in the political reward structure
implies that agencies may appear committed to serving a particular
clientele for long periods of time. (1981, p. 160)

The congressional dominance approach thus says that the legislative
structure, particularly the committee system and majority rule, facilitates
the pursuit of self-interest by legislators and leads to outcomes that are
stable and predictable. In Figure 9.4, higher subsidy levels would be
legislatively enacted for both Industry X and Industry Y. Making sure
that these subsidies actually take place depends on whether the committee can control the actions of the administrative agency delegated to
implement the policies. From the committee's viewpoint, the risk of
adverse selection exists; the wrong agency may be chosen to implement
the policy, or the wrong regulatory means may be used to guide the
agency. Moral hazard is also a problem for the committee; without
monitoring and in-course corrections, the agency may pursue its own
goals and objectives instead of those of the committee.

Those who argue most strongly for congressional dominance feel
that Congress and its committee system are capable of dealing with these
risks, especially moral hazard, through congressional oversight of the
agencies. They argue that Congress, through its committees, has ultimate
power; it controls budgets, mandates that certain activities be done and
others not be done, controls appointments, and generally oversees
projects and progress. As we noted, this doesn't require constant
monitoring by legislative committees. Instead, they can rely on the "fire
alarm" when the agencies shirk or change course. Calvert, Moran, and
Weingast summarize the oversight procedure this way: "Bureaucrats
know what types of policies they need to pursue in order to survive and
advance. . . . Interest groups monitor congressmen because they, unlike
congressmen, have the incentive to follow the day-to-day actions of
agencies. . . . And finally, congressmen claim credit from their constituents for aggressively pursuing agencies that fail to provide benefits and
otherwise insuring that the benefits continue to flow" (1987, p. 501). The
nature of Congressional oversight thus tends to be low-key and indirect,
rather than high-key and direct: "The lack of regular, public congressional hearings and investigations in no way implies a lack of congressional
influence. Attention, which is all the more effective when it is focused
through the more effective 'fire alarm' system, induces bureaucrats to
anticipate and serve Congressional interests" (1987, p. 500). And even a
critic of the approach describes it basically the same way: "According to
this perspective on oversight, then, we should normally observe sporadic,
superficial, poorly attended committee hearings . . . , and legislators who

are often quite ill-informed about agency performance, structure, or personnel. . . . What political scientists have for decades castigated as the height of congressional irresponsibility is . . . symptomatic of just what it appears not to be: effective oversight and control" (Moe, 1987, p. 479).

A major test of the congressional-dominance approach has been whether, for example, it can explain the extent to which the Federal Trade Commission (FTC) altered its enforcement activities in the early 1980s in response to changes in congressional committees. The following sketch of the evidence and arguments illustrates some of the difficulties in applying simple models to complex situations.

Fact #1: A majority of consumer-oriented members of the oversight committee between 1964 and 1976 supported an activist FTC role. "Examples of the wide range of FTC investigations included advertising aimed at children . . . , the used car market, the insurance industry, the self-regulating professional organizations such as undertakers, and several . . . major anti-trust suits" (Weingast and Moran, 1983, p. 776).

Fact #2: The FTC then came under close scrutiny by Congress, tumultuous hearings occurred, and the FTC was scolded by Congress for regulatory abuse. In 1980, the agency was even closed down by Congress for two days.

Fact #3: Over the year and a half following this closure, the FTC ceased nearly all its controversial regulatory actions and antitrust suits. It then began to concentrate on less controversial matters.

The standard bureaucratic interpretation of these three facts is that the FTC had run amuck, shirking extensively on its implicit contract with Congress: "Congress finally caught a runaway, out of control agency. This demonstrated . . . the lack of congressional attention: the FTC had operated independently for nearly a decade and, if not stopped by Congress, would have continued along these lines" (Weingast and Moran, 1983, p. 776). The congressional dominance interpretation is: "What occurred in the late 1970s was that congressional support for an activist FTC disappeared. Between 1976 and 1979, the dominant coalition on the relevant congressional committees changed from favoring to opposing an activist FTC. This resulted from the nearly complete turnover of those on and in control of the relevant Senate oversight committee" (Weingast and Moran, 1983, p. 777).

The evidence appears to be mixed. Congressional dominance proponents claim that the FTC caseload over the 1964-1976 period can be statistically explained by the degree of liberalism and activism among subcommittee members. The more activist the committee, the more the FTC pursued consumer cases. Among the fourteen of the Senate Commerce Committee's Subcommittee for Consumers, twelve left for a variety of reasons after 1976 (Calvert, Moran, and Weingast, 1987). The new subcommittee then began to reinstate the more traditional FTC role of protecting small business against unfair business competition. Muris (1986), however, claims that appropriate measures of caseload weren't used. Moe (1987) argues that the FTC role changed because of a major reorganization and revitalization in 1970-1971, but he attributes this to presidential initiatives rather than to a change in committee composition.

9.6 Agenda Control and the Median Voter

In this section, the median voter is brought into the principal-agent framework that we have developed in the previous two sections. Having considered the legislature as principal and the bureau as agent, let's step farther back in the democratic process and consider how effective the voter would be as a principal, and in particular, how effective the median voter would be. It is, of course, a fundamental precept of democratic theory that the will of the people should be done; in theory at least, the median voter is supposed to play an important role in expressing the will of the people under majority rule.

9.61 Is the Median Voter an Effective Principal?

Several complications arise when we consider the voter as principal. For one, the voters, like members of a legislature, may simply not agree on what the agent should do. If so, agreement has to be reached on a voting rule. If majority rule is used, this means that the median voter is the key principal, rather than those voters with more extreme preferences.[12] Having identified the principal by specifying a voting rule, we may then ask whether principal-agent problems would also exist for voters and legislators. In some respects, the answer is clearly yes. There is likely to be asymmetric information between principal and agent, for example, and there are likely to be problems of adverse selection and moral hazard in selecting, instructing, and monitoring an agent.

There is one very major difference, however, between the voter as principal and the legislator as principal, a difference that has been with us since Chapter 5. This is the incentive or disincentive to take action. A legislator who has intense preferences can form a coalition or logroll with another legislator to better express those preferences. Once a partner is found, the coalition has to be negotiated and means of monitoring the agreement must be explored. This might take some time and effort, but legislators do it routinely. The number of coalition partners is usually not large, and most of the costs are probably small. Thus, there is usually some incentive and opportunity for legislators to take political action; indeed, this is what we expect them to do.

A voter who has intense preferences, however, is usually faced with a more hostile incentive framework for expressing these preferences. She might agree with other voters that they should support a particular course of action, but ironically, the secrecy of the voting booth may cause the costs of monitoring each other's actions to be infinitely high. And even if monitoring was costless, the free-rider problem might again rear its head. If the prospect of successful political action was available as a public good to those not taking action as well as to those taking action, this might erode the basis of support for action.

This difference in incentives suggests that legislators will be politically active but that voters will be politically inactive—even the crucial median voter. Although we might want voters to act as principals in instructing the legislature and guiding the agencies, there will be a general lack of incentive for them to do so. This means that agenda control will likely be exercised by the legislature or by the agencies.

9.62 Reversion Budgets and Budget Maximizers

One form of agenda control that can thwart a principal-agent relationship based on the voter as principal can be found in the public provision of primary and secondary education. This good has a tradition of local control. Local people have usually wanted to maintain control over curricula, textbooks, teachers, and, implicitly, over community values. Local school boards (legislatures) are elected to govern this process; they, in turn, appoint school administrators to operate the schools. Local school boards run the gamut from low-key, informal political processes to highly politicized processes. School board members usually serve without pay; these positions often attract community leaders who view school board memberships as a form of community service and sometimes as a stepping stone to higher office or more successful businesses.

Voters are thus involved in public-school matters primarily through election of school board members. In most states, voters do not vote directly on the level of school funding. Historically, financial support for local schools has evolved away from locally imposed property taxes and toward state-imposed income and sales taxes. The amount of tax revenues available to run the schools in these cases usually depends on tax collections and legislative formulas for distribution. Federal funding of primary and secondary education is largely limited to facilities and programs for special target groups such as the handicapped.

In a few states, however, local school districts still rely heavily on the local property tax as a revenue source. In Oregon, for example, the citizens vote on a property tax "levy," the amount of property taxes to be collected and used to operate the public schools during a school year. This process begins when school boards and administrators determine the need for spending, and thus property the tax levy that will be presented to voters. The levy amount, together with the *reversion budget*, or the property tax level that would occur if the voters rejected a proposed tax levy, determines the extent of spending from local resources. The reversion budget gives the school boards and administrators agenda control over rationally inactive voters, as we'll see. As a result, the principal may be controlled by the agent.

The preferences for different levels of school spending (and hence, tax levies) are shown in Figure 9.5 for three equal-sized groups of voters. One group (V_l) prefers a low level of spending, another (V_h) prefers a much higher level. The median voter, or group of voters (V_m) in this case, prefers an intermediate level of school spending. Under majority rule, spending level S_m would be preferred over S_r by V_m and V_h, and it would be preferred over S_b by V_m and V_l; thus, the median voter group would appear to be decisive in determining the outcome. S_m, the spending level that the median voter group would prefer, however, might only be reached after a large number of elections; and school boards might not allow this to happen.

If the number of elections is limited, the reversion budget becomes crucial in determining the outcome (Romer and Rosenthal, 1984). If the

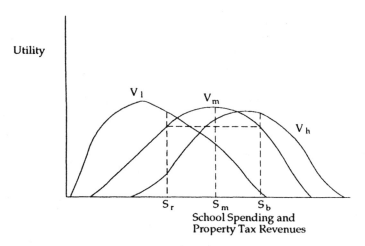

FIGURE 9.5 Voter Preferences for School Spending

reversion budget is zero, no tax revenue can be raised or spent until *some* levy amount gains approval from the voters. If a levy amount of $5.0 million is defeated by the voters, for example, nothing can be spent until a second election results in the passage of (say) a $4.5 million levy.

9.63 Voting on School Budgets in Oregon

A zero-level reversion budget thus appears to introduce instability into the funding of local schools. The State of Oregon tried to address this in 1917 when it allowed units of local government, including school districts, to establish a tax base, or the maximum amount of property taxes they could levy (tax) without voter approval. For many districts, the base was equal to their taxing level in 1916; a district was allowed to tax and spend at this level (plus a 6 percent annual growth rate) without going to the voters for approval of a levy amount. Districts were allowed to ask the voters for even more money as an "excess levy," that is, over and above the tax base plus the 6 percent growth rate. If the voters said no, the district's tax base served as the reversion budget; this was the maximum amount that could be levied without voter approval.

As the years passed, however, several factors combined to cause these tax bases to become inadequate in terms of operating the schools. Inflation, population growth, enrollment growth, and rising demands for education all contributed to the inadequacy of the tax bases. Voters approved larger bases in some districts, but the general lag persisted into the mid-1980s when one-third of Oregon's school districts either had no tax base or one that was clearly inadequate for providing a quality education. These school districts were forced each year to seek voter approval of excess levies. A typical district, for example, might have this funding structure:

> $3 million in state aid (voter approval not required)
> + $1 million in property tax base (voter approval not
>   required)
> + $6 million in excess levy (voter approval required)
> ————
> $10 million

With this funding situation, repeated elections were often needed to determine an excess levy that the voters were willing to approve. Oregon law allowed districts to hold as many as six budget elections.[13] In many cases, school had actually started in the fall before an excess levy was approved. In about 20 to 25 highly publicized cases, schools had to be closed due to lack of funds.

Did low property tax bases lead to instability and low funding for the public schools? Yes, according to most school officials. No, however, was the surprising conclusion of Romer and Rosenthal (1984), who studied the Oregon school situation in the mid-1970s. In their view, the low tax bases served as reversion budgets that allowed budget-maximizing school boards and school administrators to extract *greater* spending levels than desired by the median voter. If S_r was the existing tax base, for example, a levy setter who tried to satisfy the median voter would ask for $(S_m - S_r)$ as an excess levy (Figure 9.5). Romer and Rosenthal argued that instead, levy setters acted like Niskanen bureaucrats by attempting to maximize the spending level. Instead of asking for $(S_m - S_r)$ as an excess levy, a budget maximizer would ask for nearly $(S_b - S_r)$; this was the largest spending level that would be favored over the reversion budget by the median voter.

In other words, a low tax base could be used as a form of agenda control, creating a "hammer" that would fall on parents and children alike if parents didn't vote for the proposed tax levy. Romer and Rosenthal found that if the tax base was below a threshold level such that school closures might result, district spending was 15 percent higher than it would otherwise have been. Stevens, Kerkvliet, and Mason (1992) later found that this effect was related to district enrollment; large districts tended to use reversion budgets to enhance spending more than did small districts.

Four additional comments might be added on reversion budgets as a form of agenda control. First, it isn't clear who is most responsible for exercising agenda control—elected school boards or appointed school administrators. By tradition, school administrators make budget proposals that are then whittled down by school boards and their advisory budget committees. Second, local school funding involves a variety of high-demand and low-demand interest groups. One can think of local iron triangles made up of certain school administrators, certain school board members, and parents of children with certain attitudes, abilities, or interests. One triangle might include fixed-income and retired taxpayers and their elected representatives. Third, it isn't clear that budget maximization is "bad"; no one really knows the true demand curve for the output of the public schools. And fourth, the example suggests that voters are not very strong principals in the principal-agent relationship with school boards and school officials.

9.7 Summary

Collective choice analysts don't agree on whether elected legislators or nonelected bureaucrats usually have the upper hand. They do agree that self-interest motivations apply to each, usually reelection prospects for legislators and budget sizes for bureaucrats. How strictly they apply, however, is often at issue.

The early concept of iron triangles, or subgovernments, was based on consensus rather than conflict. Small clusters of representatives, agency heads, and interest groups would work together to decide and implement policy in particular areas such as water resources. Niskanen's (1971) budget-maximization model was based on conflict between a requesting agency, which has better information on supply costs and demand, and on a legislative committee, which has control of the agency's budget. The two usually bargain in a bilateral monopoly context. If the agency is successful in maximizing the size of the budget granted by the committee, the net economic value of its output is driven to zero by excessive output levels.

A more recent approach to bureaucracy is based on the economics of organization, and in particular, on the idea of principal-agent relationship; the legislature is the principal and the bureau is its agent. Agency problems will arise if the interests of the principal and agent are in conflict, if they have different information, and if they have different incentives to reveal that information. All of these are likely to happen, creating problems of adverse selection (hidden information) or moral hazard (hidden actions) for the principal. Four measures for dealing with the agency problem are suggested by Kiewiet and McCubbins (1991): screening and selection of agents, contract design, monitoring and reporting, and institutional checks.

Contrary to Niskanen's view of strong bureaus, the congressional dominance approach argues that Congress effectively controls the bureaus through structure—induced equilibrium. This happens because of the system of congressional committees, a form of agenda control that reduces instability and generates predictable outcomes. Agency direction will change only if committee composition changes; this takes us back to Chapter 8 and legislative markets, PAC money, and voters who have strong incentives to be apathetic.

Agenda control can also be viewed through school spending at the local government level. Democratic theory suggests that voters should act as principals and that school boards and administrators should act as agents. The use of reversion budgets by the latter, however, can thwart this and cause spending under majority-rule voting to exceed the level preferred by the median voter.

Terms and Concepts for Review

public administration
iron triangles and subgovernments
Niskanen model of bureaucracy
bilateral monopoly
asymmetric information
budget maximization
organizations
hierarchy organizations and conflict of interest
shirking
team members
principal-agent relationship
adverse selection
moral hazard
agency problem
screening and selection
contract design
monitoring and reporting
police patrol oversight
fire alarm oversight
administrative procedures
institutional checks
congressional dominance
structure-induced equilibrium
electorally induced preferences
reversion budgets
pivotal voter

10

Administrative Government:
Part 2

10.0 Principals, Agents, and Decision Frameworks

Now that we see the interaction between legislatures and administrative agencies as a principal-agent relationship with uncertain outcome, let's consider something that those in the academic world are fond of dispensing—advice. The social sciences, life sciences, physical sciences, engineering, and humanities have long traditions of advising government, but self-interested legislators and bureaucrats don't always want this advice. Analyses are not always timely; the demander may not want whatever is recommended, and the supplier may be reluctant to make recommendations. Legislators may seek advice only when they want to improve their chances of reelection; agencies may provide information or present their analyses only if their self-interest will be enhanced.

At other times, however, advice will be expected and even welcomed. For one thing, it is often uncertain whether agency analyses will antagonize or please legislative constituents. Also, agencies may not always be budget maximizers, and legislators may not always be reelection-minded. Disciplinary norms and other types of allegiance among agency personnel may stand in the way of budget maximization (Wilson, 1989). Some personnel may see themselves as economists first or biologists first, for example, and as employees of a particular agency second.

When advice is offered or sought, several *decision frameworks* exist for organizing and presenting this advice, including benefit-cost analysis (Lave, 1981). These frameworks involve the collection, analysis, and presentation of information for evaluation of programs or policies. This may occur ex ante (before the fact) or ex post (after the fact). Other information is also needed for day-to-day administration, but the decision frameworks that we'll be discussing are the most relevant to program or policy evaluation. Some of these have been mandated by the enabling legislation for an agency; others were created when legislators approved acts and assigned them to agencies for implementation. Decision frameworks may be very structured, requiring agencies to collect specific information and perform specific analyses, or they may leave considerable discretion to the agency.

At least nine decision frameworks have been discussed by Lave (1981) and Smith (1986). One additional framework (program evaluation) is added here. These decision frameworks fall into two categories. The first is technical—how best to meet a certain objective. This category includes what Lave calls a "no-risk" framework (avoiding any additional risk), technology-based standards, the balancing of good and bad through "risk-risk" analysis, and cost-effectiveness analysis to ensure accomplishing an objective at lowest cost. The second category is normative, involving a choice among objectives. This category includes risk-benefit analysis, environmental impact statements, economic impact analysis, multiple-objective programming, program evaluation, and benefit-cost analysis.

The order in which these frameworks are mentioned ranges from those that require the least theory, information, and analysis to those that require the most. At the low end is the no-risk framework. The so-called Delaney Clause of the Food, Drug, and Cosmetic Act passed by Congress in 1958, for example, banned any cancer-causing food additive. Benefit-cost analysis is the most demanding in its need for theory, data, and analysis. In spite of these greater needs, it also offers the most insight into the extent to which efficiency is increased or decreased by public policies. This suggests that we should take a closer look at benefit-cost analysis than at the other decision frameworks.

10.01 Decision Frameworks: A Brief History

Jules Dupuit set the stage for systematic analysis and decision frameworks with his engineering studies of public works projects in mid-nineteenth century France (Gramlich, 1990). Benefit-cost analysis, the oldest of the decision frameworks, was mandated for use in water resource planning by the Flood Control Act of 1936. This act was passed by Congress after severe flooding occurred in the Ohio and Mississippi River valleys. It instructed the water agencies to ensure that project benefits "to whomsoever they accrue" would be greater than project costs. Economists later viewed this as a mandate by Congress that projects be built only if they would generate potential Pareto improvements (Eckstein, 1958). A less omniscient interpretation is that Congress simply wanted to prevent graft and corruption when it instructed agencies to follow proper accounting practices in their haste to build dams and prevent flooding. A report of the U.S. Federal Inter-Agency River Basin Committee, the "Green Book" (1950), later sought to establish ground rules on how agencies would conduct benefit-cost analyses, a need that arose when the water agencies began to actively compete for local political support.

The next major decision framework was the Planning Programming Budgeting System, adopted by the Johnson administration in the 1960s. Fueled by the public spiritedness and analytical skills of "whiz kids" like Robert McNamara and Charles Hitch, the PPB system was highly touted as a rational-comprehensive way to make budget decisions. Agencies would set objectives, measure outputs and costs, and then devise least-cost ways of meeting these objectives. One effect of the PPB system may have been to centralize power at higher administrative levels as a means of reducing principal-agent problems within an agency. The system eventually died, however, because it required extensive resource commitments that competed with providing regular agency output and because it interfered with legislative prerogatives. Elements of the PPB system still exist in federal and state governments.

The next major decision framework, the environmental impact statement, came into being with the National Environmental Policy Act of 1969. Designed to display information on a variety of environmental impacts, the act reached full bloom in the 1980s. By causing information on adverse impacts to be supplied, it provided a strategic device that enabled environmental groups to more effectively use the judicial process to limit or prevent adverse actions. Conservative political forces led to the issuance of Executive Order 12291 by President Reagan in 1981. This order required federal agencies to assess the benefits and costs of any proposed major regulations that would have an annual impact on the economy of more than $100 million or those that would result in other major changes and adverse effects. This order also specified that regulatory action should be undertaken only if the likely social benefits were greater than the likely social costs; inefficient regulation should not be undertaken.

10.02 The Need for Advice

We thus have on paper, so to speak, a variety of legislative and executive acts that force—or allow—agencies to provide information and analysis. One would like to be able to say how effective these acts are, how good the information is, and how well the decision frameworks serve the people. This is more than can we do here, if it can be done at all. We can, however, reflect back on how the various legislative and administrative models of Chapters 8 and 9 deal with the "need" for information and analysis. Specifically, let's reconsider four models of legislative regulation (the Stigler, Peltzman, and Becker models and "voting your district") and two means by which legislative principals might reduce the agency problem (contract design, monitoring).

Producers dominated consumers in the Stigler model (1971) because they are few in number, usually large, and often quite homogenous. Information did not play a major role; the producers were bound to win. A later version, the Peltzman model (1976), opened the door for strategic use of information. Both the support function and the opposition function allowed information to play a significant role in the making of legislative decisions about the size of the beneficiary group, the size of the implicit tax, and the amount of wealth transfer.[1] The beneficiaries are likely to know that they are indeed beneficiaries, but it is less likely that non-beneficiaries have the same degree of knowledge, because their per capita losses will often be small. Those who will suffer substantial losses are probably aware of that fact. Others, however, are likely to be members of a latent group, to use Mancur Olson's (1965) term for those who are rationally inactive even though there are potential group gains from action. Those decision frameworks that function as disclosure acts—benefit-cost analysis, environmental impact statements, and economic impact analysis—make it more likely that nonbeneficiaries will be made aware of adverse consequences and thus become more open to the pleas of interest groups (Section 7.6) and vote-seeking legislators who appeal to unrepresented interests (Section 8.2).

The Becker (1983, 1985) model of regulation makes it even more likely that nonbeneficiaries will have a stake in the action. It does so, however, with a bold and sweeping assumption that is too strong for many analysts to accept. Becker assumes that deadweight losses, no matter how small, trigger political responses. If so, proposed investments or regulations that involve more cost than benefit are bound to fail. Knowing this, regulators would not propose them. Information in the Becker model would thus enhance efficiency in government. The voting-your-district model, however, generates exactly the opposite conclusion. Legislators in this model take a very parochial view—they disregard all benefits that occur outside their district. Efficiency would suffer even with good information because of this narrow outlook.

Very different views about the role of information thus exist in the models of legislative regulation, but information does play a central role in the principal-agent models of legislative-administrative interaction. In Kiewiet and McCubbins's (1991) view, for example, information and analysis play explicit roles in reducing the agency problem. One means of control is appropriate contract design; another is monitoring and reporting. The latter activities would implement a contract by specifying the type, amount, and timing of information and analysis.

Some ways of providing information—environmental impact statements, for example—are likely to open up the political process. Others, however, are likely to maintain the political status quo. Executive Order 12291, for example, called for detailed analysis of the impacts of proposed regulations. Bentkover characterizes its implications: "Executive Order 12291 has several implications. Briefly, it now requires: Increased time requirements for the proposal, approval, and promulgation of regulations. More rigorous demonstration of the *benefits* of the proposed actions, to the extent of weighing benefits against the societal costs. Explicit analysis and selection of alternatives with the lowest societal cost. More detailed and substantive analysis to support rulemaking" (1986, pp. 3-4). Executive Order 12291 thus provided a new contract design with a new method of monitoring and control. It lengthened the time frame and raised new hurdles prior to the taking of additional regulatory action; this "fire alarm" oversight gives vested interests time and incentive to resist proposed changes that would harm them.

10.1 Benefit-Cost Analysis

As we take a closer look at benefit-cost analysis, we'll find that much of the relevant theory has already been presented in Chapters 2, 3, and 5. What remains is to put this theory into a benefit-cost context.

10.11 General Concepts

In the most general terms, *benefit-cost analysis* is a method for identifying the gains (benefits) and losses (costs) of a public policy or program and evaluating them in dollar terms, properly adjusted for when they occur in time. The benefit-cost framework relies heavily on theory to identify effects. It is also comprehensive in assessing the scope of effects and demanding in terms of quantitative measurement. In its purest form, benefit-cost analysis is very much a rational-comprehensive decision method (Chapters 1 and 2). An efficiency objective is agreed upon (at least the analyst presumes that it is), and alternatives for attaining this objective are comprehensively explored. Realistically, the analysis is usually less than comprehensive. A forest management agency, for example, may put most of its analytical efforts into evaluation of just two or three competing management plans.

The purpose of benefit-cost analysis is to evaluate the likely extent of the net gains that would be associated with a government program, policy, or project (hereafter, these terms are used interchangeably). The involvement of government may take a variety of forms. Many benefit-cost concepts come from the water resource development era with its massive investment in physical structures. Today, there is more emphasis on investment in human capital through education and health policies and on the regulation of safety in food, in the environment, in transportation, and in the workplace.

Several normative characteristics of benefit-cost analysis define what a "good" analysis should do. The first characteristic is that social rather than just private gains and losses should be evaluated. This is done by evaluating any external effects of policies, as well as intended effects, by evaluating nonmarket goods as well as market goods and by considering future generations as well as the current generation.

A second characteristic of good benefit-cost analysis is that it takes the perspective of some political jurisdiction. There is no "best" perspective, but the perspective should be made clear. Analyses of federal programs are generally from a national perspective, but a regional, state, or local perspective is usually more appropriate for programs initiated at these levels of government. The latter perspectives, however, may also help federal decisionmakers understand the likely impacts and the political reactions at lower levels of government.

Third, benefit-cost analysis should be done on a "with and without" basis; analysts need to portray the situation with and without the policy or program. Evaluation on a simple before and after basis involves the risk—indeed the certainty—that other forces will change over time, making it less likely that the consequences of the policy will be accurately identified.

Fourth, the analytical focus should be on changes in quantities of goods and services resulting from the government policy. As discussed in Chapter 2, this allows us to ask whether too much or not enough of a good or service is currently being produced (Figure 2.8) and whether the proposed policy would increase or decrease efficiency. Because benefit-cost analysis is based on the assumption that efficiency is the single objective for policy, it can be useful in gauging whether we would be moving toward or away from that objective.

Fifth, benefit-cost analysis should focus on changes in net economic value that would be associated with changes in the quantities of these goods and services. The change in net economic value for any good will be the sum of changes in consumers' surplus and producers' surplus. To think in net terms, the analyst will need to consider both the value of the good (how much consumers are willing to pay for it) and its cost (how much suppliers have to be paid to create it or part with it). Comparison of the two amounts determine whether the Kaldor-Hicks compensation test (Chapter 2) is satisfied. If the net economic value of all affected goods and services is positive, the gainers could compensate the losers and a potential Pareto improvement in efficiency would exist.

Sixth, changes in net economic value should be adjusted for their time of occurrence with an appropriate discount rate. It was particularly important in the water resource development era that the large "one-time" construction costs could be compared with the smaller ongoing amounts of future benefits. Even with today's focus on human capital and safety regulation, the comparability of benefits and costs is still important. Many investments in education, for example, involve current costs and lifetime benefits.

Seventh, any benefit-cost analysis is bound to be a partial analysis, rather than a general-equilibrium analysis. This is particularly true for two reasons. One is that the prices and quantities of goods other than those directly affected by a policy are assumed to remain constant; the second assumption is that the real income of consumers does not change because of price changes brought about by the policy. Both assumptions make analyses more tractable, but at the expense of realism.

These seven characteristics of benefit-cost analysis make it possible to avoid blind alleys. For example, it might instead be suggested that programs be evaluated on the basis of money spent on a good or service to be produced by the program. One problem with this approach is that the good may be a nonmarket good; the government may choose not to sell it (access to neighborhood playgrounds, for example), or it may be nearly impossible to package and sell (clean air, for example). Second, even if the good can be sold, the price may not accurately reflect its social value. Externalities may be generated by production or consumption of the good; these would often not be reflected in market price. Third, the good may be sold in imperfectly competitive markets; the marginal benefits to users exceed the marginal cost to producers because of restricted supply (Figure 3.5).

Consider, for example, a program that would bring about an increase in domestic oil production. Use of the current market price of oil as a measure of value could have at least three defects. First, the current price of oil might be "too low" because negative externalities are often generated by oil production. Second, this price might be "too high" if oil producers have sufficient market power to restrict supply and raise the price. Even if neither of these things happened, total expenditures on oil would decline if an inelastic demand for oil caused prices to fall sharply when the additional production occurred. This would make it appear that the new oil had a negative value. A benefit-cost focus on the change in oil output and on the associated changes in net economic value to consumers and producers would avoid these ambiguities.

10.12 Valuation Where Markets Exist

The simple principles from Chapter 2 can aid the benefit-cost analyst in valuing project-related changes in the quantities and net economic values of market goods and services. In this section, we'll use these principles to value social benefits and social costs in dollar terms.[2] Exactly how the principles are applied, however, depends on whether markets exist for those goods and whether these markets are competitive. Let's first assume that the good to be produced (or another product derived from that good) would be exchanged in competitive markets; then we will consider some effects of imperfect competition. We will also consider how useful these examples are and speculate about empirical measurement of benefits and costs.

Benefits. In the simplest case of competitive markets, the good is available prior to government action at a constant cost of P_0 (Figure 10.1). An efficient market price and quantity of $P_0 Q_0$ has been established; there is no incentive for firms to produce more, and it would be inefficient for the government to expand production. The marginal benefits to demanders at output Q_1, for example, would be less than the marginal costs to producers. If, however, government action could make all units of output available at a lower cost (P_1), consumers would be bet-

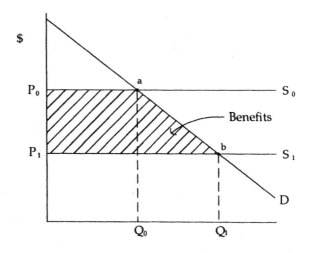

FIGURE 10.1 Benefit Evaluation: Constant Costs

ter off by having to pay less for the good. An example: Increased productivity of labor might be gained if we had more educated, higher skilled, and healthier workers. This would lower the supply function for those goods and services provided by labor from S_0 to S_1. This, in turn, would allow consumers' surplus and net economic value to increase by P_0 abP_1. There would be no producers' surplus because of the assumption of a constant supply cost.

The theory is straightforward, but there is an apparent irony: If markets work well enough to provide Q_0 output, why would we consider government intervention to enlarge the output? One answer has to do with the collective action problem. Individual workers and firms may not have the incentive to take efficient measures that would lead to increased labor productivity unless they could capture a share of the gain. Publicly supported programs might offer a means of overcoming this problem.

Benefits may also exist in situations in which the cost per unit of output increases as more output is produced (Figure 10.2). In these situations, either labor and capital are less productive at higher output levels or their prices have been bid up as output expands. This increasing-cost case is more likely to be the general situation than is the constant-cost case, especially in the short run. Increases in net economic value can occur with increasing costs, however, as well as with constant costs. Even if wage rates were bid up as output expanded (moving along S_0, for example), a more skilled and healthy labor force would be a more

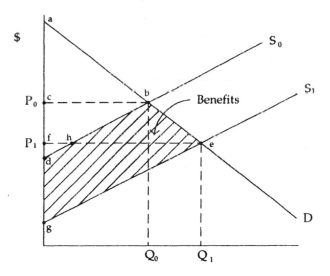

FIGURE 10.2 Benefit Evaluation: Increasing Costs

productive labor force (comparing S_1 with S_0). The economic benefits would be the increase in net economic value from related goods and services, or area begd.[3] Of this amount, area beh is new consumers' surplus, area hegd is new producers' surplus, and area cbhf is a transfer of producers' surplus to consumers' surplus. Consumers would clearly be better off because of increased productivity, but producers could be worse off because area cbhf (their losses) might be larger than area hegd (their gains).

Benefits can also be evaluated if markets are not perfectly competitive. Two major sources of market imperfections are the creation of externalities (Figures 3.3 and 3.4) and the use of market power to restrict supply, drive up price, and create excess profit (Figure 3.5). Taking externalities into account in benefit evaluation simply combines principles from Chapter 3 with the principles in the previous paragraphs. If government action increased labor productivity through investments in education, health, and safety, for example, the supply function for goods produced with that labor would fall from S_0 to S_1 (Figure 10.3). If these goods were produced at constant cost, the increase in consumers' surplus from market goods would be area P_0 abP_1. In addition, positive externalities might lead to nonmarket benefits from increased productivity, health, and safety ($D_t - D_p$). The workers' increased resistance to communicable disease, for example, is a service that might not easily be withheld from others. In this case, gains of area cdba would accrue to others as a non-

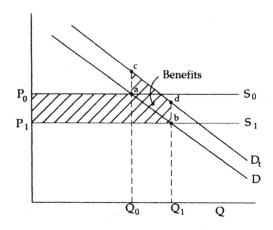

FIGURE 10.3 Benefit Evaluation: Constant Costs and Positive Externalities

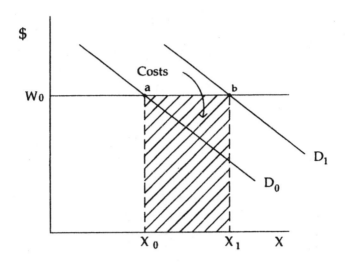

FIGURE 10.4 Cost Evaluation: Constant Costs

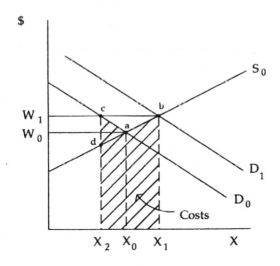

FIGURE 10.5 Cost Evaluation: Increasing Costs

market benefit. Any external benefits from outputs less than Q_0 or greater than Q_1 would not be attributable to the policy under consideration.

Costs. The costs of government policies and projects can also be evaluated through changes in the net economic value of affected goods and services. Let's continue to consider the enhancement of labor skills and health as the proposed action. We know that to produce these outputs of labor skills and health, we would need other inputs of capital and labor. If one of these labor inputs is available at constant cost (W_0 in Figure 10.4), the net economic value that is "used up" by using that input is simply its monetary cost. This would be measured by the amount of the input ($X_1 - X_0$) multiplied by the wage rate (W_0). If there are no externalities generated by labor use and if the price of labor isn't bid up by the project, labor costs are simply area abX_1X_0.

The wage rate may rise, however, because of a project-induced shift in the demand for labor (Figure 10.5). If we were to evaluate labor costs as though they were fixed and constant, the result would be an underestimate for two reasons. First, all but the first unit of labor would have to be paid more than the initial W_0 wage rate. Second, an opportunity cost arises when wages rise to W_1 because of the project. At this higher wage, other demanders of labor would use only X_2 units of labor. This would create a "crowd-out" cost (area cad) in forgone net economic value of other goods and services (note the "with and without" analysis). Because only X_2 units of labor are used by other demanders at the higher wage rate, the money cost of the project is not just abX_1X_0 but is dbX_1X_2. The shaded area in Figure 10.5 is equal to this cost plus the crowd-out tri-

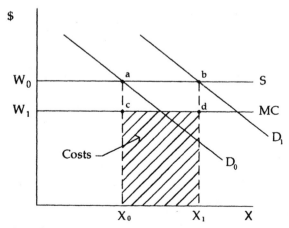

FIGURE 10.6 Cost Evaluation: Constant Costs and Imperfect Factor Markets

angle. In other words, the project cost becomes larger if there is competition for the resources that it uses.

Market imperfections may also affect the evaluation of project cost. Negative externalities imposed on others add to social costs, just as positive externalities added to social benefits in Figure 10.3. A second source of discrepancy between monetary costs and social costs may occur if a project buys inputs from a noncompetitive supplier. This was illustrated in Figure 3.5. Because of imperfect competition, the selling price for the supplier, a in Figure 10.6, is greater than c, the marginal cost. As a result, evaluating project costs as abX_1X_0 would overstate the social cost—part of this area is actually monopoly rent or excess profit. The social cost would be cdX_1X_0, which is a lesser amount than abX_1X_0.

10.13 Valuation of Nonmarket Goods

Valuation of nonmarket goods is a relatively new area of benefit-cost analysis. The basic theory for valuation of nonmarket goods is straightforward, but the measurement side is difficult and challenging. Not many years ago, benefit-cost analysts had to largely ignore environmental and other nonmarket goods. Markets didn't exist to generate values for them, and research on nonmarket valuation was in its infancy. It was little wonder that benefit-cost analysis acquired a bad reputation among environmentalists. Nonmarket valuation is now a central aspect of benefit-cost analysis in health and in consumer and workplace safety as well as for the policies concerning the environment and natural resources. Not all nonmarket goods can be evaluated, however, and not all environmentalists are convinced that research progress has been made. Nevertheless, the results may be useful in setting policy.

The basic theory behind valuation of nonmarket goods is shown in Figure 10.7, which is a slightly more complex formulation than Figure 2.6, which we discussed earlier. Increases in the availability of goods and services are valued according to the consumer's willingness to pay (WTP) for the additional amounts; decreases in availability are valued according to the consumer's willingness to accept (WTA) compensation for the reduced amounts. WTP values usually represent program benefits; WTA values represent program costs. Based on a starting point, a, which represents Q_0 of the good and Y_0 of consumer income, increased availability of the good due to the project would make the consumer better off by allowing her to reach b. In dollar terms, the extent to which she becomes better off is bc, or Y_0Y_1. This is the WTP—the maximum amount that she would pay for increased availability of the good; paying any larger amount would leave her worse off than she was at the starting point.

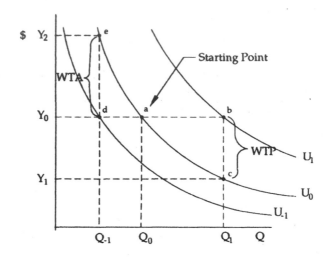

FIGURE 10.7 Benefit or Cost Evaluation: Nonmarket Good

Reduced availability of a nonmarket good might be from Q_0 to Q_1. This could happen if a project used a good as an input or if it generated a negative externality that reduced the availability of some other good. In dollar terms, a consumer would be worse off by amount ed, or Y_2Y_0. This is the WTA—the minimum compensation that she would accept for reduced availability of the good. Compensating her by more than this amount would leave her better off than she was at the starting point.

The measurement of WTP and WTA amounts is complicated for several reasons. First, there are usually no markets for these goods, at least none that work well; this is why government action is proposed. Second, appropriate units of measurement for nonmarket goods are less obvious than those for market goods. Agreement on a 10 percent improvement in air quality may be a complicated matter. Third, the public good nature of many nonmarket goods means that consumers have little incentive to think about how much they value a good.

Researchers have to be creative and ingenious in discovering the WTP and WTA values of consumers. V. Kerry Smith describes it this way: "Benefit analysis often resembles detective work (Natural Academy of Sciences 1975). The analyst must appraise whether the actions of individuals (or firms) . . . provide clues about their respective valuations of the nonmarketed goods or services. As with any form of detective work, there are several ways to find these clues" (1986, p. 19). A key aspect of looking for these clues is to find a physical or behavioral link between a nonmarket good, on one hand, and a market good or observable action by a household, on the other hand. For example,

- Improved air quality may lead to better health and fewer medical costs.
- A new reservoir may create valuable building sites along the shoreline.
- Increased aircraft noise may reduce property values near airports.
- More dangerous jobs call for higher wage rates.
- A survey respondent may state a high WTP or WTA value for some recreational activity or exposure to physical harm.

In each case, there is a change in quantity of a nonmarket good (air quality, noise, risk); each of these may have an impact on *related markets* (health costs, property values, wage rates) or on household behavior (WTP or WTA values). For the past thirty years, researchers have explored both indirect and direct methods of determining the monetary values that are associated with these and other nonmarket goods. Indirect methods were considered first, partly because economists believed that many nonmarket changes (air pollution, for example) would be reflected in the values of goods exchanged in related markets (health care). Also, economists have tended to trust what people do, not what they say they will do. Two indirect methods, the travel cost method and the hedonic method, are briefly described. Direct methods of valuing nonmarket goods have emerged more recently as economists have gained familiarity with elicitation techniques. The contingent valuation method, which we discussed in Chapter 5, is the major direct method of valuing nonmarket goods.

Travel Cost Method. Public outdoor recreation in this country has a long tradition of being available to users regardless of their income level. Even though facilities such as parks can be viewed as a nonmarket good because of the general absence of full-cost admission charges, most people would agree that these goods have value to users. Early researchers such as Hotelling (1949), Clawson (1959), and Clawson and Knetsch (1966) reasoned that the markets for travel and lodging would be those most affected by changes in the nonmarket good; this method became known as the *travel cost method*. Recreationists incur auto expenses and perhaps extra lodging and food costs because recreation sites are often located some distance from their homes.

In the typical research, travel costs are estimated for users who live various distances from the recreation facility; it is then assumed that users would view an increase in admission charge ($1 more per day, for example), as adding to costs in the same way that an increase in auto expenses would add to costs. Because facility use usually tapers off with the greater distance and higher costs faced by more distant users, raising

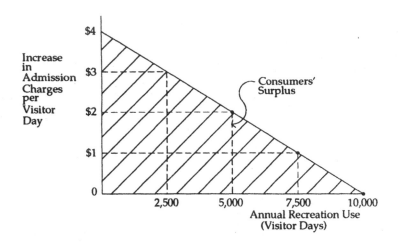

FIGURE 10.8 Recreation Demand Function: Travel Cost Method

the entrance fee would also cause use to taper off. This allows a demand function to be derived for a facility. It also permits an estimate of willingness to pay by users who gain consumers' surplus from use of the facility without having to pay the higher costs of the more distant users. The consumers' surplus from the facility shown in Figure 10.8, for example, is the entire area under the demand function, or $20,000 per year.[4]

Hedonic Method. The value of nonmarket goods may be reflected in a variety of actions that are taken by consumers in related markets. The so-called *hedonic method* has come into use as a means for estimating benefits from public policies regarding air and water quality, noise, recreation, and crime. Often the level of a nonmarket good varies geographically and its level is beyond the control of individual households. These households may adapt, however, by seeking residential locations that offer higher levels of the nonmarket good. The values of single-family residences tend to be higher, for example, in neighborhoods with better air quality, lower noise levels, and lower crime rates; the values of these nonmarket goods become imbedded in the value of private residences.

The first step in this method is to estimate a hedonic price function, where the value of a residence is a function of housing attributes including the nonmarket good. That is,

$$P = (S, H, Q), \tag{10.1}$$

where   P = value of residence
   S = structural characteristics of the residence, including size, number of rooms, and age
   N = neighborhood characteristics, including accessibility to work, stores, and shopping
   Q = the nonmarket good (air quality, for example).

This equation is usually estimated from a cross section of residences. One well-known study used data from 634 single-family residences in neighborhoods of greatly different air quality within the Los Angeles metropolitan area (Brookshire et al., 1982).

When neighborhood and structural factors are statistically held constant (the age of the house, for example), home values are usually higher in neighborhoods with higher levels of air quality (Figure 10.9). The rate of increase in housing values, however, usually tapers off at higher levels of air quality. The DD function in Figure 10.10 shows the *implicit marginal price* of buying a higher level of air quality through purchase of a home in a better area.[5] The high willingness to pay by the ith household, $d_i d_i$, would cause it to move from residence *a* to residence *b*, and thus into equilibrium. Other households might be willing to pay

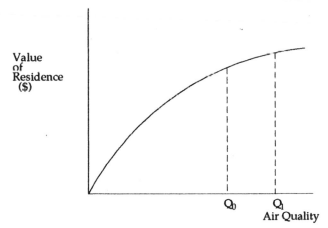

FIGURE 10.9 Residential Values and Air Quality: Single Family Residence

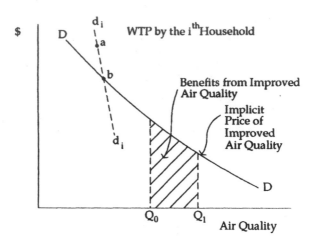

FIGURE 10.10 Household Willingness to Pay for Improved Air Quality

less, but all are assumed to be along the DD function; there they would be paying exactly (but only) what they would have to pay for increments of air quality in the residential market.

Suppose that an improvement in air quality from Q_0 to Q_1 was proposed for a community with a medium level of air quality (Q_0) compared to other communities. The benefits from this improvement would be the shaded area in Figure 10.10. This would be sum of households' willingness to pay for improved air quality between the current and proposed levels of air quality. For example, the benefits from improving air quality from "fair" to "good" in the Los Angeles study would have been between $33 and $128 per household in 1978, depending on community income. These figures reflect imputed monthly rent rather than value of residence, but the same ideas apply in either case.

10.14 Special Considerations

In addition to identifying the various benefits and costs of public actions and attaching dollar values when possible, the benefit-cost analyst must take several other topics into consideration. One is what to do if benefits and costs occur at different points in time, which they often do. Second, we need to consider the secondary benefits issue, that is, whether benefits are real or whether they are displaced from some other use. Third, some goods and services—like human life—are unique; they deserve special treatment even though economists are criticized for treating them like any other commodity.

Present Values and Discounting. The need for making benefits and costs comparable is especially crucial if they occur at very different points in time. A $10 million flood-control dam would incur most of its costs early in the project life. The benefits, however, would occur for many years into the future. Simply adding the costs on one hand and the benefits would ignore the fact that economists—and most other people—believe that getting a dollar today or a dollar a year from now are not equally attractive alternatives, even if both are certain to happen. The benefit-cost analyst has to reduce future benefits and costs to their *present value*, which is the amount of money that would have to be invested today to accumulate to a specified amount at a specified time in the future. The present value of $1 million in benefits that will occur ten years from now is $614,000 at a *discount rate* of 5 percent. That is, $614,000 invested today at 5 percent will yield $1 million ten years from now. If the discount rate is higher, say 8 percent, the present value of $1 million to be received ten years from now is only $463,000. Invested at 8 percent, this is the amount that will accumulate to $1 million in ten years.

By this reasoning, a flood-control dam that is expected to yield annual benefits of $1 million has a present value of these benefits that gets progressively smaller the farther into the future we go (Figure 10.11). At a 5 percent discount rate, the present value of $1 million to be received ten years from now is $614,000, but the present value is only $87,000 if the $1 million is received fifty years from now. This amount is smaller because it has a longer period over which to grow. Not only do present values become smaller for benefit streams farther into the future, they also become smaller at higher discount rates. These higher rates cause the pattern shown in Figure 10.11 to shift downward, making present values less at any given discount rate. At a discount rate of .08, for example, the present value of $1 million to be received fifty years from now is only $21,000. This doesn't seem like much compared to $1 million, but it is all one would need to eventually have $1 million.

What does this mean for policy? For public investments where the annual benefits are small compared to initial costs (water resource development, for example) or where the benefits occur in the far distant future (reforestation), the discount rate may be crucial in determining the present value of future benefits and costs (Tietenberg, 1988, p. 81). It is also important for other types of investment and regulation because costs and benefits usually do not occur in the same proportion each year. Investments in education and health, for example, often have benefits that extend far into the future.

Economists don't generally agree on the choice of a discount rate. They do agree, however, that there are two major approaches to the topic. Chapter 3 on market failure can help us here. One approach is that

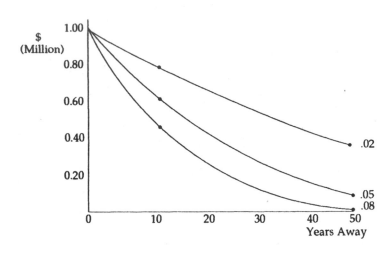

FIGURE 10.11 Present Value of a $1 Million Benefit Stream at Different
Discount Rates

markets, including capital markets, usually work well. This is often called
the *opportunity cost* approach. In theory, a purely competitive capital
market would equate an individual's rate of time preference—how much
he or she would prefer a dollar now over a dollar later—to the opportunity cost of capital—how much that dollar could earn if put to work in
the private sector. The second approach is that markets may fail to bring
about an efficient allocation of resources over time. Advocates believe
that a *social discount rate*, a rate less than the opportunity cost of capital,
would be better.

There are several sources of alleged market failure, including the
collective action problems of whether enough will be saved and invested
to enhance future consumption and who should do the saving. Other
complications with markets include imperfect competition, taxes, and
uncertainty. At present, the social discount rate is increasingly popular
among economists. Lind (1982), a key advocate of this approach feels that
we should use a social discount rate that reflects the willingness of
society to exchange present consumption for future consumption; but he
also thinks that we need to consider the extent to which private-sector
investment would be displaced by public investments. His estimates of
the social discount rate are under 5 percent, which is far less than most
opportunity-cost estimates.

Distributional Effects.   Benefit-cost analysis addresses an efficiency
objective rather than a distributional objective, although public policies
have distributional effects that are of obvious interest to policy makers.

There is one particular aspect of distribution, however, that relates directly to efficiency analysis. This is the issue of *secondary benefits*, or the extent to which the impacts and spin-offs of a project should be counted as project benefits. New highways attract new businesses. Better educated people tend to earn more and spend more. How much, if any, of this related spending gives rise to social benefits in the sense that we have discussed?

This question dates back to the 1950s, when agency analysts counted income gains to equipment sellers and food processors as social benefits from federal irrigation projects. Critics objected to this as double counting. They argued that the local gains were illusory from a national perspective, that they simply displaced activity someplace else. The benefit-cost literature of that time made a distinction between primary benefits, those resulting from the "primary purpose" for which the costs were incurred, and secondary benefits, those induced by or stemming from the project. By this definition, the primary purpose of a public irrigation project was to raise crops and livestock. The preceding chapters should make one wary of this particular definition. That is, the purpose of a project may have been to raise crops, but it may also have been to generate political benefits and thus help reelect local representatives (Weingast, Shepsle, and Johnsen, 1981).

There is little doubt that economic ripples are generated by public actions and that these can be important in "voting your district" by legislators (Section 8.15). From a benefit-cost perspective, however, whether these secondary effects are real or whether they simply displace activity elsewhere depends upon the opportunity costs of the inputs (Eckstein, 1958; Haveman and Weisbrod, 1975). If these inputs could earn just as much elsewhere as they would earn on the project, there are no real secondary benefits, only displaced activity. However, if some of the inputs would otherwise be unemployed or if they would be imperfectly mobile among uses, resources that would not otherwise be used might be put to use. Secondary benefits would exist in a real sense.

This distinction may sound good, but there is a temptation for self-interested agencies to exploit imperfect knowledge about the opportunity costs of inputs and to claim that secondary benefits exist. The economy has often been at less than full employment, especially in certain regions (Appalachia, for example) and in certain industries and occupations, but there has been little research on the extent to which benefits and costs should be adjusted for this factor. Haveman and Krutilla's early research (1968) is still noteworthy; they found that water resource projects varied widely by type and location in the likelihood that they would draw on unemployed resources. In general, economists have not made much headway in building a knowledge base that would allow inclusion of secondary benefits when appropriate and disallow them when not appropriate.

The Value of Human Life. The most controversial aspect of benefit-cost analysis is probably the *valuation of human life* in monetary terms. Many people simply do not approve of considering human life in dollar terms, as if it were any other economic commodity. Some of this concern involves a faulty understanding of the way economists pose the analytical issues. For example, the question is not about the life or death of any particular person. This is essentially a situation of ransom, where the "value" of life would be limited by the amount of money that relatives and friends could raise to free the hostage.

Instead, the focus is on implicit valuation of small differences in the probability of life or death, differences that arise from differences in the degree of risk and human safety. These valuations can be used to assess policies that involve safety on highways, in the workplace, in the environment, and with respect to health in general. Because improvements in safety come at a cost, it may be helpful for policymakers to know what particular types of safety should be promoted. When the question is posed this way, the implicit decision framework is cost-effectiveness (which we'll discuss later). What is the least expensive way to save a life? When put this way, the analyst can ignore the values of life. The benefit-cost analysis framework, however, asks an efficiency question: How many lives should be saved, given the cost of saving lives? Even though the beneficiaries are faceless statistical entities, not particular people, this is a controversial question.

Early attempts to measure the value of human life used data on lost earnings and medical costs. These, however, were minimum estimates; people would-and-do pay more than just their doctor bills and lost earnings to gain increased safety and health. Later the human capital approach used data on forgone lifetime earnings to reflect the value of human life. This approach was also criticized because it was not related to a person's willingness to pay for increased safety.

The accepted form of valuation is now the hedonic method, which was discussed in Section 10.13. This method assumes that enhanced human safety is a nonmarket good whose value may be determined by analysis of related market values. In this case, the related market is usually the labor market with its substantial differences in safety among workers in different occupations and industries. The hedonic method involves estimating an earnings equation such as that shown by Viscusi (1986, p. 199):

$$w = \alpha + \sum_{i=1}^{m} \beta_i x_i + \gamma_0 p + \gamma_1 q + u \qquad (10.2)$$

where w = wage rate or annual earnings
    x_i = explanatory variables (i = 1, 2, ... m) such as education,
        age, race, sex, job experience, occupation, and industry
    p = risk of death
    q = risk of nonfatal injury
    u = random error term

and α, B_i, γ_o, and γ_1 are parameters to be estimated. A careful specification of personal and job-related characteristics is crucial if we are to make good estimates of the wage premiums that employees receive for taking greater risks of death and nonfatal injury. Other things equal, risky jobs involve higher wages. Other things aren't always equal, however; coal miners may be poorly paid for their risky work because of their limited ability to get other types of jobs.

Monetary estimates of the value of human life are becoming less controversial, more refined, and more useful in policy. Kip Viscusi, a leader in this research, notes that these values were becoming part of the policy debate as early as 1984 (1986, p. 207). In proposing a particular safety standard in the construction industry, for example, the Occupational Safety and Health Administration (OSHA) argued for a $3.5 million value of life for the average blue collar worker. The Office of Management and Budget (OMB) wanted only a $1 million value; a congressional supporter of higher safety standards urged a $7 million figure. Viscusi notes that the willingness-to-pay approach was accepted by each of these three parties, along with the idea of using labor market studies as a way to derive the estimates.[6]

10.2 Other Frameworks

In addition to benefit-cost analysis, there are other useful and generally less-demanding frameworks for policy analysis. These were listed in Section 10.1. Lave (1981) lists four criteria for comparing frameworks. The first, comprehensiveness, is whether all issues and consequences are considered. The second is the extent of the intellectual foundation and associated knowledge, assumptions, and value judgments. The third criterion is the resource requirement, and the fourth is felicitousness, or the ability to deal first with first-order issues. Benefit-cost analysis has high data needs and demands, but it also offers prospects for providing useful policy information if there is a common denominator in dollar terms. Not all effects of policies can be monetized, however, and not all decisionmakers want analyses that arrange information according to the single criterion of economic efficiency. The continuing popularity of the other frameworks is partly because decisionmakers want the options, alternatives, and flexibility that the less comprehensive frameworks offer.

Technology-based Standards. In the past, analysts have been unable to fully identify, let alone monetize, all the health and safety effects of policy proposals regarding air and water pollution. Because of this, agencies have often required firms to use the best available control technology for controlling waste discharges, rather than insisting that they find the most efficient level of treatment (benefit-cost analysis) or determine the type and level of effluent disposal that would minimize some waterborne or airborne health risk (cost-effectiveness analysis). A technology-based standard would cause the effluent to be treated according to a certain technology. This approach relies on engineering judgments and does not require evidence of benefits, costs, or risks. As Smith (1986, p. 28) notes, the best technology is often not obvious; instead, there may be different objectives that could be satisfied by the choice of one technology over another.

Cost-Effectiveness Analysis. This framework would select the policy that would minimize the costs of attaining a stated goal or objective. Lowering the death rate from cancer might be one objective. Several alternatives exist for meeting this objective, including reductions of carcinogens in the environment, early detection, public education, various existing types of treatments, new forms of treatment, and basic research. Each alternative has some relationship to the cancer death rate, other factors held constant, and health budgets could be allocated according to these relationships. As Lave points out, "Mathematically, this is a problem of maximization under constraints; the solution is to equate the effectiveness of the last dollar spent on each activity" (Lave, 1981, p. 20). The first increment of funds would go to that agency or rate-reducing alternative that would save the most lives. The next increment of funds would be allocated on the same basis, perhaps to the same agency or alternative. When all the allocated funds are spent, each source of rate-reduction should yield the same reduction in the cancer death rate at the margin. Otherwise, funds could be reallocated and assigned to a program with a higher payoff.

The main advantage of cost-effectiveness analysis is that the analyst is spared the task of placing a dollar value on human life. This need is overridden by the stated policy objective, which is to save as many lives as possible with a given budget. The main disadvantage—and here the ice gets thinner—is that we don't know how many lives should be saved by lowering the cancer death rate as opposed to saving lives in some other manner. (Economics was labeled the "dismal science" because of early pessimism by Malthus about population growth, not, as one might suspect, because of statements like this.) If one knew the value of human life, the marginal benefits from saving lives through the cancer alternatives might exceed the marginal costs. In this case, most people would agree that more should be done. Benefit-cost analysts, however, would go further and insist that we should promote those forms of death reduction that have the highest payoff in an efficiency sense.

Risk-Benefit Analysis. The next two frameworks have a common feature—they display information without any assumption that one particular criterion is most important. Benefit-cost analysts try to enhance economic efficiency; cost-effectiveness analysts try to minimize the costs of reaching a stated objective. Risk-benefit analysis and environmental impact statements are information-based methods that inform citizens and interest groups. Moreover, they offer flexibility to elected and appointed suppliers because there are many implicit objectives. The sheer volume of information opens up the political process and offers ample grounds for debate, but these methods often strike the benefit-cost analyst and the cost-effectiveness analyst as too vague to be effective.

Information-based frameworks lend themselves to an open democratic process; criteria-based frameworks lend themselves more to technocratic rule. Lave characterizes the risk-benefit framework as follows: "Under the risk-benefit framework, regulators would . . . balance the general benefits of a proposed regulation against its general risks. This framework is intended to be somewhat vague, with all effects being enumerated, but with full quantification and valuation being left to the general wisdom of the regulators" (Lave, 1981, p. 18). For example, a medical drug known to have widespread benefits in preventing heart disease might also be found to involve carcinogens that promote cancer. Should the drug be withdrawn from use? The benefits and risks in this case both involve health, but there may also be other benefits such as convenience or consumer preferences.

The main advantage of risk-benefit analysis is that it causes agencies to consider a very broad set of outcomes, whether or not these outcomes can be monetized or even quantified. The disadvantages are vagueness and a lack of commensurability. Outcomes simply do not compare easily. On balance, however, risk-benefit analysis will remain popular for this reason: "The framework has an immediate appeal to congressmen and regulators since it is a general instruction to consider all social factors in arriving at a decision. While no one can oppose considering all relevant factors, no one has specified precisely how this is to be done" (Lave, 1981, p. 18).

Environmental Impact Statements. Mandated by the National Environmental Policy Act (NEPA), this framework might be viewed as a form of risk-benefit analysis because it requires agencies to balance economic and environmental benefits. It explicitly requires consideration of environmental effects even though we are often unable to assign willingness-to-pay or willingness-to-accept values to these goods. The framework recognizes that many environmental effects are unknown or dimly known and that monetization of all costs and benefits is not possible. The primary advantage, as with risk-benefit analysis, is that it opens up the political process; the disadvantage is lack of commensurability among outcomes.

Multiple-Objective Programming. As noted in Chapter 1, practitioners in the field of policy analysis recognize that multiple objectives, not single objectives, dominate the political process. Like benefit-cost analysis, multiple-objective programming is a rational-comprehensive process in which an end is specified and policies are evaluated in that light. In multiple-objective programming, however, weights are assigned to indicate the relative importance of two or more objectives. These may include efficiency and equity, but more likely they will reflect specific results, outcomes, or criteria that are relevant to a program area (Zeleny, 1982). One result of a neighborhood safety program, for example, might be reductions in the crime rate against persons (murder, rape); a second result might be reductions in the crime rate against property (theft, arson). Different combinations of inputs, including police patrols, surveillance, and public education might affect the two outcomes somewhat differently, however. One set of inputs might be best for protecting people, another set might be best for protecting property. Identifying the "best" set would be possible only if weights were assigned to the two types of crime rates. An example of weight assignment might be

$$S = -0.67 \text{ PE} - 0.33 \text{ PR}, \qquad (10.3)$$

where PE and PR are reductions in crime rates against persons and property, respectively, and S is the weighted objective of neighborhood safety. In this formulation, reductions in the personal crime rate would count more than reductions in the property crime rate.

The major advantage of this framework is that it forces agencies to specify objectives, to consider how these objectives might be reached, and to identify how the objectives might conflict with each other. The disadvantage is that weight selection is usually difficult and arbitrary. Analysts might try to learn, for example, how city councils have made decisions in the past; one finding might be that protection against property crimes, not personal crimes, has been given the greatest weight. This finding might be useful to critics who claim that more attention should be given to protecting people than to protecting property. The finding wouldn't necessarily indicate what the current city council should do or what it is likely to do; each council wants to make that decision for itself.

Program Evaluation. Those using this decision framework try to look back at what actually happened with a policy or program and, on this basis, to inform future decisions. *Program evaluation* is the application of social science research methods to analysis of the process by which programs are implemented (Langbein, 1980; Rossi and Freeman, 1989). Evaluation research is bound to be controversial because agencies and legislators tend to muddle through (Chapter 1), rather than set clear, specific objectives. In spite of the lack of explicit objectives, there is often a clamor by interest groups and legislators for evaluation of programs. Analysts use descriptive data, statistical methods, and optimizing techniques to address questions like the following:

- Was the program implemented according to guidelines?
- What facilities and resources did it use?
- Who participated in the program?
- Did the target audience participate?
- Did the program produce intended outcomes?
- To what extent were outcomes due to other factors?

As Langbein notes, program evaluation operates within the system, thus it is partly scientific and partly political. That is, it "uses methods that are as scientific as possible to answer questions that the evaluator believes his nonscientific audience has posed" (1980, p. 3).

10.3 Summary

The academic disciplines have advice to give government, but government may not want that advice if it jeopardizes reelection, budget size, or other dimensions of self-interest. At times, however, legislatures and bureaus will want advice; hence, academics should be ready.

Several decision frameworks exist for organizing and presenting advice. Benefit-cost analysis is the most ambitious of these; it calls for identifying all social benefits and social costs associated with a government program and valuing these in present value monetary terms—no small job. Ideally, analysts attempt to determine the changes in net economic value for each good and service that would be affected by a proposal to see if those who would gain could compensate those who would lose and still have something left over. If so, the benefits will exceed the losses; efficiency will be enhanced by enacting the program.

Valuation of market goods in benefit-cost analysis is fairly simple in concept, but most public programs are likely to involve nonmarket goods. These are more difficult than market goods to value in monetary terms. Analysts usually look for related private markets such as the residential housing market to determine what people are willing to pay for nonmarket goods such as better air quality and reduced noise. Direct methods of determining monetary values, particularly the contingent valuation method from Chapter 5, are also used. Special problems in benefit-cost analysis include choosing an appropriate discount rate, determining whether secondary benefits exist, and estimating monetary values for human life.

Other decision frameworks are less demanding and less comprehensive than benefit-cost analysis. Some, like benefit-cost analysis, are criteria-based. Cost-effectiveness analysis may be helpful in selecting a policy to meet a single criterion such as minimizing costs. Multiple-objective programming finds the best option for satisfying two or more objectives, but weights need to be assigned to reflect the relative importance of the objectives.

Other decision frameworks are information-based rather than criteria-based. Program evaluation looks back at what actually happened. Risk-benefit analysis and environmental impact statements bring future impacts and risks out into the open for democratic dialogue, whether or not monetary values can be assigned to goods and services. The alternatives usually lack comparability in these frameworks, but this may be a political advantage to self-interested legislators and agency administrators who want room to maneuver.

Terms and Concepts for Review

decision frameworks
benefit-cost analysis
benefit and cost valuation with constant costs
benefit and cost valuation with increasing costs
benefit and cost valuation with externalities
benefit and cost valuation with imperfect factor markets
benefit and cost valuation for nonmarket goods
related markets
travel cost method
hedonic method
implicit marginal price of a nonmarket good
present value
discount rate
opportunity cost

social discount rate
secondary benefits
valuation of human life
technology-based standards
cost-effectiveness analysis
risk-benefit analysis
environmental impact statements
multiple-objective programming
program evaluation

11

Federated Government

11.0 Introduction

We now need to recognize that there are usually several levels of government within a nation. The three-tiered system in the United States, for example, consists of a federal government, fifty state governments, and over 80,000 units of local government, including cities, counties, townships, school districts, and other special districts (Ostrom, Ostrom, and Bish, 1988, p. 2). In this chapter, we will consider efficiency and equity as two reasons for the existence of such a system. We will then consider funding methods by which higher levels of government can affect outcomes at lower levels. This will involve some new terminology: intergovernmental grants, revenue-sharing, block grants, formula grants, categorical and noncategorical grants, matching and nonmatching grants, open-ended and closed-ended grants.

As with Chapter 10, most of the economic concepts that we need for understanding these terms have been presented in earlier chapters, but the outcomes of various types of intergovernmental grants are often difficult to predict. This problem will need to be considered in principal-agent terms. Among the factors that give rise to uncertain outcomes are these: Political incentives may vary at different jurisdictional levels, the production function for services may be different than we have believed it to be, and most goods are neither pure public goods nor pure private goods, but somewhere in between.

11.1 Fiscal Federalism

The theme of this book has been whether to let markets decide how much of a good or service will be produced or whether government should make this decision. The matter of federalism involves a related

choice: What level of government should decide? *Federalism* is the name
usually given the division of powers and responsibilities between a
central government and lesser units of government. As Oates notes (1972,
p. 14), the outcome is usually a compromise between unitary government
and decentralized government. Political scientists often view federalism
in terms of the power reflected in laws and constitutional provisions that
protect autonomy at different levels of government. Counties, for
example, are usually creatures of the state; they have no legal standing
on their own. State governments can create them, change them, or abolish
them.

Economists tend to view federalism in somewhat more narrow terms
as *fiscal federalism*, or the allocation of economic functions among levels
of government. In particular, they are interested in the effects of various
fiscal incentives on resource allocation and income distribution at lower
levels of government. Wallace Oates, whose *Fiscal Federalism* (1972) is still
a standard reference on the topic, describes the usual focus of economists:
"While, as many political scientists have stressed, the fiscal structure of
a particular country is no doubt largely the result of the unique political
and social history of that nation, it may still be true that certain types of
economic incentives have predictable impact on the structure and
operation of the public sector" (p. vi).

11.11 Who Should Do What?

The choice of jurisdictional level starts with the basic idea that
government has three economic functions—an allocation function, a
distribution function, and a stabilization function (Musgrave, 1959). The
conventional wisdom has been that the federal government should play
the major role in distribution and stabilization functions but that federal,
state, and local governments each have responsibility for the allocation
function (Oates, 1972). The three economic functions of government and
their roles are as follows:

- the *allocation function* involves deciding how resources will be
  used and what goods and services will be produced.
- the *distribution function* involves deciding how income should
  be distributed.
- the *stabilization function* involves using fiscal and monetary
  policy to move an economy toward greater output and
  employment, at stable prices.

Let's first consider the stabilization function. It is usually agreed that
the use of fiscal and monetary policy for purposes of stabilization is

something that the federal or central government should be responsible for. If people are allowed to freely move about within a nation, something we take for granted as a basic right, the boundaries between governments will be porous to flows of labor and capital and purchases of goods and services. Economies will be open by design, rather than closed, and the leakages from public (and private) spending will be large enough that states and cities will find it unproductive to engage in countercyclical fiscal policy. States may have an effect on national macroeconomic conditions if they run budget surpluses, for example, but the primary responsibility for stabilization is clearly at the federal level.

The distribution function is somewhat more complex. Economists would probably assign primary responsibility to the federal government while recognizing that states may take some responsibility for distribution, at least more so than for stabilization. And the states apparently agree because many have a variety of redistributive policies, especially in health, education, and welfare. As with stabilization, the need for involvement by higher levels of government arises from the mobility of people across political boundaries. If one city adopts a policy of aggressively taxing and spending for redistributive purposes, low-income people may move to that city to gain the benefits. High-income residents may move out for the same reason. People are more likely to move between cities or states than between nations; thus, the distribution function is usually seen as most effectively handled at the federal level of government.

11.12 Local Public Goods

Choosing what jurisdictional level will be responsible for the allocation function involves a question that we have discussed before: How "public" is a public good? As we saw in Chapter 2, governments need to provide pure public goods if they are to be provided—markets for public goods will not exist because of lack of incentives for buyers and sellers alike. And as we saw in Chapter 5, there are impure public goods—those that are subject to crowding and congestion. In this chapter, we recognize that there are also *local public goods*, those whose consumption is largely limited to residents of the political jurisdiction in which the goods are provided.

Imagine a community, for example, where people gather to visit and relax in the town square and to shop in nearby stores. If only a few other people are present in the square, I can use it as a pure public good; my use does not deny use or quality of use to others, and vice versa. As the number of people in the square increases, however, this good may become impure because of congestion: Some value is lost because of excessive use. A local public good, however, is more like the light that is cast by a street lamp along the square; its value to me diminishes as I walk past it. Instead of losing value because of crowding, local public goods lose value because of distance between the good and the user.

The conventional wisdom of economists is that the federal or central government should provide pure and impure public goods—those for which the benefits to users do not depend on distance and geographic location. National defense is probably the closest that we come to this. Local public goods, however, are most efficiently provided at lower levels of government because most of the benefits accrue to local residents. Access to a city's fire department isn't worth much if the city is too far away, just as a city library is primarily useful to those who live or work in that community. But higher levels of government should—for efficiency reasons—encourage the production of goods that have positive externalities—those that also generate some benefits for people who live outside the local jurisdiction. Left to their own political and economic incentives, cities and towns will produce Q_0 of a local public good if the demand by their citizens is D_r and if $S = MC$ is the marginal cost (Figure 11.1). To be efficient in a larger perspective, they need to be induced to also consider D_n, the demand by nonresidents, and thus to produce Q^*.[1] Only if the political jurisdiction that determines the level of Q includes

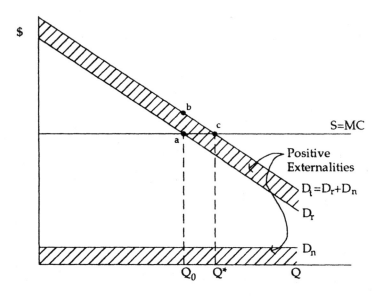

FIGURE 11.1 Positive Externalities in the Production of Local Public Goods

the same individuals who consume Q will there be *perfect correspondence* in its provision (Oates, 1972, Chapter 2). Because different goods would likely have different benefit regions, this could lead to the conclusion that there should be a different and efficient-sized jurisdiction for every good. One could envision a different (but overlapping) unit of special government for each good or service. In reality, cities and counties are multiproduct jurisdictions; grants from higher levels of government are often used to stimulate production of those goods that spill over to other jurisdictions.

11.13 Voting with Your Feet

One other reason for making allocation decisions at lower levels of government is that the preferences of citizens may vary because of differences in incomes and other factors. If so, lower levels of government may be able to respond to this efficiently. In the section on clubs (Chapter 5), we discussed the "voting with your feet" model of Tiebout (1956), which is a cornerstone in the theory of local public finance (Rubinfeld, 1987; Schwab and Oates, 1991). According to this model, under certain conditions—when mobility is costless and when incomes aren't affected by mobility—mobile consumers search for and find the community that best satisfies their preferences for local public goods. In equilibrium, the people in any one community have identical demands, and communities are homogenous. This voluntary sorting process is not only efficient but also reduces the need for interference by higher levels of government in the production of local public goods.

As we noted in Chapter 5, however, many of the assumptions in the Tiebout model do not hold. Preferences for local public goods of the traditional type—parks, police, fire protection—have not been very important in explaining why people move from one community to another. Also, incomes depend on residential location, at least for most people. And many communities have decided not to compete in the market for nonresidents. In the spirit of "pulling up the drawbridge," no-growth advocates—often those who have just moved to an attractive community—have waged political battles with growth advocates in many cities and towns.

But there is a hint of reality in the Tiebout model, one that has caused it to be long-lived. Like people do tend to cluster together. However, even if the model were valid, would we always want to live close to only others like ourselves? Sorting ourselves into homogenous enclaves could mean isolating rich communities from poor communities. This is objectionable to many. Even though each household has a demand for local public services and a supply of skills and resources, demand and supply won't necessarily balance out. Communities will usually be better off or worse off, not unaffected, when people move in or out (Breton, 1974). In particular, the flight to the suburbs from U.S. cities in the 1950s and 1960s left many central cities impoverished as poorer in-migrants replaced well-to-do out-migrants. Poor communities in a Tiebout world might be efficient communities, but they would still be poor.

11.2 Intergovernmental Grants

There are several reasons for higher governments intervening in the way lower governments allocate resources. Voting with your feet may work imperfectly in matching up people and public services, and we might not like the equity overtones even if it worked well. Also there is not likely to be perfect correspondence between benefit regions and taxing regions for a good. Benefits will often spill over to those outside the state or local government that provides the good; too little will be produced if lower governments fail to consider this. Higher government may intervene for efficiency reasons (there may be too little production of a good that spills over) or for equity reasons (certain people and regions may fare too poorly).

We need, then, to discuss several aspects of principal-agent relations in federated governments, including the likely outcomes of intergovernmental grants. We can also speculate about how self-interest among voters, interest groups, legislators, and administrators at granting and receiving levels of government might affect outcomes. We should also note that the "stick" as well as the "carrot" can be used to affect resource allocation at lower levels of government. Grants can be made to affect spending, but higher government can also regulate the affairs of lower government. For example, the federal government lowered the speed limit on interstate highways to fifty-five miles per hour in the late 1980s, much to the chagrin of truckers and others. Random checks of traffic flows were used to grant or deny states access to federal funds. As a second example of regulatory power, state governments usually specify who can attend local schools (setting an entry age), who must attend (mandatory attendance ages), and how many days the local school districts must be in session.

11.21 Types of Grants

There are many types of intergovernmental grants; the following definitions should help in understanding their nature and outcomes.

- *Revenue-sharing*: A political catch-all term for grants to lower governments that are financed from taxes or other revenues collected at higher levels.
- *Categorical grants*: Those grants made for specific programs within a policy area such as health or welfare.
- *Noncategorical or block grants*: Those grants that lower levels of government can use for unspecified purposes, although these are usually within a policy area such as health or welfare.
- *Formula grants*: Those grants that are based on specific factors such as the number of schoolchildren or the per capita income. (These are usually categorical grants.)
- *Matching grants*: Those grants that specify a cost-sharing formula. (The interstate highway system involved a 9:1 federal to state match, but a 1:1 match is much more common.)
- *Closed-ended grants*: Those matching grants that specify an upper limit that may be received.
- *Open-ended grants*: Those matching grants that do not specify an upper limit.

11.22 Categorical Matching Grants Versus Block Grants

Even a quick reading of these definitions suggests that lower levels of government may prefer some types of grants over others. It seems likely, for example, that cities and counties would prefer a simple block grant with no strings attached rather than a categorical grant with a requirement of local matching funds. This would give local units more flexibility in making decisions. One of the oldest constructs in fiscal federalism is a diagram to show that such preferences are likely. It also reveals the fundamental agency problem that a principal must face in making intergovernmental grants; the two levels of government may simply have different needs and different goals.

Consider, for example, a city and the preferences of its residents for public health programs (Q) that the state government is trying to promote through categorical matching grants. Let's assume that the preferences that count the most at the city level are those of the median voter. As we saw in Chapter 6, this voter will be decisive under majority rule, although we learned in subsequent chapters that supply-driven political processes, particularly legislative or bureaucratic agenda setting, may be preemptive. The median-voter model is thus a useful starting point, but we need to keep its limitations in mind.

Without a categorical matching grant, the city's median voter would face the P_0 price line for public health services and buy Q_0 units (Figure

11.2). The median voter would give up Y_0Y_1 income for these services. The vertical axis represents income as access to private goods and all other public services; thus, $0Y_1$ income is left for these purposes.

The state's 1:1 matching grant for public health services would shift the price line out to Y_0P_1. Twice as much output could now be bought, and only \$0.50 would be needed to buy \$1.00 worth of output; the two are equivalent statements. Because of the cheaper price, the median voter would now favor Q_1 output (*b*). She would have to spend only Y_0Y_2 for public health services, leaving more income ($0Y_2$) available for other things.[2] The matching grant would thus increase the median voter's utility from U_0 to U_1.

Both the state and the city's median voter are now better off—the state because it has induced the city to use more public health services, the median voter because she has more money and more public health services. This voter could become even better off, however, if the amount of subsidy received from the state through the categorical matching grant (bc) could be spent in some other manner (Oates, 1972). And she does, in fact, receive a subsidy, because it costs her only Y_0Y_2 to gain services that actually cost someone Y_0Y_3. Converting the categorical matching grant to an equal-sized block grant with no strings attached would result in a new price line, P_0'. This would restore the original (full) price for public health services, but it would also shift this new price line outward by the amount of subsidy (bc = Y_4Y_0). This would give local leaders more flexibility in causing public money to be spent as the median voter pleases and allow a higher U_2 utility level to be reached at point *c*.[3] Even more money would then be available for the median voter to spend on private goods and all other public services. Public health spending would be between Q_0 and Q_1—more than it was originally, but less than the state would like it to be. A categorical matching grant is thus stimulative, but it also constrains the choices that are available to the recipient.

11.23 The Principal's Options

The likelihood of conflict between principal (higher government) and agent (lower government) should now be clear. The principal will want to have some options for dealing with this agency problem. These options include the offering of various other types of grants.

Revenue-Sharing. Both the attractiveness to lower levels of government of nonrestrictive grants and the loss of control by higher government are illustrated by Figure 11.2. But some votes have been gained in the past by legislators at both higher and lower levels from political platforms that called for revenue-sharing. Revenue-sharing grants offer

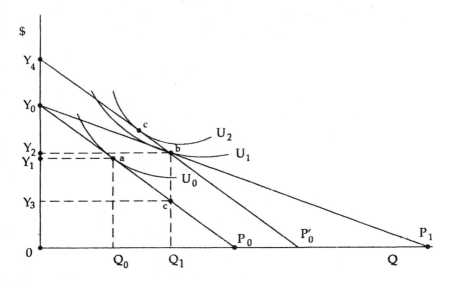

FIGURE 11.2 A Categorical Matching Grant and a Block Grant

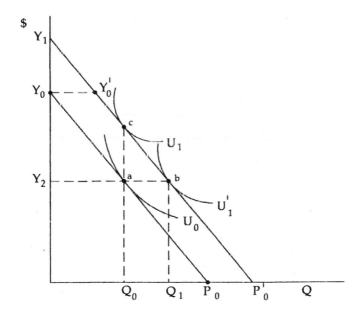

FIGURE 11.3 A Revenue-Sharing Grant

flexibility to state and local governments, but their use has declined since the mid-1980s. They totaled about $4 billion in 1986 but declined to $75 million in 1987; after that, they were not shown separately in the national income and product account tables (*Survey of Current Business*, January 1992, Table 3.16).

When a political jurisdiction receives revenue-sharing funds without strings attached, the price line is shifted outward by the amount of the grant ($Y_0Y_1 = P_0P_0'$ in Figure 11.3). Consider again the impact on public health services at the local level. The most likely outcome of this type of grant, depending on the median voter's preferences, would lie between *b* (where the entire grant would be used to enhance spending on public health), and *c* (where the entire grant would be used for other public services or returned to taxpayers for private spending).[4] There is a tremendous difference between these two outcomes, but let's defer discussion of this until we consider other types of grants.

Nonmatching Categorical Grants. Another type of grant is the nonmatching categorical grant (Figure 11.4).[5] These are made by higher-level government for the purpose of enhancing spending by lower government within a general policy area, but they do not involve matching requirements. They may involve a lump sum for each unit of government, but they are more likely to be allocated on a formula basis that considers population, incomes, previous performance, and other factors.

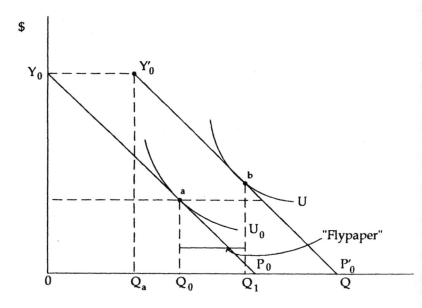

FIGURE 11.4 A Nonmatching Categorical Grant

Nonmatching categorical grants simply shift the price line outward in a parallel manner. Prices remain unchanged. It is stipulated, however, that lower government (a school district, for example) would have to spend at least the amount of the grant within a specified policy area ($0Q_a$ = Y_0Y_0' in Figure 11.4).[6] How would a school district spend this grant? Remember, it is not certain that the entire amount of the grant would be spent on a specified purpose, because the median voter gains utility from three sources—school spending, spending on other public services, and private goods.

Matching Closed-Ended Categorical Grants. These are grants in which higher government provides matching money for specific programs within policy areas, but there is an upper limit to the total grant. State aid to school districts in New York, for example, was on a matching basis for operating costs of less than $1,200 per student in 1975-1976 (Romer, Rosenthal, and Munley, forthcoming). At spending levels above this limit (Q_c), local districts would face the initial price of P_0', rather than a subsidized price (Figure 11.5). This introduces a kink into the price line. The median voter in a district might prefer to be at point c on indifference curve U_2, but the closed-ended nature of the grant would prevent this. He would have to settle for the upper funding limit, point b, where the slope of the indifference curve would be less than the slope of the lower portion of the P_0' price line. The median voter's willing-

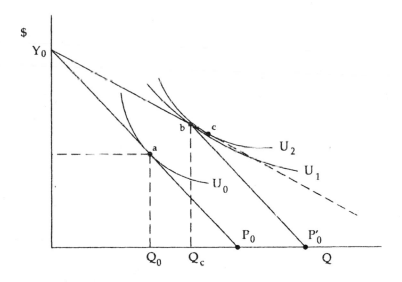

FIGURE 11.5 A Matching Categorical Closed-End Grant

ness to give up income to get additional school funding would be less than the price; thus, he would choose to remain at the kink, so to speak.

11.24 The Flypaper Effect

It is known that consumers spend more on a variety of goods and services when their income increases, but they don't spend the entire amount on any one good. This, however, has happened differently with intergovernmental grants. The *flypaper effect* is a name for the situation in which lower governments spend matching categorical grants differently than would the median voter if his or her income rose by an equivalent amount. These grants to lower governments usually "stick where they land," thus inviting the very descriptive term "flypaper." The flypaper effect is an apparent deviation from the expected partial spending of a similar-sized increase in income; instead, spending on the designated categorical purpose has been estimated to increase by nearly the entire amount of the grant (for example, Q_1Q_0 in Figure 11.4) (Gramlich, 1977; Courant, Gramlich, and Rubinfeld, 1979; Craig and Inman, 1982).

A variety of explanations have been advanced for the flypaper effect. Most have to do with self-interested bureaucrats, legislators, or interest groups nudging aside the median voter and competitive electoral processes. Dougan and Kenyon (1988), for example, claim that interest-group politics are crucial. Then too, *fiscal illusion* may exist if voters fail to accurately perceive either the consequences of spending or the availability and cost of resources. In their research on Oregon school spending from property tax revenues, Romer and Rosenthal (1984) argued that local voters were largely unaware that school districts also received considerable state aid (Section 9.5). The fact that state aid is not mentioned in the property tax ballot's description of financial consequences offers support for the argument of fiscal illusion.

Whatever the best explanation for the flypaper effect, it appears to happen in spite of *fungibility*, which makes it possible for grant money to be spent for purposes other than those specified by the principal in the categorical grant. Zampelli describes some of these options from the agent's viewpoint: "For example, when conditional aid is intended to apply to increases in local public output beyond current levels, the local government can reduce its own normal funding of the subsidized output, use a project that was going to be undertaken anyway as the means for securing a matching grant, redefine budget categories, or reallocate overhead costs to transform some or all of the aid into fungible resources" (1986, p. 33). State education officials can verify, for example, that a $3 million categorical grant to a school district is used only for designated purposes—paying teachers, fixing roofs, and so forth. Unless they are omniscient, however, they don't know how much the district would have spent *without* the grant. In other words, point *a* in Figure 11.4 cannot be observed, especially if the grant program has been in existence for some time. As long as the district spends more than $3 million, they can usually claim that the $3 million state grant was spent for education.

11.3 Emerging Knowledge

Fiscal federalism has been one of the oldest and best-established areas of collective choice involving government. The conventional wisdom, largely formalized several decades ago by Musgrave (1959) and Oates (1972), has been that the federal government should be responsible for distribution and (especially) stabilization. The allocation function should be shared with state and local government because of variations in preferences and because of local public goods. Some positive externalities will occur when lower units of government produce goods and services; thus, intergovernmental grants should be used to stimulate production. Matching categorical grants are best for stimulating production, but lower units of government prefer grants that allow them to spend as they wish. The conventional wisdom has also been that a "flypaper effect" exists; lower units of government will actually spend categorical grants for their designated purpose even though this money could often be converted to other uses.

Now, fiscal federalism is again becoming one of the more exciting areas of collective choice because there have been major advances in knowledge about the production and demand for local services. This is fortunate, because state and local levels may have additional spending responsibilities in the future. Alice Rivlin (1991), a distinguished economist and public servant, believes that the 1990s will see a return to an intellectual tradition that emphasizes a clean and neat distinction between state and federal functions. Why? In Rivlin's view, states are now more capable governments than they used to be because the federal government is preoccupied with international affairs and because people have negative attitudes toward government that may cause more decisions to be made at lower levels of government.

11.31 The Production of Services

The economist's view of local public goods goes directly back to the Tiebout model of Section 11.13 (Schwab and Oates, 1991; Rubinfeld, 1987). If people could vote with their feet for communities with different sets of public services, this could lead to an efficient outcome, but perhaps not an equitable one. We would have efficient rich communities and efficient poor communities.

The Tiebout model, however, assumes that all communities have the same technology and the same cost structure for producing public services. This assumption is now being challenged (Bradford, Malt, and Oates, 1969; Oates, 1981; Hamilton, 1983; Schwab and Zampelli, 1987; Craig, 1987; Schwab and Oates, 1991). The challenge is that the character- istics of the residents may affect the costs of production. Community income is a key factor that affects the demand for local services, but it may also affect the costs of providing such important services as eduction and public safety. A high-income community may get more out of an identical set of purchased inputs—police personnel and communication devices, for example—than would a low-income community because it is better able to use these inputs. For one thing, better-maintained and -lighted streets in a high-income community may reduce response time by the police. Police personnel and communication devices are important inputs in the production of personal safety, but they are only inputs— what is more important is the output of safety.

Let's look more closely at public safety. Researchers see a difference between the output produced by the public sector and the final output of safety, as perceived by residents (Bradford, Malt, and Oates, 1969). Schwab and Oates say that:

> By combining police officers with other police inputs, a local government produces a vector of D-output, including . . . police patrols, traffic controls at busy intersections, etc. A resident of the jurisdiction, however, is primarily interested in the level of public safety (C-output) which depends not only on D-output but also on the characteristics of the community. Poor communities, for instance, burdened with high unemployment and individu- als with a high propensity to commit crimes, will exhibit lower levels of safety for any given vector of D-outputs than will more affluent communi- ties. (1991, p. 220)

These authors are saying that public safety is produced by a variety of factors. The only one under the direct control of local government is the level of deployment of police personnel and associated inputs. In Craig's (1987) study of seventy-nine Baltimore neighborhoods, police did not produce safety directly. Instead, they produced apprehensions of suspects. This could be measured as an arrest rate, which was an intermediate output that enhanced personal and property safety.[7] Safety was also enhanced by several residential characteristics. These included home ownership and high incomes, both of which were associated with higher-than-average levels of private goods such as lighting and warning systems.

Education provides another example. Consider this view by Schwab and Oates: "Likewise, the level of educational attainment . . . depends not only on the teaching staff, library facilities, and other inputs, but in fundamental ways on the characteristics of the pupils themselves" (1991, p. 220). These characteristics can influence educational attainment in two ways—through the household's own characteristics (income, for example) and through the characteristics of other households (peer group effects, in particular). These characteristics upset the Tiebout conclusion that it would be efficient for people to sort themselves into homogenous communities of safety-seekers or education-seekers. In fact, a heterogeneous community would mean that some residents would have certain characteristics such as above-average income that would enhance community safety. The implication, to cite Schwab and Oates, is that "efficient community composition no longer involves homogenous communities. The gains from interaction in the production of local public goods must be played off against the gains from having populations that are homogenous in demand" (1991, p. 218).

Any individual's presence in the community thus involves positive or negative externalities; each person will have a "bottom line" in terms of generating benefits to others and costs for others. As with most externalities, the conventional wisdom has been to levy a tax if costs are imposed on others. But who would be taxed the most in this case? The poor, because they drive up the costs of providing public safety by not having lighting and warning systems in their homes.

This irony was recognized by Schwab and Oates, who label an externality tax on the poor as superregressive. They show that a system of equalizing intergovernmental grants—the largest grants going to the lowest-income communities—would improve equity and enable poor households to pay the tax. This would lead to efficient output of local public services. The argument for equalizing grants would no longer be just an equity argument, it would be an efficiency argument as well. Diversity within communities would become a good thing, and the rich would no longer flee the city to avoid the poor, as they have traditionally done. Instead, they might view the grants as just compensation for their own subsidies of the less well off.

11.32 *The Flypaper Effect Again*

The failure of economists to recognize community characteristics as a factor of production has caused a reinterpretation of the research results on the flypaper effect, that is, lower levels of government spend more from categorical grants than might be expected given that these grants are usually quite fungible. In particular, governments spend more from grants than they would from an equivalent increase in household income.

Hamilton (1983) offered a benchmark explanation for this along the lines of the previous paragraphs: Household income is different than grant money. Grants can provide more teachers, but they can't add to the ability of households to supplement and support the education of youngsters. He says, "The flypaper effect is due to the fact that transfer income, unlike own income, is not an input in the production of local public services. Own income . . . is combined with purchased inputs to produce the output, local public service" (1983, p. 348). Grant money can increase the use of "purchased inputs" such as teachers and maintenance, but "own income" can enhance the productivity of good teachers. Hamilton argues that an increase in own income has two rather complex effects, not unlike the price and income effects that were discussed in the appendix to Chapter 4. Other things equal, an increase in own income would substitute for some purchased inputs. Because own income is a productive factor, however, the cost of producing education would fall; more would be demanded at a lower price. This would stimulate the demand for purchased inputs. Hamilton shows that if the first (substitution) effect is larger than the second (price) effect, spending from grant income will always be more than spending from own income, thus accounting for the flypaper effect. In a later article, Schwab and Zampelli (1987) confirmed Hamilton's findings.[8] We now know that household income and other community characteristics can play a vital role in determining the spending of grants, but this, as all authors note, doesn't rule out the possibility that fiscal illusion and interest groups can also cause a higher level of spending from grant income.

11.33 *The Degree of Publicness*

There are other types of new knowledge that are transforming fiscal federalism from its somewhat stodgy former self into an exciting new area of study. One study (Craig, 1987), for example, asks, Are what we call "local public goods" really public goods, and why are they particularly local? One might go on to say, Pittsburgh's police force may not be much help if you are in New York, but is this because we've defined the responsibilities in a certain way or is there something inherently local about the provision of public safety through city police departments? Is public safety really a public good, whereby I can have more without you having less? Or does it tend to be a private good?

Craig's approach to these questions involved several concepts that have been discussed in previous chapters. One is Buchanan's idea of clubs as ways to organize the production of impure public goods, those that are subject to congestion (Chapter 5). Members would decide on the most efficient club size by balancing the marginal gains from cost-sharing against the marginal costs from additional congestion. (Remember, clubs needn't be voluntary; a unit of local government can be considered a club in some respects.) If local public goods are really local, we might observe the relationship shown in Figure 11.6 for public safety, where the utility from safety becomes less at larger population sizes due to the sharing of a fixed set of police resources by more and more people. Gridlock would occur at N^*; both safety output and utility would fall to zero.

A second aspect of Craig's model is how local public services are affected by the characteristics of residents. One of these characteristics is population size, as reflected in two production functions. The first is for an intermediate output of arrests, A_i:

$$A_i = A_i [P_i, Y_i, (N^* - N)_i],$$ (11.1)

where $A_i =$ the arrest rate or clearance rate for crime in the ith neighborhood
$P_i =$ level of police deployment
$Y_i =$ a vector of physical variables that characterize the neighborhood
$(N^* - N)_i =$ the lack of congestion, where N^* is the gridlock population.

Police personnel and neighborhood characteristics produce arrests; these in turn deter crime and produce public safety (Q_i) for residents in the second production function:

$$Q_i = Q_i [A_i, X_i, (N^* - N)_i],$$ (11.2)

where $X_i =$ another vector of neighborhood characteristics that affect safety.

If safety is a local public good, congestion could occur in either production function; it could affect the production of arrests or the production of public safety. The severity of congestion would vary with population size (Figure 11.6). Without congestion (N°), safety would be a pure public good; I could have more without less for you. At some level of congestion (N^*), safety would become a pure private good. Gridlock would be a Hobbesian jungle; if I'm safe, you're not.

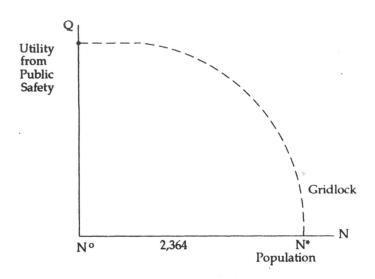

FIGURE 11.6 Congestion and Gridlock with Local Public Goods

Craig tested his model with data from seventy-nine police beats in Baltimore during 1972. Data were available on crime rates, police deployment, arrest rates, neighborhood characteristics, and neighborhood population. For a neighborhood of average size (2,364 people) and for neighborhoods twice that large, public safety was nearly a pure public good. At a neighborhood population of 10,716, however, the N^* gridlock was reached, primarily through congestion in the production of arrests. Police personnel assigned to one case were unavailable for other duties that could lead to arrests. Public safety thus became a private good in the largest neighborhood in the study.

Does this mean that neighborhoods should not be larger than about 10,000 residents? Not necessarily. If police deployment and other resources could increase proportionately with population size, then it is possible that congestion would not occur. Could the Pittsburgh police force be effective in New York? Not if it was stationed in Pittsburgh, because proportionality wouldn't exist; police response time would be too long. If this obstacle was removed—if the Pittsburgh police were redeployed to New York—they might be effective.

The nature of local public goods, as Craig has shown for public safety, thus seems to be that they *are* "local"—congestion occurs and the goods become less valuable. Knowing this, we tend to define them as local public goods and keep the Pittsburgh police in Pittsburgh neighborhoods, where their response time is reasonable.

11.4 Summary

The full regalia from Chapters 1 through 10 can be brought to bear on fiscal federalism, which is the allocation of economic responsibility among different levels of government. Traditional normative issues of what government should do are giving way to related issues of why government doesn't behave in the way our models predict, and how higher government can deal with lower government in a principal/agent relationship.

The traditional advice of economists has been on how federal, state, and local government should share responsibility for resource allocation and how intergovernmental grants should be designed. Some advice is well established; the voluntary sorting of people into homogenous communities might reduce the need for higher-level intervention, but it would also raise equity issues. Higher and lower levels of government will have different "first choices" among types of grants due to differing objectives. Higher government will offer matching categorical grants to stimulate spending on certain programs, but lower government will want the flexibility to divert spending to other purposes.

The emerging knowledge in fiscal federalism involves how local services are produced (partly through the characteristics of the residents themselves), what this implies for local government (heterogeneous communities may be both efficient and equitable), why governments actually spend categorical grant money on the designated purpose when it could be diverted to other uses (it is less valuable than the incomes of residents themselves), and whether local public goods are really local (it appears that they are). Each of these is a substantive improvement in knowledge about collective choice in federated government. Joined with tradition, these new insights invigorate fiscal federalism as a challenging and exciting area of study.

Terms and Concepts for Review

federalism
fiscal federalism
distribution function
stabilization function
allocation function

local public goods
perfect correspondence
revenue-sharing
categorical grants
noncategorical (block) grants
formula grants
matching grants
nonmatching grants
closed-ended grants
open-ended grants
flypaper effect
fiscal illusion
fungibility

Notes

Chapter 1

1. Key terms are italicized when first used. Providing a definition in your own words will enhance learning.
2. Keeney and Raiffa (1976) is an example of earlier work; Weimer and Vining (1989) is a leading current text.
3. See Mitchell (1983) for an insightful account of the evolution of rational choice.

Chapter 2

1. Vilfredo Pareto was an Italian scholar at about the turn of the nineteenth century.
2. The Edgeworth box diagram is named after Sir Frances Edgeworth, a prominent turn-of-the-century British economist.
3. If Smith and Jones had the same MRS at a, the slopes of their indifference curves would be the same. J_0 and S_0 would then be tangent to each other and there would be no incentive for exchange.
4. We assume, for convenience, that all goods cost money and that money is the only constraint on their consumption. In fact, most goods require time for their consumption, and time is a limited resource for consumers. Adding time as a second constraint greatly complicates the analysis.
5. A procedure for separating the income and substitution effects of a price change is shown in the appendix to Chapter 4.
6. Standard references to theoretical and applied welfare economics include Mishan (1967), Boadway and Bruce (1984), and Just, Hueth and Schmitz (1982). For a policy analysis slant, see Jenkins-Smith (1990).
7. Francis W. Bator's 1957 article, "The Simple Analytics of Welfare Maximization," is a classic statement of these three assumptions, although it isn't particularly simple.
8. This situation draws primarily on the first assumption, that of efficient production. The second (efficient exchange and consumption) and third (efficient linking of production and consumption) are most pertinent to a market situation.
9. No higher level of social welfare than c can exist: Economists playfully call it the *bliss point* or Omega. This point is both efficient (it is on the utility possibility frontier) and desirable (it is on the highest social indifference curve). It represents *welfare maximization* with respect to use of a set of resources.

Chapter 3

1. Sections 3.31 and 3.32 draw on a classification of market failure developed by Steiner (1977).

2. Between Q_0 and Q^*, the consumers' surplus would increase by acQ^*Q_0 if the good were free—which it is not—but the increase in cost is only bcQ^*Q_0.

Chapter 4

1. The section "Social Mobility in America" in the Winter 1987 issue of the *Wilson Quarterly* offers an excellent synopsis of this topic.

2. For one provocative view, see Henry Fairlie's article entitled "Talkin' 'Bout My Generation," *The New Republic*, March 28, 1988. The cover page for this issue is a cartoon labeled "Greedy Geezers."

3. After calling it "voodoo economics" during the presidential primaries in 1984, candidate George Bush came to appreciate the idea more fully as Vice President and President George Bush.

4. Of the three, A (additive utility) comes closest to classical utilitarianism, which maintained that social well-being depends on adding the utilities of individuals (Buchanan, 1985, p. 55). The other two are important historical variants with different functional forms and much different policy implications. To some economists, A is the true utilitarian approach, and M and G are "Rawlsian" and "egalitarian" approaches, respectively.

5. OD is drawn at a 45° angle to show equal incomes for the two groups.

6. This can be seen by drawing a new wage line (W_0) parallel to W_1 and tangent to the initial indifference curve (U_0) at B. This shows that a worker would substitute leisure for income at the new wage rate if utility could be held constant at U_0. This analytical procedure is known as the separation of a wage change into substitution and income effects. The difference between L_0 and L_B on the horizontal axis shows that leisure would increase and labor would decrease because of the substitution effect.

7. Because the net effect of the tax is the difference between points E_0 and E_1 and because the substitution effect is negative with respect to work (moving from E_0 to B), the income effect (B to E_1) must be both positive with respect to work *and* larger than the substitution effect.

Chapter 5

1. According to Hardin (1982, pp. 16-25), this specific model of social interaction was stimulated by von Neumann and Morgenstern (1944), developed

in about 1950 by Merrill Flood and Melvin Dresher (Flood, 1958), and elaborated by Luce and Raiffa (1957).

2. This section reflects the influence of Michael Taylor's insightful and readable book *The Possibility of Cooperation* (1987).

3. This model was presented by Lindahl ([1919] 1967) and revived by Buchanan (1968).

4. Contrary to what many economists believe and have been taught, Coase himself was under no illusion that transactions costs would actually be zero.

5. Other favorites, in order, were community campaigns (e.g., United Way), medical charities (e.g., March of Dimes), social welfare groups, international relief and assistance (e.g., Food Aid), colleges and universities, hospitals, environmental groups, and libraries and art groups.

6. Russell Hardin's *Collective Action* (1982) has excellent discussions of free-riding and of interest-group formation (e.g., pp. 31-35 and Chapter 7).

7. Interest-group membership is considered again in Section 7.6.

8. Some donors may feel too comfortable, in the opinion of Felix and Elizabeth Rohatyn. They serve on boards of dozens of charities and were quoted as being concerned with ethical aspects of the dazzling opulence of charity balls and benefit dinners (*New York Times*, January 5, 1986, p. 23). The opportunity to see and be seen, however, is a powerful private good that may be a great help in fund-raising.

9. Political scientist Russell Hardin tells how he found out that economists are different. "One afternoon some time ago, I was involved in a conversation around a table at the Hoover Institution. We were debating the meaning of a word. . . . one of my colleagues noted that this was essentially a factual question, which should therefore be settled by reference to the relevant factual authority: 'one who believes that human conduct is motivated wholly by self-interest.' The work whose definition we had sought and just heard was, of course, 'cynic.' . . . Of those who instantly said 'economist' that day, I was the only noneconomist, I said it with a slightly accusing tone. The others, I am convinced, said it with pride. I have since occasionally wondered who was more in the right" (1982, pp. xiv-xv).

10. Whether consumer preferences are revealed or whether they are constructed by CV questioning is a critical issue that is still being debated. Recent psychological research (particularly Slovic, Griffin, and Tversky, 1990) suggests that the latter is often the case.

11. It has been possible in some cases to compare contingent valuation results with those from other research methods. Poor air quality and aircraft noise, for example, have been shown to depress property values in certain neighborhoods. In one key study, Brookshire et al. (1982) compared contingent valuation results with property value differences in the Los Angeles airshed and concluded that the two methods gave comparable results. In most other cases, there has been a lack of market values with which CV results might be compared.

12. An article in 1976 by Robert Willig was titled "Consumer's Surplus Without Apology." Willig contended that it usually doesn't matter that there are many definitions of consumer's surplus. He showed that if the quality changes are small and payment or receipt of payment doesn't greatly alter the wealth

position of users, the various consumer's surplus measures will give about the same results.

Chapter 6

1. In *Liberalism Against Populism* (1982, Chapter 3), Riker presents three desirable properties of a voting rule that simple majority rule may satisfy as a voting method if there are only two alternatives. These properties reflect a blend of technical and moral considerations (p. 51). With monotonicity, when individual valuations of an alternative rise, so does social valuation. With undifferentiatedness (anonymity), one person's vote cannot be distinguished from that of another (for example, secret ballots). With neutrality, the voting method doesn't favor either alternative (it may favor the status quo, for example). In Riker's view, a major problem with majority rule is that restricting choice to two alternatives violates the neutrality property.

2. The term "dictatorial" may be troubling to some, but remember that it is used as shorthand in a mathematical proof. Substitute, if you prefer, "unresponsive to popular preferences."

3. Sen (1966) proved that the Arrow problem isn't a problem if preferences are single-dimensioned. This is not likely to happen except in the simplest situation. According to Mueller, "Issues must all be of the one dimensional variety: the number of guns, the number of schoolbooks. The voters cannot simultaneously consider both the number and kind of books. And their preferences must be single peaked in one dimension. . . . If some individuals have multiple peaks, they must somehow be isolated and excluded from the community, or an impossibility result can again emerge" (1989, pp. 392-393).

4. See Enelow and Hinich (1984, Chapter 2) and Mueller (1989, Chapter 5).

5. See Enelow and Hinich (1984, Chapter 3), Mueller (1989, Chapter 5), and Riker (1986, pp. 142-152).

6. The use of circular indifference curves indicates that the consumer also gains utility from goods and services that are excluded from the diagram. In this case, it is reasonable to think of after-tax income, or money *not* spent for schools, as a third good or service.

7. William Riker, in his very readable book *The Art of Political Manipulation* (1986, pp. 142-152), discusses how the manipulation of dimensions is commonly used with agenda control to seek political advantage and stabilize outcomes. With Figure 6.12, this could be done by introducing a new dimension (tenure for teachers, for example) or by neutralizing an existing dimension (freezing budget size at current levels, for example).

8. See Dougan and Munger (1989) for an expanded treatment of ideology.

9. See Poole (1984), Poole and Romer (1985), Poole and Rosenthal (1984), Poole, Romer, and Rosenthal (1987), and Romer and Rosenthal (1984).

10. It seems ironic that C. L. Dodgson, the English author, mathematician, and logician who wrote the delightful and well-known fantasy *Alice's Adventures*

in Wonderland under the pseudonym of Lewis Carroll more than a century ago, also wrote about inconsistencies in majority-rule voting.

11. This section draws on Mueller's discussion of voting rules (1989, Ch. 7).

Chapter 7

1. Downs also dealt with multiple-party case, but for simplicity, only the two-party system is considered here.

2. Downs (1960) later argued that government would tend to be too small because there would be a lack of information among voters about future activities that would generate net benefits. This would penalize parties that propose efficient activities in the future.

3. Decisions on how, whether, and how much voting information to acquire can also be portrayed with this model. P would reflect the value of information in facilitating a "better" vote on the individual's part, and D could reflect "politics as entertainment"—a private benefit to the voter. For a recent work on the dynamics of voter information as applied to presidential primary elections, see Bartels (1988).

4. Those who are paid to prepare proposals and make presentations are better off because of rent-seeking. As Congleton (1988) shows, however, opportunity costs must be considered. Only if these resources would otherwise be unemployed will waste due to rent-seeking not occur. Normally, the people who are paid to prepare and present the proposals would be doing something else of equal value if they weren't involved in rent-seeking.

5. Jeffrey Berry (1989) has an excellent presentation of interest-group issues in his book *The Interest Group Society*.

6. In more current terms, electoral slack weakens the principal-agent relationship between voters and elected suppliers (see Chapter 9).

7. Breton didn't explicitly include uncertainty; thus, he mentions only three factors instead of four.

8. With respect to whether corporations, consumers, or workers actually pay the corporate income tax, for example, Joseph E. Stiglitz, a leading authority on the topic, states that "There is no agreement among economists about the incidence of the corporation tax . . . or about the nature of the distortions it introduces" (1988, p. 564).

9. Although this wasn't explicit in Chapter 2 (Figure 2.4, for example), DD represents an income-compensated demand curve. There are no income effects of price changes, only substitution effects (see the Appendix to Chapter 4). Willig (1976) demonstrated that there are usually only slight differences in consumers' surplus between this theoretically pure demand curve and an uncompensated or ordinary demand curve where price changes make consumers a little better off or a little worse off.

10. For simplicity, the supply of the commodity is assumed to be perfectly elastic at P_o.

11. Working generates income along a price line (wage rate) for labor; leisure is consumed by not working. The appendix to Chapter 4 explains these concepts in more detail.

12. The original producers' surplus was P_oJA; the producers' surplus after the tax would be P_1EA. The difference is P_oJEP_1. Although the new price at the pump would be $P_1 + t$, the price to the retailer would be only P_1; the difference is the tax per gallon of EF.

Chapter 8

1. Mitchell (1990) and Mitchell and Munger (1991) provide excellent reviews of how interest groups can affect legislative outcomes.

2. Although regulation is often used to mean the implementation of a set of rules, a much broader legislative connotation is intended here. "Regulation" makes it explicit that gainers and losers are defined by the way the rules are written. "Regulator" can mean an individual legislator or a legislative body.

3. Stigler also saw that industry could gain by limiting substitutes and by price-fixing, but these would be most effective if entry was also limited.

4. Arnold (1990, Chapter 8) provides a companion account of this and previous tax-reform acts.

5. Some public choice analysts have been critical of Peltzman's idea that legislators try to maximize the vote margin; they argue that this wastes too many other opportunities to do good for society or to get rich. Riker's (1962) concept of a minimum winning coalition is in sharp contrast to Peltzman's formulation (see Section 6.43).

6. The two remaining triangles, fga and dbh, are deadweight losses, that is, they are reductions in efficiency because of reduced use of the cheapest source of raw material. See Section 7.73 for a general discussion of deadweight losses resulting from taxation.

7. The loss of consumers' surplus in Figure 8.2 is larger than the increase in producers' surplus (cfae) because of the tariff (fdhg) and the deadweight loss (fga plus dhb).

8. Interest groups representing homebuilders and realtors might also oppose the regulator because their sales—and producers' surplus—would decline as home values increased.

9. Mitchell and Munger (1991) argue that this result is a spin-off of the Coase theorem, which said that waste (the effects of inefficient resource allocation) will be reduced to zero, regardless of the initial assignment of property rights, if transaction costs are zero.

10. The notion that pressure group outcomes may be "good" may worry those who are skeptical about political influence. Becker neatly sidesteps this by assuming that both groups have equal access to political influence.

11. These are short, persuasive TV messages about candidates, useful mainly for a quick trip to the refrigerator.

12. Accepting too many campaign contributions from outside interests may be costly to a representative if they appear to conflict with the needs of district constituents.

13. The focus of this section is on PACs at the federal level, but they have also proliferated at the state level (Alexander, 1984, Chapter 7). State laws on PACs vary widely in scope and detail.

14. Grier and Munger (1986) offer a concise summary of PAC history, Berry's (1989) chapter on PACs is excellent, and Alexander (1984) is also a useful reference.

15. See Dom Bonafede, "Some Things Don't Change—Cost of 1982 Congressional Races Higher than Ever," *National Journal*, October 30, 1982, pp. 1832-1836.

16. Denzau and Munger (1986) incorporate a legislator's productivity directly into his supply function for legislative effort. Being a committee member, in particular, would reduce the cost of gaining a favorable outcome; interest groups would search for low-cost suppliers. Making the demand function explicit may be a more familiar procedure for students.

17. If there are two legislators with equal productivities and equal demands (D_u, for example) but different supply costs (S_u and S_{nv}, for example), their campaign contributions will depend on the elasticity of demand for their services. In general, the demand for a factor of production tends to be inelastic if there are few substitutes for it. In this case, the House Education and Labor Committee might be the only committee that could initiate the workplace safety bill. Total revenues increase as one moves up an inelastic demand curve; thus, a larger contribution would be needed to obtain the services of the legislator who has the more reluctant constituency.

18. It is this prospect, not just coincidence or efficient time management, that leads to simultaneous voting on a number of water resource development projects in the form of an omnibus water bill. Each project would usually benefit only a small geographic constituency, generally at the taxpayer's expense. With simultaneous voting, I have to vote for your project to get my own.

19. Another serious ethical issue is raised by the fact that House incumbents who were elected prior to 1980 are legally able to convert any campaign surplus to personal use if they retire from Congress by 1993. Unspent campaign funds totaling about $40 million are held by 166 representatives, including 20 who each hold more than $500,000 in leftover money (*Congressional Quarterly Weekly Report*, January 12, 1991, pp. 72-79).

Chapter 9

1. A more negative view about bureaucracy was held by another prominent writer of the time, Ludwig von Mises (1944), an Austrian advocate of laissez faire.

2. Chapter 8 of Berry (1989) is especially useful for understanding this concept.

3. Niskanen used the terms bureau, bureaucracy, and bureaucratic government to mean the same as agency and administrative government.

4. These and many other interesting facts can be gleaned from a current edition of the *Washington Information Directory* or the *Congressional Staff Directory*, both of which are available at most public libraries. The subcommittee structure varies from session to session, depending on the wishes of the House and Senate leaders.

5. There are obviously two sponsors—one in each chamber—but differences can be worked out through conference committees and other ·congressional institutions. Thus, Niskanen could treat the two as one.

6. A more precise statement is that agencies will try to maximize the total budget as long as it equals or exceeds total cost. Output Q_n in Figure 9.1 would involve a slightly larger budget (B_n) than would output Q_a (B_a) but the agency wouldn't want Q_n because it would cost more to produce (C_n) than the sponsor would provide in budget.

7. This has to happen for the total budget to equal the total cost in Figure 9.1.

8. Sections 9.4 and 9.5 draw on an overview of the economics of organization by Moe (1984) and a recent work on delegation of congressional authority by Kiewiet and McCubbins (1991).

9. These two problems are identified in more straightforward terms as the hidden information problem and the hidden action problem (Kiewiet and McCubbins, 1991, Chapter 2). The hidden information problem, of which adverse selection is one variant, arises from the fact that certain information is either unavailable to the principal or costly to obtain. The hidden action problem, like moral hazard, arises when an outcome generated in part by an agent is not conducive to the principal's best interests. Kiewiet and McCubbins also define a third agency problem, Madison's dilemma, arising when "resources or authority granted to an agent for the purpose of advancing the interests of the principal can be turned against the principal" (p. 26). This problem is especially severe when the agent occupies a leadership position, as Congress does, for example.

10. Lying on his back during a hold in the countdown to blast off for an early space flight, astronaut and later senator John Glenn said it occurred to him that "the whole thing had been put together by a low bidder."

11. This, as Kiewiet and McCubbins note (1991, p. 25), is the crux of Niskanen's model of bureaucracy.

12. The median voter is actually decisive under majority rule only if everyone votes, which usually doesn't happen. Voting abstentions among those at the low end of the preference scale, for example, will create a new median voter—one who prefers a larger amount than does the true median voter. *Pivotal voter* refers to the median voter among those voting.

13. An amendment to the Oregon constitution in 1987 created a safety net for school districts. They were able to levy, without popular vote, an amount equal to the previous year's operating levy, but without the 6 percent annual growth rate. This effectively updated their tax base, but school funding problems have persisted.

Chapter 10

1. There is no administrator in the Peltzman model, which is one reason that political scientists are lukewarm (at most) about it.

2. This section draws on Gramlich (1990), which is useful for an expanded treatment of benefit-cost procedures.

3. It may be difficult to estimate the size of the shaded area in Figure 10.2. There may be uncertainty about what the two supply functions would look like at lower levels of price because these levels may be outside our range of experience. However, we may have greater confidence in statistical estimates of the demand function around the neighborhood of the current price. If so, the constant-cost case might be assumed even though increasing returns actually exist.

4. That is, ($3)(2,500) + (½)($4 - $3)(2,500 - 0) + ($2)(5,000 - 2,500) + (½)($3 - $2)(5,000 - 2,500) . . . = $20,000.

5. The implicit marginal prices of Q are the partial derivatives of residential value with respect to Q. The DD function itself is estimated as a second step:

$$\frac{\partial P}{\partial Q} = f(Q, I, A_i),$$

where I is household income and A_i are other household attributes (Freeman, 1979, pp. 121-129).

6. If a relaxation of safety standards was proposed, the willingness to accept compensation for increased risk would be a more appropriate measure of value.

Chapter 11

1. Political jurisdictions can also generate negative externalities, in which case they would be producing too much at Q^*.

2. The median voter would be left with more income if the positive income effect of the price change (in this case, the matching grant) was larger than the negative substitution effect on other goods and services (see appendix to Chapter 4). The opposite would tend to happen with small-grant programs; the income effect would be small and the net effect would be a reduction in spending for other goods and services.

3. A critic of the median voter model would point out that there might be three different median voters in Figure 11.2, one for each funding situation (*a*, *b*, and *c*). This is because the distribution of income among city residents could be different for each situation.

4. Outcomes above *c* on the new price line would happen only if the income elasticity for public health was negative, which is unlikely. The U_1 and U_1' indifference curves reflect different patterns of preferences and are not meant to be on the same indifference map.

5. Matching and nonmatching categorical grants from federal to state and local governments in 1990 totaled $132 billion and included the following categories (*Survey of Current Business,* January 1992, Table 3.16): Medicaid, $43.3 billion; welfare and social services, 31.3 billion; highways, 14.1 billion; elementary and secondary education, 7.8 billion; urban renewal and community development, 3.1 billion; transit, 3.1 billion; labor training programs, 2.8 billion; water and sewerage, 2.3 billion for a total of $107.8 billion. These categories accounted for over 80 percent of the total. This aid amounted to about 16 percent of total revenues of state and local governments in that year (*Economic Report of the President,* 1991, Table B-82).

6. The school district in Figure 11.4 would have spent more Q_0 than the grant amount (Q_a) without the program, so this particular grant would have an income effect but no substitution effect (see appendix to Chapter 4). If O_0 was less than Q_a, the grant would be partially a matching grant and would thus have both price and income effects on school spending. If Q_0 was $5 million and Q_a was $10 million, each local dollar would "earn" $2 in state aid.

7. Craig's measure of safety was obtained by subtracting the per capita crime rate from a constant term (1987, p. 335). Those neighborhoods with larger values for safety were thus safer neighborhoods.

8. Schwab and Zampelli (1987) also estimate an income elasticity of price as well as conventional income and price elasticities of demand for police protection.

Bibliography

Abrams, Burton, and Mark D. Schmitz. 1978. "The 'Crowding-Out' Effect of Governmental Transfers on Private Charitable Contributions." *Public Choice* 33: 29-39.

_____. 1984. "The Crowding-Out Effect of Governmental Transfers on Private Charitable Contributions: Cross-Section Evidence." *National Tax Journal* (December): 563-568.

Alchian, Armen A., and Harold Demsetz. 1972. "Production, Information Costs, and Economic Organization." *American Economic Review* 62 (December): 777-795.

Alexander, Herbert E. 1984. *Financing Politics.* 3rd ed. Washington, D.C.: CQ Press.

Allman, William F. 1984. "Nice Guys Finish First." *Science 84* 5 (October): 24-32.

Anderson, Terry L., and Peter J. Hill. 1980. *The Birth of a Transfer Society.* Stanford, Calif.: Hoover Institution Press.

Arnold, R. Douglas. 1990. *The Logic of Congressional Action.* New Haven: Yale University Press.

Arrow, Kenneth J. 1951. *Social Choice and Individual Values.* New York: John Wiley.

Babcock, Bruce A., Colin A. Carter, and Andrew Schmitz. 1990. "The Political Economy of U.S. Wheat Legislation." *Economic Inquiry* 28 (April): 335-353.

Bartels, Larry M. 1988. *Presidential Primaries and the Dynamics of Public Choice.* Princeton, N.J.: Princeton University Press.

Bator, Francis M. 1957. "The Simple Analytics of Welfare Maximization." *American Economic Review* (March): 22-59.

Baumgartner, Frank R., and Jack L. Walker. 1988. "Survey Research and Membership in Voluntary Associations." *American Journal of Political Science* 32 (November): 908-928.

Becker, Gary S. 1964. *Human Capital.* New York: National Bureau of Economic Research.

_____. 1983. "A Theory of Competition Among Pressure Groups for Political Influence." *Quarterly Journal of Economics* 98 (August): 371-400.

_____. 1985. "Public Policies, Pressure Groups, and Dead Weight Costs." *Journal of Public Economics* 28 (December): 329-347.

Bentham, Jeremy. 1948. *An Introduction to the Principles of Morals and Legislation.* New York: Hafner. (Originally published in 1780.)

Bentkover, Judith D. 1986. "The Role of Benefits Assessment in Public Policy Development," in Judith D. Bentkover, Vincent T. Covello, and Jeryl Mumpower, eds., *Benefits Assessment: The State of the Art.* Pp. 1-12. Dordrecht, Holland: D. Reidel.

Berry, Jeffrey M. 1989. *The Interest Group Society.* 2nd ed. Glenview, Ill.: Scott, Foresman.

Birnbaum, Jeffrey H., and Alan S. Murray. 1988. *Showdown at Gucci Gulch*. New York: Vintage Books.

Bishop, Richard C., and Thomas A. Heberlein. 1979. "Measuring Values of Extramarket Goods: Are Indirect Measures Biased?" *American Journal of Agricultural Economics* 61 (December): 926-930.

Black, Duncan. 1958. *The Theory of Committees and Elections*. Cambridge: Cambridge University Press.

Boadway, Robin W., and Neil Bruce. 1984. *Welfare Economics*. Oxford: Basil Blackwell.

Bradford, David F., R. A. Malt, and Wallace E. Oates. 1969. "The Rising Cost of Local Public Services: Some Evidence and Reflections." *National Tax Journal* 22: 185-202.

Breimyer, Harold F. 1973. "An Analysis of the Market for Food Stamps: Comment." *American Journal of Agricultural Economics* 55 (February): 110-112.

Brennan, Geoffrey, and James M. Buchanan. 1988. "Is Public Choice Immoral? The Case for the 'Nobel' Lie." *Virginia Law Review* 74: 179-189.

Breton, Albert. 1974. *The Economic Theory of Representative Government*. Chicago: Aldine.

Brookshire, David S., and Don L. Coursey. 1987. "Measuring the Value of a Public Good: An Empirical Comparison of Elicitation Procedures." *American Economic Review* 77 (September): 554-566.

Brookshire, David S., Mark A. Thayer, William D. Schulze, and Ralph C. d'Arge. 1982. "Valuing Public Goods: A Comparison of Survey and Hedonic Approaches." *American Economic Review* 72 (March): 165-177.

Brown, David L., and John M. Wardwell, eds. 1980. *New Directions in Urban-Rural Migration*. New York: Academic Press.

Bryant, W. Keith. 1972. "An Analysis of the Market for Food Stamps." *American Journal of Agricultural Economics* 54 (May): 305-314.

_____. 1973. "An Analysis of the Market for Food Stamps: Reply." *American Journal of Agricultural Economics* 55 (February): 112-115.

Buchanan, Allen. 1985. *Ethics, Efficiency, and the Market*. Totowa, N.J.: Rowman and Allanheld.

Buchanan, James M. 1965. "An Economic Theory of Clubs." *Economica* 32 (February): 1-14.

_____. 1968. *The Demand and Supply of Public Goods*. Chicago: Rand McNally.

Buchanan, James M., and Gordon Tullock. 1962. *The Calculus of Consent*. Ann Arbor: University of Michigan Press.

Buchanan, James M., Robert D. Tollison, and Gordon Tullock, eds. 1980. *Toward a Theory of the Rent-Seeking Society*. College Station: Texas A&M Press.

Bush, Winston C., and Lawrence S. Meyer. 1974. "Some Implications of Anarchy for the Distribution of Property." *Journal of Economic Theory* 8 (August): 401-412.

Calabresi, Guido. 1968. "Transaction Costs, Resource Allocation, and Liability Rules—A Comment." *Journal of Law and Economics* 11 (April): 67-73.

Calvert, Randall L., Mark J. Moran, and Barry R. Weingast. 1987. "Congressional Influence over Policy Making: The Case of the FTC," in Mathew D.

McCubbins and Terry Sullivan, eds., *Congress: Structure and Policy.* Pp. 493-522. Cambridge: Cambridge University Press.

Carter, John R., and Michael D. Irons. 1991. "Are Economists Different, and If So, Why?" *Journal of Economic Perspectives* 5 (Spring): 171-177.

Clark, Peter B., and James Q. Wilson. 1961. "Incentive Systems: A Theory of Organizations." *Administrative Science Quarterly* 6 (September): 129-166.

Clarke, Edward H. 1971. "Multipart Pricing of Public Goods." *Public Choice* 11 (Fall): 17-33.

_____. 1977. "Some Aspects of the Demand-Revealing Process." *Public Choice* 29 (Spring): 37-49.

Clawson, Marion. 1959. "Methods of Measuring the Demand for and Value of Outdoor Recreation." RFF Reprint No. 10. Washington, D.C.: Resources for the Future, Inc.

Clawson, Marion, and Jack L. Knetsch. 1966. *Economics of Outdoor Recreation.* Baltimore: Johns Hopkins University Press.

Clotfelter, Charles T. 1985. *Federal Tax Policy and Charitable Giving.* Chicago: University of Chicago Press.

Coase, Ronald. 1937. "The Nature of the Firm." *Economica* 4 (November): 386-405.

_____. 1960. "The Problem of Social Cost." *Journal of Law and Economics* 3 (October): 1-44.

Collier's Encyclopedia. 1990. New York: Macmillan Educational Co.

Common Cause. 1989. "Congressional Campaign Financing: The Case for Reform." Washington, D.C.: Mimeo.

Congleton, Roger D. 1988. "Evaluating Rent-Seeking Losses: Do the Welfare Gains of Lobbyists Count?" *Public Choice* 56 (February): 181-184.

Conover, Pamela, and Stanley Feldman. 1981. "The Origin and Meaning of Liberal-Conservative Self-Identification." *American Journal of Political Science* 25 (November): 617-645.

Courant, Paul N., Edward M. Gramlich, and Daniel L. Rubinfeld. 1979. "The Stimulative Effects of Intergovernmental Grants: Or Why Money Sticks Where It Lands," in Peter Miezkowski and William H. Oakland, eds., *Fiscal Federalism and Grants-In-Aid.* Pp. 5-21. Washington, D.C.: The Urban Institute.

Coursey, Don L., John L. Hovis, and William D. Schulze. 1987. "The Disparity Between Willingness to Accept and Willingness to Pay Measures of Value." *Quarterly Journal of Economics* (August): 679-690.

Craig, Steven G. 1987. "The Impact of Congestion on Local Public Good Production." *Journal of Public Economics* 32 (April): 331-353.

Craig, Steven G., and Robert P. Inman. 1982. "Federal Aid and Public Education: An Empirical Look at the New Fiscal Federalism." *Review of Economics and Statistics* 64 (November): 541-552.

Crandall, Robert W. 1984. "Import Quotas and the Automobile Industry: The Costs of Protectionism." *The Brookings Review* 2 (Summer): 8-16.

Cyert, Richard M., and James C. March. 1963. *A Behavioral Theory of the Firm.* Englewood Cliffs, N.J.: Prentice-Hall.

Dahl, Robert A. 1961. *Who Governs?* New Haven: Yale University Press.

_____. 1970. *After the Revolution: Authority in a Good Society*. New Haven: Yale University Press.

Davidson, Roger H., and Walter J. Oleszek. 1990. *Congress and Its Members*. 3rd ed. Washington, D.C.: CQ Press.

Dawes, Robyn M., John M. Orbell, Randy T. Simmons, and Alphons J. C. van de Kragt. 1986. "Organizing Groups for Collective Action." *American Political Science Review* 80 (December): 1171-1185.

Denzau, Arthur T., and Michael C. Munger. 1986. "Legislators and Interest Groups: How Unorganized Interests Get Represented." *American Political Science Review* 80 (March): 89-106.

de Tocqueville, Alexis. *Democracy in America*. 1969. J. P. Meyer (ed.). Garden City, N.Y. Anchor Books. (Originally published in 1835.)

DiIulio, John J. 1991. "Notes on a Contrarian Scholar." *Public Administration Review* 51 (May/June): 193-195.

Donahue, John D. 1983. "The Political Economy of Milk." *The Atlantic* 253 (October): 59-68.

Dougan, William R., and Daphne A. Kenyon. 1988. "Pressure Groups and Public Expenditures: The Flypaper Effect Reconsidered." *Economic Inquiry* 26 (January): 159-170.

Dougan, William R., and Michael C. Munger. 1989. "The Rationality of Ideology." *Journal of Law and Economics* 32 (April): 119-142.

Downs, Anthony. 1957. *An Economic Theory of Democracy*. New York: Harper.

_____. 1960. "Why the Government Budget is Too Small in a Democracy." *World Politics* 12 (July): 541-563.

Dye, Thomas R., and Harmon Ziegler. 1990. *The Irony of Democracy: An Uncommon Introduction to American Politics*. 8th ed. Monterey, Calif.: Brooks/Cole.

Eckstein, Otto. 1958. *Water Resource Development*. Cambridge: Harvard University Press.

Editors Comment. 1987. *Wilson Quarterly* 11 (Winter): 6.

Enelow, James M., and Melvin J. Hinich. 1984. *The Spatial Theory of Voting*. Cambridge: Cambridge University Press.

Fama, Eugene F. 1980. "Agency Problems and the Theory of the Firm." *Journal of Political Economy* 88 (April): 288-307.

Federal Elections Commission. 1991. Press Release on 1989-90 Election Cycle, March 31, 1991. 42 pp. Washington, D.C.

Fenno, Richard F. 1973. *Congressmen in Committees*. Boston: Little, Brown.

_____. 1978. *Home Style: House Members in Their Districts*. Boston: Little, Brown.

Ferejohn, John A. 1974. *Pork Barrel Politics: Rivers and Harbors Legislation, 1947-1968*. Stanford, Calif.: Stanford University Press.

Fesler, James W. 1980. *Public Administration: Theory and Practice*. Englewood Cliffs, N.J.: Prentice-Hall.

Fiorina, Morris P. 1974. *Representative, Roll Calls, and Constituencies*. Lexington, Mass.: Lexington Books.

_____. 1982. "Legislative Choice of Regulatory Forms: Legal Process or Administrative Process?" *Public Choice* 39: 33-66.

_____. 1989. *Congress: Keystone of the Washington Establishment*. 2nd ed. New Haven: Yale University Press.

Flood, Merrill M. 1958. "Some Experimental Games." *Management Science* 5 (October): 5-26.

Freeman, A. Myrick, III. 1979. *The Benefits of Environmental Improvement*. Baltimore: Johns Hopkins University Press.

Friedman, Milton. 1953. *Essays in Positive Economics*. Chicago: University of Chicago Press.

_____. 1962. *Capitalism and Freedom*. Chicago: University of Chicago Press.

Fullerton, Don. 1982. "On the Possibility of an Inverse Relationship Between Tax Rates and Government Revenues." *Journal of Public Economics* 19 (October): 3-22.

Gardner, Bruce L. 1987. "Causes of U.S. Farm Commodity Programs." *Journal of Political Economy* 95 (April): 290-311.

Gibbard, Allan. 1973. "Manipulation of Voting Schemes: A General Result." *Econometrica* 41 (July): 587-602.

Ginzberg, Eli. 1976. "The Pluralistic Economy of the United States." *Scientific American* (December): 25-26.

Gordon, George J. 1982. *Public Administration in America*. 2nd ed. New York: St. Martin's Press.

Gramlich, Edward M. 1977. "Intergovernmental Grants: A Review of the Empirical Literature," in Wallace E. Oates, ed., *The Political Economy of Fiscal Federalism*. Pp. 219-239. Lexington, Mass.: Lexington Books.

_____. 1990. *A Guide to Benefit-Cost Analysis*. 2nd. ed. Englewood Cliffs, N.J.: Prentice-Hall.

Green, Donald Philip, and Jonathan S. Krasno. 1988. "Salvation for the Spendthrift Incumbent: Re-estimating the Effects of Campaign Spending in House Elections." *American Political Science Review* (November): 884-907.

Green, Mark. 1982. "Political PAC-Man." *The New Republic* 187 (December 13): 18-25.

Gregory, Robin. 1986. "Interpreting Measures of Economic Loss: Evidence from Contingent Valuation and Experimental Studies." *Journal of Environmental Economics and Management* 13: 325-337.

Gregory, Robin, and Lita Furby. 1987. "Auctions, Experiments and Contingent Valuation." *Public Choice* 55: 273-289.

Gregory, Robin, and Tim McDaniels. 1987. "Valuing Environmental Losses: What Promise Does the Right Measure Hold?" *Policy Sciences* 20: 11-26.

Grenzke, Janet. 1988. "Comparing Contributions to U.S. House Members from Outside Their Districts." *Legislative Studies Quarterly* 13 (February): 83-103.

Grier, Kevin B., and Michael C. Munger. 1986. "The Impact of Legislator Attributes on Interest-Group Campaign Contributions." *Journal of Labor Research* 7 (Fall): 349-361.

_____. 1991. "Committee Assignments, Constituent Preferences, and Campaign Contributions." *Economic Inquiry* 29 (January): 24-43.

Grier, Kevin B., Michael C. Munger, and Brian E. Roberts. 1991. "The Industrial Organization of Corporate Political Participation." *Southern Economic Journal* 57 (January): 727-738.

Griffith, Ernest. 1939. *Impasse of Democracy*. New York: Harrison-Hilton Books.

Groves, Theodore. 1973. "Incentives in Teams." *Econometrica* 41 (July): 617-631.

Groves, Theodore, and John Ledyard. 1977. "Optimal Allocation of Public Goods: A Solution to the 'Free Rider' Problem." *Econometrica* 45 (May): 783-809.

Guither, Harold D. 1986. "Tough Choices: Writing the Food Security Act of 1985." *American Enterprise Institute Occasional Paper*. Washington, D.C.: American Enterprise Institute.

Gulick, Luther. 1937. "Notes on the Theory of Organizations," in Luther Gulick and Lyndall Urwick, eds., *Papers on the Science of Administration*. Pp. 1-45. New York: Institute of Public Administration.

Hamilton, Bruce W. 1983. "The Flypaper Effect and Other Anomalies." *Journal of Public Economics* 22 (December): 347-361.

Hansmann, Henry B. 1986. "The Role of Nonprofit Enterprise," in Susan Rose-Ackerman, ed., *The Economics of Nonprofit Institutions*. Pp. 57-84. New York: Oxford University Press.

Hardin, Russell. 1971. "Collective Action as an Agreeable n-Prisoners' Dilemma." *Behavioral Science* 16 (September): 472-481.

_____. 1982. *Collective Action*. Baltimore: Johns Hopkins University Press.

Haveman, Robert H. 1988a. "The Changed Face of Poverty: A Call for New Policies." *Focus* 11 (Summer): 10-14.

_____. 1988b. *Starting Even*. New York: Simon and Schuster.

Haveman, Robert H., and John V. Krutilla. 1968. *Unemployment, Idle Capacity, and the Evaluation of Public Expenditures*. Baltimore: Johns Hopkins University Press.

Haveman, Robert H., and Burton A. Weisbrod. 1975. "Defining Benefits of Public Programs: Some Guidance for Policy Analysts." *Policy Analysis* (Winter): 169-196.

Heclo, Hugh. 1978. "Issue Networks and the Executive Establishment," in Anthony King, ed., *The New American Political System*. Pp. 87-124. Washington, D.C.: American Enterprise Institute.

Hettich, Walter, and Stanley L. Winer. 1988. "Economic and Political Foundations of Tax Structure." *American Economic Review* 78 (September): 701-712.

Hicks, John R. 1939. "The Foundations of Welfare Economics." *Economic Journal* 49 (December): 696-712.

_____. 1946. *Value and Capital*. 2nd ed. London: Oxford University Press.

Hiemstra, Stephen J. 1973. "An Analysis of the Market for Food Stamps: Comment." *American Journal of Agricultural Economics* 55 (February): 109-110.

Higgins, Richard S., William F. Shughart II, and Robert D. Tollison. 1985. "Free Entry and Efficient Rent Seeking." *Public Choice* 46: 247-258.

Hinich, Melvin J., and Walker Pollard. 1981. "A New Approach to the Spatial Theory of Electoral Competition." *American Journal of Political Science* 25 (May): 323-341.

Hirschman, Albert O. 1970. *Exit, Vote and Loyalty*. Cambridge, Mass.: Harvard University Press.

Hochman, Harold M., and James D. Rogers. 1969. "Pareto Optimal Redistribution." *American Economic Review* 59 (September): 542-557.

Hofstadter, Richard. 1974. *The American Political Tradition*. New York: Vintage Books.

Holcombe, Randall G. 1988. *Public Sector Economics*. Belmont, Calif.: Wadsworth.

Hotelling, Harold. 1929. "Stability in Competition." *Economic Journal* 39 (March): 41-57.

_____. 1949. Letter quoted in *The Economics of Public Recreation: An Economic Study of the Monetary Evaluation of Recreation in the National Parks*. Washington, D.C.: National Park Service, U.S. Department of the Interior.

Inman, Robert P. 1987. "Markets, Governments, and the 'New' Political Economy," in Alan J. Auerbach and Martin Feldstein, eds., *Handbook of Public Economics*. Vol. 2. Pp. 647-777. Amsterdam: North-Holland.

Jacobson, Gary C. 1980. *Money in Congressional Elections*. New Haven: Yale University Press.

_____. 1985. "Money and Votes Reconsidered: Congressional Elections, 1972-1982." *Public Choice* 47: 7-62.

Jenkins-Smith, Hank C. 1990. *Democratic Politics and Policy Analysis*. Pacific Grove, Calif.: Brooks/Cole.

Jensen, Michael C. 1983. "Organization Theory and Methodology." *Accounting Review* 8 (April): 319-337.

Johnson, Paul Edward. 1990. "We Do Too Have Morals: On Rational Choice in the Classroom." *PS: Political Science & Politics* 23 (December): 610-613.

Just, Richard E., Darrell L. Hueth, and Andrew Schmitz. 1982. *Applied Welfare Economics and Public Policy*. Englewood Cliffs, N.J.: Prentice-Hall.

Kahneman, Daniel, and Amos Tversky. 1979. "Prospect Theory." *Econometrica* 47 (March): 263-291.

_____. 1981. "The Framing of Decisions and the Psychology of Choice." *Science* 211 (January): 453-458.

_____. 1984. "Choices, Values and Frames." *American Psychologist* 39 (April): 341-350.

Kaldor, Nicholas. 1939. "Welfare Propositions of Economics and Interpersonal Comparisons of Utility." *Economic Journal* 49 (September): 549-552.

Kalt, Joseph P., and Mark A. Zupan. 1984. "Capture and Ideology in the Economic Theory of Politics." *American Economic Review* 74 (June): 279-300.

Kau, James B., and Paul H. Rubin. 1981. *Congressmen, Constituents and Contributors*. Boston: Martinus Nijhoff.

Kau, James B., Donald Keenan, and Paul H. Rubin. 1982. "A General Equilibrium Model of Congressional Voting." *Quarterly Journal of Economics* 97 (May): 271-293.

Keeney, R. L., and Howard Raiffa. 1976. *Decisions with Multiple Objectives*. New York: Wiley.

Keim, Gerald, and Asghar Zardkoohi. 1988. "Looking for Leverage in PAC Markets: Corporate and Labor Contributions Considered." *Public Choice* 58 (July): 21-34.

Kelman, Steven. 1987a. *Making Public Policy*. New York: Basic Books.

_____. 1987b. "'Public Choice' and the Public Spirit." *Public Interest* 87 (Spring): 80-94.

Kiewiet, D. Roderick, and Mathew D. McCubbins. 1991. *The Logic of Delegation*. Chicago: University of Chicago Press.

Kingma, Bruce Robert. 1989. "An Accurate Measurement of the Crowd-out Effect, Income Effect and Price Effect for Charitable Contributions." *Journal of Public Economics* 97 (October): 1197-1207.

Knoke, David. 1990. *Organizing for Collective Action.* New York: Aldine de Gruyter.

Kramer, Gerald H. 1973. "On a Class of Equilibrium Conditions for Majority Rule." *Econometrica* 41 (March): 285-297.

Krueger, Anne O. 1974. "The Political Economy of the Rent-Seeking Society." *American Economic Review* 64 (June): 291-303.

Langbein, Laura Irwin. 1980. *Discovering Whether Programs Work.* Santa Monica, Calif.: Goodyear.

Lave, Lester B. 1981. *The Strategy of Social Regulation: Decision Frameworks for Policy.* Washington, D.C.: The Brookings Institution.

Laver, Michael. 1983. *Invitation to Politics.* Oxford: Basil Blackwell.

Levy, Frank. 1988. *Dollars and Dreams.* New York: Norton.

Lind, Robert C. 1982. *Discounting for Time and Risk in Energy Policy.* Washington, D.C.: Resources for the Future.

Lindahl, Erik. 1958. "Just Taxation—A Positive Solution," in Richard A. Musgrave and Alan T. Peacock, eds., *Classics in the Theory of Public Finance.* Pp. 168-176. New London: MacMillan. (Originally published in 1919.)

Lindblom, Charles E. 1959. "The Science of 'Muddling Through.'" *Public Administration Review* 19 (Spring): 79-88.

Lindsay, Cotton M., and Michael T. Maloney. 1988. "Party Politics and the Price of Payola." *Economic Inquiry* 26 (April): 203-221.

Lowi, Theodore J. 1991. "The Pernicious Effects of Economics on American Political Science." *The Chronicle of Higher Education* 38 (December 11): B1-B2.

Luce, R. Duncan, and Howard Raiffa. 1957. *Games and Decisions.* New York: Wiley.

Magat, Wesley A. 1981. "Introduction: Managing the Transition to Deregulation." *Law and Contemporary Problems* 44 (Winter): 1-8.

March, James G., and Herbert A. Simon. 1958. *Organizations.* New York: John Wiley & Sons.

Marwell, Gerald, and Ruth E. Ames. 1981. "Economists Free Ride, Does Anyone Else?" *Journal of Public Economics* 15 (June): 295-310.

Mayhew, David R. 1974. *Congress: The Electoral Connection.* New Haven: Yale University Press.

McCann, Michael W. 1986. *Taking Reform Seriously: Perspectives on Public Interest Liberalism.* Ithaca, N.Y.: Cornell University Press.

McCubbins, Mathew D. 1985. "The Legislative Design of Regulatory Structure." *American Journal of Political Science* 29 (November): 721-748.

McCubbins, Mathew D., and Thomas Schwartz. 1984. "Congressional Oversight Overlooked; Police Patrols Versus Fire Alarms." *American Journal of Political Science* 28 (February): 165-179.

McCubbins, Mathew D., Roger G. Noll, and Barry R. Weingast. 1989. "Structure and Process, Politics and Policy: Administrative Arrangements and the Political Control of Agencies." *Virginia Law Review* 75 (March): 431-482.

McKelvey, Richard. 1976. "Intransitivities in Multidimensional Voting Models and Some Implications for Agenda Control." *Journal of Economic Theory* 12 (June): 472-482.

McLean, Iain. 1987. *Public Choice: An Introduction.* Oxford: Basil Blackwell.

Mill, John Stuart. 1871. *Principles of Political Economy.* 7th ed. London. (Originally published in 1848.)

Miller, Gary J., and Terry M. Moe. 1983. "Bureaucrats, Legislators, and the Size of Government." *American Political Science Review* 77 (June): 297-322.

_____. 1986. "The Positive Theory of Hierarchies," in Herbert F. Weisberg, ed., *Political Science: The Science of Politics.* Pp. 167-198. New York: Agathon.

Miller, Tim R. 1985. "Recent Trends in Federal Water Resource Management: Are the 'Iron Triangles' in Retreat?" *Policy Studies Review* 5 (November): 395-412.

Miller, Warren E., and Donald E. Stokes. 1969. "Constituency Influence in Congress," in Robert V. Peabody and Nelson W. Polsby, eds., *New Perspectives on the House of Representatives.* 2nd ed. Pp. 31-53. Chicago: Rand McNally.

Mishan, E. J. 1967. *Welfare Economics: Five Introductory Essays.* New York: Random House.

Mitchell, Robert Cameron. 1979. "National Environmental Lobbies and the Apparent Illogic of Collective Action," in Clifford S. Russell, ed., *Collective Decision Making.* Pp. 87-121. Baltimore: Johns Hopkins University Press.

Mitchell, William C. 1982. "Textbook Public Choice: A Review Essay." *Public Choice* 38: 97-112.

_____. 1983. "Fiscal Behavior of the Modern Democratic State: Public Choice Perspectives and Contributions," in Larry L. Wade, ed., *Political Economy.* Pp. 69-113. Dordrecht, The Netherlands: Kluwer-Nijhoff.

_____. 1990. "Interest Groups: Economic Perspectives and Contributions." *Journal of Theoretical Politics* 2: 85-108.

Mitchell, William C., and Michael C. Munger. 1991. "Economic Models of Interest Groups: An Introductory Essay." *American Journal of Political Science* 35 (May): 512-546.

Mitnick, Barry M. 1980. *The Political Economy of Regulation.* New York: Columbia University Press.

_____. 1981-1982. "Regulation and the Theory of Agency." *Policy Studies Review* 1: 442-453.

Moe, Terry M. 1980. *The Organization of Interests.* Chicago: University of Chicago Press.

_____. 1984. "The New Economics of Organization." *American Journal of Political Science* 28 (November): 739-777.

_____. 1987. "An Assessment of the Positive Theory of 'Congressional Dominance.'" *Legislative Studies Quarterly* 12 (November): 475-520.

Monroe, Kristen, ed. 1991. *The Economic Approach to Politics.* New York: HarperCollins.

Mueller, Dennis C. 1989. *Public Choice.* 2nd ed. Cambridge: Cambridge University Press.

Muris, Timothy J. 1986. "Regulatory Policymaking at the Federal Trade Commission: The Extent of Congressional Control." *Journal of Political Economy* 94 (August): 884-889.

Musgrave, Richard A. 1959. *The Theory of Public Finance*. New York: McGraw-Hill.

Musgrave, Richard A., and Peggy B. Musgrave. 1989. *Public Finance in Theory and Practice*. 5th ed. New York: McGraw-Hill, 1989.

Nachmias, David, and David H. Rosenbloom. 1980. *Bureaucratic Government USA*. New York: St. Martin's Press.

Niskanen, William A., Jr. 1971. *Bureaucracy and Representative Government*. Chicago: Aldine-Atherton.

Nozick, Robert. 1974. *Anarchy, State, and Utopia*. New York: Basic Books.

Oates, Wallace E. 1972. *Fiscal Federalism*. New York: Harcourt Brace Jovanovich.

_____. 1981. "On Local Finance and the Tiebout Model." *American Economic Review* 71 (May): 93-98.

Olson, Mancur. 1965. *The Logic of Collective Action*. Cambridge: Harvard University Press.

Oser, Jacob. 1970. *The Evolution of Economic Thought*. 2nd ed. New York: Harcourt, Brace and World.

Ostrom, Vincent. 1989. *The Intellectual Crisis in American Public Administration*. 2nd ed. Tuscaloosa, Ala.: University of Alabama Press.

Ostrom, Vincent, Elinor Ostrom, and Robert Bish. 1988. *Local Government in the United States*. San Francisco: ICS Press.

Peltzman, Sam. 1976. "Toward a More General Theory of Regulation." *Journal of Law and Economics* 19 (August): 211-240.

Plott, Charles R. 1967. "A Notion of Equilibrium and Its Possibility Under Majority Rule." *American Economic Review* 57 (September): 787-806.

_____. 1982. "Industrial Organization Theory and Experimental Economics." *Journal of Economic Literature* 20 (December): 1485-1527.

Poole, Keith T. 1984. "Least Squares Metric, Unidimensional Unfolding." *Psychometrika* 49 (September): 311-323.

Poole, Keith T., and Thomas Romer. 1985. "Patterns of Political Action Committee Contributions to the 1980 Campaigns for the United States House of Representatives." *Public Choice* 47: 63-111.

Poole, Keith T., and Howard Rosenthal. 1984. "The Polarization of American Politics." *Journal of Politics* 46 (November): 1061-1079.

Poole, Keith T., Thomas Romer, and Howard Rosenthal. 1987. "The Revealed Preferences of Political Action Committees." *American Economic Review* 77 (May): 298-302.

Posner, Richard A. 1975. "The Social Costs of Monopoly and Regulation." *Journal of Political Economy* 83 (August): 807-827.

Ramsey, Frank. 1927. "A Contribution to the Theory of Taxation." *Economic Journal* 37: 47-61.

Randall, Alan. 1972. "Market Solutions to Externality Problems: Theory and Practice." *American Journal of Agricultural Economics* 54 (May): 175-183.

Rawls, John A. 1971. *A Theory of Justice*. Cambridge: Harvard University Press.

Reisner, Marc. 1986. *Cadillac Desert*. New York: Viking.

Riker, William H. 1962. *The Theory of Political Coalitions*. New Haven: Yale University Press.

_____. 1982. *Liberalism Against Populism*. Prospect Heights, Ill.: Waveland Press.

_____. 1986. *The Art of Political Manipulation*. New Haven: Yale University Press.

Riker, William H., and Peter C. Ordeshook. 1973. *Introduction to Positive Political Theory*. Englewood Cliffs, N.J.: Prentice-Hall.

Rivlin, Alice M. 1991. "Strengthening the Economy by Rethinking the Role of Federal and State Governments." *Journal of Economic Perspectives* 5 (Spring): 3-14.

Romer, Thomas, and Howard Rosenthal. 1984. "Voting Models and Empirical Evidence." *American Scientist* 72 (September-October): 465-473.

Romer, Thomas, Howard Rosenthal, and Vincent G. Munley. Forthcoming. "Economic Incentives and Political Institutions: Spending and Voting in School Budget Referenda." *Journal of Public Economics*.

Rose-Ackerman, Susan. 1986. "Introduction," in Susan Rose-Ackerman, ed., *The Economics of Nonprofit Institutions*. Pp. 3-17. New York: Oxford University Press.

Ross, Stephen A. 1973. "The Economic Theory of Agency: The Principal's Problem." *American Economic Review* 63 (May): 134-139.

Rossi, Peter H., and Howard E. Freeman. 1989. *Evaluation: A Systematic Approach*. 4th ed. Newbury Park, Calif.: Sage.

Rousseau, Jean Jacques. 1952. "The Social Contract," in Robert Maynard Hutchins, ed., *Great Books of the Western World*. Vol. 38. Pp. 387-439. Chicago: Encyclopaedia Britannica. (Originally published in 1762.)

Rubinfeld, Daniel L. 1987. "The Economics of the Local Public Sector," in Alan J. Auerbach and Martin Feldstein, eds., *Handbook of Public Economics*. Vol. 2. Pp. 571-645. Amsterdam: North-Holland.

Ruttan, Vernon W. 1980. "Bureaucratic Productivity: The Case of Agricultural Research." *Public Choice* 35: 529-547.

Salisbury, Robert H. 1969. "An Exchange Theory of Interest Groups." *Midwest Journal of Political Science* 13 (February): 1-32.

Salisbury, Robert H., John P. Heinz, Edward O. Laumann, and Robert L. Nelson. 1987. "Who Works with Whom?" *American Political Science Review* 81 (December): 1225-1228.

Samuelson, Robert J. 1988. "An Economic Missile Gap." *Newsweek* (September 19): 49.

Sandler, Todd, and John T. Tschirhart. 1980. "The Economic Theory of Clubs: An Evaluative Survey." *Journal of Economic Literature* 18 (December): 1481-1521.

Satterthwaite, M. A. 1975. "Strategy-Proofness and Arrow's Conditions: Existence and Correspondence Theorems for Voting Procedures and Social Welfare Functions." *Journal of Economic Theory* 10 (April): 187-217.

Schlozman, Kay Lehman, and John T. Tierney. 1986. *Organized Interests and American Democracy*. New York: Harper and Row.

Schofield, Norman. 1985. "Anarchy, Altruism and Cooperation." *Social Choice and Welfare* 2: 207-219.

Schooler, Dean, and Helen Ingram. 1981-1982. "Water Resource Development." *Policy Studies Review* 1: 243-254.

Schultz, Theodore W. 1961. "Investment in Human Capital." *American Economic Review* (March): 1-17.

_____. 1971. *Investment in Human Capital.* New York: Free Press.

Schwab, Robert M., and Wallace E. Oates. 1991. "Community Composition and the Provision of Local Public Goods." *Journal of Public Economics* 44 (March): 217-237.

Schwab, Robert M., and Ernest M. Zampelli. 1987. "Disentangling the Demand Function from the Production Function for Local Public Services." *Journal of Public Economics* 33 (July): 245-260.

Sen, Amartya. 1966. "A Possibility Theorem on Majority Decisions." *Econometrica* 34 (April): 491-499.

Shavell, S. 1979. "Risk Sharing and Incentives in the Principal and Agent Relationship." *Bell Journal of Economics* 10 (Spring): 55-73.

Shepsle, Kenneth A. 1979. "Institutional Arrangements and Equilibrium in Multidimensional Voting Models." *American Journal of Political Science* 23 (February): 27-60.

Shepsle, Kenneth A., and Barry R. Weingast. 1981. "Structure-Induced Equilibrium and Legislative Choice." *Public Choice* 37: 503-519.

_____. 1984. "Political Solutions to Market Problems." *American Political Science Review* 78 (June): 417-434.

Simon, Herbert. 1946. "The Proverbs of Administration." *Public Administration Review* 6 (Winter): 53-67.

_____. 1947. *Administrative Behavior.* New York: Macmillan.

_____. 1957. *Models of Man.* New York: Wiley.

Slovic, Paul, Baruch Fischhoff, and Sarah Lichtenstein. 1980. "Facts and Fears: Understanding Perceived Risk," in Richard C. Schwing and Walter A. Albers, Jr., eds., *Societal Risk Assessment: How Safe Is Safe Enough?* Pp. 181-214. New York: Plenum.

Slovic, Paul, Dale Griffin, and Amos Tversky. 1990. "Compatibility Effects in Judgement and Choice," in Robin M. Hogarth, ed., *Insights in Decision Making: Theory and Applications.* Pp. 5-27. Chicago: University of Chicago Press.

Smith, Adam. 1937. *An Inquiry into the Nature and Causes of the Wealth of Nations.* Edwin Cannan (ed.). New York: Random House. (Originally published in 1776.)

Smith, V. Kerry. 1985. "A Theoretical Analysis of the 'Green Lobby.'" *American Political Science Review* 79 (March): 132-147.

_____. 1986. "A Conceptual Overview of the Foundations of Benefit-Cost Analysis," in Judith D. Bentkover, Vincent T. Covello, and Jeryl Mumpower, eds., *Benefits Assessment: The State of the Art.* Pp. 13-34. Dordrecht, Holland: D. Reidel.

Smithies, A. 1941. "Optimum Location in Spatial Competition." *Journal of Political Economy* 49 (June): 423-439.

Spence, Michael. 1974. *Market Signaling.* Cambridge: Harvard University Press.

Spence, Michael, and Richard Zeckhauser. 1971. "Insurance, Information, and Individual Action." *American Economic Review* 61 (May): 380-387.

Spiegel, Henry William. 1983. *The Growth of Economic Thought.* Rev. ed. Durham, N.C.: Duke University Press.

Steinberg, Richard. 1987. "Voluntary Donations and Public Expenditures in a Federalist System." *American Economic Review* 77 (March): 24-36.

Steiner, Jurg. 1990. "Rational Choice Theories and Politics: A Research Agenda and a Moral Question." *PS: Political Science & Politics* 23 (March): 46-50.

_____. 1991. "We Need More Politicians like Havel, and We Should Tell Our Students So." *PS: Political Science & Politics* 24 (September): 430-431.

Steiner, Peter O. 1977. "The Public Interest and the Public Sector," in Robert H. Haveman and Julius Margolis, eds., *Public Expenditures and Policy Analysis.* 2nd ed. Pp. 27-66. Chicago: Rand McNally.

Stephens, Glenn. 1991. "On the Critique of Rational Choice." *PS: Political Science & Politics* 24 (September): 429-430.

Stevens, Joe B. 1980. "The Demand for Public Goods as a Factor in the Nonmetropolitan Migration Turnaround," in David L. Brown and John M. Wardwell, eds., *New Directions in Urban-Rural Migration.* Pp. 115-135. New York: Academic Press.

Stevens, Joe B., Joe R. Kerkvliet, and Robert Mason. 1992. *Reading the Tea Leaves: Oregon's School Budget Elections, 1981-86.* WRDC 38. Corvallis, Ore.: Western Rural Development Center.

Stigler, George J. 1971. "The Theory of Economic Regulation." *Bell Journal of Economics* 2 (Spring): 3-21.

Stiglitz, Joseph E. 1988. *Economics of the Public Sector.* 2nd ed. New York: W. W. Norton.

Stokey, Edith, and Richard Zeckhauser. 1978. *A Primer for Policy Analysis.* New York: W. W. Norton.

Taylor, Michael. 1982. *Community, Anarchy and Liberty.* Cambridge: Cambridge University Press.

_____. 1987. *The Possibility of Cooperation.* Cambridge: Cambridge University Press.

Thurow, Lester C. 1981. "Saving Social Security." *Newsweek* (October 26): 71.

Tideman, T. Nicolaus, and Gordon Tullock. 1976. "A New and Superior Process for Making Social Choices." *Journal of Political Economy* 84 (December): 1145-1160.

Tiebout, Charles M. 1956. "A Pure Theory of Local Expenditures." *Journal of Political Economy* 64 (October): 416-424.

Tietenberg, Tom. 1988. *Environmental and Natural Resource Economics.* 2nd ed. New York: HarperCollins.

Truman, David B. 1951. *The Governmental Process.* New York: Knopf.

Tullock, Gordon. 1967. "The Welfare Costs of Tariffs, Monopolies, and Theft." *Economic Journal* 5 (June): 224-232.

U.S. Federal Inter-Agency River Basin Committee, Subcommittee on Benefits and Costs. 1950. *Proposed Practices for Economic Analysis of River Basin Projects.* Washington, D.C.: U.S. Government Printing Office.

van den Doel, Hans. 1979. *Democracy and Welfare Economics*. Cambridge: Cambridge University Press.

Verba, Sidney, and Norman H. Nie. 1972. *Participation in America: Political Democracy and Social Equality*. New York: Harper and Row.

Vickrey, William. 1961. "Counterspeculation, Auctions and Competitive Sealed Tenders." *Journal of Finance* 16 (May): 8-37.

Viscusi, W. Kip. 1986. "The Valuation of Risks to Life and Health: Guidelines for Policy Analysis," in Judith D. Bentkover, Vincent T. Covello, and Jeryl Mumpower, eds., *Benefits Assessment: The State of the Art*. Pp. 193-210. Dordrecht, Holland: D. Reidel.

von Mises, Ludwig. 1944. *Bureaucracy*. New Haven: Yale University Press.

von Neumann, John, and Oskar Morgenstern. 1944. *The Theory of Games and Economics Behavior*. Princeton, N.J.: Princeton University Press.

Walker, Jack L. 1983. "The Origins and Maintenance of Interest Groups in America." *American Political Science Review* 77 (June): 390-406.

Weaver, R. Kent. 1985. "Are Parliamentary Systems Better?" *The Brookings Review* 3 (Summer): 16-25.

Weber, Max. 1946. "Bureaucracy," in H. H. Gerth and C. Wright Mills, eds., *From Max Weber: Essays on Sociology*. Pp. 196-244. New York: Oxford University Press.

Weimer, David, and Aidan Vining. 1989. *Policy Analysis: Concepts and Practice*. Englewood Cliffs, N.J.: Prentice-Hall.

Weingast, Barry R. 1981. "Regulation, Reregulation, and Deregulation: The Political Foundations of Agency Clientele Relationships." *Law and Contemporary Problems* 44 (Winter): 147-177.

Weingast, Barry R., and William J. Marshall. 1988. "The Industrial Organization of Congress; or, Why Legislatures, like Firms, Are Not Organized as Markets." *Journal of Political Economy* 96 (February): 132-163.

Weingast, Barry R., and Mark J. Moran. 1983. "Bureaucratic Discretion or Congressional Control? Regulatory Policymaking by the Federal Trade Commission." *Journal of Political Economy* 91 (October): 765-800.

Weingast, Barry R., Kenneth A. Shepsle, and Christopher Johnsen. 1981. "The Political Economy Approach to Distributive Politics." *Journal of Political Economy* 89 (August): 642-664.

Weisbrod, Burton A. 1986. "Toward a Theory of the Voluntary Nonprofit Sector in a Three-Sector Economy," in Susan Rose-Ackerman, ed., *The Economics of Nonprofit Institutions*. Pp. 21-44. New York: Oxford University Press.

_____. 1988. *The Nonprofit Economy*. Cambridge: Harvard University Press.

Weisbrod, Burton A., and Nestor D. Dominguez. 1986. "Demand for Collective Goods in Private Nonprofit Markets: Can Fundraising Expenditures Help Overcome Free-Rider Behavior?" *Journal of Public Economics* 30 (June): 83-96.

Williamson, Oliver E. 1975. *Markets and Hierarchies*. New York: Free Press.

Willig, Robert. 1976. "Consumer's Surplus Without Apology." *American Economic Review* 66 (September): 589-597.

Wilson, Graham K. 1981. *Interest Groups in the United States*. New York: Oxford University Press.

Wilson, James Q., ed. 1980. *The Politics of Regulation*. New York: Basic Books.

_____. 1989. *Bureaucracy: What Government Agencies Do, and Why They Do It.* New York: Basic Books.

_____. 1990. "Interests and Deliberation in the American Republic, or, Why James Madison Would Never Have Received the James Madison Award." *PS: Political Science & Politics* 23 (December): 558-562.

Wilson, Woodrow. 1885. *Congressional Government.* Boston: Houghton Mifflin.

Wright, John R. 1985. "PACs, Contributions, and Roll Calls: An Organizational Perspective." *American Political Science Review* 79 (June): 400-414.

Zampelli, Ernest M. 1986. "Resource Fungibility, The Flypaper Effect, and the Expenditure Impact of Grants-In-Aid." *Review of Economics and Statistics* 68 (February): 33-40.

Zeleny, Milan. 1982. *Multiple Criteria Decision Making.* New York: McGraw-Hill.

Zodrow, George R., ed. 1983. *Local Provision of Public Services: The Tiebout Model After Twenty-Five Years.* New York: Academic Press.

About the Book and Author

The study of government policy and public decision-making has experienced a renaissance in recent years as economists and political scientists have come together to form the new field of collective, or public, choice.

The Economics of Collective Choice is a breakthrough text in this field. It is the first to approach the public policy process with a sophisticated understanding of both economics and government and to present these ideas with a grace and accessibility entirely appropriate to undergraduates. Collective choice economics as presented by Professor Stevens is a mix of applied welfare economics and public choice analysis and does not presuppose a knowledge of intermediate microeconomics.

Professor Stevens credits both the conservative insight that government intervention is often worse than what it is intended to cure and the liberal view that efficiency and justice are sometimes best served by intervention. This approach allows students to find their own balance between these ideological views.

This unique book is designed as a core text for courses on public choice and public policy analysis. It will also find wide use in courses on public administration or public affairs and as a supplementary text in courses on public sector economics and public finance.

Joe B. Stevens is professor of agricultural and resource economics at Oregon State University. He has twenty-five years of multidisciplinary research and teaching experience in the area of applied collective choice.

Index

Printed in the United States
23838LVS00002B/237

9 780813 315676